Tourist Satisfaction and Complaining Behavior: Measurement and Management Issues in the Tourism and Hospitality Industry

TOURIST SATISFACTION AND COMPLAINING BEHAVIOR: MEASUREMENT AND MANAGEMENT ISSUES IN THE TOURISM AND HOSPITALITY INDUSTRY

ATILA YÜKSEL

EDITOR

Nova Science Publishers, Inc.

New York

NOTICE TO THE READER

The Publisher has taken reasonable care in the preparation of this book, but makes no expressed or implied warranty of any kind and assumes no responsibility for any errors or omissions. No liability is assumed for incidental or consequential damages in connection with or arising out of information contained in this book. The Publisher shall not be liable for any special, consequential, or exemplary damages resulting, in whole or in part, from the readers' use of, or reliance upon, this material. Any parts of this book based on government reports are so indicated and copyright is claimed for those parts to the extent applicable to compilations of such works.

Independent verification should be sought for any data, advice or recommendations contained in this book. In addition, no responsibility is assumed by the publisher for any injury and/or damage to persons or property arising from any methods, products, instructions, ideas or otherwise contained in this publication.

This publication is designed to provide accurate and authoritative information with regard to the subject matter covered herein. It is sold with the clear understanding that the Publisher is not engaged in rendering legal or any other professional services. If legal or any other expert assistance is required, the services of a competent person · should be sought. FROM A DECLARATION OF PARTICIPANTS JOINTLY ADOPTED BY A COMMITTEE OF THE AMERICAN BAR ASSOCIATION AND A COMMITTEE OF PUBLISHERS.

LIBRARY OF CONGRESS CATALOGING-IN-PUBLICATION DATA

Tourist satisfaction and complaining behavior : measurement and management issues in the tourism and hospitality industry / Atila Yüksel, (editor).   *p. cm.*
ISBN 978-1-60456-002-2 (hardcover)
1. Hospitality industry--Management. 2. Tourism--Management. I. Yüksel, Atila.
TX911.3.M27T69 2008
647.94'068--dc22   *2007035018*

Published by Nova Science Publishers, Inc. ≃ New York

CONTENTS

PREFACE

Determining customer satisfaction is fundamental to effective delivery of services. Successfully being able to judge customers' satisfaction levels and to apply that knowledge potentially gives managers an advantage over competitors via such benefits as increased customer retention and positive word-of-mouth communication. Given the vital role of customer satisfaction, one should not be surprised that a great deal of research has been devoted to investigating the process by which customers form judgments about a service experience. As a result, noticeable progress has been achieved in the application of customer-satisfaction information within service industries, despite the fact that perhaps no other area has generated as many theoretical and methodological difficulties (Yuksel and Rimmington, 1998). Reviewed literature suggests that there is no consensus on how best to conceptualize customer satisfaction and there is a divergence of interest between academics and practitioners (Engeset and Heide, 1997). Attempting to provide a theoretical explanation of the concept, academics seem to have largely focused on conceptual issues and underlying processes. While these attempts are critical to understanding the concept, from a practitioner viewpoint, they may not be readily transferable into managerial actions. Hence, in contrast to academics, practitioners seem to be giving less attention to the underlying processes of the construct, and are more concerned with pragmatic task of measurement.

The concept of satisfaction appears to be complex, beset by numerous debates as to its definition, measurement, and management, and that individuals (staff, managers, and customers) differ in what they perceive to be satisfactory fuels the complexity in its management. On the one hand, satisfaction may mean minimum acceptability to some customers, while on the other hand it may mean near perfection to others. Depending on the situation, consumer satisfaction may (or may not) result from a complex process, involving simultaneous processing of one or more referent points at different stages of the service delivery, and it may be determined by exogenous and interpersonal elements that are beyond management. The complex and variable nature of satisfaction may suggest that development of a universal definition of the concept, and measurement framework that can fully capture the diverse elements of the consumer satisfaction in every consumption situation may not be possible (Yuksel and Yuksel, 2001). Nevertheless, a comprehensive understanding of how satisfaction judgments evolve (the structure of the satisfaction construct) in hospitality and tourism service experiences is essential to provide guidelines on ways in which customer's service experiences can be better managed.

Researchers seem to diverge on the conceptual and practical issues relating to similarities, differences, and causality between customer satisfaction and such other constructs as service quality concepts. Given the current controversy as to the relationship between these two constructs, empirical research is badly needed to provide an enhanced understanding of the similarity, and if any, differences between these two concepts. An interesting area of research would be to explore whether these two concepts are distinguishable in hospitality and tourism customers' minds and whether service quality and customer satisfaction concepts have different consequential effects on behavioral outcomes (Yüksel and Yüksel, 2001). The tenability of the proposition suggesting that customers use different forms of standards in reaching their satisfaction and quality judgments remains to be adequately explored within different hospitality and tourism contexts.

Accurate measurement of customer satisfaction is a prerequisite for developing effective management strategies. Only with reliable customer feedback, gathered through an adequate and appropriate assessment framework, can destination and facility managers be in possession of facts that will allow them to implement satisfaction improvement programs. While several frameworks have been suggested in the literature, based on the complexity inherent in customer satisfaction measurement, it might be appropriate to state that measurement and management of customer satisfaction is likely to entail difficulties. Some researchers claim that performance measures are all that are needed in satisfaction research, while others maintain that satisfaction measurement should incorporate expectations and performance. Performance bears a pre-eminent role in the formation of customer satisfaction because it is the main feature of the consumption experience. While perceived performance seems to be more straightforward and convenient, however, it is not free of shortcomings. Firstly, performance ratings alone may not lead to useful and incisive data. Secondly, it is not clear that performance only measures provide the greatest predictive power. Thirdly, it explains little about the thought processes involved in satisfaction judgments.

Hence, some researchers maintain that attribute performance must be weighted by its importance. However, whether to include importance in measuring satisfaction is also controversial. There is growing controversy over the following points: What is the best and uncontaminated way to assess attribute importance? How reliable is self-reported importance scores? Is it really necessary to weigh attribute importance by its performance, if performance ratings already contain importance information? Does weighting really add anything to our understanding of consumer behaviour or is it just an academic preference?

There are conflicting results as to the reliability and validity of these conventional assessment frameworks, used in the hospitality and tourism satisfaction research. Could adoption of models, theories, and scales developed in other service areas, dissimilar to tourism and hospitality services, account for this conflict and inconsistency in the results? Might pre and post-purchase decision-making processes, and behavior of hospitality and tourism customers be different from customers using bank or hospital services? In short, a comparative research on the reliability and validity of disconfirmation, performance and attribute importance frameworks in measuring customer satisfaction and the contribution of these to the various models' predictive power is needed. This is particularly essential because managers in hospitality and tourism need to build their management and marketing strategies on customer satisfaction research results with high reliability and validity.

One of the main difficulties with the use of the Expectancy Disconfirmation Paradigm (EDP) is the fact that it views expectations as the primary determinant of customer dissatisfaction. However, the cause of dissatisfaction may not be the disconfirmation of expectations alone. The conventional EDP suggests that if the product performance is consistent with consumer expectations, then tourists will be satisfied and they will be more likely to repurchase. However, as common experience suggests, such relationships between disconfirmation, satisfaction and repurchase intentions may not always hold in the hospitality and tourism settings. For example, a cost conscious customer may feel highly dissatisfied with the service when he/she finds out that the cost of the same service, to another customer was less, even though the customer's scores on predictive expectations minus perceived performance may suggest satisfaction. Similarly, restaurant customers may develop dissatisfaction if their perception of service transaction fairness (for example, price paid vs. level of service delivered) is beyond the acceptable range. Alternatively, a hotel customer may be satisfied even though the performance delivered, lagged behind what s/he had predicted, but was above the minimum acceptable level. Hence, in order to increase the model's ability in accounting for customer satisfaction, and provide a much richer picture of it, the effects of equity perceptions and customer tolerance levels on the development of customer satisfaction judgments need to be recognized and incorporated into the assessment framework.

Anecdotal evidence suggests that travelers may switch to competitive destinations even if their predictive expectations are met or exceeded. This raises questions about whether only the fulfillment of brand expectations, created by advertisement, plays the most important role in the determination of post-purchase behavior such as repurchase, switching, and recommendations. Based on the reviewed literature, it can be argued that there might be a difference between the extent of the influence of different standards on the formation of affective (i.e., satisfaction) and behavioral outcomes (i.e., repurchase). The point in question is that will different decision processing be in operation when customers reach satisfaction and behavioral intention judgments? Satisfaction may be determined by evaluating a product's ability to fulfill one's current desires, wants, needs, or expectations. The brand expectations, however, might be less influential in the formation of behavioral intentions in the tourism and hospitality settings (Gupta and Stewart, 1996). In addition to product availability and accessibility, the behavioral intentions may simply be determined by the extent to which the destination or organization performs better or worse in comparison to other alternative destination(s) or organization(s).

This implies that hospitality and tourism customers' post-purchase decision processing might be more extensive than the conventional EDP suggests. If this is the case, then developing management and marketing strategies for repeat business, based on results of disconfirmation of expectation measures alone is inadvisable. Further empirical research is necessary to determine the ability of expectations in predicting behavioral intentions, and understand whether hospitality and tourism customers use different comparison standards when arriving at their satisfaction and behavioral intention judgments. Additionally, it would be interesting to investigate whether comparing predictive expectations, perceived desires or experience-based norms to performance will yield the same results in terms of customer satisfaction in the tourism and hospitality contexts.

While researchers acknowledge that customers engage in processing of information relating to alternative products/services in their pre-purchase decision stage, the fact that customers may follow a similar information processing approach in post-purchase evaluations has received little recognition. There might be a multitude of factors, other than brand expectations, influencing hospitality and tourism customers' post-purchase evaluation, and favorable evaluation of unchosen alternatives might be one of them. The point in question is that will overall dis/satisfaction and behavioral intentions be dependent on the level of satisfaction with the attributes of the chosen service/product only? Or, will past satisfaction with the unchosen alternative(s) be actively processed in consumers' post-purchase evaluations and determine overall judgment as much as satisfaction with the chosen service/product could? Is focusing on service attributes as indicators of satisfaction deceptive?

The conventional assessment frameworks used in the hospitality and tourism satisfaction research suffer from a common limitation. They fail to produce information that diagnoses relative organizational strengths and weaknesses, which is imperative in developing competitive actions against competitors. As the majority of customers have experiences with other hospitality and tourism organizations, it is likely that in their evaluation they will make implicit or explicit comparisons between the facilities, attractions, and service standards of alternative organizations (Laws, 1995). Hence, it is possible that the extent and nature of tourists' past experiences with similar or different destination(s), for instance, may set the standard against which the present experience is judged. A negative (positive) discrepancy between what other destination(s) (e.g., the one most recently visited) offered and what the current destination was able to render may lead to the feelings of dissatisfaction (satisfaction) about the outcome and may influence future travel decisions, as well as, the image held for the destination.

An understanding of customers' perceptions of the organization (or destination) operating in the tourism and hospitality industry relative to other organizations (destinations) that are directly or indirectly in competition is imperative. It may enable comparison of performance elements between organizations and may provide a better understanding of how a given organization performs (Baum, 1999; Laws, 1995; Pearce, 1997). It may provide more objective foundation for evaluating the strengths and weaknesses of the company, provide better understanding of how competitive advantage can be gained (Pearce, 1997), and provide useful insights in to the design of a positioning strategy (Baloglu & McCleary, 1999). Despite its potential contribution to management knowledge, the potential influence of performance gaps, perceived by tourists, between a given destination's services and other destinations, on tourists' holiday evaluations has not been widely studied. Thus, development of research approaches that can capture the potential effect of customers' perceptions of alternative products' performance on judgments in regard to the chosen product/service is needed.

Another interesting area, which thus far has been relatively under-researched in customer satisfaction literature, is the relationship between customers' cultural orientations and their service perceptions and product evaluations. It should be noted that while the role of culture in customer service evaluation has received little attention, its importance has not gone completely unnoticed. A number of researchers have noted significant differences between customers from different cultures in their expectations for hotel and restaurant services. Given the potential effects of cultural orientations on expectations for and assessment of hospitality and tourism services, tourism and hospitality managers must first ascertain the dominant values in each targeted cultural group. They then must determine how to promote and manage services desired by different cultural groups. Indeed, if the key to an effective strategy is to meet customer needs as precisely as possible, then hospitality and tourism services must be defined relative to customer's culturally driven needs. Unless there is adequate knowledge

Implementation issues

While the literature is replete with conceptual and theoretical arguments, effective ways to develop and implement customer satisfaction building programs for the use of tourism and hospitality managers have not been adequately discussed.

EDITOR'S NOTE

The responsibility for the facts stated, conclusions reached etc., is entirely that of the Author. The Publisher is not responsible for them, whatsoever.

ACKNOWLEDGEMENT

I would like to express my sincere gratitude to those researchers whose knowledge, experience and guidance have helped me complete the present work. During this ongoing search for "excellence in research", I have received, and continuing to receive, the greatest support from my beloved family (Fisun, A. Berra and A. Erkut), my sister (Mediha Azizağaoğlu) and my parents (Ali and Şadiye Yüksel). For their admirable patience, enthusiasm, determination, and foresight, I am very much indebted.

Atila Yüksel (Ph. D)
Head of School
Didim Vocational School
Adnan Menderes University
TURKEY
ayuksel@adu.edu.tr

In: Tourist Satisfaction and Complaining Behavior
Editor: Atila Yüksel

ISBN 978-1-60456-002-2
© 2008 Nova Science Publishers, Inc.

Chapter 1

INTRODUCTION TO CUSTOMER DISSATISFACTION MANAGEMENT

Atila Yüksel[*]

Adnan Menderes University, Turkey

Customer satisfaction is a complex research topic. Continuing debates on its definition, its relationship with other constructs, and its theories, clearly show that this area of academic research is replete with difficulties. First, the literature lacks conclusive studies examining the reliability and validity of the proffered customer satisfaction measurement models. Second, the relationship as well as the difference between customer satisfaction and service quality constructs is confusing. Third, the comparison standard issue is considered crucial, however, there is limited understanding of whether the use of different standards yields different results in terms of satisfaction. Fourth, academics have been largely concerned with the conceptual antecedents of customer satisfaction, while insufficient attention has been paid to its content, particularly in hospitality and tourism service settings. The conceptual frameworks have been largely borrowed from general consumer behavior literature, and their applicability in explicating tourist satisfaction in all cases may be questionable. As a consequence, little seems to be known concerning what satisfies tourists, for example with restaurant services, shopping services etc.

"Tourism can be an epicurean experience, an indulgence, an enhancement not only of ego but also of the body. Like many human activities, it has both a positive and negative side. To try to understand the tourist experience requires not only a consideration of perceived needs and actualities of the beach and the great outdoors, but also the noise and the din of the disco and the sweat of the massage parlor" (Ryan, 1997a, p. 25). The tourist experience is a highly complex phenomenon which may be explained through a number of linked stages, starting with the translation of holiday needs and wants into motivation, followed by the experiences of various destination services, and ending with memories of the destination after returning home. As research into tourist experience has developed, several frameworks, which attempt

---

[*] Atila Yüksel (Ph. D) Head of School Didim Vocational School Adnan Menderes University, Turkey
ayuksel@adu.edu.tr

to capture the complexity of the tourist experience, have been proffered. Drawing on Engel and Blackwell's (1982) well-known consumption decision process, Van Raaij and Franken (1984), for instance, suggested a framework consisting of five stages: generic decision (whether to take holiday or not); information acquisition; decision making (selection of the alternative); vacation activities; and satisfaction and complaints. Gunn (1989) proposes a modified travel experience model consisting of seven stages. These include the accumulation of mental images about vacation experiences; modification of those images by further information; decision to take a vacation trip; travel to the destination; participation at the destination; return travel; and new accumulation of images based on experience. A somewhat different five-phase process to explain travel experience is suggested by Clawson and Knetch (1990). These are anticipation (planning and thinking of a trip); travel to the site (getting to the destination); on-site behavior (behavior at the destination); return travel (travel home); and recollection (recall, reflection and memory of trip).

The proposition shared in these multi-staged models is that a tourist, in making a purchase decision, goes through several stages, starting from need recognition, information search, an evaluation of alternatives, a choice of product or service and a post purchase evaluation (Chon, 1990). Thus, the process of choosing and of anticipating the holiday may become part of the overall tourism experience, and people may be motivated as much by the prospects of having a holiday as by the assumed benefits of the holiday itself (Sharpley, 1994). In addition, although the physical state of being on holiday terminates when the individual returns home, the memories and images of a holiday may remain much longer. In other words, the holiday may last much longer than the actual period spent away.

The context, meanings and experiences of tourists can vary from holiday to holiday, and from tourist to tourist, and "to talk of the tourist experience seems to imply a homogeneity which in reality is not always present" (Ryan, 1997a, p. 28). This is largely because tourists encounter directly with not just one, but with several members of the production chain (Van-Rekom, 1996). Holidays, as Crompton (1979) states, can be seen as periods when family bonding can be reinforced, or as Ryan (1991) more cynically notes, they can be catalyst for divorce and occasions when adults can regress into childhood in order to play (cf. Ryan, 1997b). Several researchers have stated the dialectic of tourism as being a tension between the search for and the fear of the new, and the want for either or both social interaction and isolation (Iso-Ahola, 1982). The tourist experience is then "both a sense of insularity and a degree of integration into a new environment" (Schmidt, 1979, p. 372, cf. Ryan, 1997). The tourist is pursuing a quest for authenticity, yet wishes to do so within the safety of a protected bubble (Ryan, 1997b). "In sum the tourist experience is a highly subjective and sometimes contradictory one with a content tension between promise and performance, thrift and luxury, illusion and reality" (p. 43). The nature and quality of this experience is the outcome of many individual activities with a range of people and organizations involved in the tourist experience.

WHY DO PEOPLE TRAVEL?

The key question of why do people travel has attracted considerable attention from the academics, and as a consequence, a number of different paradigms have been developed. In his attempt to bring an answer to this crucial question, Dann (1977) proposed pull and push factors, which make tourists travel. The push factors are those socio-psychological factors that are internal to the individual and which explain the desire to go on holiday. The need for relaxation, exploration, social interaction, and enhancement of kinship are regarded as the dominant push motives involved in a vacation decision (Crompton, 1979). In contrast, pull factors are those which affect the consumers destination choice (Pearce, 1992), and include factors such as scenic attractions, and historical sights, cultural characteristics (culinary) and other destination characteristics (Bello and Etzel, 1985).

Crompton (1979) extended the push/pull paradigm to accommodate the basic restorative functions of holidays. Crompton's model of vacation motivation conceives of pleasure vacationing as an essential break from routine that is necessary to facilitate the resolution of disequilibrium, which is a state of tension due to circumstances and pressures that disrupt balance in a person's life. Mayo and Jarvis (1981) have developed a four-category travel motivation: physical motivators which include physical rest, participation in sports; cultural motivators (the desire for knowledge of other countries, folklore, religion); interpersonal motivators (the desire to meet new people, to visit friends); and status and prestige motivators (the desire for recognition, attention, appreciation and good reputation). Similarly, Ragheb and Beard (1982) proposed a four-category motivation scale (cf. Ryan, 1997b); the intellectual component (learning, exploring, discovering, or imagining), the social component (the need for friendship and interpersonal relationships, and the need for the esteem of others), the competence-mystery component (master, challenge, and compete), and the stimulus-avoidance component (the drive to escape and get away from over-stimulating life situations).

Tourist motivation studies demonstrate that the adjectives and the categories of tourist motivations may differ in number, but similar themes recur (Ryan, 1997b). For example, "holidays are seen to arise from the need to escape from everyday surroundings for purposes of relaxation and discovering new things, places and people, and may be periods of self-discovery" (p. 27). A holiday is, therefore, said to be for recuperation and regeneration, compensation and social integration, escape, communication, freedom and self-determination, self-relation, happiness and to broaden the mind (Krippendorf, 1987).

Pizam, Neuman and Reichel (1979) noted that compared to what is known about motivation in general and motivation to travel in particular, relatively little is known about tourism satisfaction, its components, measurements, determinants, and consequences. While this statement might have been true at the time of its writing, it probably represents an overstatement today. The concept has been receiving an increased amount of attention since then and important findings have been elicited with respect to its measurement and its consequences. Before proceeding with the review of tourist satisfaction studies, it is important to note that though conceptually linked and positively related to one another, motivation and satisfaction cannot be equated because motives, by definition, occur before the experience, and satisfaction occurs after it (Ross and Iso-Ahola, 1991).

A number of researchers have attempted to identify sources or components of experiences which contribute to user enjoyment and satisfaction (Dorfman, 1979; Haber and Lerner, 1999; Lam and Zhang, 1999; Lounsburry and Hoopes, 1985; Pizam, Neuman and Reichel, 1978; Qu and Ping, 1999; Tribe and Snaith, 1998; Van Raaij and Franken, 1984; Weber, 1997; Zalatan, 1994). The results of these studies, generally based on the pre-post trip approach (i.e., the Expectancy Disconfirmation Paradigm), indicate that tourist satisfaction is a multifaceted concept consisting of a number of independent components or dimensions. Some studies indicate that destination related attributes (attractions, services, etc) account for tourist satisfaction, while others argue that consumer related factors such as personality, socio-economic status, demographics, and the familiarity with the destination play an important role in tourist satisfaction. Reviewed studies also suggest that sources of satisfaction and dissatisfaction might be different.

Pizam, Neuman and Reichel (1978) were among the first researchers undertaken research into tourist satisfaction concept. In their seminal study, these researchers analyzed tourists' perceptions of a number of destination attributes and concluded that there were eight dimensions influencing holiday satisfaction. The dimensions emerged after a factor analysis of tourist perception mean scores were hospitality, beach opportunities, cost, eating and drinking facilities, accommodation facilities, environment, campground facilities and extent of commercialization. Although this early study contributed to the understanding of the multifaceted nature of tourist satisfaction, managerial implications of the study are rather limited. This is largely because Pizam and his colleagues did not address which of the dimension(s) matter most in tourist satisfaction judgments and future behavioral intentions. Secondly, their study seems to assume that there is only one single homogeneous tourist market and thereby does not take the possible discrepancy that might exist between the drivers of satisfaction of different subsets of total tourist markets in to account. Investigating the perceptions of 685 tourists in the States, their research implicitly predicts that these eight dimensions would be the generic set affecting satisfaction of any subset of the total tourist market (for example, first time visitors and repeat visitors). The validity of this assumption is questionable, as drivers of satisfaction might differ between different consumer groups.

In his research on user satisfaction with recreation facilities (camping), Dorfman (1979) identified the following five factors; absence of negative conditions (annoying and inconsiderate neighboring campers, crowding and pollution), social-interpersonal relationships, naturalism (wilderness, flora, scenic beauty, fauna, sights), relaxation, and quality camping conditions (facilities and convenience, resources for camping, good terrain). Although Dorfman has not run a regression analysis to explore the impact of individual attributes on satisfaction, analyzing the variance explained by the emergent factors, he suggested that some attributes might weight more heavily in campers' satisfaction judgments and that the rank of attributes might differ between different groups. For instance, the absence of negative conditions was the most significant factor for one of the three samples in determining the levels of satisfaction, while relaxation was the most significant contributor of satisfaction for two of the other samples. The results of his study further suggested that causes of campers' dissatisfaction might be different from causes of satisfaction and the presence of certain camp attributes might not necessarily create satisfaction.

Lounsburry and Hoopes's (1985) examined vacation satisfaction in relation to demographic, work-related, and vacation-related variables. Their study brought out that there were five satisfaction dimensions, relaxation and leisure, natural environment, escape, marriage and family, and food and lodging. A correlation analysis performed on demographic, work, and vacation variables (21 variables) elicited that overall satisfaction was most strongly related to satisfaction with relaxation and leisure and also significantly related to satisfaction with escape opportunities, marriage and family satisfaction, satisfaction with food and lodging, and the level of education attainment. They found that vacationers with higher levels of formal educational attainment reported lower levels of vacation satisfaction and vice-versa. This could be because vacationers with higher levels of academic attainment may differ in terms of what they want out of a vacation, they may bring rather complex needs to vacation setting which are more difficult to satisfy in the setting. In order to explore the relative weights of the 21 study variables, they performed a stepwise regression analysis on the data obtained from 129 respondents to both pre and post-vacation questionnaires. The results revealed that the satisfaction with relaxation and leisure dimension accounted for the greatest effect on overall satisfaction. Lounsburry and Hoopes concluded that vacation satisfaction stems from person-environment-fit, wherein satisfaction increases as the fit between individual needs and motives and the ability of vacation to satisfy these needs and motives is maximized. As their pre- and post vacation questionnaires were not similar, Lounsburry and Hoopes suggested that future studies needed to measure specific expectations prior to a vacation and subsequently examine vacation satisfaction in the light of whether these expectations were met on the vacation. However, operationalisation of this approach is replete with difficulties as explained in the previous chapter.

In their study on satisfaction with organized tours, Geva and Goldman (1989) identified four factors contributing to overall satisfaction with tours. These are the instrumental aspects of the tour (hotels, meals and local services, which are perceived to be under the control of the tour operator); the social activities taking place in the tour (mutual relationships among participants, and touring in an organized manner); the performance of the tour guide (his/her relationship with the participants, and the order and the organization of the tour); and the personal experiences (the richness of the experience, entertainment on the tour, allocation of time, utilization of free time and tour itinerary). Their study suggested that as the tour consumption takes place over time and a large amount of tourist learning takes place over the duration, tourist perceptions of organized tours would not stay static and change over time. They observed that in the initial stage of the tour, the tour operator, the guide, and the group (attributes that consumer can evaluate prior to purchasing the product) were the most salient and most relevant, and thus they were the focus of consumers' early evaluations of the tour. At the end of the tour, however, the instrumental aspects of the tour (those attributes that can only be evaluated during or after the consumption such as hotels, meals, and local services) were more important. Note that the nature of these dimensions fits into the search, experience, and credence properties explicated earlier. In essence, this finding suggests that the nature and quality of the experience might be affected by different attributes at different points over the tour's duration.

In a study conducted in, 1996, Danaher and Arweiler surveyed tourists about their overall satisfaction with the tourism sector of New Zealand. These researchers attempted to determine the factors that influence overall tourist satisfaction and identify cross-cultural differences among tourists that might arise when evaluating satisfaction levels with their vacations. Using summary judgmental scales in their research (better than expected/worse than expected), the researchers investigated tourist satisfaction with transportation, accommodation, activities and attractions and their sub-components. Their regression analysis showed that activities accounted for one third of the explainable variation, with accommodation and attractions each accounting for over one fourth of the variation. However, the low R2 (10%) value achieved in their regression analysis means that the researchers seem to have omitted some critical components, such as satisfaction with hospitality and foodservice experiences, in their variable list.

Chadee and Mattsson (1996) attempted to measure the quality of tourist experiences of students from different cultures and how different factors affect the global satisfaction of tourists. Using scenarios exhibited on set of pictures for four different tourist encounters (eating out, hotel accommodation, renting a car and going on a sightseeing tour), they found that different variables impact on overall satisfaction with the specific encounter differently. For example, the impact of cleanliness on eating-out satisfaction was seven times higher than that of the prices of the meal. They also found that culture might play a role in the levels of satisfaction derived from the experience. Their results showed that compared to European students, Asians derived lower levels of overall satisfaction from the eating out experience. Culture plays significant role in how individuals form their perceptions and satisfaction.

Based on the summary judgmental scale employed by Danaher and Arweiler, Juaneda and Sastre (1997) investigated tourist satisfaction in the Balearic Islands. They found that satisfaction with local hospitality, prices, accommodation, and attractions has the strongest impact on overall satisfaction with the holiday. Their study differed from that of Danaher and Arweiler in that they attempted to incorporate comparative approach into tourist satisfaction studies in order to identify the strengths and weaknesses of the Balearic Islands' tourist product. These researchers, however, did not analyze whether tourists perceptions of their holidays in other destinations bear any impact on the levels of satisfaction derived from the current holiday experience and whether future intention to visit the present destination would be affected by past holiday experiences in other destinations.

In their motivational investigation into the structure of service experience and satisfaction in tourism, Otto and Ritchie (1996) identified four dimensions. The first factor was hedonics, accounting for 33% variance, in which consumers stated the need to be doing what they loved, to have their imaginations stirred, and to be thrilled by the service activities. The second significant factor was peace of mind in which consumers cited the need for both physical and psychological safety and comfort. The third factor, involvement, deals with the need for to participate in activities and to be educated and informed. The final factor, the recognition, suggests that consumers want to derive a sense of personal recognition from their service providers, such that they could feel important and confident that they are being taken seriously. These researchers suggested that satisfaction was a function of these dimensions only. While critical to the understanding of the concept, it seems that their research focused on the affective (emotional) side of the service experience only. These researchers overlooked the significance of so called technical aspects of a holiday (what is being delivered, e.g., accommodation and meals) as well as functional aspects (how it is being delivered, service quality) in the formation of tourist satisfaction. As they have not included the technical and functional aspects of a holiday into their research instrument, it is not possible to assess whether these aspects affect the fulfillment of consumer motivations and satisfaction. There might be a maintenance factor without which satisfaction would not be achieved (Noe and Uysal, 1997). For instance, the need for relaxation and to participate in activities will never be attained when the tourist suffers from an upset stomach.

In a recent study, Haber and Lerner (1999) argued that that tourist satisfaction is positively related to the attractiveness of the tourism venture's location; the areas of strength of the ventures and the number of services offered; and the entrepreneur's management skills and personal entrepreneurial features. The environmental dimension consists of tourist-related infrastructure, which includes auxiliary services such as restaurants, shopping, transportation, places of entertainment, information, options for excursions, and supply of activities for children, range of tourism activities in the area, the scenery, the climate. The organizational element comprises of the quality of the service, employee professionalism, price, product innovativeness, facilities, customer service, and location. The final dimension that was discussed in Haber and Lerner's study is the entrepreneurial dimension, which includes desire for independence, locus of control, risk tasking, and persistence.

Yuksel and Yuksel (2001) identified sixteen factors, with ten of them seemingly being more influential in affecting tourist satisfaction than the remaining. Among the identified factors,. the hospitality factor, consisting of the attitudes of local people and service employees towards tourists, ranked the highest in significance. The service quality emerged as the second most important factor influencing tourist satisfaction (Yuksel and Yuksel, 2001). This factor relates to service courtesy, friendliness, efficiency, and responsiveness of service personnel to tourist requests and complaints. The emergence of hospitality and service quality as significant factors affecting satisfaction is not a surprising finding. Previous studies have also identified that the positive perception of the behavior, both verbal and non-verbal, of the employees and local people could have a significant role in the formation of tourist satisfaction. It is appropriate to state that negative tourist perceptions of local people and service quality may induce dissatisfaction and deter tourists from returning to the destination. Positive tourist perceptions of local people and service quality could however enhance the experience and motivate tourists to return.

The emergence of accommodation and its facilities as another significant factor affecting tourist satisfaction suggests that provision of both physically and psychologically comforting accommodation facilities may be essential to the generation of quality holiday experiences (Yuksel and Yuksel, 2001). The findings also indicated that tourists' foodservice experience, an inseparable part of the holiday experience, might be instrumental and important in engendering tourist satisfaction. Indeed, tourists' foodservice experiences may lay the foundation for and shape the nature of holiday experience. All the joy, thrills, and other expectations of the holiday may disappear if the tourist becomes ill due to the food eaten or upset because of the low service quality delivered (Yuksel and Yuksel, 2001). Yuksel and Yuksel's findings also suggest that the convenience factors, such as the location of accommodation facility, restaurants, and the operating hours of tourist facilities, may play an important part in tourists' holiday evaluation. The preservation of natural environment, the cleanliness of beaches, the range of facilities available on beaches and the provision of comfortable sunbathing could be among the variables influencing tourist evaluation. The efficiency, courtesy, and quality of services offered at tourist facilities, the noise level, the prices charged for services, and the availability of water sports also emerge as significant considerations in tourists' holiday evaluation (Yuksel and Yuksel, 2001). This study further suggests that, as what the competition has to offer can play an important role in determining consumer behavior, the provision of comparative information is required to assist destination managers in planning appropriate competitive actions against competitors. Yuksel and Yuksel employed a modified experience-based norm model, suggested by Woodruff et al., in order to understand how tourists perceived the destination relative to other destinations, and whether experiences with other destinations affected their holiday evaluation. Their study found a relation between tourists' impressions of their previous holiday destinations and their evaluation of current holidays. The findings suggest that those respondents, who stated that their most recent holiday in another destination was better, rate significantly lower scores on current satisfaction, likelihood to return, and likelihood to recommend variables. This confirms the contention that performance levels, delivered by other destination(s), might affect tourist satisfaction and future intentions toward the present destination. That is, the perceived performance or capabilities of other destinations may set the standard against which the current experience is judged.

Studies with specific tourism products (e.g., shopping on vacation) suggest that satisfaction is not necessarily derived from acquiring goods. In this context, the shopping habitat itself may become part of the shopper's experience and influence subsequent behaviors (Yuksel, 2007). Previous research demonstrates that retail environment can be controlled by manipulating various cues, and in turn, store patrons behavior can be affected (Babin et al., 2004; Kotler, 1974). Stimulus-Organism-Response (S-O-R) paradigm postulates that the environment is a stimulus (S) containing cues that combine to affect people's internal evaluations (O), which in turn create approach/avoidance responses (R) (Mehrabian and Russell, 1974). Drawing on the S-O-R, Mehrabian and Russell (1974) postulate that all responses to an environment can be considered as approach or avoidance behaviors. Approach behaviors include all positive behaviors that might be directed at the environment; for example a desire to remain in a store and explore its offerings could be stated as approach behavior. Avoidance behaviors reflect contrasting responses; that is, a desire to leave a store or not to browse represents avoidance behaviors (Spangenberg, Crowley and Henderson, 1996). Approach behaviors are suggested by increased willingness to interact with others (including salespeople) in an environment, increased willingness to spend time and return to an environment, and an increased willingness to spend money. Individuals are expected to have greater approach behaviors in pleasant environments creating positive affects and greater avoidance behaviors in unpleasant environments creating negative affects (Mehrabian and Russell, 1974).

Researchers have investigated several aspects of in-store environment. This has produced a significant body of information describing various customer reactions caused by manipulating specific ambient cues. In a recent review of 60 experiments manipulated portions of a store's complex atmosphere, Turley and Milliman (2000) note that each of these studies found some statistically significant relationship between atmospherics and shopping behavior. For example, color has been found to affect liking of the store and perceptions of the merchandise (Belizzi, Crowley and Hasty, 1983; Bellizzi and Hite, 1992). Clutter in the environment brought out negative effects on satisfaction and attributions made concerning services (Bitner, 1990). Crowding can change the use of in-store information, satisfaction and enjoyment of the shopping environment (Eroglu and Machleit, 1990). Increasing the tempo and intensity of in-store music has been shown to reduce time consumers spend in the store (Milliman, 1982), emotional responses to waiting in banks (Hui, Dube, and Chebat, 1997) and sales in restaurants (Milliman, 1986). Music manipulations were found to affect consumers' patience, emotional reactions and approach behaviors (Chebat et al., 2001; Yalch and Spangenberg, 1990). Manipulating the odors in a shopping environment was found to influence consumers' purchase intentions and time spent-shopping (Spangenberg et al., 1996).

Previous studies have shown that exterior environment plays an important role, both positive and negative, in customers' impression formation (Bitner, 1992). Service environment provides cues to customers and creates an immediate perceptual image in customers' minds (Kotler, 1973; Lin, 2004). That is, various environmental cues and physical components in a shopping location help tourists form a holistic picture of the overall place. Tourists are not expected to evaluate a specific service location based on only one environmental stimulus, as consumers do process atmospheric characteristics holistically more than piecemeal (Michon et al., 2004). "All discrete pieces are combined to form a holistic picture of the macro environment" (Lin 2004, p., 171). This mental picture will then stimulate an emotional and behavioral response. The macro environment deserves more attention in that exterior climate (e.g., building architecture, the surrounding area, storefronts, activities, density, noise level, social temperature etc.) is the first set of cues normally seen by a tourist. If these variables are not managed well, the rest of the atmosphere may not matter. The macro environment must be pleasing and induce approach behaviors for the retail sector to be successful.

Only a few studies have examined the impact of the macro environment of a shopping district on shopping satisfaction and behaviors. Grossbart, Mittelstaedt, Curtis and Rogers (1975 cf. Turley and Milliman, 2000) found that external attributes of a shopping district have an influence on the behavior of retail customers. Other research examining the links between evaluations of the store environment as a whole and purchase behaviors has identified similar strong relationships. Adapting Fisher's (1974) Environmental Aesthetics Scale, Crowley (1993) and Spangenberg et al. (1996) studied two dimensions of environment: affective (attractive, relaxed, comfortable and good) and activating environments (lively, bright, motivating and interesting). Crowley (1993) and Spangenberg et al's (1996) research suggest a direct relationship between activating nature of the environment and evaluations of the product in that environment and purchase intentions. In another study, a high-load (arousing) environment was found to produce approach behaviors, whereas high-load unpleasant environment produced avoidance behaviors, and a low-load environment was not activating enough to motivate any measurable approach/avoidance behaviors (Donovan and Rossiter, 1982). Evidence further suggests that physical elements matching in terms of their arousing nature create more pleasing combinations, leading to increased spending and higher satisfaction than do combinations comprised of an inappropriate arousal level (Mattila and Wirtz, 2001). Similarly, Babin et al (2004) identified that when perceptual environmental appropriateness was diminished, customers reported lower positive affect, lower product quality ratings, lower perceptions of personal shopping value and fewer approach behaviors. Chebat and Michon (2003) found that favorable perceptions of the mall environment as a whole increased shopper's spending. A recent study (Yuksel, 2007) states shopping environment deserves attention in that macro climate is the first set of cues normally seen by a tourist. If macro environment is not attractive and inviting, the rest of the in-store atmosphere may not matter. The environment of shopping locations at destination must be pleasing and induce approach behaviors for the retail sector to be successful.

Decisions relating to activities whilst on holiday entail risk and possible loss, as the consequences associated with the decisions are generally uncertain. Consumers' perceptions of risks are considered to be central to their evaluations, choices, and behaviours (Campbell and Goodstein, 2001). While perceived risks are likely to influence the tourist's current and future decisions (George, 2003; Sönmez and Graefe, 1998b), surprisingly they have not been adequately integrated into hospitality and tourism domains. The majority of previous research has dealt with shopping satisfaction of mall customers. Despite its importance, shopping tourists and their risk perceptions have attracted no or limited attention from the researchers and marketers. Perceived risks can influence behaviour in large part because they alter one's feelings. Satisfaction with the shopping experience and the expressed intention of loyalty can then be affected by the perceived risk-induced emotional states of pleasure and arousal of customers. Mehrabian and Russell propose that three basic emotional states mediate behaviours in environmental situations. These emotional responses, known by the acronym PAD, are Pleasure, Arousal and Dominance. Their model posits that any environment, including that of a tourist shopping habitat will produce an emotional state in an individual that can be characterised in terms of the three PAD dimensions (Donovan and Rossiter, 1982). Pleasure-displeasure refers to the degree to which the person feels good, joyful, happy, or satisfied in the situation. Arousal-nonarousal refers to the degree to which a person feels excited, stimulated, alert or active in the situation. Dominance-submissiveness refers to the extent to which the individual feels in control of, or free to act in, the situation. Donovan and Rossiter (1982) applied an abbreviated version of the PAD scale to retailing research. They found that pleasure-arousal dimensions were adequate to represent individual's emotional responses to a wide range of environments and shopping behaviours were not related to measures of Dominance. There has been a considerable consensus in respect to this bi-dimensional character of emotions (Pleasure-Arousal) in recent marketing research (Bigne, Andreu and Gnoth in press). Emotions experienced while shopping has been shown to affect a variety of responses such as approach behaviour (Hui et al., 1997), spending levels (Donovan and Rossiter 1982), retail preference and choice (Dawson, Bloch and Ridgway, 1990), willingness to buy (Baker, Levy and Grewal, 1992), and shopping satisfaction (Machleit and Eroglu, 2000; Machleit and Mantel, 2001).

Findings of these studies suggest that overall tourist satisfaction may be evaluated along two broad dimensions. First, the instrumental dimension and second the expressive dimension. Instrumental dimension relates to the physical performance of the product such as cleanliness. In contrast, the expressive dimension corresponds to the "psychological" level of performance (for example, comfort, hospitality, and relaxation). Some researchers argue that tourist satisfaction with the psychological performance of a product is extremely important. For instance, based on a study of tourism in India, Ohja (1982) reports that there were tourists who were satisfied despite some problems with the physical product offered, yet there were tourists who were dissatisfied with the best physical product. Drawing on this study, Ohja concludes that tourist satisfaction does not come only from good sights but from the behavior one encounters, from the information one gets, and from the efficiency with which needs are served. Discussing the relative significance of these two dimensions, Reisinger and Turner (1997) remark that even the best physical product cannot compensate for psychological dissatisfaction. This suggests that when assessing tourist satisfaction with destinations, along with the "instrumental" dimension of satisfaction (satisfaction with physical performance), the "expressive" dimension of satisfaction (satisfaction with psychological performance) should also be assessed (Reisinger and Turner, 1997). The relative significance attached to each of these two dimensions, however, may vary from individual to individual or from situation to another.

In addition to the significance of the expressive dimension, several studies have shown that instrumental dimension (practical aspects) of the holiday could contribute measurably to tourist satisfaction (Noe and Uysal, 1997). For instance, Herzberg, Mausner, and Snyderman's (1959) research on work motivation suggests that hygiene factors (for example, cleanliness) cannot be compensated for if not fulfilled, and which lead to dissatisfaction. Similarly, in Lounsburry and Hoopes's research (1985), although it explained only a small portion of the variance (6%), the "lodging and food" dimension emerged among vacationers important satisfaction dimensions. In Whipple and Thach (1988) research, along with the more expressive attributes of sightseeing, two instrumental service features, including a tour escort service and point of departure, were singled out as significantly contributing to satisfaction of the trip. In another study on organized tours, it was also evident that tourist satisfaction was influenced by factors unrelated to long term or planned motivational considerations (Geva and Goldman, 1991). Such practical aspects of the pace of the tour, opportunities to use facilities, comfort, and cleanliness of the bus, figured noticeably among the satisfaction dimensions. This may suggest that motivations (such as knowledge seeking and escape) may be more easily achieved if such practical aspects are taken into account and catered for on sightseeing tours. In other words, such instrumental aspects as accommodation and food service quality may have the potential to facilitate or inhibit the fulfillment of the holiday motivations. The practical implications of all this is that destination authorities should always try to satisfy the hygiene (or the basic) factors first and then the motivational factors (Ross and Iso-Ahola, 1991).

Reviewed literature suggests that tourist satisfaction is a very complex and has been receiving growing attention from researchers. Over the last three decades, some studies have investigated tourist satisfaction from anthropological, sociological and psychological perspectives. While these perspectives are critical to understanding of the concept, they are not readily transferable into managerial actions. Some studies indicated that destination related attributes that management can directly manipulate account for tourist satisfaction, while others argued that consumer related factors such as personality, socio-economic status, demographics, and the familiarity with the destination play an important role in tourist satisfaction. Some studies considered tourist market as homogenous and contended that generic dimensions affect tourist satisfaction, while others defended that drivers of satisfaction between different subsets of the market might be different, which requires managerial attention. Researchers in the tourist satisfaction area also seem to have paid inadequate attention to comparative studies, although it is important to know the relative performance for the success in both short and long terms. The possibility that the performance level delivered by a competitor might affect tourist satisfaction and future intentions with the present destinations appears to be under researched. Assessment of performance relative to main competitors can help destination managers develop better focus in catch-up and differential strategies.

Despite these continuing debates, there are two elements on which there appears to be an agreement. First, tourist satisfaction is not a universal phenomenon, not everyone gets the same satisfaction out of the same holiday experience, and second, tourist satisfaction may be a multifaceted concept. This is partly because unlike material products and pure services, the holiday experience is a blend of different tangible and intangible products brought together. As tourism is an experience made up of many different independent parts, some more tangibles than others, tourist satisfaction, as was discussed earlier, may be treated as a cumulative measure of total consumption experience. In other words, satisfaction with a holiday experience may be based on the sum total of satisfactions with the individual attributes of all the products and services that compose the holiday experience and that the relative weight of these attributes in the formation of tourist satisfaction might be different.

Even though customer satisfaction has become the most frequent application of market research in the 1990s, there are a number of issues imposing difficulties to its measurement. Yüksel and Yüksel (Chapter 2) start with presenting several definitions of service and customer satisfaction which are important to the development of this research. The term customer satisfaction is first examined generically and then explained within the context of tourism. There is no universally accepted definition of customer satisfaction and because no one gets the same satisfaction out of the same service consumption, defining what constitutes tourist satisfaction seems to be difficult. Yuksel and Yuksel (Chapter 2) suggest that, to better understand tourist satisfaction, it may be best to frame the concept in terms of a tourism experience that is cumulative in nature. This cumulative view of satisfaction is logical, as holiday experiences generally involve several independent components. The focus of the next section in Chapter 2 is on the similarity and differences between satisfaction and two other related concepts, namely attitude and service quality, as it is imperative to the understanding of the satisfaction concept and to the development of the research. A critical review of the literature undertaken in this section reveals that there are two different thoughts with respect to the similarity/ differences between customer satisfaction and service quality constructs. To some, the distinction between the two is extremely important because "service providers need to know whether their objective should be to have customers who are satisfied with their performance or to deliver the maximum level of perceived service quality" (Cronin and Taylor, 1992: 56). Conversely, others argue that there is no need for such distinction and practitioners are not interested in the difference between these two constructs per se. Management would rather be more interested in both concepts mainly as predictors of customer behavior, for example repeat purchase and word-of-mouth recommendations, which directly affects the viability and profitability of the firm (Dabholkar, 1995).

Researchers supporting the difference seem to have failed to address what precisely are the differences between satisfaction and service quality and what does each add to understanding of and ability to predict consumer behavior? In addition, from a management viewpoint, attempting to differentiate between the two concepts might be pointless, particularly if they do not affect consumers' post-purchase behavioral outcomes differently. Moreover, such distinction may be considered unnecessary because in most cases a positive perception of service quality enhances customer satisfaction, and a negative quality perception brings about customer dissatisfaction. At present, there is limited research evidence in the literature concerning whether service quality and customer satisfaction are distinguishable. As Spreng and Mackoy (1996) quite rightly put it, if they are distinct constructs, "then we need to understand how different they are. If they are not distinct then we do not have to waste time on surveys asking for both or confuse managers by telling them they have to be concerned with both " (p. 202).

Boksberger (Chapter 3) discusses customer value - one of the most important measures for gaining competitive edge - in detail. Since customer value reveals the relative benefits and sacrifices of a purchase to customers, it represents a challenge for customer orientation in the tourism and hospitality industry. Given the fact that service quality and customer satisfaction are the predominant constructs in the literature, the growing body of knowledge of customer value is fragmented and does not specifically attest to the characteristics of tourism services. Likewise, the role of perceived risk has attracted little attention from academicians and practitioners. Having outlined that services are perceived to be riskier than goods, Boksberger systemises the particularities of tourism and hospitality services, perceived risk and the sources of value. That is, a theoretical analysis of the characteristics of services and the value constructs along with definitions and limitations is presented, based on an extensive literature review. By integrating the concept of perceived risk and a multidimensional typology of value, Boksberger proposes a conceptual framework of customer value for the tourism and hospitality industry. Boksberger provides a genuine theoretical contribution, as well as, several implications for management practice in the tourism and hospitality industry.

Yüksel and Yüksel (Chapter 4) present a number of frameworks developed to explain customer satisfaction in the literature. The theories explicated in this chapter include the Dissonance Theory, the Contrast Theory, the Expectancy-Disconfirmation Theory, the Comparison Level Theory, the Value-Percept Theory, the Attribution Theory, The Equity theory, the Person-Situation Fit concept, and the Importance-Performance model. There is widespread consensus among these satisfaction theories that satisfaction is an evaluative judgment, which results from a comparison of product performance to some forms of evaluation standard. The majority of these theories, for example the Expectancy Disconfirmation Paradigm, the Comparison Level Theory, and the Evaluative Congruity Theory concur that product performance exceeding prior expectations or some form of standards signifies satisfaction, whereas dissatisfaction is the outcome when product performance falls short of that standard. Thus, the disparity concept between the actual outcome and the expected constitutes the core of the majority of the satisfaction theories.

Early theories of the satisfaction concept assume that consumers may either exaggerate (the Contrast Theory) or adjust (the Dissonance Theory) the perceived disparity between the product performance and the initial expectations or the norm. As these early theories have not been applied in tourism and hospitality settings, the validity of their assumptions remains unclear. Based on the logic of the Dissonance Theory, some researchers suggest that in order to have a higher product evaluation, companies should raise customer expectations substantially above the product performance. This assumption is criticised on the grounds that it does not take into account of the concept of tolerance levels. Drawing on these two early satisfaction theories, Oliver developed the Expectancy-Disconfirmation paradigm which postulates that if the outcome of a product is judged to be better than or equal to the expected, the consumer will feel satisfied. If, on the other hand, actual outcome is judged not to be better than expected, the consumer will be satisfied. The EDP has gained growing support from researchers and it has become the most widely applied framework in studies assessing customer satisfaction with tourism and hospitality services.

Last decades also saw the development of other models to explain customer satisfaction. In contrast to EDP which assumes satisfaction resulting from disconfirmation of predictive expectations, LaTour and Peat's (1979) Comparison Level Theory views satisfaction as a function of comparison between product performance and consumers' past experiences and experiences of other consumers. Westbrook and Riley (1983) introduced the Value-Percept Theory which proposes that satisfaction is an emotional response that is triggered by a cognitive evaluative process in which the perceptions of an offer are compared to one's values, needs, wants or desires, in contrast to expectations suggested in Oliver's EDP model. Sirgy's Evaluative Congruity Model views satisfaction as a function of evaluative congruity, which is a cognitive matching process in which a perception is compared to an evoked referent cognition for the purpose of evaluating a stimulus object/action. The Importance-Performance model, borrowed from Fishbein and Ajzen's consumer behaviour model, and adapted to hospitality services by Barsky, assumes that consumer satisfaction is a function of beliefs about an object's attributes (that is a product possesses a particular attribute) and the strenght of these belief (that is, the relative importance of each attribute to the customer's overall satisfaction with the product or service). As stated earlier, majority of these theories suggest that customer satisfaction is a relative concept and judged in relation to a standard. While several comparison standards have been proposed in the literature, no consensus exists concerning which standard might be the most appropriate (which standard best predicts customer satisfaction) (Cote, Foxman and Cutler, 1989; Erevelles and Leavitt, 1992).

Yüksel and Yüksel (Chapter 5) state that the concept of customer satisfaction is integral to marketing thought. Various theoretical frameworks, based on various standards, have been developed to explain this important concept. Researchers have not converged on the exact conceptualisation of the comparison standard and disconfirmation constructs (Tse and Wilton, 1988). Several researchers concur that consumers may use expectations but other kinds of baselines may be operative in the formation of satisfaction judgments. As early as 1977, Miller, for instance, developed a classification scheme by using four different kinds of comparisons: expected, deserved, ideal and minimum tolerable performance. Predictive expectations have been widely adopted as the comparison standard in many tourism and hospitality research investigations. However, the marketing literature is replete with evidence demonstrating that expectations-based dis/confirmation measures, at best, have yielded only modest correlations with satisfaction measures. As a result, the validity of using expectations as the sole pre-consumption antecedent of the dis/confirmation process and as the basis for predicting its outcomes has become disputable. Expectations have been elevated to some grand conceptual status "but there is no compelling theoretical or empirical reason that expectations per se must be the comparison for judgement" (Iacobucci et al 1994, p. 25). Past research may have attached " unwarranted importance to expectations as the standard of performance influencing feelings of satisfaction" (Cadotte et al 1987, p. 306). There is a very little justification for consumers using only focal brand expectations to judge performance after purchase (Westbrook and Reilly, 1983).

Review in Chapter 5 suggests that some standards of comparison may be better than others at explaining satisfaction and that the relationship between disconfirmation, performance, and satisfaction may change depending on the standards used to measure them. However, at present there is no consensus of an appropriate standard, and some researchers have suggested that the standard that is used is contingent upon a number of consumer and situational factors (Spreng and Dixon, 1992). The comparison standard, for example, has been conceptualised as expected (Oliver, 1980), ideal (Sirgy, 1984), or normative performance (Woodruff et al 1983). Some researchers have suggested that consumers may not only use a single standard but may also engage in multiple comparisons in customer satisfaction/dissatisfaction formation. Although there seems to be an agreement as to the fact that customer satisfaction can be a function of multiple standards, it is not clear, however, which combination of standards is more applicable to different consumption situations, and to different products and services. It is important to note that in spite of the emphasis placed on the different types of standards, only a few have received much empirical attention. For instance, predictive expectation as a standard has been studied extensively in marketing literature in general and in tourism and hospitality literature in particular. Other standards have not been examined as well in the tourism and hospitality literature. A review of customer satisfaction literature in Chapter 5 clearly manifests that researchers in marketing and consumer behavior in general and hospitality and tourism in particular have favored the use of Expectancy-Disconfirmation paradigm, which employs predictive expectations as the comparative standard. Despite the fact that no model or theory is complete, limited research has been carried out whether the dominant Expectancy-Disconfirmation paradigm possesses any theoretical and/or methodological shortcomings and whether it could be possible to apply the model in every situation.

Gutierrez, Agudo and Rodriguez (Chapter 6) note that knowledge of the customer satisfaction process, a psychological process which the individual goes through during the pre-encounter and post-encounter stages with services, is a critical issue in tourism research. Variables such as attitudes, prior beliefs, service assessments and behavioral intentions can play a significant role in this psychological process. In this context, one of the most important and unexplored trends is the move away from a single comparison standard (expectations) toward multiple standards in the customer satisfaction process. On the other hand, image has been extensively analyzed as a key psychological variable in the individual's choice process. Unfortunately, little research has been done on the influence of provider image during the different stages of the customer satisfaction process. With this in mind, Gutierrez et al. try to enhance the body of knowledge on tourist satisfaction in two ways: (1) by exploring the effect of multiple comparison standards on customer satisfaction; and (2) by examining the influence of image during the different stages of the customer satisfaction process (pre, during and after the tourist service encounter). Their results, obtained from a qualitative and quantitative research in the travel agency sector, suggest that in contrast to the traditional views of tourist satisfaction: (1) multiple comparison standards (i.e. ideal and predictive expectations) operate simultaneously in the customer satisfaction process; and (2) image takes part in all the stages of this psychological process (i.e. formation of expectations, satisfaction and customer loyalty).

Measuring tourist satisfaction is not an option but an essential part of destination management information system. Tourism and hospitality managers who measure satisfaction against what customers are really after would seem to receive far more powerful data to act upon than do present surveys where things are checked off from a list that may or may not have relevant items on them. Yüksel and Yüksel (Chapter 7) use a modified version of the research approach originally developed by Kreck (1998) in order to (1) identify critical destination attributes that are important to tourists, (2) assess their current performance, and (3) benchmark how the destination (in this case Turkey) performs on these attributes compared to one of its rivals. Results showed differences, as well as similarities, between attributes important to tourists when compared to attributes included in other satisfaction surveys.

Tourism is a multi-cultural industry. The significant role that culture holds in affecting travelers' buying behavior has led growing number o researchers to study differences, particularly between Western and Asian cultures. Consequently, many interesting cultural differences have been discovered. Cross-cultural research (CCR) is however replete with inadequately addressed methodological and practical difficulties. Firstly, the conventional operationalisation of culture is highly questionable, which may bring about misleading and costly marketing implications. Secondly, the extent to which cross-cultural studies are equipped with adequate research approaches to explore differences and similarities within-between cultures reliably and validly is debatable. Last but not least, the stability and predictability of one's culture is a contentious issue. Solnicar, Grün and Le (Chapter 8) criticize that response styles can distort survey findings. Culture-specific response styles (CSRS) are particularly problematic to cross-cultural and empirical tourism researchers using multi-cultural samples because the resulting data contamination can lead to inaccurate conclusions about the research question under study. This is particularly the case when constructs such as satisfaction are measured, which are difficult to operationalise. Nevertheless, possible culture-specific response style effects are typically ignored, thus jeopardizing the validity of reported findings. This chapter raises awareness of the problem, illustrates the problem empirically and presents a method that enables researchers to assess the robustness of empirical findings on cross-cultural differences in satisfaction to CSRS. This approach avoids the disadvantages of ignoring the problem and interpreting spurious results or choosing one single correction technique that potentially introduces new kinds of data contamination.

Segment based satisfaction studies are on increase. Market segmentation is one of the most useful methods which can help travel marketers to enhance their understanding of why different people like to travel, and what underlying issues are important as tourists process holiday information and proceed along all of decision stages in the course of putting a trip together (Fitzgibbon, 1994). Since Smith's pioneering article in 1956, which argued that groups of consumers could be defined in such a way that their purchasing behavior would be relatively homogeneous, numerous marketing studies have been completed that have used and improved concepts of segmentation (Smith, 1989). These studies aimed at obtaining more accurate and effective segments and employed different segmentation criteria and the methods of analysis (Legoherel, 1998). Several practical guidance have been proffered for marketers to follow during and after the segmentation process in order to improve implementability of segmentation solutions and their impact on business performance (Dibb, 1998; Simkin and Dibb, 1998). The most commonly cited guidance is that of Kotler's (1984), which states that segments should demonstrate measurability, so that segment size and potential can be measured; substantiality, in order that segments are sizeable enough to be profitable; accessibility, so that customers in the segments to be reached; actionability, allowing segments to be effectively served with marketing programs and; stability, so that resources can be safely invested.

While there is guidance readily available for marketers during and after the segmentation process, little research has directly dealt with the question of causes of success/failure that can be considered before the segmentation process (Dibb, 1998). Some contributions however have been made to the debate. Well designed planning, commitment and involvement of senior managers, readiness to respond to market changes, and creative thinking have all been referred to as potential success factors (Dibb, 1998). The choice of variables that will identify prospective segments, more amenable to the appeal of the product/service as reflected in advertising and sales messages is a crucial factor. Another issue, which might affect the outcome of segmentation research, is the erraticism and unpredictability of human behavior over various stages of the purchasing process (Fitzgibbon, 1994; Legoherel, 1998). That is, the consumer may sometimes be statutory-oriented, and sometimes convenience-oriented with respect to the same product/service category.

The notion of instability of consumer behavior and changing composition of benefit segments over time has been noted by a number of researchers. These researchers debated that if one segment could describe the consumption of a product at a given time, no guarantee existed that it would be still relevant at another time (Woodside and Jacobs, 1985). Trends in fashion or economics and competition could affect the configuration of segments (Haley, 1985). Researchers therefore suggest that segmentation analysis is more effective when it is performed on a regular basis because it helps to detect and assess trends and changes in the market place (Formica and Uysal, 2000). An additional contention is that changes in consumer behavior, and thus segment instability, may not only occur over time (seasons, years) but also over the duration of service/product consumption experience. That is, the consumer at the end of the consumption experience may not belong to the same segment identified by information solicited prior to the experience.

It is theorized that a consumer's buying process is multi-staged. That is, a consumer, in making a purchase decision, goes through the stages of need recognition, information search, evaluation of alternatives, choice of product/service, and post purchase evaluation. With respect to vacationers, Clawson and Knetsch (1966) put forward that vacation experience consists of five different phases. These include anticipation and planning, travel to the destination, on-site experiences, travel back, and evaluation. Their contention is that vacationers may differ across all or some of these phases. The difference in information, situational factors, and complex rules of dissonance reduction suggest that the vacationer at the end of the journey may not be the same individual at the beginning of the journey in terms of needs, motivations, expectations and preferences. Possible modifications in tourist behavior that occur during the course of the purchasing process (intention, travel to destination, on-site experiences, and post-trip phase) may induce instability among the groups of tourists determined during segmentation studies (Legoherel, 1998). If so, from the marketing managerial point of view, the usefulness of launching a promotion campaign based solely on tourists' stated preferences before the visit would be called into question.

It should be noted that the majority of segmentation research have looked specifically at what tourists would like to do (stated preferences) and solicited their motivations, expectations or the importance assigned to certain supply attributes prior to the experience (Frochot and Morrison, 2000). Although uses of these variables have resulted in many interesting segmentation schemes, focusing solely on pre-visit phase of consumer decision making process nevertheless has some shortcomings. The holiday is an unfolding experience, an evolving product in that consumption takes place over time and a large amount of consumer learning takes place over the holiday duration (Geva and Goldman 1989). Tourists' pre-visit motivations, expectations, and assigned importance to destination attributes might not be similar to that of their post-visit. They may be shaped by the actual experience and that the configuration of segments may differ as a result. Inevitably, this requires modifications in marketing communications.

Salih and McIntosh (Chapter 9) evaluate tourist satisfaction within the context of a specific segment (diving tourism) and present the findings of an empirical research undertaken with more than 200 divers in the Maldives. Travel destination and leisure activity choice are similarly dependent on the perceived satisfaction and beneficial outcomes sought from the activity. However, leisure experiences within destinations are consumed in different ways. The satisfaction sought by divers differs from other recreationists. As such, a focus on the experiential nature of the leisure activity itself is required in relation to advancing the measurement and evaluation of tourist satisfaction.

Diving is an activity that embodies many experiential characteristics (Gunter, 1979; 1987); underwater exploration, entrance into the mysterious "deep blue", the experience of weightlessness, being mesmerised and fantasized by the beauty beneath the sea. Generally, divers' preferences and behaviour depend on their experience and level of commitment to the sport (Bloch and Bruce, 1984). Thus, many factors influence the nature of divers' satisfaction, which are often beyond the control of the service providers but require consideration in the conceptualization of tourist satisfaction. A large number of studies have attempted to understand consumer satisfaction (for example, Danaher et al., 1996). However, few studies have sought to understand tourist satisfaction in relation to scuba diving. This special segment of the tourism industry needs to be studied further, especially in the context of island nations such as the Maldives where tourism is not only the main source of revenue, but divers comprise almost one-third of their annual tourist arrivals.

Yüksel and Yüksel (Chapter 10) use empirical data from a recent cross-national research on British and German travelers to explore their personal motivations for taking overseas holidays and their attribute-seeking patterns. Due to possibility of differences among travelers from the same nation in terms of their motivations and the importance that they attach to specific destination attributes, within-nation variations are also explored. Results of the study suggest that travelers have multiple travel motives and the push and pull factors are nationality-sensitive. Importance levels attached to push and pull forces were found to vary within British travelers. Dolnicar and Le (Chapter 11) note that despite a long history in empirical tourism research and satisfaction research, yet little work has been done at the cross-roads of these two areas. Dolnicar and Le make a step towards filling this gap by (1) reviewing prior work in data-driven market segmentation with a specific focus on satisfaction, (2) analyzing managerial recommendations resulting from these studies, and (3) providing empirical examples of how commonsense and data-driven segmentation studies could be conducted using satisfaction as discriminating criterion between tourists.

Failures are likely to happen even in the best-run organizations despite the service provider's attempt to provide consistent and high quality services to consumers. This is partly because service delivery is heterogeneous across service encounters and there are internal and external factors that may impact on the delivery process. Customers' pre-purchase expectations are negatively disconfirmed when they perceive a failure with respect to any dimensions of service quality (outcome and/or process). Broken service promise and unmet expectations will cause the customer cognitively and affectively evaluate the service failure and determine which step (e.g., exit or voice - complaining to the service provider, friends, relatives or third parties) (Day and Landon, 1977), if any, will be taken to redress the situation (Levesque and McDougall, 2000; Susskind, 2000, 2002). Complaint handling is a critical moment of truth for companies in their efforts to satisfy and keep customers (Strauss and Seidel, 1998). Unfortunately, research shows that the majority of customers are dissatisfied with companies' service recovery efforts (Andreassen, 2001; Tax, Brown and Chandrashekaran, 1999).

A service recovery refers to the actions a service employee takes in response to a service failure (Brown, Cowles and Tuten, 1996; Gronroos, 1988). The aim of service recovery efforts is basically to move a customer from a state of dissatisfaction to a state of satisfaction (Zemke, 1994). Recovery to failures can take many forms. These actions range from "do nothing to whatever it takes to fix the problem" (Bitner et al., 1990; Hart et al., 1990; Hoffman et al., 1995; Kelley, Hoffman and Davies, 1993). The effectiveness of recovery strategies depends on the situation and is influenced by such factors as importance and type of service. Effectiveness is also dependent on the way in which the service provider handles the problem. Responsiveness, empathy and understanding improve the effectiveness of the recovery strategy (Bitner et al., 1990; Hart et al., 1990). Thus, not only what is done but also how it is done will contribute to the effectiveness of the recovery.

Dissatisfied customers may engage in specific complaint behavior(s) and this is probably based on a complex decision-making process, which includes expectancy of outcomes, costs and benefits involved, attributions of blame, and attitude towards the act of complaining (Day, 1984; Singh and Widing, 1991). Attitude toward complaining is defined as the personal tendency of dissatisfied consumers to seek compensation from the firm (Richins, 1980). This attitude is conceptualized as the overall affect of the "goodness" or "badness" of complaining to sellers and is not specific to a specific episode of dissatisfaction (Singh and Widing, 1991). Hirschman (1970) posited that voice behavior is partly dependent on the ability and willingness of the consumer to complain. Consumers with positive attitudes toward complaining, compared with those who are reluctant to seek redress, are expected to be less likely to engage in negative intention and behavior, such as negative word-of-mouth communication and exit (Day and Landon, 1976). Thus, those consumers who have a more favorable attitude toward complaining are expected to be more likely to express their complaint intention to the firm. Blodgett et al. (1995) in their discussion of the empirical evidence on attitude to complaining found that consumers who have a favorable attitude to complaining will be more likely to seek redress from a retailer. These authors also posited that consumers who are averse to seeking redress will instead just silently exit and/or engage in negative word-of-mouth behavior. Kim, Kim, Im and Shin (2003) found empirical support for their hypothesis that complaint intention is positively influenced by increases in favorable attitudes toward complaining. Some of the negative attitudes that prevent people from complaining could be culture related (i.e., propensity to complain, fear of confrontation, losing face, etc.). Some customers with a specific cultural background may believe that complaining is a necessary, worthwhile and important function of consumerism, others may not. Given the probable relationship between consumer attitudes and behaviors, examining differences between cultures in their attitudes to complaining is managerially important in order to design actions to impact on consumers' tendency to complain directly to the organization instead of elsewhere (Davidow and Dacin, 1997, cf. Kim et al., 2003). Using a scenario, involving a core service failure and no recovery action, Yuksel et al. (2006) examined differences and similarities in complaining attitudes and behaviors of British, Israeli, Dutch and Turkish hotel customers. Results have shown that respondents from these countries had favorable attitude toward complaining. That is, they will do something about their dissatisfaction. A moderate relationship between attitudes and choice of complaining behavior was reported (Yuksel et al., 2006). Respondents with favorable attitudes to complaining were more likely to engage in voice behaviors; whereas, respondents with negative attitudes were more likely to display switch or loyalty behavior. The study concludes that the more negative about complaining the less likely that consumer will engage in voice behavior. Mediating role of consumer attitudes related to consumer complaint behavior needs further empirical attention.

O'Neill and Mattila (Chapter 12) focus on hotel service recovery strategy and present the concepts of stable and unstable service failure and service recovery. Findings from a survey of actual hotel guests indicate that guests' overall satisfaction regarding service failure and recovery are higher when they believe that service failure is unstable and recovery is stable. In addition, guests indicate they are more likely to return to the same hotel when they believe that service failure is unstable and recovery is stable. Moreover, their results suggest that guests are more satisfied with their guest room when they believe that recovery is stable.

Research on consumer complaining behavior (CCB) suggests that a vast majority of consumers do not report their dissatisfaction; rather they switch companies and spread negative word-of-mouth. Ro and Mattila (Chapter 13) propose an integrated conceptual framework of consumer complaining behavior by using cognitive appraisal theory as its foundation. The proposed model starts with a service failure as an input into the evaluation process. A service failure will trigger an immediate affective response (initial dissatisfaction) that enables consumers to engage in a cognitive appraisal process. A cognitive appraisal process consists of four components: importance of the event, seriousness of the problem, attribution, and coping potential. Negative emotions are generated as a result of the cognitive appraisal process and the elicited emotions influence the type of coping strategies used by the consumer. Specifically, their model includes four negative emotions: anger resulting from controllable causes attributes to others, disappointment resulting from uncontrollable causes attributed the situation, regret from self-blame, and worry from uncertainty. Problem-based coping and emotion–based coping are manifested as consumer complaining behaviors. Voice and third-party actions are considered as problem focused coping strategies, while negative word-of-mouth, switching, and no-action are considered as emotion-focused coping strategies. Individual differences and industry characteristics also influence consumers' cognitive appraisal processes and their complaint behaviors.

Yuksel and Cengiz (Chapter 14) note that like any spoken language, body language has words, sentences and punctuation. Each gesture is like a single word and one word may have several different meanings. Non-verbal behavior (NVB) can thus have several functions in a service recovery situation. It can clarify verbal message (i.e., communication depends largely on what individuals are doing vocally and bodily while saying it). NVB can also help establish a relationship between staff and customer and help establish staff credibility (i.e., customer's perception of staff competence, trustworthiness and character). Service recovery is a very delicate, interaction-intensive and emotionally-driven moment-of-truth, in which customer may become extremely vigilant to any kind of cue. Empirical negligence of the likely effects of NVB on customers' recovery emotions and their evaluations of the service provider is therefore curious. Yüksel and Cengiz explored whether staff's NVB during a service recovery could shape customers' emotional reactions, their evaluation of the staff and their behavioral intentions. A quasi experiment, manipulating two forms of kinesics (i.e., open/closed body posture and appropriate/inappropriate eye contact), was conducted with tourists. Empirical evidence in the study suggests that NVB during a recovery could, to a large extent, determine customers' judgments. An open body posture, accompanied with an appropriate eye contact leads to positive emotions and favorable perceptions of the service personnel. Staff displaying such positive NVB is seen more credible, competent, courteous and trustworthy. Favorable NVB appears to have significantly increased the respondents' ratings on behavioral intentions and contacting with the same staff (i.e., trust and empathy building) in the case of experiencing another problem.

Complaint handling is fast-growing research field and a crucial success factor in the business environment. Many service firms invest heavily on understanding their ever-sophisticated customers whose perceptions, values, and attitudes are constantly changing. Conventional methods, including in-house surveys, focus groups etc. have been widely used to trace trends in customer recovery expectations, goals, consumption emotions and so on. Different from these obtrusive methods, Tanrısevdi (Chapter 15) argues that extensive use of the Internet by the Internet-literate customers, both before and after the service consumption, urges hotel managers to scan customers' expressions about their and/or other similar organizations. Based on a content analysis of over two hundred and twenty seven e-complaints, gleaned from three separate web-based complaint forums, Tanrısevdi argues that e-complaints are important source for managerial feedback, and subsequent improvements and maintenance.

Research in-so-far has provided empirical evidence about effects of such environmental cues as noise, lighting, color, atmosphere, crowd density etc. on customers' perceptions, evaluations and approach-avoidance behaviors. Recent arguments suggest that there are yet other factors in the direct control of destination authorities which can have effects on tourists' onsite evaluations, and approach/avoidance behaviors (Yuksel, 2006). Yuksel and Efendi (Chapter 16) propose that marketing efforts that decrease the level of uncertainties associated with a service experience, as well as, unawareness level about a place and its attractions may induce positive evaluations and approach behaviors. Provision of additional information (e.g., what is available, at what cost and how to get there) through exposure of onsite promotions/advertisements, for example may help reduce uncertainties. Continuous communication with visitors in this form can increase interest and awareness about offerings of the place. It can compensate likely inefficiencies and incompleteness resulting from initial (if any) communication efforts which are likely to be constrained by time, space and other limitations. Repeated exposure to destination promotion materials/messages may result in gradual learning and ultimately further visitations, and extra buying behaviors on holiday (McWilliams and Crompton, 1997). Literature further shows that buyers would feel reassured that a wise purchase decision has been made when they are presented with such post purchase promotions.

Bilim and Yüksel (Chapter 17) argue that consumption of holiday products/destinations carries a symbolic meaning. They state that destinations may possess a personality that travelers either use as an avenue for self-expression or to experience the anticipated emotional benefits that differentiate one destination from another. These perceived destination personalities may emerge through the different ways that destinations present themselves. However, research on brand personality and the symbolic use of brands largely has been restricted to how consumers express themselves by choosing brands. Moreover, brand personality has often been discussed with clear reference to products and corporate brands, but not to destinations and how this can be communicated via holiday postcards. The contention of Bilim and Yüksel is that destination personality (if any) conveyed by postcards (i.e., indirect experiences) may positively influence consumer preference through a congruence effect. Extent of the congruence depends on the postcards' ability in evoking favorable affective image and a fit between depicted personality and the individual's holiday motivations, and his/her self-image.

Mil and Yüksel (Chapter 18) question the method of querying the existence of something, in this case customer satisfaction and ask what we measure is really customer satisfaction.

Mil and Yuksel's presumption that the existence shall be searched at a contrary existence is creating a very critical point in the research developed with a qualitative point of view.

REFERENCES

Andreassen, T. W. (2000). Antecedents to satisfaction with service recovery. *European Journal of Marketing*, 34 (1/2), 156-175.

Armistead, C. G., Clarke, G., and Stanley, P. (1995). Managing Service Recovery. Cranfield. *School of Management.*

Babin, J. B., Darden, R. W., and Griffin, M. (1994). Work and/or fun: measuring hedonic and utilitarian shopping value. *Journal of Consumer Research,* 20, 644-656.

Baker, L., Grewal, D., and Parasuraman, A.(1994). The influence of store environment on quality inferences and store image. *Journal of Academy of Marketing Science*, 22(4), 328-339.

Baker, L., Levy, M., and Grewal, D. (1992). An experimental approach to making retail store environmental decisions. *Journal of Retailing*, 68(4), 445-460.

Bellizzi, A. J., Crowley, E. A., and Hasty, W. R. (1983). The effects of colour in store design. *Journal of Retailing*, 59(1), 21-45.

Bellizzi, J.A., and Hite, R.A. (1992). Environmental colour, consumer feelings and purchase likelihood. *Psychology and Marketing*, 9(3), 347-363.

Bello, D.C., and Etzel, M. J. (1985). The role of novelty in the pleasure travel experience. *Journal of Travel Research*, 24, 20-26.

Bigne, E. J., Andreu, L., and Gnoth, J. (In press). The theme park experience: an analysis of pleasure , arousal and satisfaction. *Tourism Management.*

Bitner, M. (1992). Servicescapes: the impact of physical surroundings on customers and employees. *Journal of Marketing*, 56, 57-71.

Bitner, M. J. (1990). Evaluating Service Encounters: The Effect of Physical Surrounding and Employee Responses. *Journal of Marketing*, 54, April, 69-82.

Blodget, J.G., Hill, D. J., and Tax, S.S. (1997). The effects of distributive, procedural and interactional justice on postcomplaint behaviour. *Journal of Retailing,* 73, 185-210.

Brown, S. W., Cowles, D. L., ve Tuten, T. L. (1996). Service Recovery Its Value and Limitations as Retail Strategy. *International Journal of Service Industry Management*, 7 (5): 32-46.

Cadotte, E. R., Woodruff, R. B ., Jenkins, R. J. (1987). Expectations and Norms in Models of Consumer Satisfaction. Journal of Marketing Research, 24 August: 305-14.

Chadee, D. D., and Mattsson, J. (1996). An Empirical Assessment of Customer Satisfaction in Tourism. The Services Industries Journal, 16 (3): 305-320.

Chebat, J., and Michon, R. (2003). Impact of ambient odors on mall shoppers' emotions, cognition, and spending. *Journal of Business Research*, 56, 529-539.

Chon, K. S. (1990). The role of destination image in tourism: A review and discussion. *The Tourist Review*, 2, 2-9.

Churchill, G. R., and Surprenant, C. (1982). An Investigation into Determinants of Customer Satisfaction. *Journal of Marketing Research*, 19, 491-504.

Clawson, M., and Knetsch, J. L. (1966). *Economics of outdoor recreation*. Baltimore, USA: John Hopkins.

Cote, J. A., Foxman, E. R., and Cutler, B. D. (1989). *Selecting an appropriate standard of comparison for post-purchase evaluations, Advances in Consumer Research*, 16, 502-506.

Crompton, J. L. (1979). Motivations for pleasure vacation. *Annals of Tourism Research, 6* (4): 408-424.

Cronin, J .J. Jr., and Taylor, S. A. (1992). Measuring Service Quality: A Re-examination and Extension. *Journal of Marketing* 56: 55-68.

Crowley, A. E. (1993). The two dimensional impact of color on shopping. *Marketing Letters, 4,* 59-69.

Czepiel, J. A., Rosenberg, R. J., and Akerele, A. (1974). *Perspectives on consumer satisfaction*. AMA Educator's Proceedings, Chicago, IL, USA: American Marketing Association, 119-123.

Dabholkar, A. P. (1995). A contingency framework for predicting causality between customer satisfaction and service quality. *Advances in Consumer Research*, 22: 101-108.

Danaher, P. J., and Haddrell, V. (1996). A comparison of question scales used for measuring customer satisfaction. *International Journal of Service Industry Management*, 17 (4): 4-26.

Danaher, P. J., and Arweiler, W. (1996). Customer satisfaction in the tourism industry, a case study of visitors to New Zealand. *Journal of Travel Research.* 89-93.

Dann, G. (1977). Anomie, ego-enhancement and tourism. *Annals of Tourism Research*, 4 (4), 184-194.

Dawson, S., Bloch, P., and Ridgway, N. (1990). Shopping motives, emotional states and retail outcomes. *Journal of Retailing*, 66, 408-427.

Day, R. L. (1984). Modeling choices among alternate responses to dissatisfaction. *Association of Consumer Research Proceedings*, (11), 496-499.

Day, R.L., and London, E. L. (1977). *Toward a theory of consumer complaining behaviour*, in Woodside, A. G., Sheth, J., and Bennett, P (eds). *Consumer and Industrial Buying Behaviour*, Elsevier North-Holland Inc., Amsterdam, Netherlands. 425-37.

Day, R.L., and Landon, Jr. E. L. (1977). *Toward a theory of Consumer Complaining Behavior*, in A. Woodside, J. Sheth and P. Bennett (eds), *Consumer and Industrial Buying Behavior*. Amsterdam, Netherlands: North Holland Publishing Company, 425-437.

Dibb, S. (1998). Market segmentation: strategies for success. *Marketing Intelligence and Planning* 16(7): 394-406.

Dorfman, P. W. (1979). *Measurement and Meaning of Recreation Satisfaction: A Case study in camping. Environment and Behaviour.* 11 (4):483-510.

Donovan, R. J., and Rossiter, J. R. (1982). Store atmosphere: an environmental psychology approach. *Journal of Retailing*, 58, 34-57.

Engel, J., and Blackwell, D. R. (1982). *Consumer Behaviour*, New York, Holt, Rinehart, and Winston.

Erevelles, S., and Leavitt, C. (1992). A Comparison of Current Models of Consumer Satisfaction/Dissatisfaction. *Journal of Consumer Satisfaction /Dissatisfaction and Complaining Behavior*, 5: 104-114.

Eroglu, S. A., and Machleit, K. (1990). An empirical study of retail crowding : antecedents and consequences. *Journal of Retailing*, 66(2), 2001-221.

Eroglu, S. A., Machleit, K., and Barr, T. F. (2004 In Press). Perceived retail crowding and shopping satisfaction: the role of shopping values. *Journal of Business Research*.

Fisher, J. D. (1974). Situation specific variables as determinants of perceived environmental aesthetic quality and perceived crowdedness. *Journal of Research in Personality*, 8, 177-188.

Fitzgibbon, R. J. (1994). Market segmentation research in tourism and travel. In Formica, S, and M. Uysal. (1998). Market segmentation of an international cultural-historical event in Italy. *Journal of Travel Research*, Sping:16-24.

Frochot, I., and Morrison, A. M. (2000). Benefit segmentation: a review of its applications to travel and tourism research. *Journal of Travel and Tourism Marketing*, 9 (4): 21-45.

Geva, A., and Goldman, A. (1989). Changes in the perception of a service during its consumption: a case of organised tours. *European Journal of Marketing*, 23 (12): 44-52.

George, R. (2003). Tourist's perceptions of safety and security while visiting cape town. *Tourism Management*, 24, 575-585.

Gronroos, C. (1988). Service Quality: six criteria of Good Perceived Service Quality. *Review of business*. 9(3), 10-13.

Gunn, C. A. (1989). *Vacationscape: Designing Tourist Regions*. Second Edition, New York, USA: Van Nostrand Reinhold Publishers: 23-28.

Gunter, B. G. (1979). *Some properties of leisure*. In H. Ibrahim and R. Crandall (Eds.), Leisure: A psychological approach. Los Alamitos, CA, USA: Hwong.

Gunter, B. G. (1987). The leisure experience: Selected properties. *Journal of Leisure Research*, 19(2), 115-130.

Haber, S., and Lerner, M. (1999) Correlates of Tourist Satisfaction. *Annals of Tourism Research*, 26 (1): 197-201

Hart, C. W. L., Heskett, J.L., and Sasser, W.E. (1990). The Profitable Art of Service Recovery. *Harvard Business review*, 68 (4), 148-156

Hirschman, A.O. (1970). *Exit, Voice and Loyalty: Responses to Decline in Firms, Organizations and States*. Cambridge, UK: Harvard University Press.

Hoffman, K.D., Kelley, S.W., and Rotalsky, H.M. (1995). Tracking Service Failures And Employee Recovery Efforts. *Journal of Services Marketing*, 9 (2), 49-61.

Hui, M.K., Dube, L., and Chebat, J. (1997). The impact of music on consumers' reactions to waiting for services. *Journal of Retailing*, 73, 87-104.

Iacobucci, D., Grayson, A. K., and Ostrom, A. L. (1994*). The Calculus of Service Quality and Customer Satisfaction: Theoretical and Empirical Differentiation and Integration. in Advances in Service Marketing and Management*, Swarts et al (eds) 3 JAI Press Greenwich, CT, UK: 1-67.

Iso-Ahola, S.E. (1982). Toward a social psychological theory of tourism motivation: a rejoinder. *Annals of Tourism Research*, 12 (1), 256-262.

Juaneda, C., and Sastre, F. (1997). *Destination choice and customer satisfaction in the tourist industry*, a case study of visitors to Majorca.

Kelley, S. W., Hoffman, K.D., and Davis, M.A. (1993). A Typology Of Retail Failures And Recoveries. *Journal of Retailing*, 69(4), 429-452.

Kim, S., and Littrell, A. M. (2001). Souvenir buying intentions for self versus others. *Annals of Tourism Research*, 28-3: 638-657.

Kim, C., Kim, S., Im, S., and Shin, C. (2003). The effect of attitude and perception on complaint intentions. *Journal of Consumer Marketing*, 20(4), 352-371.

Kotler, P. (1973-1974). Atmospherics as a marketing tool. *Journal of Retailing*, 49, 48-61.

Kotler, P. (1984). *Marketing Management: Analysis, Planning and Control.* 5th Edition, Prentice- Hall, 443-64.

Krippendorf, J. (1987). *The holiday makers*; understanding the impact of leisure and travel. Heinemann.

Lam, T., and Zhang, Q. H. (1999). Service quality of travel agents: the case of travel agents in Hong Kong, *Tourism Management*, 20: 341-349.

LaTour, S. T., and Peat, N. C. (1979). Conceptual and Methodological issues in consumer satisfaction research, *Advances in Consumer Research*, 6: 431-437.

Legoherel, P. (1998). Toward a market segmentation of the tourism trade: expenditure levels and consumer behaviour instability. *Journal of Travel and Tourism Marketing* 7(3): (19-29.

Levesque, T., and McDougall, G. (2000). Service problems and recovery strategies: an experiment. *Canadian Journal of Administrative Sciences,* 17(1), 20-37.

Lin, Y. I. (2004). Evaluating a servicescape: the effect of cognition and emotion. *International Journal of Hospitality Management*, 23, 163-178.

Lounsburry, L. W., and Hoopes, L. L. (1985). An Investigation of factors Associated with Vacation Satisfaction. *Journal of Leisure Research*, 17: 1-13.

Machleit, K. A., and Eroglu, S. (2000). Describing and measuring emotional response to shopping experience. *Journal of Business Research*, 49, 101-111.

Machleit, A. K., and Mantel, P. S. (2001). Emotional response and shopping satisfaction: moderating effects of shopper attributions. *Journal of Business Research*, 54, 97-106.

Mattila, A. S., and Wirtz, J. (2001). Congruency of Scent And Music As A Driver Of In-Store Evaluations And Behavior. *Journal of Retailing*, 77; 273-289.

Mayo, E. J., and Jarvis, L. P. (1981). *The psychology of leisure travel: effective marketing and selling of travel services.* MA: CBI Publishing Company.

Mehrabian, A., and Russell, J.A. (1974). *The basic emotional impact of environments. Perceptual and Motor Skills*. 38, 283-301.

Michon, R., Chebat, J., and Turley, L. W. (2004 in Press). Mall atmospherics: the interaction effects of the mall environment on shopping behaviour. *Journal of Business Research*.

Milliman, R. E. (1982). Using background music to affect the behaviour of supermarket shoppers. *Journal of Marketing*, 46, 286-289.

Milliman, R. E. (1986). The influence of background music on the behaviour of restaurant patrons. *Journal of Consumer Research*, 13, 86-91.

Ohja, J. M. (1982). Selling Benign Tourism: Case references from Indian scene, *Tourism Recreation Research*, June, 23-24.

Oliver, R. L. (1980). A Cognitive Model of the Antecedents of Satisfaction Decisions. *Journal of Marketing Research,* 17, 46-49.

Otto, E. J., and Ritchie, B. R. J. (1996). The service experience in tourism. *Tourism Management,* 17, (3): 165-174.

Pearce, P. L. (1982). *The social psychology of tourists behaviour.* New York, USA: Pergamon.

Pizam, A., Neumann, Y., and Reichel, A. (1978). Dimensions of tourist satisfaction with a destination area. *Annals of Tourism Research*, July/September: 314-322.

Qu, H., and Ping, E. Y. W. (1999). A service performance model of Hong Kong cruise travellers' motivation factors and satisfaction. *Tourism Management*, 20: 237-244.

Ragheb, M.G., and Beard, J. G. (1982). Measuring leisure attitudes. *Journal of Leisure Research*, 14, 155-162.

Reisineger, Y., and Turner, L. (1997). Tourist Satisfaction with Hosts: A Cultural Approach Comparing Thai tourists and Australian Hosts. *Pacific Tourism Review*, 1: 147-159.

Richins, M. L. (1980). Consumer Perceptions of costs and benefits associated with complaining. In Hunt, H. K., and Day, R. L. (Eds.). *Refining the concepts and measures of consumer satisfaction and complaining behavior* (pp. 50-53). Bloomington, Indiana, USA,University Press.

Ross, D. L. E., and Iso-Ahola, S. E. (1991). Sightseeing tourists' motivation and satisfaction. *Annals of Tourism Research*, 18, 226-237.

Ryan, C. (1991). *Recreational Tourism: A Social Perspective*. Routledge, New York, USA.

Ryan, C. (1997). From Motivations to Assessment, in *The Tourist Experience: The New Introduction*, (ed.) Chris Ryan, Cassell, London, UK.

Sharpley, R. (1994). *Tourism, tourist and society*. Elm, London, UK.

Simkin, L., and Dibb, S. (1998). Prioritising target markets. *Marketing Intelligence and Planning* 16 (7): 407-17. (Smith, L. J. S. (1989). Tourism analysis: a handbook. London, UK: Longman Scientific and Technical.

Singh, J., and Widing, E. R. (1991). What occurs once consumers complain? A theoretical model for understanding satisfaction/dissatisfaction outcomes of complaint responses. *European Journal of Marketing*, 25 (3), 30-45.

Sirgy, J. M. (1984). *A social cognition model of CS/D: an experiment, Psychology, and Marketing*, 1, 27-44.

Sönmez, S. F., and Graefe, A. R. (1998). Determining future travel behaviour from past travel experience and perceptions of risk and safety. *Journal of Travel Research*, 37(2), 171-177.

Spangenberg, E. R., Crowley, A. E., and Henderson, P. W. (1996). Improving the store environment: do olfactory cues affect evaluations and behaviours. *Journal of Marketing*, 60, 67-89.

Spreng, R. A., and Dixon, A. L. (1992). *Alternative Comparison Standards in the Formation of Satisfaction/Dissatisfaction*, in Enhancing Knowledge Development, In Leone and Kumar (eds) Marketing, Chicago, LL, USA: American Marketing Association: 85-91.

Spreng, R. A., and Mackoy, R. D. (1994). A dynamic model of affect, disconfirmation and satisfaction judgement, A paper presented at the 1994 *Annual Conference of Journal of Consumer Research*, Boston, USA.

Susskind, A. M. (2000). Efficacy and outcome expectations related to customer complaints about service experiences. *Communication Research*, 27 (3), 353-378.

Tax, S. S., Brown, W. S., and Chandrashekaran, M. (1998). Customer evaluations of service complaint experience: implications for relationship marketing. *Journal of Marketing*, 62, 60-76.

Tribe, J., and Snaith, T. (1998). From Servqual to Holsat: holiday satisfaction in Varadero, Cuba. *Tourism Management*, 19: 125-34.

Turley, W. L., and Milliman, E. R. (2000). Atmospheric effects ob shopping behaviour: a review of the experimental evidence. *Journal of Business Research*, 49, 193-211.

Tse, D. K., and Wilton, C. P. (1988). Models Of Customer Satisfaction Formation: An Extension. *Journal of Marketing Research*, 25, 204-212.

Van Raaij, W. F., and Francken, D. A. (1984). *Vacation Decisions, Activities and Satisfactions*. 11: 101-112.

Weber, K. (1997). Assessment of Tourist Satisfaction, Using the Expectancy disconfirmation theory, a study of German Travel Market in Australia, *Pacific Tourism Review*, 1: 35-45.

Westbrook, R. A., and Reilly, M. D. (1983). *Value-Percept disparity: an alternative to the disconfirmation of expectations theory of customer satisfaction*, in Bogozzi, P. R. and Tybouts, A. (eds) Advances in Consumer Research, Association for Consumer Research, 10, Ann Arbor, MI, USA: 256-61.

Whipple, W. T., and Thach, V. S. (1988). Group Tour Management: Does Good Service Produce Satisfied Customers. *Journal of Travel Research*, Fall, pp. 16-21.

Woodruff, R. B., Ernest, R. C., and Jenkins, R. L. (1983). Modeling Consumer Satisfaction Processes Using Experience-Based Norms. *Journal of Marketing Research*, Vol. 20, August, pp. 296-304.

Woodside, A.G., and Jacobs, L. W. (1985). Step two in benefit segmentation: learning the benefits realised by major travel markets. *Journal of Travel Research*, 24, 7-13.

Yalch, R.F., and Spangenberg, E. (1990). Effects of store music on shopping behaviour. *Journal of Consumer Marketing*, 7, 55-63.

Yüksel, A., and Yüksel, F. (2001). Measurement and Management Issues in Customer Satisfaction Research: Review, Critique and Research Agenda. *Journal of Travel and Tourism Marketing*, 10(4), 47-111.

Zemke, R. (1994). *Service recovery. Executive Excellence*, 11 (9), 17-18.

In: Tourist Satisfaction and Complaining Behavior
Editor: Atila Yüksel

ISBN 978-1-60456-002-2
© 2008 Nova Science Publishers, Inc.

Chapter 2

TOURIST SATISFACTION: DEFINITIONAL AND RELATIONAL ISSUES

Atila Yüksel and Fisun Yüksel

Adnan Menderes University, Turkey

INTRODUCTION

The provision of tourist satisfaction and quality tourism experience is fundamental for organisations and destination authorities for a number of reasons (Yuksel, 2000). First, satisfaction "reinforces positive attitudes toward a brand, leading to a greater likelihood that the same brand will be purchased again…dissatisfaction creates a negative attitude toward a brand and lessens the likelihood of buying the same brand again" (Assael, 1987, p. 47). Depending on the degree of their dis/satisfaction, tourists may either return, recommend a destination to other tourists, or may not return and express negative comments that may damage the reputation of the destination (Pearce, 1988). Destination managers need to focus on the provision of high quality tourist experiences as "the consequences of customer dissatisfaction can be sudden and harsh" (Maddox, 1985, p. 2). Moreover, tourists may respond to negative (unsatisfactory) experiences "in a more physically destructive way, and various acts of vandalism, notably, property damage, theft and graffiti may be seen as an extreme expression of visitor dissatisfaction" (Pearce and Moscardo, 1984, p. 21).

Second, the generation of satisfaction is a cost-effective approach to maintaining a business (Murray, 1992). Recent studies have brought out that it is highly likely that a dissatisfied customer never returns (Dube, Reneghan and Miller, 1994), and to get a new customer costs more than to keep an existing one (Stevens, Knutson and Patton, 1995). For instance, while it costs about $10 in advertising, public relations, price incentives and other promotions to get a new customer, the cost to keep a satisfied customer is only about $1 (ibid.). Similarly, other studies suggest that it costs three to five times as much to attract a new customer as it does to retain an old customer (Fierman, 1994; La Boeuf, 1987). Capturing new customers from competitors is costly because a greater degree of service improvement is needed to induce customers to switch from a competitor (Anderson and Sulvian, 1990).

Third, studies have also elicited that the generation of satisfaction with services leads to word-of-mouth recommendations which is suggested to be more effective at enhancing volume and profit in many companies and destinations than marketing, promotion or advertising activities. For instance, based on the results of a Gallup study, Stevens et al (1995) state that of the consumers going to a restaurant for the first time, 44% went because of a recommendation and another 10% went with someone who had been there before. In a study of restaurant customers, Plymire (1991) found that 91% of a restaurant's dissatisfied customers will never come back and they will typically tell eight to ten others about their negative experience. Similarly, Becker's and Wellins's (1990) study brings out that while only 38% of restaurant customers tell their friends about an excellent service, 75% of restaurant customers share information about poor service (cf. Sundaram, Jurowski and Webster 1997). It was found that on average a problem related to service quality causes a 20% decline in customer loyalty (Murray, 1992). In his study on the fast-food industry, Wallace (1995) reported that small changes in loyalty and consumption patterns could have a disproportionate impact on a firm's profitability. Wallace estimates that 5% reduction of customer defection will result in a 25% increase in profits (cf. Pettijohn, Pettijohn and Luke 1997). In another study, Fornell (1997) estimates that if 92 percent of the tourists to Spain return for more visits at least once during the next five years, there will be an $1.4 billion increase in the revenue. This suggests that the cost associated with ignoring tourist dis/satisfaction can be tremendous. Destinations that fail to pay attention to the provision and improvement of satisfaction and overlook their shortcomings stand to loose their market share. Therefore, understanding customer dis/satisfaction lies at the very heart of effective provision and management of the concept, and thus, accurate measurement of this concept is a vital ingredient in the success of destinations in both short and long term.

Customer satisfaction measurement has become the most frequent application of market research in the 1990s, however, this area of research is still with fraught with difficulties (www.allenymarketing.com/Cust_satis.htm, 1998). Even though "there is a consensus that customer satisfaction is central to success in the delivery of tourist and leisure services, satisfaction remains an elusive, indistinct and ambiguous construct" (Crompton and Love, 1995, p. 11). To this end, the following section presents current debates in relation to definition of customer satisfaction and its similarities and distinction with related constructs. The chapter starts with the definition of services and moves on to outlining a number of alternate conceptual definitions of customer satisfaction proposed by the researchers. This is followed by a discussion on the difference/ similarity between satisfaction and two other related concepts, namely attitude and service quality, as illustrating the similarity and differences between satisfaction and these concepts is imperative to advance the understanding of the satisfaction concept and to the development of the research.

TOURISM AND HOSPITALITY SERVICES

Tourism and hospitality services (or products) are a multifaceted phenomenon, which occur in specific environments and are closely related to managerial issues, which range from marketing and consumer behaviour analysis, to employee relations and organisational behaviour (Murray, 1992). In its simplest form, a service can be described as an intangible but identifiable activity providing the satisfaction of needs (Kotler, 1984), and services are related to performance as opposed to objects (Parasuraman, Zeithaml and Berry, 1985). Within the tourism and hospitality industry, a service can signify either an escape from daily life or a means of self-fulfilment (Ryan, 1991). The service does not represent possession of a physical product, but leads customers to acquire and fulfil dreams. Services are the procedures affecting the product flow to customers and the manner in which staff delivers the product (Martin, 1986).

The definition of service has changed over time. In addition to more traditional components of the definition such as employee courtesy, product knowledge, helpfulness, and enthusiasm, it has been expanded to include service aspects such as convenient location, breadth of selection, category dominance, speed of transaction, and competitive prices. Tschohl (1991) simply defines service as "whatever your customer thinks it is". In spite of the fact that sometimes customers can be illogical or uninformed, what customer thinks seems all that matters. Expressed in terms of attitude, service can be seen as thoughtfulness, courtesy, integrity, reliability, helpfulness, efficiency, availability, friendliness, knowledge, and professionalism (Tschohl, 1991 cf. Murray, 1992). Service clearly involves maintaining old customers, attracting new ones, and leaving all of them with an impression that induces them to do business again with the restaurant or the destination again (Murray, 1992).

Three main characteristics of services, namely their tangible and intangible composition, the simultaneity of production and consumption, and their heterogeneous nature impose difficulty to their evaluation and measurement (Lee and Hing, 1995). It is important to note that these service features are not mutually exclusive but are, in many cases, conjoint. The most recognised service feature is its intangibility. This implies that services cannot be measured, touched, and evaluated before they are purchased (Cowell, 1984). Most services are performance rather than objects, and therefore a service exists in time, but not in space (Shostack, 1984). For this reason, when a customer purchases a service such as a hotel stay or a vacation, she goes away empty handed, but she does not go away empty headed. However, apart from souvenirs and photographs, she has nothing to show for the purchase but she has memories to share with others (Lewis, 1989).

Services and products are thought to be distinct in that the former is produced (tangible) and the latter is performed (intangible). However, this traditional view is rather rigid, as products and services may have both tangible and intangible characteristics (Teare et al., 1994). For example, Kotler (1984) defines product as "anything that can be offered to a market for attention, acquisition, use, or consumption that might satisfy a want or need. It includes physical objects, services, persons, places, organisation and ideas" (p. 463). Similarly, a service involves direct consumption of physical goods and use of physical facilities (tangibles), as well as, the interaction with service providers (Nightingale, 1985). Shostack (1977) argues that consumer decisions concerning an intangible-dominant entity will be based on the tangible clues surrounding it, and people use appearance and external impressions to make judgements about realities. For instance, customers generally judge the ambience of restaurant services by observing such physical forms as architecture, layout, design, and dress of the personnel (Haywood, 1983).

Another feature of service that makes its definition and measurement difficult is simultaneous production and consumption (Gronroos, 1984). Services are first sold then produced and consumed simultaneously (Cowell, 1984). Therefore, unlike manufactured products, services cannot be subjected to quality control checks prior to consumption. Service providers are human, and customer-provider interaction is, though staged, both simultaneous and spontaneous, making the control of service a difficult and complex issue (Czepiel, 1980, cf. Kandampully, 1997). Production and consumption of a service can only take place through buyer-seller interactions (Vandamme and Leunis, 1993) which occur in the provider's premises and not in the customer's home environment. Customers are the co-producers of service products, as they share decision-making responsibilities with service providers in the production of services to accomplish the desired level of service outcomes (Davidow and Uttal, 1990; McMahon and Schemeizer, 1989).

Another important feature of services is their heterogeneous nature. This implies that assurance of a uniform service in tourism cannot be guaranteed, as provision of consistent behaviour from the service personnel is difficult to attain.

> "In a service business you are dealing with something that is primarily delivered by people, to people. Your people are as much of your product in the customer mind as any other attribute of that service. People's performance day in and day out fluctuates. Therefore, the level of consistency that you can count on and try to communicate to the customer is not a certain thing" (Kinsley 1979, cf. Kandampully, 1997, p. 6).

As not all hospitality and tourism services are routines, deviations from the routine norms are quite common (Haywood, 1983). Inconsistencies can occur because different service providers perform a given service differently on different occasions. Therefore, what management intends to deliver might be quite different from what customers receive (Parasuraman et al., 1985).

Tourism services are experiential in nature, which fosters evaluation of service both during and after service delivery. That is, the tourist is integral part of the service enabling him or her to make an evaluation while the service is being performed, as well as, after it has been performed. The evaluation of tourism and hospitality services is argued to be more complex than that of goods (Reisinger and Waryszak, 1996; Zeithaml, 1981). This may be partly because of the fact that tourism and hospitality services contain high percentage of experience and credence properties, whereas search properties are dominant in goods. Search properties refer to those attributes that a consumer evaluates before engaging in the service (for example, price, size, and colour). These properties are primarily tangibles, which are physical representations of the service, such as facilities, equipment, appearance of personnel, and other recipients of service (Mackay and Crompton, 1988). Experience properties are those attributes that can be only assessed after purchase or during consumption (taste, purchase satisfaction) (Zeithaml, 1981). Credence properties are the attributes that the consumer finds impossible to evaluate even after purchase and consumption (for example, the hygiene conditions in the restaurant kitchen). In general those services that are high in experience properties are argued to be difficult to evaluate and those services that are high in credence properties, like tourism and hospitality services, may be the most difficult to evaluate (Reisinger and Waryszak, 1996).

It is important to note that tourism product is an amalgam or package of tangible and intangible elements centred on activities at a destination (Medlik and Middleton, 1983; Medlik, 1988; Moutinho, 1995; Smith, 1994). It is the "collection of physical and service features together with symbolic associations which are expected to fulfil the wants and needs of the buyer" (Jefferson and Lickhorish, 1988, p. 211). It comprises the actual and perceived attractions of a destination, the activities, the facilities, and the destination's accessibility. Tourism product is the complete experience of the tourist from the time one leaves home to the time one returns. Thus, the nature and quality of tourist product is the outcome of many individual activities with a range of people and organisations involved in the tourist experience (Hughes, 1989, 1991; Whipple and Thach, 1988).

In a holiday experience, tourists encounter directly with not just one, but with several members of the production chain (Van-Rekom, 1996), thus there are more than one tourist-provider encounters. For instance, the travel agent (when booking a trip) is the first member of the product chain which tourists meet. Then, a hostess of the tour operator at the airport and the airline personnel during the flight attend tourists. Once in the country of destination, a coach company (another member of the production chain), hired by the tour operator, transfers them to their hotels. During the holiday, tourists meet different service providers, for example, restaurateurs, hoteliers, local people, etc. Many transient impressions and experiences occur during this total consumption, and it is this total experience that is consumed and evaluated (Teare, 1998; Weirmair, 1994). These experiences affect the consumer's state of mind during and at the end of the consumption, which forms the basis for subsequent travel decisions. Understanding which parts in this product chain matter and how they could be best combined to produce the desired experience is of significant importance to destination managers.

CUSTOMER SATISFACTION

The concept of satisfaction is complex partly because

> "the most important thing to know about intangible products is that customers usually do not know what they are getting into until they don't get it... only then do they become aware of what they bargained for, only on dissatisfaction do they dwell...satisfaction is, as it should be, mute, its existence is affirmed only by its absence" (Levitt, 1981, p. 96).

While everyone knows what satisfaction means, it clearly does not always mean the same thing to everyone (Oliver, 1997). On the one hand, satisfaction may mean minimum acceptability to some customers while on the other hand it may mean near perfection to others (Day, 1980). As a result of this complexity, researchers have defined satisfaction in a variety of ways. For instance, customer satisfaction is defined as a cognitive evaluation of the attributes the consumer attaches to the service (Chadee and Mattsson, 1996), or as "the customer's subjective evaluation of a consumption experience, based on some relationship between the customer's perceptions and objective attributes of the product" (Klaus, 1985, p. 21). Satisfaction is regarded as a level of happiness resulting from consumption experience; or a cognitive state resulting from a process of evaluation of performance relative to previously established standards; or a subjective evaluation of the various experiences and outcomes associated with acquiring and consuming a product relative to a set of subjectively determined expectations. Satisfaction with a product or service is the consumer's evaluation of the extent to which the product or service fulfils the complete set of wants and needs which the consumption act was expected to meet (Czepiel, Rosenberg and Akarel, 1974). Satisfaction has also been defined as a two factor process of evaluating a set of satisfiers and a set of dissatisfiers associated with a product (Maddox, 1981); or one step in a complex process involving prior attitude towards a brand, a consumption experience resulting in a positive or negative disconfirmation of expectations, followed by feelings of satisfaction or dissatisfaction which mediates post consumption attitude which subsequently influences future purchase behaviour (Day, 1980).

Satisfaction is also defined as "the buyer's cognitive state of being adequately or inadequately rewarded in a buying situation for the sacrifice he has undergone. The adequacy is a consequence of matching actual past purchase and consumption' experience with the reward that was expected from the brand in terms of its anticipated potential to satisfy the motives served by the particular product class (Howard and Sheth, 1969, p. 145). Oliver (1997, p. 13) proposes that satisfaction is "the consumer's fulfilment response. It is a judgement that a product or service feature, or the product or service itself, provided (or is providing) a pleasurable level of consumption-related fulfilment, including the levels of under-or-over fulfilment". These definitions represent the scope of the concept which ranges from a simplistic "black box" happiness perspective to a very complicated set of concepts, and there appears to be an absence of general consensus among satisfaction researchers as to how to define satisfaction.

Drawing on these definitions, the concept of customer satisfaction may be viewed as "either an outcome or as a process" (Yi, 1990, p. 68). Some definitions suggest that customer satisfaction is an outcome resulting from the consumption experience. For example, Howard and Sheth (1969, p. 145) suggest that satisfaction is "the buyers cognitive state of being adequately or inadequately rewarded for the sacrifice he has undergone", while Westbrook and Reilly (1983, p. 145) define customer satisfaction as "an emotional response to the experiences provided by and associated with particular products or services purchased" (in Yi 1990). In parallel, Churchill and Surprenant (1982) define satisfaction as the outcome of purchase and use, resulting from the buyer's comparison of the rewards and costs of the purchase in relation to the anticipated consequences. In this line, Oliver (1981, p. 27) views satisfaction as "the summary psychological state resulting when the emotion surrounding dis/confirmed expectations is coupled with the consumer's prior feelings about the consumption experience".

Customer satisfaction has also been defined as "an evaluation rendered that the consumption experience was at least as good as it was supposed to be" (Hunt, 1977, p. 459). By the same token, Tse and Wilton (1988, p. 204) view satisfaction as "the consumer's response to the evaluation of the perceived discrepancy between prior expectations (or some norm of standards) and the actual performance of the product (service) perceived after consumption". Translated into a tourism context, this implies that satisfaction is a psychological concept that involves a feeling of well being and pleasure resulting from the interaction between a tourist's experience at the destination area and the expectations formed about that destination (WTO, 1985). Defined by Hughes (1991, p. 166) tourist satisfaction may be seen "a multifaceted concept, primarily determined by visitors' attitudes both before and after".

These definitions define the key concepts and the mechanism by which the concepts interact, and each of these recognises that satisfaction is the end state of a psychological evaluation process (Oliver, 1997). This process oriented approach, as opposed to the outcome-oriented approach, sounds useful that "it spans the entire experience and emphasises the process, which may lead to customer satisfaction with unique measures capturing prominent aspects of each stage"(Yi, 1990, p. 69). As Yi quite rightly puts it, this process-oriented approach appears to place much importance on evaluative and psychological processes that generate customer satisfaction, and is therefore gained much support from researchers.

In addition to the outcome-process debate, one of the most frequently raised questions regarding the definition of satisfaction has been whether it is a cognitive process or an emotional state (Oh and Parks, 1997). For example, Howard and Sheth (1969) described satisfaction as "the buyer's cognitive state of being adequately or inadequately rewarded for the sacrifice he has undergone". Similarly, satisfaction is defined as an evaluation (cognitive) of a chosen alternative that is consistent with prior beliefs with respect to that alternative (Engel and Blackwell, 1982). On the other hand, Westbrook (1980, p. 49) argues that satisfaction is not solely a cognitive phenomenon, rather "it also comprises an element of affects or feeling, in that consumers feel subjectively good in connection with satisfaction, and bad in connection with dissatisfaction". While some advocate that satisfaction is either a cognitive process or an emotional state, others suggest that satisfaction should be defined to reflect the link between both the cognitive and emotional processes, because "customer satisfaction is an emotional feeling in response to a process of confirmation/ and/or disconfirmation (cognitive)" (Woodruff, Ernest and Jenkins, 1983). Customer satisfaction may be more than a simple cognitive evaluation process (Oh and Parks, 1997). This is to say that customer satisfaction is a complex human process involving extensive cognitive, affective and other undiscovered psychological and physiological dynamics (ibid.).

As can be seen, the concept of consumer satisfaction has been defined differently. Variations among these alternative definitions set forth here indicate that the concept does not have a single universally accepted meaning (Maddox, 1981), and thus pinning down a generally agreed definition of consumer satisfaction is difficult. Nevertheless, the conceptualisation that appears to have received greatest support is the view that satisfaction is regarded as a consumer's subjective post-consumption evaluative judgement concerning benefits obtained from specific purchase consumption.

As tourism is an experience made up of many different independent parts, some more tangibles than others, tourist satisfaction may be treated as a cumulative measure of total consumption experience. Tourist satisfaction may be defined at least at three levels. These are the total satisfaction, the dimensional (component) satisfaction, and the product-service satisfaction. Product-service level satisfaction refers to tourist satisfaction with the individual product-service experiences delivered by a single organisation in the production chain. For example, satisfaction with service personnel in a restaurant represents the individual product-service level satisfaction. Dimensional level satisfaction results from the summation of satisfactions derived from individual products and services within the given component of tourism. For example, sum of satisfactions with room, service personnel, restaurant, and facilities in a hotel constitutes dimensional level satisfaction. Total satisfaction embraces all of the individual products-service level satisfactions and dimensional level satisfactions accumulated by the tourist. In other words, satisfaction with a holiday experience may be based on the sum total of satisfactions with the individual attributes of all the products and services that compose the holiday experience (Haber and Lerner, 1999; Pizam, 1994; Teare,

1998). It is important to note that the nature and quality of this experience is usually outside the direct influence of destination authorities as the activities of many individuals and organisations can influence the tourist experience considerably (Hughes, 1989). Tourist satisfaction is not a universal phenomenon in that not everyone gets the same satisfaction out of the same holiday experience. In addition, tourist satisfaction or dissatisfaction with one of the components may lead to satisfaction or dissatisfaction with the total holiday experience. That is the negative impression of one component may override well-executed quality in other areas (carry-over effect).

CUSTOMER SATISFACTION AND ATTITUDE

In addition to the debate on its definition, there seems to be widespread confusion among researchers as to its relationship with other related constructs, most specifically with the concepts of attitude and service quality. A number of researchers, for instance, have regarded satisfaction as an attitude. As early as 1979, LaTour and Peat emphasised that given that attitude and satisfaction are both evaluative responses to products, it is not clear whether there are any substantial differences between the two. "In fact it may be more parsimonious to consider satisfaction measures as post consumption attitude measures" (p. 434). Correspondingly, Czeipel and Rosenberg (1977, p. 93) view satisfaction as a form of attitude " in the sense that it is an evaluative orientation which can be measured. It is a special kind of attitude because by definition it cannot exist prior to purchase or consumption" (cf. Yi, 1990).

However, several others argue that satisfaction is conceptually different from attitude (Oliver, 1980; Westbrook and Reilly,1983). To Oliver (1997) satisfaction is different from attitude because of the disconfirmation of expectation, which is a central concept in satisfaction. Satisfaction is an evaluation of the total purchase situation relative to its expectations, whereas attitude is the liking of the product that excludes the element of comparison. While satisfaction is relatively transient and is consumption specific, attitude is a consumer's relatively enduring effect toward an object or experience and does not involve surprise as a central concept (Yi, 1990). Attitude is a predisposition toward a service created by learning and experience (Moutinho, 1986), and can be regarded as more general to a product or experience and is less situationally oriented. In the context of consumer behaviour, the attribute is defined as a consumer's constant evaluative inclinations toward or against any element in his or her market domain (Chon, 1989). The attitude and satisfaction concepts are separate, however they may be intrinsically related. In a dynamic framework, customer satisfaction with a specific service encounter may be affected by pre-exceeding attitudes about the product (Cronin and Taylor, 1992) and customers post usage attitudes may be influenced by satisfaction (Bolton and Drew, 1994).

CUSTOMER SATISFACTION AND SERVICE QUALITY

There also appears to be growing confusion among researchers about the distinction (and the relationship) between the concepts of customer satisfaction and service quality. This confusion is largely due to the fact that both the customer satisfaction and service quality concepts have been founded on a similar conceptual and theoretical framework. For example, customer satisfaction researchers maintain that customer satisfaction and dissatisfaction is an evaluation based on the perceived discrepancy between customers' prior expectations of a product and the actual performance of that product as perceived after consumption (the Expectancy-Disconfirmation paradigm) (Tse and Wilton, 1988). Analogously, service quality researchers generally define service quality to be a comparative function between consumer expectations and actual service performance (the Gap Model). Given the similarity, some researchers consider service quality and customer satisfaction as similar constructs (for example, Dabholkar, 1993, 1995; Spreng and Singh, 1993), while others maintain that these are two distinct constructs (Cronin and Taylor, 1992; Oliver, 1993; 1997; Parasuraman, Zeithaml and Berry, 1988; Taylor, 1994).

Those supporting the distinction argue that differentiation between the two is extremely important to managers and researchers alike. According to this group "service providers need to know whether their objectives should be to have customers who are satisfied with their performance or to deliver the maximum level of perceived service quality" (Cronin and Taylor, 1992, p. 56). In contrast, others supporting the similarity argue that these two constructs might be different operationalisations of the same construct, and attempting to differentiate between the two may be unnecessary. From a management viewpoint, striving to differentiate between the two might be futile, particularly if they do not have differential effect on post-purchase behavioural outcomes (i.e., satisfaction creates more repeat business than high service quality perception or vice versa). To this end, the following section first provides a definition of service quality. Next, the debates relating to the similarity and distinction between customer satisfaction and service quality concepts are outlined.

SERVICE QUALITY: DEFINITION

Many of the suggested quality definitions have originated from the manufacturing sector and are seemingly inappropriate for services due to the unique features (for example, intangibility, simultaneous production and consumption, perishability and heterogeneity). In the product quality tradition, Crosby (1979) views quality as conformance to standards, while Garwin (1983) suggests that quality is achieved through the prevention of internal failures (defects before the product leaves the factory) and external failures (defects after product use). These definitions such as conformance to requirements or internal and external failures are argued to be too product oriented and technical to be of great use in service contexts (Gilbert and Joshi, 1992) and are found insufficient to understand service quality (Parasuraman, Zeithaml and Berry, 1985).

A clearer understanding of service quality and its measurement has been provided by the expanding search for quality during the last decade (Lewis, 1987). This search for service quality has produced several definitions. For example, some viewed service quality as "the degree of excellence intended and the control of variability in achieving that excellence in meeting customers' requirements" (Wycoff, 1984, p. 78), while others argued that service quality results from the comparison of customer expectations of service with their perceptions of the actual service outcome (Gronroos, 1984; Lewis and Booms, 1983; Parasuraman et al. 1985). Definitions of this kind, embracing expectations and perceptions of customers, are often used in tourism and hospitality services because the customer is significantly involved in the service production process (King, 1984). In this domain, two distinct schools of research have made major contributions to conceptualisation of service quality. These are the Nordic School of Quality Research (NSQR) led by the Norwegian researchers such as Gronroos and Gummesson, and the North American School of Quality Research (NASQR), led by American researchers, notably by Parasuraman, Berry and Zeithaml.

The NSQR view quality from a service/product perspective. One of the major contributions of this school is the suggestion that service quality occurs in three dimensions; first technical, second functional and third reputation (Gronroos, 1984). The technical dimension is concerned with the outcome of service encounters, such as food in a restaurant. The functional dimension is concerned with the process of service delivery, for example, friendliness of an employee, while the reputation dimension involves both technical and functional dimensions and may reflect a corporate image. By classifying service quality dimensions, this school suggests that because of the nature of service, for example, intangibility, heterogeneity, simultaneity, functional quality is quite important, sometimes more important than the technical quality (Gronroos, 1984). This implies that there exist different service dimensions and these may be evaluated differently by customers.

The North American School of Quality Research focuses on the delivery aspects of service quality (Brogowicz, Delene and Lyth, 1990). The current conceptualisation of this school is that service quality is a result of the gap between what customers expect and what they experience during the service delivery (Parasuraman et al., 1985). More specifically, the NASQR regards quality as an outcome of a comparative process between the desired service and the perceived service (ibid.). This comparative process leads to the formation of distinct gaps, which influence the judgement of perceived quality (ibid.).

This school of research suggests that the difference between expected and actual service constitute the true measurement of service quality (Parasuraman et al 1985). Conducting in-depth interviews with executives from large firms in different sectors (for example, banking, retailing, and dry cleaning), this school initially produced ten service quality dimensions (Parasuraman et al 1985). These were reliability, responsiveness, competence, access, courtesy, communication, credibility, security, rapport, and appearance. In a follow-up research, Parasuraman et al. (1988) subsequently refined these ten dimensions into five. Reliability, responsiveness and tangibles remained, but the other seven components were combined into two aggregate dimensions: assurance and empathy. In the light of successive pilot tests, this school developed a service quality model, the Servqual, which formulates the service quality construct as a difference between consumer expectations and perceived performance of a given product/service. Although the model has received growing criticism in recent years, the Servqual model has also been employed in assessing customer satisfaction with tourism and hospitality services in a number of studies (Saleh and Ryan, 1991; Tribe and Snaith, 1998).

This review of literature given above clearly demonstrates that the conceptualisation and operationalisation (measurement) of service quality is very similar to that of customer satisfaction, which is causing confusion among researchers. According to Oh and Parks (1997) this confusion needs to be clarified immediately because the current theoretical and methodological debates among customer satisfaction and service quality researchers are causing a delay in introducing customer satisfaction and service quality paradigms into hospitality research. The following section, therefore, discusses similarity and distinction between these two concepts.

SATISFACTION AND SERVICE QUALITY: ARE THEY DISTINGUISHABLE?

From a conceptual viewpoint, it may seem possible to distinguish between service quality and customer satisfaction, though empirically it might be difficult (Dabholkar, 1993). For instance, service quality can be viewed as perceptions of a service experience or the consumers overall impression of the relative inferiority or superiority of an organisation and its service, while customer satisfaction is tied to disconfirmation and contains an element of comparison or surprise (Bitner and Hubbert, 1994; Bolton and Drew, 1992; Cronin and Taylor, 1992; Gronross, 1993; Oliver, 1997). Oliver (1997) suggests a number of ways that may help distinguish customer satisfaction from service quality. These are:

Expectations for quality are based on ideal or perceptions of excellence, whereas a large number of non-quality issues can help form satisfaction judgements (for example, needs, equity, perceptions of fairness).

The dimensions underlying quality judgements are rather specific, whereas satisfaction can result from any dimension, regardless of whether or not it is quality related.

The perception of quality does not require experience with the service or provider whereas satisfaction judgements do.

Quality is believed to have fewer conceptual antecedents than does satisfaction.

It is, however, controversial whether these provide a reliable basis on which these two concepts could be differentiated. The following section, therefore, presents the controversy pertaining to similarities and differences between these concepts.

DIFFERENCE BASED ON GLOBAL VERSUS TRANSACTIONAL VIEWS?

The most common explanation of the difference between the two concepts is that perceived service quality is a form of attitude, a long-run evaluation, whereas satisfaction is transaction specific (Bitner, 1990; Bolton and Drew, 1991; Parasuraman et al 1988). This implies that perception of quality is more holistic, developed and maintained over a long period of time as a result of experience with service performance, whereas customer satisfaction is viewed as encounter specific, and may be a more immediate reaction to a specific service experience (Cronin and Taylor, 1992; Parasuraman et al 1988).

While above argument seems logical, it restricts the conceptualisation of customer satisfaction to a particular experience and the conceptualisation of service quality to a global concept, a long run evaluation occurring across experiences or over time. It seems likely that, for example, consumers are in fact able to evaluate service quality immediately after each individual encounter in a hotel stay experience. That is, the consumer might develop individual quality perceptions with respect to check-in experience, room and its facilities, the service in the hotel restaurant and etc. It is also true that consumers can develop a general feeling of satisfaction or dissatisfaction (summary dis/satisfaction) with a firm after a number of experiences (Bolton and Drew, 1991; Drew and Bolton, 1991; Spreng and Singh, 1993), so it is not necessarily encounter specific. This suggests that a customer can evaluate quality or satisfaction for both a single encounter and may form from this a longer-term perception (Bitner and Hubert, 1994; Iacobucci, Grayson and Ostrom, 1994; Rust and Oliver, 1994). This indicates that customer satisfaction and service quality can be both conceptualised either in terms of a given experience or in the longer term (Dabholkar, 1993). Therefore, the use of duration to separate customer satisfaction and service quality is not adequate (Iacobucci et al., 1994; Spreng and Sing, 1993). Operational separation of the two constructs is unlikely if both are viewed as transactional or longer term (Drew and Bolton, 1991). It is important to note that attempts to distinguish service quality and customer satisfaction on the basis of encounter-specific and holistic concepts seem sub-optimal as they are untested and arbitrary (Iacobucci et al 1994).

DIFFERENCE BASED ON COMPARISON STANDARDS?

Those advocating the difference further maintain that the standards against which performance is compared are different in service quality and customer satisfaction constructs (Oliver 1993; Parasuraman et al 1988). To Oliver (1997), satisfaction and service quality judgements may result from comparison with different expectations for the same attribute; in this case ideal (for quality) and predicted expectations (for satisfaction). Similarly, service quality researchers (for example, Bitner 1990; Bolton and Drew, 1991; Parasuraman et al 1988, 1994; Zeithaml, Berry and Parasuraman, 1993) propose that in measuring service quality, the level of comparison is what a consumer should expect against what is received, whereas in measures of customer satisfaction the appropriate comparison is what a consumer would expect against what is received.

However, the proposition suggesting different standards are used in service quality and satisfaction judgements is doubtful, as similar standards might be used in both constructs (Dabholkar, 1993). The service quality literature has generally called the standard "an expectation", but it seems that it uses some other type of standard used in consumer satisfaction literature. For example, in their early work Parasuraman et al (1985) stated that quality "…involves a comparison of expectations with performance". Although they do not explicitly define expectations, given their examples (p.46), it appears that they are talking about beliefs about a product's performance which would be termed a "predictive expectation" in satisfaction literature (Spreng and Singh, 1993). In a later study, Parasuraman et al (1988) suggest a change in the comparative standard that is used as perceptions of service quality "stems from a comparison of what they feel service firms should offer with their perceptions of the performance of firms providing services". They maintained that in the service quality literature, expectations did not mean predictions, but rather expectations were viewed as desires or wants of consumers, i.e., what they feel service provider should rather than would offer. Finally in their recent work Parasuraman, Berry and Zeithaml (1991) use " an excellent company" (for example, employees of excellent companies will have neat appearance) as a standard.

It appears that as a standard the service quality literature is using something very similar to some standards used in the satisfaction literature (for example, desires or experience-based norms discussed in Chapter 3) (Dabholkar, 1993). The service quality literature, however, claim that satisfaction is formed from a comparison with predictive expectations (Bolton and Drew, 1991; Bitner, 1990; Parasuraman et al 1988, 1994; Oliver, 1993; Rust and Oliver, 1994; Zeithaml et al., 1993). However, there are studies suggesting that ideals or desires might be important antecedents to satisfaction (Barbeau 1985; Cadotte, Woodruff and Jenkins, 1987; LaTour and Peat, 1979; Spreng and Olshavsky, 1993; Swan and Travick, 1979; Westbrook and Reilly, 1983). For instance, Swan and Trawick (1979) found that only confirmation of desired expectations would lead to satisfaction, whereas confirmation of predicted expectations would lead to indifference. Some researchers emphasise that researchers who employ the Servqual and its scoring algorithm (performance minus ideal expectation) "appear to be essentially capturing a measure more closely related to consumer satisfaction than service quality" (Hemmasi, Strong and Taylor, 1995, p. 27). Therefore, unless otherwise is empirically confirmed, the standard against which performance is compared cannot be confidently used to discriminate between service quality and satisfaction (Spreng and Mackoy, 1996; Spreng and Singh, 1993).

DIFFERENCE BASED ON ACTUAL EXPERIENCE?

In service quality judgements, word-of-mouth communications, past experiences and external communications of the firm are considered to be the antecedents of quality (Bolton and Drew, 1991). This implies that quality might be judged on the basis of some external criteria such as Consumer Reports or Tour Operator Ratings for a destination, whereas satisfaction requires some direct experience, and involves internal judgement (Oliver, 1993; Iacobucci et al 1994). Similarly Callan (1994) states that standard used in quality judgements concerning hospitality services may be set by the consumer, tour operator or some external authority or all three. Following this, it may be argued that service encounters are the providers' only chance of satisfying a customer, as service experiences cannot be undone, whereas ability to build service quality perceptions through advertising and other indirect means is possible (Oliver, 1993). Therefore it is reasonable to argue that customer satisfaction is purely experiential and also unique to customers and internal (Oliver, 1993). However, service quality does not always require experience. "A five star hotel may be perceived as being of high quality although it has never been visited" (Meyer and Westerbarkey, 1996: 186).

The proposition suggesting that quality does not always involve experience, whereas satisfaction is an experiential concept and more internal might seem to distinguish between the two concepts. It is, however, important to note that two types of quality have been suggested in the literature; the objective service quality and the perceived service quality. Objective service quality could be defined as the technical superiority or inferiority of the product which can be derived from external sources such as Consumer Reports, and does not involve an experience with the product (Zeithaml, 1988). On the other hand, perceived service quality could be defined as the consumer perception about the product performance after it is consumed, involving a subjective evaluation of the experience. This may suggest that objective quality and satisfaction are different from each other, while the difference between satisfaction and perceived service quality is less clear-cut.

DIFFERENCE BASED ON OTHER FACTORS?

As stated earlier, some argue that ideal or excellence based expectations may be used as a reference point for quality judgements. However, a number of non-quality referents, including needs, and equity, fairness perceptions, can be used in satisfaction and dissatisfaction judgements (Iacobucci et al. 1994; Oliver, 1993). In this respect, the dimensions underlying service quality judgements are assumed to be rather specific, whereas satisfaction judgements can be derived from all potential salient attributes whether or not they are quality related (Oliver, 1993). Oliver, for example, argues that it is possible to be satisfied with a low quality service encounter if a consumer expects a minimal performance. Dissatisfaction may result from high-quality performance "if expectations exceed the maximum potential of a service provider" (Oliver, 1993: 66). Moreover, unexpected events such as parking problems before entering a five-star hotel can result in dissatisfaction, though high quality perception of the hotel may remain the same (Bitner, 1990). Additionally, the fairness of the exchange process (Oliver and Desarbo, 1988), or a comparison of the outcome with others' experience can condition the satisfaction judgement, for example, an employee's interest toward certain customers and ignorance of others during the service experience. Moreover mood, usage frequency and situation can affect satisfaction judgements (Westbrook and Reilly, 1983). This implies that a customer in a high quality restaurant may be dissatisfied when some elements of service delivery are not up to personal standards. The above proposition seems to provide some degree of evidence concerning the distinctiveness of the concepts. However, this contention which holds that fairness of the exchange process or a comparison of the service outcome with other's experience does not impact on perceived service quality has not been empirically tested and verified.

CASUAL LINK BETWEEN SATISFACTION AND SERVICE QUALITY

A review of the emerging literature suggests that there appears to be a considerable level of consensus among marketing researchers that service quality and customer satisfaction are separate constructs, yet they are conceptually closely related. There have been a number of recent empirical attempts to validate the specific nature of the relationship between service quality and customer satisfaction (Bitner, 1990; Cronin and Taylor, 1992). However, the literature has demonstrated conflicting results as to the casual order between the two concepts. Some argue that customer satisfaction with a given service would lead to an overall global attitude about service quality of a product (Bitner, 1990; Oliver, 1981; Parasuraman et al 1988). In contrast, others argue an alternate casual order in that service quality is an antecedent to customer satisfaction. That is, in a given situation service quality will lead to overall customer satisfaction over time (Cronin and Taylor, 1992; Drew and Bolton, 1991; Such, Lee, Park and Shin, 1997).

Woodside, Fray and Daly (1989) report empirical results suggesting that consumer satisfaction is an intervening variable that mediates the relationship between service quality judgements and repurchase intentions. Their results suggest the following casual order; service quality→ customer satisfaction→ purchase intentions. On the other hand, based on her study of the service quality and consumer satisfaction perceptions of 145 travellers at an international airport, Bitner suggests an alternative ordering of service quality and satisfaction constructs (i.e., satisfaction→ service quality→ purchase intentions). The empirical results of Cronin and Taylor's (1992) LISREL-based analyses indicate the opposite of Bitner's findings. Cronin and Taylor directly assessed the service quality/customer satisfaction relationship across four different industries: banking, pest control, dry cleaning, and fast food. Cronin and Taylor's results support Woodside et al's (1989) conclusion that service quality appears to be a casual antecedent of customer satisfaction. Consistent with findings of Cronin's and Taylor's (1992) research, Such et al (1997) found that perceived service quality is an antecedent to customer satisfaction and repurchase intention, and customer satisfaction influences repurchase intentions directly. A similar finding was obtained in Gotlieb, Grewal and Brown's (1994) study on hospital patients. Using an identical approach of Cronin and Taylor, they found that only the quality to satisfaction path was significant.

A number of researchers maintain that rather than focusing on one, better results can be achieved for the prediction of customer behaviour by integrating these two concepts. Taylor and Baker (1994, p. 173), for instance, report that "conceptualising satisfaction and service quality as acting jointly to impact on purchase behaviour increases our ability to explain more of the variance in consumers' purchase intentions than existing models". In their study it was found that the highest level of purchase intentions was observed when both service quality and customer satisfaction judgements were high. Similarly, Woodside et al (1989) proposed that overall consumer satisfaction with a service would be positive and substantial when the consumer perceives high service quality. These findings suggest that practically, an attempt to improve one of the constructs will improve the other. That is, in order to predict consumer behaviour better, these two constructs may need to be integrated. The causality between customer satisfaction and service quality may be relevant for understanding of consumers' evaluation but not necessarily for managerial considerations (Iacobucci et al 1994).

REFERENCES

Anderson, W. E., and Sullivan, W. M. (1993). The antecedents and consequences of Customer satisfaction for firms, *Marketing Science*, 12, 125-143.

Assael, H. (1987). *Consumer Behaviour and Marketing Action*, 3rd edition, Boston, PWS,- Kent.

Barbeau, B. J. (1985). Predictive and Normative Expectations in consumer satisfaction, a utilisation of adaptation and comparison levels in a unified framework, in Hunth, K. H., and Day, L. R. (Eds) *Conceptual and Empirical contributions to Consumer Satisfaction and Complaining Behaviour*, 27-32.

Bitner, M. J. (1990). Evaluating Service Encounters: The Effect of Physical Surrounding and Employee Responses, *Journal of Marketing*, 54, April, 69-82.

Bitner, M. J. and Hubbert, A. R. (1994). Encounter Satisfaction versus Overall Satisfaction versus Quality, In Rust, T. R. and Oliver, R. L. (eds.) *Service Quality New Directions in Theory and Practices*, Sage Publications, London, UK. 72-95.

Bolton, N. R. and Drew, J. H. (1991). A longitudinal analysis of the impact of service changeson customer attitudes. *Journal of Marketing*, 55, 1-9.

Bolton, R. N. and Drew, H. J. (1994). Linking customer satisfaction to service operations and outcomes, in Rust, T. R. and Oliver, R. L. (eds.) *Service Quality New Directions in Theory and Practices*, Sage Publications, London, UK, 173-201.

Brogowicz, A. A., Delene, L. M. and Lyth, M. D. (1990). A Synthesised Service Quality Model with Managerial Implications. *International Journal of Service Industries Management*, 28, 27-45.

Cadotte, R. E., Woodruff, B. R., and Jenkins, R. L. (1982) Norms and Expectation predictions: how different are the measures, Proceedings, 7th Annual Conference on Consumer Satisfaction, Dissatisfaction and Complaining Behaviour: 49-56.

Chadee, D. D. and Mattsson, J. (1996). An Empirical Assessment of Customer Satisfaction in Tourism. *The Services Industries Journal* 16 (3), 305-320.

Chon, K. (1989). Understanding Recreational Traveller's Motivation, Attitude and Satisfaction. *Tourist Review* 1, 3-6.

Churchill, G. R.and Surprenant, C. (1982). An Investigation into Determinants of Customer Satisfaction. *Journal of Marketing Research* 19: 491-504.

Cowell, D. (1984). *The marketing of services*, Butterworth - Heinemann, London.

Crosby, P. (1979). Quality is free, New York, 1-304

Shostack, G. L., (1984). Designing Services That Deliver. *Harvard Business Review,* 133-39.

Crompton, L. J., and Love, L. L. (1995). The Predictive Validity of Alternative Approaches to Evaluating Quality of a Festival. *Journal of Travel Research,* 34 (1), 11-25.

Cronin, J .J. Jr. and Taylor, S. A. (1992). Measuring Service Quality: A Re-examination and Extension. *Journal of Marketing,* 56, 55-68.

Dabholkar, A. P. (1995). A contingency framework for predicting causality between customer satisfaction and service quality, *Advances in Consumer Research*, 22, 101-108.

Dabholkar, A. P. (1993) .Customer Satisfaction and Service Quality: two constructs or one?, in Cravens, D., and Dickson, P. (Eds) *Enhancing Knowledge Development in Marketing*, 4, American Marketing Association, Chicago, 10-18.

Davidow, H. W. and Uttal, B. (1990). *Total Customer service: the Ultimate Weapon*, Harpercollins, New York.

Day, R. (1980). How satisfactory is research on consumer satisfaction? *Advances in Consumer Research*, 7, 593-7.

Drew, J. H., and Bolton, N. R. (1991). The structure of consumer satisfaction, effects of survey measurement, *Journal of Consumer Satisfaction, Dissatisfaction, and Complaining Behaviour*, 4, 21-31.

Dube, L., Renaghan, L. M., and Miller, J. M. (1994). Measuring Customer Satisfaction for Strategic Management, *The Cornell Hotel and Restaurant Administration Quarterly,* 35 (1), 39-47.

Engel, J., and Blackwell, D. R. (1982). *Consumer Behaviour*, New York, Holt, Rinehart, and Winston.

Fornell, C. (1992). A national customer satisfaction barometer, the Swedish experience, *Journal of Marketing*, 56: 6-21.

Garwin, D. A. (1983). Quality on the line, *Harvard Business Review*, 61, 65-73.

Gilbert, D.C. and Joshi, I. (1992). Quality management and the tourism and hospitality industry, in Cooper, C.P. and Lockwood, A. (Eds.) *Progress in tourism, recreation, and hospitality management*, 4, Belhaven, London.

Gotlieb, B. J., Grewal, D., and Brown, S. (1994). Consumer Satisfaction and Perceived Quality, Complementary or Divergent Constructs?, *Journal of Applied Psychology*, 79: 875-885.

Gronroos, C. (1984). A Service quality model and its marketing implications. European *Journal of Marketing*, 18, 36-44.

Haber, S., and Lerner, M. (1999). Correlates of Tourist Satisfaction. *Annals of Tourism Research*, 26 (1), 197-201.

Haywood, K. M. (1988). Assessing the quality of hospitality services, *Int. J. Hospitality Management*, 2, (4) 165-177.

Hemmasi, M., Strong, C. K., and Taylor, A. S. (1996). Measuring service quality for strategic planning and analysis in service firms. *Journal of Applied Business Research*, 10, (4), 24-35.

Howard, A. J. and Sheth, N. J. (1969). The theory of buyer behaviour. Wiley, New York: 147

Hughes, K. (1991). Tourist satisfaction: A Guided Tour in North Queensland. *Australian Psychologist*, 26 (3), 166-171.

Hunt, K. H. (1977). CS/D- overview, and future research directions, in Hunt, K. H. (ed) *Conceptualisation and Measurement of Consumer Satisfaction and Dissatisfaction*, Marketing Science Institute, Cambridge, MA, 455-488.

Iacobucci, D, Grayson, A. K. and Ostrom, A. L. (1994). The Calculus of Service Quality and Customer Satisfaction: Theoretical and Empirical Differentiation and Integration. *in Advances in Service Marketing and Management*, Swarts *et al* (eds) 3 JAI Press Greenwich, CT, 1-67

Kandampully, J. (1995).*Quality Service In Tourism*, In Foley, M., Lennon, J. J., and

King, A. C. (1984). Service oriented quality control. *The Cornell H. R. A. Quarterly*, November, 92-98.

Kotler, P. (1984). *Marketing Management: Analysis, Planning and Control.* 5th Edition, Prentice- Hall, 443-64.

LaTour, S. T. and Peat, N. C. (1979). Conceptual and Methodological issues in consumer satisfaction research. *Advances in Consumer Research*, 6, 431-437.

Lee, Y. K. and Hing, N. (1995). Measuring Quality in Restaurant Operations: An Application of the Servqual Instrument. *International Journal of Hospitality Management*, 14, (3/4), 293-310.

Levitt, T. (1981). Marketing Intangible Products and Product Intangibles. *Harvard Business Review* (May-June), 94-102.

Lewis, R. C. (1987). The Measurement of Gaps in the Quality of Hotel Services. *Int. J. Hospitality Management*, 6 (2), 83-88.

Lewis, R.C. and Chambers, E.R. (1989). *Marketing leadership in hospitality*, Van Nostrad, New York

Mackay, J. K., and Crompton, L. J. (1990). Measuring the quality of recreation services. *Journal of Park and Recreation Administration*, 8 (3), 47-56.

Maddox, N. R. (1981). Two-factor theory and consumer satisfaction: replication and extension. *Journal of Consumer Research*, 8, 97-102.

Maddox, N. R. (1985). Measuring Satisfaction with Tourism. *Journal of Travel Research*, Winter, 2-5.

Medlik, D. and Middleton, V. T. C. (1983). The tourist product and its marketing implications. *International Tourism Quarterly*, 28-35.

Meyer, A. and Westerbarkey, P. (1996). Measuring and Managing Hotel Guest Satisfaction., in Olsen, D. M., Teare, R. and Gummesson, E. (Eds.) *Service Quality in Hospitality Organisations*, Cassell, New York, NY, 185-204.

Nightingale, M. (1985). The Hospitality Industry: Defining Quality for a Quality Assurance Programme- A Study of Perceptions. *Service Industries Journal*, 5, (1), 9-24.

Oh, H. and Parks, C. S. (1997). Customer Satisfaction and Service Quality: A critical Review of the Literature and Research Implications for the Hospitality Industry. *Hospitality Research Journal*, 20 (3), 36-64.

Oliver, L. R. (1997). Satisfaction a behavioural perspective on the consumer. The McGraw-Hill Companies, Inc. New York.

Oliver, R. L. (1993). A Conceptual Model of Service Quality and Service Satisfaction: Compatible Goals and Different Concepts, In Swart, T. A., Bowen, D. E., and Brown, S. W. (eds.) *Advances in Service Marketing and Management*, 3, JAI Press, Greenwich, CT, 65-86.

Oliver R. L. and DeSarbo, W. S.(1988). Response Determinants in Satisfaction Judgement. *Journal of Consumer Research*, 14, 495- 507.

Parasuraman, A. Zeithaml, A. V. and Berry, L. L. (1985). A Conceptual Model of Service quality and Its Implications for Future Research. *Journal of Marketing*, 49, 41-50.

Parasuraman, A. Zeithaml, A. V. and Berry, L. L. (1988). Servqual: a Multiple Item Scale for Measuring Consumer Perceptions of Service Quality *Journal of Retailing*, 64, Spring, 12-40.

Parasuraman, A., Berry, L. L, and Zeithaml, V. A. (1991). Understanding customer expectations of services, *Sloan Management Review*, 32: 39-48.

Pearce, L. P. (1988). *The Ulysses factor: Evaluating visitors in tourist settings*. New York, Springer-Verlag.

Pearce, L. P. and Moscardo, M. G. (1984). Making Sense of Tourists' Complaints. *Tourism Management*, (March), 20-23

Pettijohn, L. S., Pettijohn, C. E., and Luke, R. H. (1997). An Evaluation of Fast Food Restaurant Satisfaction: Determinants, Competitive Comparisons and Impact on Future Patronage, *Journal of Restaurant Food Service Marketing*, 2 (3), 35-49.

Pizam, A. (1994). Planning a tourism research investigation in Ritchie, J.R.B et al (eds) Travel and Tourism and Hospitality Research; A handbook for managers and researchers John Wiley and Sons.

Reisinger, Y., and Waryszak, R. (1996). Catering to Japanese Tourists: What Service do They Expect from Food and Drinking Establishments in Australia? *Journal of Restaurant and Foodservice Marketing*, 1 (3/4), 53-71.

Rust, T. R. and Oliver, L. R. (1994). Service Quality: insights and managerial implications from the frontier, IN Rust, T. R., and Oliver, L. R. (Eds.) *Service Quality, New Directions in Theory and Practice*, Sage Publications, 1-20.

Ryan, C. (1991). *Recreational Tourism: A Social Perspective*. Routledge, New York.

Stevens, P., Knutson, B., and Patton, M. (1995). Dineserv: A Tool For Measuring Service Quality in Restaurants. *Cornell Hotel and Restaurant Administration Quarterly*, April, 56-60.

Saleh, F. and Ryan, C. (1991). Analysing Service Quality in the Hospitality Industry Using the Servqual Model. *Service Industries Journal*, 11 (3), 324-345.

Smith, M. A. (1995). Measuring service quality: is Servqual now redundant, *Journal of Marketing Management*, 11: 257-276.

Spreng, R. A. and Mackoy, R. D. (1994). A dynamic model of affect, disconfirmation and satisfaction judgement, A paper presented at the 1994 Annual Conference of Journal of Consumer Research, Boston.

Spreng, R. A. and Sing, A. K. (1993). An empirical assessment of the Servqual scale and the relationship between service quality and satisfaction. *American Marketing Association*, Summer,1-6

Spreng, R. A. and Olshavsky, R. W. (1993). A desires congruency model of consumer satisfaction. *Journal of the Academy of Marketing Science*, 21, 3, 169-177.

Such, H. S., Lee, H. Y., Park, Y., and Shin, C. G. (1997). The Impact of Consumer Involvement on the Consumers' Perception of Service Quality- Focusing on the Korean Hotel Industry. *Journal of Travel and Tourism Marketing*, 6 (2), 3352.

Sundaram, D. S., Jurowski, C., and Webster, C. (1997). Service Failure Recovery Efforts in Restaurant Dining: The Role of Criticality of Service Consumption. *Hospitality Research Journal*, 3.

Swan, J. and Travick, F. I. (1980) Satisfaction related to the predictive vs. desired expectations, in Hunt, H. K. and Day, R. (eds) Refining concepts and measures of consumer satisfaction and complaining behaviour, Indiana University, 7-12

Teare, E. R. (1998). Interpreting and responding to customer needs. *Journal of Workplace Learning*, 10 (2), 76-94.

Tribe, J. and Snaith, T. (1998). From Servqual to Holsat: holiday satisfaction in Varadero, Cuba. *Tourism Management* 19, 125-34.

Tse, D. K. and Wilton, C. P. (1988). Models Of Customer Satisfaction Formation: An Extension. *Journal of Marketing Research*, 25, 204-212.

Vandamme, R. and Leunis, J. (1992). Development of a multiple item scale for hospital service quality. *International Journal of Service Industries Management*, 4 (3), 30-49.

Westbrook, R. A., and Reilly, M. D., (1983). Value-Percept disparity: an alternative to the disconfirmation of expectations theory of customer satisfaction, in Bogozzi, P. R. and Tybouts, A. (eds) *Advances in Consumer Research, Association for Consumer Research*, 10, Ann Arbor, MI, 256-61.

Woodruff, R. B.; Ernest, R. C.; Jenkins, R. L. (1983). Modelling Consumer Satisfaction Processes Using Experience-Based Norms. *Journal of Marketing Research*, 20, 296-304.

Wycoff, D.D. (1984). New tools for achieving service quality. *The Cornell H. R. A. Quarterly*, November, 78-91.

Yi. Y. (1990). A Critical Review of Consumer Satisfaction, in V. A. Zeithaml (Ed.), Review of Marketing. Chicago: American Marketing Association, 68-123.

Zeithaml, V. A. (1981). How consumer evaluation process differ between goods and services. *Advances in Consumer Research*, 186-190.

Zeithaml, V. A. (1988). Consumer perceptions of price, quality and value: a means-end model and synthesis of evidence. *Journal of Marketing*, 52, 2-22.

In: Tourist Satisfaction and Complaining Behavior
Editor: Atila Yüksel

ISBN 978-1-60456-002-2
© 2008 Nova Science Publishers, Inc.

Chapter 3

CUSTOMER VALUE IN THE TOURISM AND HOSPITALITY INDUSTRY – A RISK-ADJUSTED APPROACH

Philipp E. Boksberger
University of Applied Sciences HTW Chur

INTRODUCTION

Research highlights differences in the nature of services as against products, since services are believed to create special challenges for their consumers and their marketers. The proposed definitions and classifications of services are always the result of a conducted service-good analysis on a continuum where pure goods and pure services are the hypothetical extremes. Thus, a number of schemes for classifying services have been identified: the degree of intangibility, the status of the service within the total offer, the extent of inseparability, the pattern of service delivery, the extent of people orientation, the significance of the service to the purchaser and the (un-)market-ability of the service. Although a number of these schemes have been presented in isolation, the unique nature of services is, in practice, simultaneously classified by four constitutive characteristics: intangibility, inseparability, heterogeneity and perishability (Berry and Parasuraman, 1993). Because of these characteristics, as well as the interactive character of service production and consumption, Murray (1991, p. 10) has stated: "The role of risk in the consumption of services has been addressed both conceptually [...] and empirically [...], with theory and evidence suggesting that services are perceived to be riskier than goods." This confirms that services are indeed riskier than goods (Mitchell and Greatorex, 1993). Moreover, perceived risk seems to be especially relevant for tourism and hospitality services (Cheron and Richtie, 1982; Floyd, Gibson, Pennington-Gray and Thapa, 2003; Lepp and Gibson, 2003; Roehl and Fesenmaier, 1992) since they are high in experience and credence attributes (i.e. the knowledge of these services relies either on previous personal experiences and the belief in given information). However, most risk-related research has occurred in the products sector, yet the tourism and hospitality industry may provide more theoretically valid and practically meaningful research. Taking this background into consideration, it is important that the influence of perceived risk on customer value should be well understood. In other words, the integration of perceived risk into a model of customer value seems to be judicious and warranted.

THEORETICAL BACKGROUND

Customer Value

Customer value has been considered as a crucial determinant which forces behavioural intention and, therefore, has been identified as the dominant construct in the recent scholarly discussion on behavioural service performance measurement (Holbrook 1994). Nevertheless, this construct has attracted little attention in tourism studies. Instead, service quality (Parasuraman, Zeithaml and Berry's (1988) SERVQUAL) and customer satisfaction (Cronin and Taylor's (1992) SERVPERF) are still the dominant constructs in tourism research. However, just as there is much controversy in the definitions and terminology of service quality and customer satisfaction, the discussion about the expectancy disconfirmation paradigm and the appropriate standard of comparison is equally debateable (Yüksel and Yüksel, 2001). Moreover, there is a profound conceptual discussion about differences, similarities, linkages, temporal order and relationship between service quality and customer satisfaction (Dabholkar 1993). Thus, it can be stated that the conceptualisation of service quality and customer satisfaction has been either over-simplified or too complicated, and the operationalisation has generally lacked managerial focus. Since Parasuraman (1997) has proved that the customer value is one of the most important measures for gaining competitive edge, a new 'mania' in marketing has emerged. Unfortunately few studies have explored customer value in a tourism and hospitality context, and most studies have focused on the 'value for money' paradigm and tended to focus on product-based measures of value. Overall, two issues of fundamental concern remain unresolved in the emerging literature:

For almost as long as customer value has been studied, the general nature and the specific types of value have been of interest to researchers. Debate sprang from the theoretical base of Maslow's (1943) need hierarchy, Rokeach's (1973) value survey and Kahle's (1983) list of values. This resulted, for example, in Sheth, Newman and Gross's (1991) consumption values and Holbrook's (1994) consumer values. In these typologies, values typically are relative to the consumers (personal), their stated preferences (comparative) and the specific context (situational). Therefore Woo (1992, p. 85) claims for a multifaceted value construct by discerning four levels of meaning: "First, we can take values to mean what is of true worth to people in the broad context of the well-being and survival of individuals, and by extension, of the species as a whole. ... Second, we can take value to mean what a society collectively sees as important and worthy of individual pursuits [...] regardless of whether or not such highly valued objects of consumption really contribute to his or her well-being. ... Third, we take value at the level of the individual to refer to what the individual holds to be worthwhile to possess, to strive or exchange for. ... Fourth, we take value in the most concrete sense to refer to the amount of utility that consumers see as residing in a particular object and that they aim to maximize out of a particular act of buying or consuming." In sum, the categorisation and classification of the various types of value in tourism and hospitality may vary according to research design and research context and are not terminatorally defined.

Customer value has not only been given many definitions in theoretical and empirical research but also has been linked to other marketing constructs such as service quality or customer satisfaction. Nonetheless, there is no consensus about how these three constructs are to be measured and conflicting arguments have been made as to their importance, linkages and temporal order (Caruana, Money and Berthon, 2000). Thus, a selection of empirical studies that have attempted to model the antecedent, mediating and consequent relationships among service quality, customer satisfaction, perceived value and behavioural intentions is presented in Table 1.

Table 1. Studied Relationships among Customer Value

Author(s) and Year	Construct								Study Design and Method(s)	No.	Research Context
	Dependent Variable			Mediator		Independent Variable					
	Q	S	V	S	V	S	V	BI			
Duman and Mattila (2005)		X_2			Y_2			Z_3	Mail Survey Structural Equation Modelling	392	Cruise Vacation
Petrick (2004)	X_1			Y_{11}	Y_{12}	Z_{11}	Z_{12}	Z_{13}	Mail Survey Confirmatory Factor Analysis	792	Cruising
Eggert and Ulaga (2002)			X_3	Y_3				Z_3	Phone Survey Structural Equation Modelling	301	Retail (Purchasing Managers)
Brady and Cronin (2001)	X_1			$Y11$	$Y12$	$Z11$		$Z12$	Interviews Confirmatory Factor Analysis	649	Auto Lubrication Centres, Video Rental Stores, Amusement Parks
Caruana, Money and Berthon (2000)	X_1			$Y1$	$Z1$				Interviews Moderated Regression Analysis	80	Audit Services
Cronin, Brady and Hult (2000)	X_1	X_2	X_3	Y_{11} Y_3	Y_{12} Y_2			Z_1 Z_2 Z_3	Interviews Structural Equation Modelling	1944	Health Care, Fast Food, Entertainment
Kashyap and Bojanic (2000)	X_1			Y_1		Z_{11}	Z_{12}		Mail Survey Structural Equation Modelling	444	Upscale Business Hotel

Table 1. (Continued)

Author(s) and Year	Construct								Study Design and Method(s)	No.	Research Context
	Dependent Variable			Mediator		Independent Variable					
	Q	S	V	S	V	S	V	BI			
McDougall and Levesque (2000)	X1		X3	Y1 Y3				Z1 Z3	Mail Survey Structural Equation Modelling	448	Dentist, Hair Stylist, Auto Repair, Restaurant
Tam (2000)	X1 X3			Y1 Y3		Z11 Z31		Z12 Z32	Mail Survey Structural Equation Modelling	92	Chinese Restaurant
Oh (1999)	X1			Y11	Y12	Z11		Z12	Survey Structural Equation Modelling	545	Luxury Hotels
Andreassen and Lindestad (1998)	X1		X3	Y11 Y3	Y12			Z1 Z3	Phone Survey Structural Equation Modelling	600	Package (Charter) Tour
Patterson and Spreng (1997)		X2	X3	Y3				Z2 Z3	Mail Survey Confirmatory Factor Analysis	128	Consulting Service
Sweeney, Soutar and Johnson (1997)	X1				Y1			Z1	Mail Survey Structural Equation Modelling	1068	Electrical Appliances
Fornell, Johnson, Anderson, Cha and Everitt (1996)	X1	X2		Y1	Z1			Z2	Phone Survey Partial Least Squares	44,994	Seven Major Economic Sectors of United States
Hartline and Jones (1996)	X1				Y1			Z1	Mail Survey Structural Equation Modelling	1351	Hotel Services
Chang and Wildt (1994	X1				Y1			Z1	Laboratory Experiment Regression Analysis	823	Apartments, Personal Computers

Legend: **Q** = Service Quality   **S** = Customer Satisfaction   **V** = Customer Value   **BI** = Behavioural Intentions

Reflecting these peculiarities, the proposed framework treats the value construct more comprehensively and attempts to explain it by the pivotal role of risk in consumer behaviour of services. Based on the social exchange theory, the key tenet of the behavioural perspective of value is in essence reciprocal exchange transactions or, more specifically, a social interaction. Arguably, social interaction contains an 'exchange ratio' of (tangible or intangible) activities and rewards/costs on the grounds that consumers always explain their conduct by means of its benefits and sacrifices to them. Hence, Zeithaml (1988, p. 14) defines customer value as "customer's overall assessment of the utility of a product based on perceptions of what is received and what is given." Accordingly, this assessment, or more explicitly this comparison of a service's 'get' and 'give' components, is incorporated in Woodruff's (1997, p.142) customer value hierarchy approach: "Customer value is a customer's perceived preference for and evaluation of those product attributes, attribute performances, and consequences arising from use that facilitate (or block) achieving the customer's goals and purposes in use situations." It can be concluded that customer value can be considered as a trade-off between consumers' evaluation of the benefits of using a service and the sacrifice (Bolton and Drew, 1991). Although this description takes behavioural considerations into account, it does not specify the benefits and sacrifice components for the calculation of customer valueю

BENEFITS

In respect to what consumers receive, past research has identified service quality and affective responses as well as service reputation as components of benefits (Dodds, Monroe and Grewal, 1991; Grewal, Monroe and Krishnan, 1998; Zeithaml, 1988). Previous studies consistently show that perceived service quality is one of the main antecedents of customer value (Cronin, Brady and Hult, 2000). Traditionally, service quality has been mostly measured using the cognitive-based SERVQUAL instrument. Since the literature suggests that customer value includes both cognitive and affective elements, affective responses are an important part of thoroughly measuring the service experience. In affective consumer behaviour, symbolic and hedonistic responses surround the consumption of services (Duman and Mattila, 2005). Thus, symbolic responses reflect the consumption of services to satisfy consumers' symbolic needs (self-enhancement, role position, group membership or ego identification), whereas hedonistic responses are multisensory, fantasy and emotive aspects of consumers' service experience (Leigh and Gabel, 1992). For example, research findings suggest that brand name, store name and country name have a positive effect on perceived quality in relation to consumers' perception of value (Dodds et al., 1991). Therefore, it can be argued that symbolic responses (the reputation of the service rendered) influence customer value. In this context, status-seeking was identified as a central function of symbolic consumption. Furthermore, various researchers have analysed hedonistic responses (received emotions such as joy, jealousy, fear, rage and rapture) in terms of their relationship with customer value (Teas and Agarwal, 2000). Thus, it could be concluded that the benefits consumers receive from services include emotional responses to the service (Day and Crask, 2000).

SACRIFICES

Zeithaml (1988) proposes that sacrifices include monetary and non-monetary costs of the purchase of the service, whereas monetary costs can be further analysed into transactional costs (perceived monetary price for purchase) and relational costs (perceived monetary price for maintenance, repair or replacement). Since transactional costs are consumers' perception of the purchase price of the service, they directly influence customer value (Bolton and Drew, 1991; Cronin et al., 2000). In line with this research, the effects of price bundling on customer value and state that providing an all-inclusive price package, even if actual monetary outlay is higher, will significantly increase perceptions of value for first time consumers. Chang and Wildt (1994) tested actual and reference price as predictors of perceived price and found a positive relationship between objective and perceived price and a negative relationship between reference and perceived price. In view of that, Jayanti and Gosh (1996) concluded that price-based transaction utility (based on the difference between actual and reference price) and quality perceptions are the two main determinants of customer value. Thus, it has been well established in the marketing literature that the perceived monetary price for the purchase of a service and customer value are directly negatively related. In contrast, it is argued that sacrifice expectations include perceived monetary price for maintenance, repair or replacement and, therefore, indirectly influence customer value. Moreover, in the context of waiting and delays, it can be argued that time equated with its opportunity costs is another element of sacrifice expectations. Even most studies of customer value have not measured the non-monetary costs but have looked only at the role of monetary costs in sacrifice. The following discussion outlines the most important components of non-monetary costs. According to Zeithaml (1988) non-monetary costs include time, effort, search and psychic costs. While Petrick (2002) identifies time, information search, brand image and convenience as additional non-monetary costs, Duman and Mattila (2005) take behavioural, cognitive and decisional control into account. However, Dodds et al. (1991) have been among the first to also measure the effects of non-monetary costs such as brand and store information. Similarly, Cronin, Brady, Brand, Hightower and Shemwell (1997) measured sacrifice including both monetary and non-monetary costs. In their study, sacrifice has been conceptualised by service consumers' perceptions of price, time, effort and different risk factors. Since consumers spend time and effort not only to make a decision under risk and uncertainty but also in the consumption of services, the results of their study showed significant support for a negative relationship between sacrifice (monetary and non-monetary costs) and customer value. Therefore, it is a combination of perceived monetary as well as non-monetary costs that equate to consumers' overall perceived sacrifice, which, in turn, affects their perception of service value.

MEASUREMENT

Both qualitative and quantitative methods have been used to measure the value construct. In qualitative measurements, efforts to measure customer value by using a unidimensional scale have been criticised for lacking validity (Woodruff and Gardial, 1998). Generally, those early measurements have operationalised customer value as a trade-off between price as the sacrifice and quality as the benefit. Several authors suggested that viewing customer value only as a trade-off between price and quality is too simplistic (Sweeney and Soutar, 2001). Furthermore, unidimensional measures have shown the difficulties of predicting customer value since customers may be able to identify fifty or more different attributes that shape perception of value (Gale, 1994). It can also be argued that the value construct is considered as a function of sacrifice associated with utilising the service and benefits received in exchange. In recent research, the value construct has been operationalised as quantitative measurements using multiple item scales for better measuring customer value. See Table 2 for a review of selected empirical studies.

Table 2.Measurement of Customer Value

Author(s) and Year	Construct(s)and Item(s)	Study Design	No.	Research Context
Sánchez, Callarisa, Rodríguez and Moliner (2006)	• Functional Value Establ.: 4 Items • Functional Value Person.: 4 Items • Functional Value Product: 4 Items • Functional Value Price: 3 Items • Emotional Value: 5 Items • Social Value: 4 Items	Interviews	402	Tourism packages
Heinonen (2004)	• Technical Value: more/same/fewer • Functional Value: more/same/less • Temporal Value: more/same/less • Spatial Value: more/same/less	Interviews	37	Online banking
Wang, Lo, Chi and Yang (2004)	• Functional Value: 4 Items • Social Value: 3 Items • Emotional Value: 5 Items • Perceived Sacrifices: 6 Items	Mail Survey	320	Security service
Petrick (2002)	• Quality: 4 Items • Emotional Response: 5 Items • Monetary Price: 6 Items • Behavioural Price: 5 Items • Reputation: 5 Items	Mail Survey	792	Cruising
Agarwal and Teas (2001)	• Perceived Quality: 5 Items • Perceived Sacrifice: 2 Items • Performance Risk: 2 Items • Financial Risk: 3 Items • Perceived Value: 5 Items	Experiment	530	Hand-held business calculators, wristwatches
Sweeney and Soutar (2001)	• Functional Value (Quality): 6 Items • Emotional Value: 5 Items • Functional Value (Price): 4 Items • Social Value: 4 Items	Mail Survey	635	Furniture, Car Stereo
Cronin, Brady and Hult (2000)	• Sacrifice: 3 Items • Service Quality Performance:10 tems • Overall Service Quality: 3 Items • Service Value: 2 Items	Interview	1944	Health Care, Fast Food, Entertainmet
McDougall and Levesque (2000)	• Perceived Value: 1 Item	Mail Survey	448	Dentist, Hairstylist, Auto repair, Restaurant
Sweeney, Soutar and Johnson (1999)	• Functional Service Quality: 5 tems • Technical Service Quality: 2 Items • Product Quality: 4 Items • Relative Price: 2 Items • Performance/Financial Risk: 2 tems • Perception of Value for Money: 3 Items	Mail Survey	1068	Electrica Appliance
Grewal, Monroe and Krishan (1998)	• Advertised Selling Price: 2 Price Levels • Internal Reference Price: 2 Items • Perceived Quality: 3 Items • Perceived Transaction Value: 3 Items • Perceived Acquistion Value: 9 Items	Experimental Survey	328	Bicycle

Table 2. (Continued)

Author(s) and Year	Construct(s) and Item(s)	Study Design	No.	Research Context
Sinha and DeSarbo (1998)	• Relative Quality (Manufacturer, Mile-age, Performance, Reliability, Safety) • Relative Price (Average Price, Cost Factor, Depreciation)	Experimental Survey	95	Cars
Cronin, Brady, Brand, Hightower and Shemwell (1997)	• Overall Service Value: 1 Item • Service Quality: 10 Items • Overall Service Quality: 5 Items • Sacrifice: 9 Items	Interviews	1944	Health Care, Fast Food, Entertainment
Patterson and Spreng (1997)	• Outcomes: 2 Items • Method: 3 Items • Service: 4 Items • Relationship: 2 Items • Global: 1 Item • Problem Identification: 2 Items • Value: 1 Item	Mail Survey	128	Consulting Service
Chang and Wildt (1994)	• Perceived Quality: 4 Items • Perceived Price: 2 Items • Perceived Value: 1 Item	Laboratory Experiment	823	Apartments, Personal Computers
Bolton and Drew (1991)	• Perceived Service Quality: n.a. • Perceived Service Value: n.a. • Sacrifice: n.a. • Customer Characteristics: n.a.	Mail Survey	1408	Telephone Service
Dodds, Monroe and Grewal (1991)	• Perceived Sacrifice: 5 Price Levels • Perceived Quality: 5 Items • Perceived Value: 5 Items	Experiment	585	Calculator, Stereo Headset Player
Sheth, Newman and Gross (1991)	• Functional Value: 6 Items • Conditional Value: 4 Items • Social Value: 2 Items • Emotional Value: 7 Items • Epistemic Value: 3 Items	Mail Survey	145	Cigarette Smoking (users/non-users)

PERCEIVED RISK AND CUSTOMER VALUE

Risk has always been a concern of human beings. But in our modern 'risk society' risk is not longer an option; it is rather an inescapable structural condition of advanced industrialisation (Virilio and Lotringer, 1983, p. 32): "Every technology produces, provokes, programs a specific accident [...] The invention of the boat was the invention of shipwrecks. The invention of the steam engine and the locomotive was the invention of derailments. The invention of the highway was the invention of three hundred cars colliding in five minutes. The invention of the airplane was the invention of the plane crash." In 1960 Bauer introduced the term 'perceived risk' into the scientific discussion and contended that (Bauer, 1960, p. 390): "Consumer behavior involves risk in the sense that any action of a consumer will produce consequences which he cannot anticipate with anything approaching certainty, and some of which at least are likely to be unpleasant." However, since the average consumer has limited information, a restricted number of trials to consider and a semi-reliable memory, accurate assessment of risk is made almost impossible (Mitchell, 1998). In tourism and hospitality risks arise due to the constitutive characteristics of services, the multidimensionality of elements, as well as the interactive character of service production and consumption making up the overall experience (Boksberger and Craig-Smith, 2006). It is suggested that as perceived risk increases tourists may seek benefits (such as higher quality, more customised service attention, etc.), whereas in situations of relatively less perceived risk, tourists may seek competitive costs. Moreover, it is assumed that a tourist with a high perception of risk either over- or underestimates service performance provided within a certain zone of tolerance, and, therefore, turns out to be either delighted or deluded. To explore the role of perceived risk in the determination of customer value, the difficulties that perceived risk takes on a meaning via the method of operationalisation. The most common measures of perceived risk typically use a compositional methodology including losses, significance and uncertainty whereas six types of losses have been identified in the literature: financial loss, functional loss, physical loss, psychological loss, social loss and temporal loss (Kaplan, Szybillo and Jacoby, 1974; Yates, 1992). Thus, several authors have made initial efforts to include perceived risk along with perceived value in their studies. For tangible products at brand level, functional risk and financial risk have been proved as significant mediators of perceived quality and sacrifice, and of customer value respectively (Agarwal and Teas, 2001; Sweeney, Soutar and Johnson, 1999). Accordingly, early investigations of customer value in tourism and hospitality (Jayanti and Ghosh, 1996; Bojanic, 1996; Williams and Soutar, 2000) revealed the urge for an adequate measurement for services. Taking their conclusions into account, Petrick (2002) developed a multiple item instrument (SERV-PERVAL) which was found to be reliable, and has convergent and discriminant validity within the sample of passengers on two different seven-day Caribbean cruises (Petrick, 2004). Following the approach, Petrick and Backman (2002a; 2002b), Al-Sabbahy, Ekinci and Riley (2004) as well as Sánchez, Callarisa, Rodríguez and Moliner (2006) reported only a moderate reliability of their scales and a poor explanation of overall customer value variance for golf travellers, hotel guests and package tourists. These results indicate that current measures of customer value may be inappropriate and do not capture the complexity of services in tourism and hospitality. Therefore, the proposed model of customer value (see Figure 1) is based on the assumption that the six types of losses consumers face in their decision making will be reflect in their assessment of customer value. The subject at the centre of this model are the following operational definitions of the six customer value dimensions (Agarwal and Teas, 2001; Petrick, 2002; Sheth et al., 1991; Sweeney and Soutar, 2001; Sweeney et al., 1999):

Financial value represents the perceived sacrifice in the monetary costs of the purchased service. It results from the specific situation or the context faced in the decision-making process. In other words, the financial value can be seen as the perceived value of the choice maker's second best option, which has an impact upon the consumers' assessment of the utility of the acquired service.

Functional value is related to the economic utility relative to the perceived benefit associated with the performance of the service. The underlying functional, utilitarian or physical attributes have been identified in many studies as cues for the evaluation of quality. Physical value is the perceived benefit of being in good health. Accordingly, the physical value represents the bodily well-being of the consumer and others due to the performance of the service.

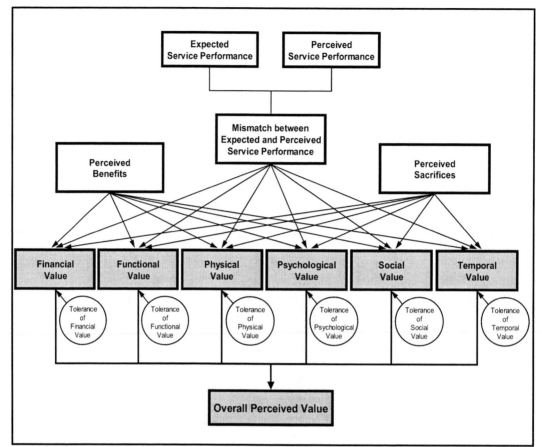

Figure 1.Customer Value Model

Psychological value or emotional value concerns the ability of a service to arouse feelings or affective states. Further, psychological value represents the ability of a service to arouse curiosity, provide novelty and/or satisfy a desire for knowledge. Social value subsumes the perceived social value in proportion to the perceived utility acquired through association with or avoidance of one or more positively/negatively stereotyped demographic, socio-economic, and cultural-ethic groups.

Temporal value represents the perceived sacrifice as a result of temporal effort associated with the decision-making process (e.g. the information search). The time loss due to a service failure and the time necessary to rectify the failure, is considered to be a key determinant of temporal value.

The proposed measurement of customer value incorporates the six types of perceived values described above, whereas each type is itself a direct function of the relevant perceived benefits and perceived sacrifices. The proposed model, presented in the Figure 1, can be described as: Customer value = ΣN [Perceived ValueN = f (PercBN, PercSN, error)], where N represents the different perceived risk dimensions.

DISCUSSION AND CONCLUSION

Due to the four main characteristics of services - intangibility, heterogeneity, perishability and inseparability - it is confirmed that services are riskier than goods (Mitchell and Greatorex, 1993). Since customers are more often motivated to avoid mistakes than to maximise their utility, it is suggested that perceived risk is a powerful determinant in explaining customers' behaviour (Mitchell, 1998). Nevertheless, existing models of customer value have not explicitly addressed the role of perceived risk (Boksberger, 2004). The development of a conceptual framework, with respect to the influence of perceived risk, may help to better determine customer value in tourism and hospitality. Particularly, in the present competitive environment of tourism and hospitality, the offering of value-added services has become a key factor for the survival. Since consumers are becoming more value conscious (i.e. are trying to purchase the service that will give more benefits for less sacrifice), managers should understand what defines customer value of their services in their consumers' minds. Thus, the cues that signal value to customers, as they choose tourism and hospitality services, need to be identified and addressed. The proposed model for customer value will give companies information about how strongly their services represent 'customer value' from the consumers' perspectives. It also reveals shortcomings where companies may not meet consumers' requirements. Generally speaking, managers who want to track insights to allocate their resources judiciously to maximise customer value can be guided by this model:

Financial Value

Companies have little control over perceived financial value unless they can reduce prices. Although price reductions are possible, it is not necessarily a desired choice, especially because higher prices are potential indicators of higher functional value.

Functional Value

In order to be in control of the performance of their services and/or the consequences associated with a service failure, companies should minimise the influence of situation- and consumer-related factors through customised service design.

Physical Value

Above all, consumers always need to experience a feeling of well-being, reassured by efficient, courteous and competent staff in every service setting.

Psychological Value

The crucial communication and interaction process between consumers and frontline employees has to be trained. Most of all, maintaining a high level of situational awareness (i.e. paying especially attention to irregular operations) must be the top priority for all staff members.

Social Value

While successful branding may provide long term reputation which will lower peer group pressure, a socially orientated relationship management may increase consumers' loyalty. This highlights the importance for companies to establish and maintain benefits for their consumer communities.

Temporal Value

While companies are able to significantly reduce consumers' temporal effort in decision-making process with adequate targeted information, advanced technology enables consumers to be in control of time-consuming services (i.e. self-check-in, e-ticketing, pre-bookable services, etc.).

In conclusion, it can be stated that companies should exhibit an honest picture of their services, as Parasuraman et al. (1991) revealed that companies have a better chance of meeting consumers' value perception when their promises reflect the service actually delivered rather than an idealised version of a service. In addition, companies should eliminate frivolous service design that creates unreasonable consumer expectations. Instead the tourism and hospitality industry should make their services less risky, less time consuming and more self-relevant. Moreover, there is a strong tendency for customers, practitioners and researchers to emphasise one or more value dimensions while ignoring others. This makes it almost impossible to determine and identify those value creation and delivery processes and activities that contribute most to the intended superior customer value. Moreover, the proposed correlation effects substantiate the salience of customer value, confirming that behavioural values should be as much a concern in tourism and hospitality as utilitarian values. In other words, the results indicate that, although consumers may believe that a company provides high levels of service quality, it does not necessarily follow that customer value will be high. Nor does it follow that, if prices are perceived to be high, the customer value will be low. Finally, it is advocated that future research will have to empirically validate the proposed model of customer value as well as to investigate the interaction of customer value with other core marketing constructs.

REFERENCES

Agarwal, S., and Teas, R.K. (2001). Perceived Value: Mediating Role of Perceived Risk. *Journal of Marketing Theory and Practice*, 9 (4), 1-14.

Al-Sabbahy, H.Z., Ekinci, Y., and Riley, M. (2004). An Investigation of Perceived Value Dimensions: Implications for Hospitality Research. *Journal of Travel Research*, 42 (3), 226-234.

Bauer, R.A. (1960). Consumer Behavior as Risk Taking. In Hancock, R.S. (Ed.), *Dynamic Marketing for a Changing World* (pp. 389-398). Chicago, USA: American Marketing Association.

Berry, L.L., and Parasuraman, A. (1993). Building a new Academic Field - The Case of Services Marketing. *Journal of Retailing*, 69 (1), 13-60.

Boksberger, P.E. (2004). Does Perceived Risk influence Perceived Value of Services? In *The 9th International Research Symposium of Service Excellence in Management* (pp. 96-105). Karlstad: Services Research Center (CTF).

Boksberger, Ph.E., and Craig-Smith, S. J. (2006). Customer Value amongst Tourists: A Conceptual Framework and a Risk-adjusted Model. *Tourism Review*, 61 (1), 6-12.

Bolton, R.N., and Drew, J.H. (1991). A Multistage Model of Customers' Assessments of Service Quality and Value. *Journal of Consumer Research*, 17 (4), 375-384.

Brady, M.K., and Cronin, J.J. Jr. (2001). Customer Orientation - Effects on Customer Service Perceptions and Outcome Behaviors. *Journal of Service Research*, 3 (3), 241-251.

Caruana, A., Money, A.H., and Berthon, P.R. (2000). Service Quality and Satisfaction - The moderating Role of Value. *European Journal of Marketing*, 34 (11/12), 1338-1352.

Chang, T.Z., and Wildt, A.R. (1994). Price, Product Information, and Purchase Intention: An Empirical Study. *Journal of the Academy of Marketing Science*, 22 (1), 16-27.

Cheron, E.J., and Ritchie, B.J.R. (1982). Leisure Activities and Perceived Risk. *Journal of Leisure Research*, 14 (2), 139-154.

Cronin, J.J. Jr. and Taylor, J.R. (1992). Measuring Service Quality: A Reexamination and Extension. *Journal of Marketing*, 56 (1), 55-68.

Cronin, J.J. Jr., Brady, M.K., Brand, R.R., Hightower Jr., R. and Shemwell, D.J. (1997). A Cross-Sectional Test of the Effect and Conceptualization of Service Value. *Journal of Services Marketing*, 11 (6), 375-391.

Cronin, J.J. Jr., Brady, M.K., and Hult, G.T.M. (2000). Assessing the Effects of Quality, Value, and Customer Satisfaction on Consumer Behavioral Intentions in Service Environment. *Journal of Retailing*, 76 (2), 193-218.

Dabholkar, P.A. (1993). Customer Satisfaction and Service Quality: Two Constructs or One? In Cravens, D.W. and Dickson, P.R. (Eds.). *Enhancing knowledge development in marketing* (pp. 10-18). Chicago: American Marketing Association.

Day, E., and Crask, M.R. (2000). Value Assessment: The Antecedent of Customer Satisfaction. *Journal of Consumer Satisfaction, Dissatisfaction and Complaining Behavior*, 13, 52-60.

Dodds, W.B., Monroe, K., and Grewal, D. (1991). Effects of Price, Brand and Store Information on Buyer's Product Evaluations. *Journal of Marketing Research*, 28 (3), 307-319.

Duman, T., and Mattila, A. (2005). The Role of Affective Factors on Perceived Cruise Vacation Value. *Tourism Management*, 26 (3), 311-323.

Floyd, M.F., Gibson, H., Pennington-Gray, L. and Thapa, B. (2003). The Effect of Risk Perceptions on Intentions to travel in the Aftermath of September 11, 2001. *Journal of Travel and Tourism Marketing*, 15 (2/3), 19-38.

Fornell, C., Johnson, M.D., Anderson, E.W., Cha, J., and Everitt, B.B. (1996). The American Customer Satisfaction Index: Nature, Purpose, and Findings. *Journal of Marketing*, 60(4), 7-18.

Gale, B.D. (1994). *Managing Customer Value*. New York, USA: The Free Press.

Grewal, D., Monroe, K., and Krishnan, R. (1998). The Effects of Price Comparison Advertising on Buyer's Perceptions of Aquisition Value, Transaction Value and Behavioural Intentions. *Journal of Marketing*, 62 (2), 46-59.

Hartline, M.D., and Jones, K.C. (1996). Employee Performance Cues in a Hotel Service Environment: Influence on Perceived Service Quality, Value, and Word-of-Mouth Intentions. *Journal of Business Research*, 35 (3), 207-215.

Heinonen, K. (2004). Reconceptualizing Customer Perceived Value: The Value of Time and Place. *Managing Service Quality*, 14 (2/3), 205-215.

Holbrook, M.B. (1994). The nature of customer value: An axiology of services in the consumption experience. In Rust, R. and Oliver, R.L. (Eds.) *Service Quality: New Directions in Theory and Practice* (21-71). Newbury Park: SAGE Publications.

Jayanti, R.K., and Ghosh, A.K. (1996). Service Value Determination: An Integrative Perspective. *Journal of Hospitality and Leisure Marketing*, 3 (4), 5-25.

Kahle, L.R., and Kennedy, P. (1988). Using the List of Values LOV to Understand Consumers. *Journal of Services Marketing*, 2 (4): 49-56.

Kaplan, L.B., Szybillo, G.J., and Jacoby, J. (1974). Components of perceived risk in product purchase: A cross-validation. *Journal of Applied Psychology*, 59 (2), 287-291.

Kashyap, R., and Bojanic, D.C. (2000). A Structural Analysis of Value, Quality, and Price Perceptions of Business and Leisure Travelers. *Journal of Travel Research*, 39 (1), 45-51.

Leigh, J., and Gabel, T. (1992). Symbolic Interactionism: Its Effects on Consumer Behavior and Implications for Marketing Strategy. *Journal of Services Marketing*, 6 (3), 5-16.

Lepp, A., and Gibson, H. (2003). Tourist Roles, Perceived Risk and International Tourism. *Annals of Tourism Research*, 30 (3), 606-624.

Maslow, S.H. (1943). A Theory of Human Motivation. *Psychological Review*, 50 (4), 370-396

McDougall, G.H.G., and Levesque, T. (2000). Customer Satisfaction with Services: Putting Perceived Value into the Equation. *Journal of Services Marketing*, 14 (4/5), 392-410.

Mitchell, V.W. (1998). Defining and measuring perceived risk. In *Academy of Marketing Conference* (pp. 380-384). Sheffield: Academy of Marketing Association.

Mitchell, V.W., and Greatorex, M. (1993). Risk Perception and Reduction in the Purchase of Consumer Services. *The Service Industries Journal*, 13 (4), 179-200.

Murray, K.B., (1991). A Test of Services Marketing Theory: Consumer Information Acquisition Activities. *Journal of Marketing*, 55 (1), 10-25.

Oh, H. (1999). Service Quality, Customer Satisfaction, and Customer Value: A Holistic Perspective. *International Journal of Hospitality Management*, 18 (1), 67-82.

Parasuraman, A. (1997). Reflections on Gaining Competitive Advantage through Customer Value. *Journal of the Academy of Marketing Science*, 25 (2), 154-161.

Parasuraman, A., Berry, L.L., and Zeithaml, V.A. (1991). Understanding Customer Expectations of Service. *Sloan Management Review*, 32 (3), 39-48.

Parasuraman, A., Zeithaml, V.A., and Berry, L.L. (1988). SERVQUAL: a Multi-Item Scale Measuring Consumer Perceptions of Service Quality. *Journal of Retailing*, 64 (1), 12-40.

Patterson, P.G., and Spreng, R.A. (1997). Modelling the Relationship between Perceived Value, Satisfaction and Repurchase Intentions in a Business-to-Business, Services Context: An Empirical Examination. *International Journal of Service Industry Management*, 8 (5), 414-434.

Petrick, J.F. (2002). Development of a Multi-Dimensional Scale for Measuring the Perceived Value of a Service. *Journal of Leisure Research*, 34 (2), 119-134.

Petrick, J.F. (2004). The Roles of Quality, Value, and Satisfaction in Predicting Cruise Passengers' Behavioral Intentions. *Journal of Travel Research*, 42 (4), 392-407.

Petrick, J.F., and Backman, S.J. (2002a). An Examination of Golf Travelers's Satisfaction, Percieved Value, Loyalty, and Intentions to Revisit. *Tourism Analysis*, 6 (3/4), 223-237.

Petrick, J.F., and Backman, S.J. (2002b). An Examination of the Construct of Perceived Value for the Prediction of Golf Traveler's Intentions to Revisit. *Journal of Travel Research*, 41 (1), 38-45.

Roehl, W.S., and Fesenmaier, D.R. (1992). Risk Perceptions and pleasure Travel: An Exploratory Analysis. *Journal of Travel Research*, 30 (4), 17-26.

Rokeach, M. (1973): *The Nature of Human Values*. New York: Free Press.

Sánchez, J., Callarisa, L., Rodríguez, R.M., and Moliner, M.A. (2006). Perceived Value of the Purchase of a Tourism Product. *Tourism Management*, 27 (3), 394-409.

Sheth, J.N., Newman, B.I., and Gross, B.L. (1991). *Consumption Values and Market Choices*. Chincinatti: South Western Publishing.

Sinha, I., and DeSarbo, W.S. (1998). An Integrated Approach toward the Spatial Modeling of Perceived Customer Value. *Journal of Marketing Research*, 35 (2), 236-249.

Sweeney, J.C., and Soutar, G.N. (2001). Consumer Perceived Value: The Development of a Multiple Item Scale. *Journal of Retailing*, 77 (2), 203-220.

Sweeney, J.C., Soutar, G. N., and Johnson, L.W. (1997). Retail Service Quality and Perceived Value. *Journal of Retailing and Consumer Services*, 4 (1), 39-48.

Sweeney, J.C., Soutar, G.N., and Johnson, L.W. (1999). The Role of Perceived Risk in the Quality-Value Relationship: A Study in a Retail Environment. *Journal of Retailing*, 75 (1), 77-105.

Tam, J. L. M. (2000). The Effects of Service Quality, Perceived Value and Customer Satisfaction on Behavioural Intentions. *Journal of Hospitality and Leisure Marketing*, 6 (4), 31-43.

Teas, R.K., and Agarwal, S. (2000). The Effects of Extrinsic Product Cues on Consumers' Perceptions of Quality, Sacrifice, and Value. *Journal of the Academy of Marketing Science*, 28 (2), 278-290.

Virilio, P., and Lotringer, S. (1983). *Pure War*. New York, USA: Semiotext(e).

Wang, Y.G., Lo, H.P., Chi, R.Y., and Yang, Y.H. (2004). An Integrated Framework for Customer Value and Customer-Relationship-Management Performance: A Customer-based Perspective from China. *Managing Service Quality*, 14 (2/3), 169-182.

Williams, P., and Soutar, G. N. (2000): Dimensions of Customer Value and the Tourism Experience: An Exploratory Study. In *ANZMAC* (pp. 1415-1421). Gold Coast: Australia and New Zealand Marketing Academy.

Woo, H.K.H. (1992). *Cognition, Value, and Price: A General Theory of Value*. Ann Arbor: University of Michigan Press.

Woodruff, R.B. (1997). Customer Value: The Next Source for Competitive Advantage. *Journal of the Academy of Marketing Science*, 25 (2), 139-153.

Woodruff, R.B., and Gardial, S.F. (1998). *Know your Customer: New Approaches to Understanding Customer Value and Satisfaction*. Malden: Blackwell.

Yates, J.F. (1992). *Risk Taking Behavior*. Chichester: Wiley.

Yüksel, A., and Yüksel, F. (2001). Measurement and Management Issues in Customer Satisfaction Research: Review, Critique and Research Agenda. *Journal of Travel and Tourism Marketing*, 10 (4), 47-111.

Zeithaml, V.A. (1988). Consumer Perceptions of Price, Quality and Value: A Means-End Model and Synthesis of Evidence. *Journal of Marketing*, 52 (3), 2-22.

In: Tourist Satisfaction and Complaining Behavior
Editor: Atila Yüksel

ISBN 978-1-60456-002-2
© 2008 Nova Science Publishers, Inc.

Chapter 4

CONSUMER SATISFACTION THEORIES: A CRITICAL REVIEW

Atila Yüksel and Fisun Yüksel
Adnan Menderes University, Turkey

INTRODUCTION

The marketing and consumer behavior literature has traditionally suggested that customer satisfaction is a relative concept, and is always judged in relation to a standard (Olander, 1977). Consequently, in the course of its development, a number of different competing theories based on various standards have been postulated for explaining customer satisfaction. The theories include the Expectancy-Disconfirmation Paradigm (EDP), the Value-Precept Theory, the Attribution Theory, the Equity Theory, the Comparison Level Theory, the Evaluation Congruity Theory, the Person-Situation-Fit model, the Performance-Importance model, the Dissonance, and the Contrast Theory.

Early researchers, including Engel, Kollat and Blackwell (1968), Howard and Sheth (1969), and Cardozzo (1965), relied on the dissonance theory developed by Festinger (1957). Subsequent studies (Anderson, 1973; Olshavsky and Miller, 1972) drew on the assimilation-contrast theories proposed by Sheriff and Hovland (1961). Later, Oliver (1977), drawing on the adaptation level theory (Helson, 1964), developed the Expectancy-Disconfirmation model for the study of consumer satisfaction, which received the widest acceptance among researchers. These frameworks generally imply conscious comparison between a cognitive state prior to an event and a subsequent cognitive state, usually realized after the event is experienced (Oliver, 1980). Following the introduction of the EDP, Westbrook and Reilly (1983) proposed the Value-Precept theory as a competing framework to study consumer satisfaction, arguing that what is expected from a product may not correspond to what is desired and valued in a product, and thus, values may be better comparative standards as opposed to expectations used in the EDP. In addition, Sirgy (1984) proposed the Evaluative Congruity model as another competing framework to explain consumer satisfaction. According to Chon (1992), the Evaluative Congruity Model is a better framework than the

EDP because of its ability in capturing the different states of satisfaction/ dissatisfaction resulting from different combinations of expectations and performance outcome. Last decades also saw the development of a number of additional frameworks such as the Attribution Theory, Importance-Performance model, and the Equity Theory for the study of consumer satisfaction. It is important to note that some of the posited theories have received intensive attention in the literature (for example, the EDP), while others have not provoked further empirical research (Oh and Parks 1997). The following section undertakes a critical review of these theories postulated to explain consumer satisfaction, as this is important to the development of the research.

THE DISSONANCE THEORY

The Dissonance Theory suggests that a person who expected a high-value product and received a low-value product would recognize the disparity and experience a cognitive dissonance (Cardozzo, 1965). That is, the disconfirmed expectations create a state of dissonance or a psychological discomfort (Yi, 1990). According to this theory, the existence of dissonance produces pressures for its reduction, which could be achieved by adjusting the perceived disparity. This theory holds that "post exposure ratings are primarily a function of the expectation level because the task of recognizing disconfirmation is believed to be psychologically uncomfortable. Thus consumers are posited to perceptually distort expectation-discrepant performance so as to coincide with their prior expectation level" (Oliver, 1977, p. 480). For instance, if a disparity exists between product expectations and product performance, consumers may have a psychological tension and try to reduce it by changing their perception of the product (Yi, 1990). Cardozzo argues that consumers may raise their evaluations of those products when the cost of that product to the individual is high. For example, suppose that a customer goes into a restaurant, which she or he expects it to be good, and is confronted with an unappetizing meal. The consumer, who had driven a long distance and paid a high price for the meal, in order to reduce the dissonance, might say that the food was not really as bad as it appeared or she likes overcooked meal, etc.

The researchers pursued this approach implicitly assume that consumers would generally find that product performance deviated in some respect from their expectations or effort expenditures and that some cognitive repositioning would be required (Oliver, 1980). This theory has not gained much support from researchers, partly because it is not clear whether consumers would engage in such discrepancy adjustments as the model predicts in every consumption situation. In his criticism of the Dissonance theory, Oliver (1977), for instance, argues that "Generally, it is agreed that satisfaction results from a comparison between X, one's expectation, and Y, product performance. Thus, it is the magnitude and direction of this difference, which affects one's post-decision affect level. X serves only to provide the comparative baseline. Moreover, consumers are under no particular pressure to resolve the X-Y difference. In fact, satisfaction/dissatisfaction is thought to arise from recognition and acknowledgement of dissonance" (p. 206).

If the Dissonance Theory holds true, then companies should strive to raise expectations substantially above the product performance in order to obtain a higher product evaluation (Yi, 1990). However, the validity of this assumption is questionable. Raising expectations substantially above the product performance and failing to meet these expectations may backfire, as small discrepancies may be largely discounted while large discrepancies may result in a very negative evaluation. This suggestion fails to take into account the concept of "tolerance level". The tolerance level suggests that purchasers are willing to accept a range of performance around a point estimate as long as the range could be reasonably expected. When perceptions of a brand performance, which are close to the norm (initial expectation), are within the latitude of acceptable performance, and then it may be assimilated toward the norm (Woodruff et al 1983). That is, perceived performance within some interval around a performance norm is likely to be considered equivalent to the norm. However, when the distance from this norm is great enough, that is perceived performance is outside the acceptable zone, then brand performance will be perceived as different from the norm, which, in contrast to this model's assumption, will cause dissatisfaction not a high product evaluation.

The Dissonance Theory fails as a complete explanation of consumer satisfaction, however, it contributes to the understanding of the fact that expectations are not static in that they may change during a consumption experience. For instance, the importance attached to pre-holiday expectations may change during the holiday and a new set of expectations may be formed as a result of experiences during the holiday. This implies that as customers progress from one encounter to the next, say from hotel's reception to the room or the restaurant, their expectations about the room may be modified due to the performance of the previous encounter (Danaher and Arweiler, 1996).

THE CONTRAST THEORY

The Contrast Theory suggests the opposite of the Dissonance Theory. According to this theory, when actual product performance falls short of consumer's expectations about the product, the contrast between the expectation and outcome will cause the consumer to exaggerate the disparity (Yi, 1990). The Contrast theory maintains that a customer who receives a product less valuable than expected, will magnify the difference between the product received and the product expected (Cardozzo, 1965). This theory predicts that product performance below expectations will be rated poorer than it is in reality (Oliver and DeSarbo, 1988). In other words, the Contrast Theory would assume that "outcomes deviating from expectations will cause the subject to favorably or unfavorably react to the disconfirmation experience in that a negative disconfirmation is believed to result in a poor product evaluation, whereas positive disconfirmation should cause the product to be highly appraised" (Oliver, 1977, p. 81). In terms of the above restaurant situation, the consumer might say that the restaurant was one of the worst he or she had ever been and the food was unfit for human consumption, etc.

If the Contrast Theory were applied to a consumption context, then the poor performance would be worse than simply poor, and good performance would be better than a rating of good would suggest (Oliver, 1997). Under the dissonance theory, the opposite effects occur, perceived performance, whether it is less or more favorable than the consumer's expectations, is drawn to the original expectation level. It is important to note that these theories have been applied and tested in laboratory settings where the customer satisfaction was tightly controlled, situation specific and individually focused. For instance, researchers investigated the ability of these theories in predicting customer satisfaction with a pen (Cardozzo, 1965), a reel-type tape recorder (Olshavsky and Miller, 1972), ball-point pen (Anderson, 1973), and a coffee brand (Olson and Dover, 1975). Thus, it is curious whether hypotheses held by these theories could be accepted or rejected when applied in a field survey research study of hospitality and tourism services (Oh and Parks, 1997). It is, for instance, not clear whether all purchase decisions in tourism and hospitality services result in dissonance.

THE EXPECTANCY DISCONFIRMATION PARADIGM

Drawing on the shortcomings of the above early theories of consumer satisfaction, Oliver (1977; 1980) proposed the Expectancy-Disconfirmation Paradigm (EDP) as the most promising theoretical framework for the assessment of customer satisfaction. The model implies that consumers purchase goods and services with pre-purchase expectations about the anticipated performance. The expectation level then becomes a standard against which the product is judged. That is, once the product or service has been used, outcomes are compared against expectations. If the outcome matches the expectation confirmation occurs. Disconfirmation occurs where there is a difference between expectations and outcomes. A customer is either satisfied or dissatisfied as a result of positive or negative difference between expectations and perceptions. Thus, when service performance is better than what the customer had initially expected, there is a positive disconfirmation between expectations and performance which results in satisfaction, while when service performance is as expected, there is a confirmation between expectations and perceptions which results in satisfaction. In contrast, when service performance is not as good as what the customer expected, there is a negative disconfirmation between expectations and perceptions which causes dissatisfaction.

This type of discrepancy theory has a long history in the satisfaction literature dating back at least to Howard's and Sheth's (1967) definition of satisfaction which states that it is a function of the degree of congruency between aspirations and perceived reality of experiences. Porter (1961) can be credited with early empirical applications of this comparative model of customer satisfaction in the field of job satisfaction (cf. Oliver, 1997). In his study, Porter, for instance, compared the worker's perception of how much of a job facet (for example, pay) there should be to the worker's perception of how much is the facet there now. In support of Porter's view, Locke (1965) proposed that this discrepancy methodology could be employed in assessing employees' job satisfaction

This literature review demonstrates that in addition to job satisfaction literature this model has found great degree of support from researchers in other disciplines, and has been widely used to evaluate satisfaction with different products and services, for example with flu treatment (Oliver, 1980), with restaurant services (Bearden and Teel, 1983; Cadotte, Woodruff and Jenkins, 1987; Swan and Trawick, 1981), with automobiles (Oliver and Swan, 1989;), with record players (Tse and Wilton, 1989) with stock market services (Oliver and DeSarbo, 1988), with video disc player (Churchill and Surprenant, 1982) with hotel and holiday destination services (Barsky, 1992; Barsky and Labagh, 1992; Pizam and Milman, 1993; Tribe and Snaith, 1998; Weber, 1997).

INFERRED VERSUS DIRECT DISCONFIRMATION

It is important to note that there are basically two methods of investigating dis/confirmation of expectations. First, the inferred approach (or the subtractive approach) and second the direct approach (or the subjective approach) (Meyer and Westerbarkey, 1996; Prakash and Lounsbury, 1992). The inferred approach involves the computation of the discrepancy between expectations and evaluations of performance. This requires researchers to draw separate information relating to customer service expectations and perceived performance. These scores are then subtracted to form the third variable, the dis/confirmation or difference score. The inferred (subtractive) disconfirmation approach (for example, LaTour and Peat, 1979), is derived from the theory of comparison (Thibaut and Kelley, 1959) and assumes that the effects of a post-experience comparison on satisfaction can be expressed as a function of algebraic difference between product performance and a comparative standard. Tse and Wilton (1988) report that the inferred approach has found considerable support from studies in cognitive psychology where psychological variables expressed as algebraic rules have been found to represent human information processes over a wide variety of situations.

The direct approach on the other hand, requires the use of summary judgmental scales to measure dis/confirmation, such as better than expected to worse than expected. The calculation of the difference scores by the researcher is avoided as the respondents can be asked directly the extent to which the service experience exceeded, met or fell short of expectations. As an alternative approach, subjective disconfirmation approach represents a distinct psychological construct encompassing a subjective evaluation of the difference between product performance and the comparison standard (Churchill and Surprenant, 1982; Oliver, 1980). That is, subjective disconfirmation encompasses a set of psychological processes that may mediate perceived product performance discrepancies. Tse and Wilton (1988) state that such processes are likely to be important in situations in which product performance cannot be judged discretely.

An important distinction between the direct and inferred approaches has been drawn by Oliver (1980) who suggests that "subtractive disconfirmation (inferred) may lead to an immediate satisfaction judgment, whereas subjective disconfirmation represents an intervening distinct cognitive state resulting from the comparison process and preceding satisfaction judgments" (p. 460). Hence, according to Oliver, subjective disconfirmation is likely to offer a richer explanation of the complex processes underlying customer satisfaction/dissatisfaction formation. Swan and Martin (1981) compared the ability of inferred and direct disconfirmation measures in predicting customer satisfaction. They found that satisfaction is more sensitive (better predicts) to inferred disconfirmation than to direct disconfirmation, which appears to be contradicting with Tse's and Wilton's (1988) finding, which suggests that direct disconfirmation yields a better prediction of customer satisfaction than inferred disconfirmation

Both the inferred and the direct methods of EDP have been used by hospitality and tourism researchers in various studies which assess international travelers' satisfaction levels as well as in studies investigating customer satisfaction with hotel services (for example, Barsky, 1992; Barsky and Labagh, 1992; Cho, 1998; Chon and Olsen, 1991; Danaher and Haddrell, 1996; Pizam and Milman, 1993; Reisinger and Turner, 1997; Reisinger and Warzyack, 1995; Weber, 1997; Whipple and Thach, 1989). It is important to remind that, the

Servqual technique, utilized by some researchers in assessing tourist satisfaction (Tribe and Snaith, 1998), employs a similar algorithm to that of the inferred disconfirmation approach.

Despite its widespread popularity, however, the EDP is not free of shortcomings. The main criticisms of this approach focus on the use of expectations as a comparison standard in measuring customer satisfaction, the dynamic nature of expectations and the timing of its measurement, the meaning of expectations to respondents, the use of difference scores in assessing satisfaction, and the reliability and validity of the EDP in predicting customer satisfaction (refer to Yuksel and Yuksel, 2001 for a detailed discussion on EDP limitations). One of the problems related to the EDP is the suggested sequence of the model, which presupposes that everyone has precise expectations prior to the service experience. It is obvious that without these prior expectations, dis/confirmation of expectations cannot occur (Halstead, Hartman, and Schmidt, 1994). However, the logic of the EDP, stating that everyone has firm expectations of all attributes prior to service experiences, might be less meaningful in situations where customers do not know what to expect, until they experience the service. Unlike tangible goods where search attributes are dominant, tourism and hospitality services are experiential in nature, and they contain high percentages of experience and credence properties (Reisinger and Waryszak, 1996). Search properties refer to those attributes, which a consumer evaluates before engaging in the service. These properties are primarily tangibles, which are physical representations of the service (for example, facilities, equipment, and appearance of personnel). Experience properties are those attributes that can be only assessed after purchase or during consumption such as taste, value, and purchase satisfaction (Zeithaml, 1981). Credence properties are the attributes that the consumer finds impossible to evaluate even after purchase and consumption (for example, the backstage hygiene conditions). In general, those services that are based heavily on experience and credence properties, such as hospitality and tourism services, may be difficult to predict and evaluate (Hill, 1985). Moreover, the variability in the service level that is provided from encounter to encounter in hospitality and tourism services may create uncertainty, which may inhibit the formation of precise pre-purchase expectations (Jayanti and Jackson, 1991). Thus, the assumption that the formation of firm and realistic attribute-specific expectations prior to every purchase in the hospitality and tourism context may be incorrect.

Customers with little or no brand experience of products and services constitute a special case in the EDP, as it is not clear how the EDP may be applied to the evaluation of services for which the consumer has little information or experience to generate a meaningful expectation (Halstead et al., 1994; McGill and Iacobucci, 1992). Customer expectations of completely unfamiliar experiences (for example, first time travel to Eastern Europe) are almost meaningless (Halstead et al., 1994). "Though one might assume that expectations based on travel to other parts of Europe would be an appropriate proximate, this too, may have little relevance to the actual experience" (Halstead et al., 1994). Lack of any kind of previous experience with the service, or not knowing what to expect as a result of the absence of pre-purchase information, may result in tentative and uncertain expectations (Crompton and Love, 1995; Mazursky, 1989; McGill and Iacobucci, 1992). In these situations, regarding expectations as firm criteria against which make evaluative judgments is likely to be fallacious (Crompton and Love, 1995)

Learning from previous service experiences may result in more accurate and stable expectations (Day, 1977). Experienced customers may, therefore, make better choices when repurchasing, they may have more realistic expectations, and they may be more satisfied with their choices (Fisk and Coney, 1982; Halstead et al., 1994; Westbrook and Newman, 1987). On the other hand, inexperienced customers may rely on external sources of information (Halstead et al., 1994), such as the organization's promotional material, and word of mouth communication shape their expectations, leading to expectations that are weaker, less complete, less stable, and superficial (Halstead et al., 1994; Mazursky, 1989; McGill and Iacobucci, 1992). Thus, measuring expectations may not be valid in situations where consumers do not have well formed expectations prior to service experience (Carman, 1990). In such situations, as Carman notes, expectations may be assumed to be zero, and that expectation measures do not need to be obtained every time the perception measures are obtained.

Another problem with the EDP is that post-purchase evaluations may not be based on initial expectations. For instance, McGill and Iacobucci (1992, p. 571) report that "in contrast to what might have been expected from the literature on the disconfirmation paradigm, that comparison of subjects' listing of features that affected their level of satisfaction in the post-experience questionnaire were not entirely consistent with the listing of factors that they expected to affect their level of satisfaction in the pre-experience questionnaire". Similarly, Whipple and Thach (1989, p.16) state that expectations may be important indicators of choice preference and "there is evidence that pre-purchase choice criteria and post-purchase choice criteria are not the same". If different evaluative criteria are used before and after a service experience then "the initial expectation framework is disregarded and is of little value for measuring satisfaction".

Another problem with the EDP relates to the meaning of expectations question to the respondent (i.e., whether the expectation question signifies the same meaning to everyone). Expectation represents a baseline, against which performance is compared, and it may vary from a minimum tolerable level of performance and estimates of anticipated performance, to some concept of ideal or perfect service (Ennew, Reed, and Binks, 1993). Given the confusion about the precise meaning of expectation, the use of this concept as a means to conceptualise comparison standards, has been criticized by a number of researchers (Woodruff et al., 1991). The expectation component of both service quality and satisfaction investigations might have serious discriminant validity shortcomings, which causes the performance-minus expectation measurement framework to be a potentially misleading indicator of customer perceptions of services. For instance, findings reported in Teas' (1993) study clearly suggest that not all respondents interpret the question of expectation in the same way, and there may be a considerable degree of confusion, among respondents, concerning the actual question being asked. Teas (1993) identified that some responses suggested that the expectation questions involved an importance measure, while other respondents used the scale to predict the performance they would expect (i.e. forecasted performance). A few respondents interpreted the question in terms of the ideal point concept (i.e., the optimal performance, what performance can be), and minimum tolerable concept (i.e., what performance must be).

If there is a difference between customers' interpretations of the expectation question, then the scores obtained from performance-minus-expectation process can be misleading. Assume that two respondents rated different scores on expectation question concerning a visually appealing restaurant (1 and 7 respectively) and rated the same score of 7 on perceived performance. As a result of the low score on expectation, the calculation suggests a positive gap (+6) in the first case, whereas the latter's ratings suggest a gap score of zero, which consequently implies that the satisfaction is higher in the first case. However, what if the respondent rated low on the expectation question because she wishes to save money and desires a visually unappealing restaurant, or the visual appealing issue is unimportant to the respondent. The last probability, in particular, represents a potential measurement validity problem. Although the first respondent rated 1 on the expectation scale because the visually appealing issue is an unimportant factor, the resultant P-E (+6) score suggests that a higher level of quality/satisfaction in that situation than the quality/satisfaction level suggested in the second respondent's case, in which the performance is high on an important attribute. Thus, it is illogical to assume that "scores with high performance on attributes of low importance items should reflect a higher service quality [satisfaction] than equally strong performance on attributes of high importance" (Teas, 1994, p. 44).

An additional problem related to the EDP is its main presumption. The current logic of the EDP predicts customers will evaluate a service favorably, as long as their expectations are met or exceeded (Iacobucci, Grayson, and Ostrom, 1994). However, this may not be the case every time. In situations where consumers are forced to buy an inferior, less desirable brand because their preferred brand is not available, then consumers may not necessarily experience disconfirmation of a pre-experience comparison standard (LaTour and Peat, 1979). "If a less desirable brand was indeed as undesirable as the customer had expected it to be, the consumer would experience no disconfirmation, and yet could be quite dissatisfied" (Iacobucci et al., 1994, p. 16). In addition, users of new brands who experience unfavorable disconfirmation of a high pre-experience standard, which was generated through advertising, may still be satisfied with the brand, if it has more of the desired attributes than competing brands (LaTour and Peat, 1979).

The key role played by expectations in determining the level of satisfaction, is questionable. Consumers may show satisfaction or dissatisfaction for aspects where expectations never existed (McGill and Iacobucci, 1992; Yi, 1990). In her research on tourist satisfaction, Hughes (1991, p. 168) reported that "surprisingly, even though experiences did not fulfill expectations, a considerable number of tourists were relatively satisfied". Similarly, Pearce (1991) maintains that tourists may be satisfied even though their experiences did not fulfill their expectations. In a study of service quality perceptions of clinic customers, Smith (1995) reports a similar finding, that respondents described themselves as extremely pleased with the clinic even where an aggregate performance-minus-expectation score was negative (P<E). Similarly, Yuksel and Rimmington (1998) found that customers might be reasonably satisfied even if the service performance does not totally meet their initial expectations. These findings cast doubts over the logical consistency of the expectancy-dis/confirmation model, as it predicts the customer to be dissatisfied when initial expectations are not met.

One possible explanation for this could be that some consumers may use minimum acceptable as a comparative standard in certain situations, and the performance above the minimum acceptable but below the predicted expectations may not necessarily create dissatisfaction. The latitude-of-acceptance (Anderson, 1973) or zone-of-indifference (Woodruff et al., 1983) concept might explain why those customers, whose expectations are unmet, report satisfaction. This concept suggests that purchasers are willing to accept a range of performance around a point estimate as long as the range could be reasonably expected (Oliver, 1997). If customer tolerance of some deviation from expectations exists, a level of service less than the expected does not generate dissatisfaction (Saleh and Ryan, 1991). Perceived performance within the zone of indifference probably does not cause much attention to be directed toward the evaluation process. In contrast, perceived performance, outside the zone of indifference is unusual and attention getting, leading to an emotional response (Woodruff et al., 1983). An alternative explanation could be that, customers might engage in a trade-off process, where strength of an attribute may compensate for the weakness(es) of another attribute, and may lead to overall satisfaction (Lewis, Chambers and Chacko, 1995).

There is a continuing debate on the timing of expectation measurement in customer satisfaction studies. Some researchers suggest that expectations should be solicited before the service experience (Carman, 1990), whereas others argue that expectations may be measured after the service experience (Parasuraman et al., 1988). Those supporting the measurement "before the experience" contend that, "to be of value expectations should be elicited prior to the service being provided, otherwise the risk is so great that expectations will be contaminated by perceptions of the actual service provided" (Getty and Thomson, 1994, p. 8). This method has been employed by a number of researchers in tourism and hospitality literature (for example, Fick and Ritchie, 1991; Johns and Tyas, 1996; Hughes, 1991; Pizam and Milman, 1993; Tribe and Snaith, 1998; Weber, 1997; Whipple and Thach, 1989). For instance, in their investigation of satisfaction among first time visitors to Spain, Pizam and Milman (1993) solicited travelers' expectations before they left and examined their perception of 21 destination attributes after they returned from their holiday. Weber (1997) adopted a similar approach in her research on satisfaction of the German travel market in Australia. Weber distributed questionnaires to tourists on their arrival and asked them to complete the pre-trip section on the day of arrival and the post-trip section at the end of their holiday.

Although adopted by a number of researchers, measuring expectations prior to service experience is problematic. It is reasonable to assume that, in some situations where the pre-post method is adopted, not all of the respondents answer to the expectation part of the questionnaire at the required time (for example, before the service experience). A number of respondents may wait to complete the expectation part after the dinner, which may produce "hindsight bias" (Weber, 1997; Yuksel and Rimmington, 1998). Prior expectations may be modified during the service encounter, and these modified expectations, may be used in the comparison process (Danaher and Mattsson, 1994; Gronroos, 1993; Iacobucci et al., 1994; McGill and Iacobucci, 1992). An observed effect (satisfaction) may be due to an event, which takes place between the pre-test and the post-test (Cook and Campbell, 1979). According to Boulding, Karla, Staelin, and Zeithaml (1993, p. 9) "A person's expectations just before a service contact can differ from the expectations held just after the service contact because of the information that enters the system between service encounters". The unpredictability of tourism events lies at the heart of vacational experience (Botterill, 1987), and events that are completely unanticipated prior to a trip may become significant contributors to overall holiday satisfaction (e.g., unanticipated sources or discoveries such as the weather, the travel companion and unexpected adventures) (Pearce, 1980; Weber, 1997).

If learning takes place during the service encounter, and expectations are modified as a consequence of this, then the use of initially measured expectations in satisfaction assessment is not logical. Satisfaction is most accurately measured at the conclusion of the transaction, and thus, the expectation referent, relevant to satisfaction, would be the one actually used by the consumer in satisfaction formation, not necessarily the one measured before consumption (Oliver, 1997). This becomes problematic if the consumer has updated (downgraded or elevated) his or her expectations during consumption. Recent studies (e.g., Zwick, Pieters, and Baumgartner, 1995) suggest that updated expectations may be more influential in satisfaction judgments than pre-consumption expectations. Given the evidence above, it seems reasonable to assume that a customer's expectations, prior to the service experience, may be different from those against which they compare the actual experience.

Given the complications that surround the measurement of expectations prior to the service experience, an alternative method of soliciting expectations is that they are measured after the service experience or simultaneously with the service experience. A number of researchers have used this method (Dorfman, 1979; Fick and Ritchie, 1991; Parasuraman et al., 1988). For example, Parasuraman et al (1988) and Dorfman (1979) asked respondents to complete both expectations and perceptions questions at the same time. Based on their previous experience with the service, respondents were asked what they expected and then were asked what they had experienced. However, this approach is also questionable, as expectations might be over/under stated if the tourists have a very negative or positive experience (Yuksel and Rimmington, 1998). In addition, respondents' capability to correctly remember prior expectations raises doubts about the validity of these measures (Lounsbury and Hoopes, 1985). It is argued that, if expectations are measured after the service experience or simultaneously with the experience, it is not the expectations that are being measured but something that has been biased by the experience. For example, Halstead (1993) found that expectations that are measured after service experience, were higher for dissatisfied customers than for satisfied customers. This suggests that recalled expectations will be biased toward the experienced performance (Oliver, 1997).

From a practical perspective, Dorfman (1979) draws attention to the fact that expectations are generally rated very highly. That is, respondents may feel motivated to demonstrate an "I-have-high-expectation" social norm, and the expected level therefore may exceed the existing level for no other reason than this type of response bias (Babakus and Boller, 1992). In the service quality area, for example, Babakus and Boller (1992, p. 257) pointed out that " in general when people are asked to indicate an expected level and an existing level of service they seldom rate the expected level lower than the existing level". If these scores are almost constant, "then there is little point in including them in an instrument, since they will not give responses significantly different from using the perception scores alone" (Crompton and Love, 1995, p. 15).

The results of Fick and Ritchie's (1991), Parasuraman et al.'s (1988; 1991; 1994), Smith (1995) and Tribe and Snaith's (1998) research reveals that, scores on expectations are indeed rated consistently higher than the scores on the performance component. For instance, Smith (1995) reports that the mean score for the expectation scale in her study was 6. 401 (standard deviation 0.347). In the study by Parasuraman et al. (1991) the mean expectation score was 6.22. Buttle (1995), in a comprehensive review of research studies on service quality and satisfaction reported that, the average score of expectations was 6.086. The results of Bojanic and Rosen's (1995) study, in a family restaurant environment, demonstrated that consumers' perceptions about the actual level of service provided, fell significantly short of their expectations. Similarly, the research undertaken by Yuksel and Rimmington (1998) revealed that the mean expectation scores for restaurant services was, significantly higher than the mean performance perception scores. These findings suggest that it would be difficult to satisfy tourists as expectations will never be met or exceeded.

In this sense, to ensure that expectations are exceeded, some researchers have suggested that service providers should understate the destination or organization's capability of delivering these experiences, in promotional efforts. For example, Pizam and Milman (1993, p. 208) suggested that "it would be more beneficial to create modest and even below realistic expectations". Though this is a sensible and potentially effective suggestion in theory, it is questionable whether it can and, should be, implemented practically (Weber, 1997). The problem is that tourists may not want to spend time and money in a destination in the first place if promotional efforts convey the possibility of the destination being unable to deliver adequate services. Moreover, establishing a threshold is difficult at which expectations are raised high enough to attract customers, but low enough to allow for expectations to be exceeded (Weber, 1997). The present logic of the EDP encourages managers to lower expectations for a given service and then having the users discover a superior outcome, than expected, leading to greater satisfaction. Obviously, low expectations would affect the motivation and would therefore reduce purchase and consumption (Williams, 1998).

Additionally, expectations are argued to have a direct positive effect on satisfaction because "without observing the performance, expectations may have already predisposed the consumer to respond to the product in a certain way (the higher the expectations, the higher the satisfaction or vice versa)" (Oliver, 1997, p. 89). If high expectations lead to more favorable ratings, then one may suggest that companies should strive to raise expectations substantially above the product performance in order to obtain a higher product evaluation (Yi, 1990). However, the validity of this suggestion is also questionable. Raising expectations substantially above the product performance and failing to meet these expectations may backfire, as small discrepancies may be largely discounted while large discrepancies may result in a very negative evaluation. Given these complications, it appears that increasing service performance may be the safest strategy.

THE COMPARISON LEVEL THEORY

A number of authors criticized the Expectancy-Disconfirmation paradigm on the grounds that this approach posits that the primary determinant of customer satisfaction is the predictive expectations created by manufacturers, company reports, or unspecified sources (Yi, 1990). For instance, La Tour and Peat (1979) argued that the EDP ignores other sources of expectations, such as the consumer's past experience and other consumer's experience with similar constructs. They proposed a modification of the Comparison Level Theory (Thibaut and Kelley, 1959). In contrast to the Expectancy-Disconfirmation paradigm which uses predictive or situationally-produced expectations as the comparison standard, the Comparison Level Theory argues that there are more than one basic determinants of comparison level for a product: (1) consumers' prior experiences with similar products, (2) situationally produced expectations (those created through advertising and promotional efforts), and (3) the experience of other consumers who serve as referent persons.

Applying the Comparison Level Theory to the confirmation/disconfirmation process, LaTour and Peat found that experience based standards or norms play a role as a baseline for comparisons in consumer's satisfaction judgments. They found that situationally induced expectations had little effect on the customer satisfaction, while expectations based on prior experiences were the major determinant of customer satisfaction. This finding suggests that consumers may give less weight to manufacturer-provided information, when they have personal experience and relevant information about other consumer experiences (Yi, 1990). Unlike the Expectancy/ Disconfirmation paradigm, the Comparison Level Theory suggests that consumers might bring a number of different comparison standards into the consumption experience. Consumers might be more likely to use predictive expectations based on external communication (advertisement) before the purchase (in their decision-making), while different standards (for example, past experience and experiences of other consumers suggested by LaTour and Peat's model) might become more likely after the purchase. There is, however, inadequate information concerning what standards that consumers bring into the consumption experience are being confirmed and disconfirmed. Theoretical discussions aside, the use of past experience suggested by the Comparison Level Theory as the comparison standard in customer satisfaction investigations may serve managers to compare their performance with their rivals, and undertake required actions to catch-up or for product differentiation.

THE VALUE PERCEPT THEORY

Similar to LaTour and Peat's argument, Westbrook and Reilly (1983) argue that the Expectancy-Disconfirmation paradigm may not be the most appropriate model to explain customer satisfaction, as customer satisfaction/dissatisfaction is more likely to be determined by comparative standards other than expectations. They proposed a Value-Percept Disparity theory, originally formulated by Locke (1967), as an alternative to the Expectation-Disconfirmation paradigm. Criticizing the predictive expectations used as a comparison standard in the traditional Disconfirmation paradigm, Westbrook and Reilly argue that what is expected from a product may or may not correspond to what is desired or valued in a product. Conversely, that which is valued may or may not correspond to what is expected. Thus, values have been proposed to be a better comparative standard as opposed to expectations in explaining customer satisfaction/dissatisfaction. According to the value-percept theory, satisfaction is an emotional response that is triggered by a cognitive evaluative process in which the perceptions of an offer are compared to one's values, needs, wants or desires (Westbrook and Reilly, 1983). Similar to the Expectancy/Disconfirmation paradigm, a growing disparity between one's perceptions and one's values (value-perception) indicates an increasing level of dissatisfaction.

In their study, Westbrook and Reilly compared the expectation-confirmation model with the value-percept disparity model. The value-disparity was defined as the extent to which the product provides the features and performance characteristics needed or desired. The disparity was assessed on a single differential scale anchored with "provides far less than my needs" and "provides exactly what I need". In contrast to their hypothesis, which states that values, as opposed to expectations, determine satisfaction, Westbrook and Reilly found that the disconfirmation of expectations had a stronger effect on satisfaction than the disparity between value and perceptions. They suggested that both constructs (expectations and values) were needed in explaining customer satisfaction, as they found neither the expectation-disconfirmation model nor the value percept model was sufficient on its own. Similarly, results of recent studies investigating the ability of value and expectations in determining satisfaction demonstrate that it might be better to integrate desires and expectations into a single framework, as they are both affecting consumer satisfaction (Spreng et al 1996). The Value-Percept theory which postulates satisfaction as the fulfillment of consumer desires, values, or wants, as opposed to their expectations, has not received as much support from researchers as the EDP did in ascertaining customer satisfaction with hospitality and tourism services.

THE IMPORTANCE- PERFORMANCE MODEL

Although the EDP has dominated as the theoretical construct with which to measure satisfaction and that predictive expectations are regarded as the comparison standard that best explains satisfaction, the impact of attribute importance is also recognized (Barsky, 1992; Martilla and James, 1977; Oh and Parks, 1997). Satisfaction is seen as a function of customer perceptions of performance and the importance of that attribute. Based on the expectancy-value model, developed by Fishbein and Ajzen (1975), in which attribute importance and beliefs play a central role, Barsky (1992) posited that overall satisfaction/dissatisfaction toward a product/service are dictated by the importance of specific characteristics and the degree to which that product provides the specific characteristics. This model predicts that people generally have a belief about an attribute, but each attribute may be assigned important weighting relative to other attributes (ibid.). This implies that customers' satisfaction levels are related to the strength of their beliefs regarding attribute importance multiplied by how well these attributes meet their expectations (Barsky, 1992) (a modified version of EDP to measure customer satisfaction).

Researchers in marketing have used importance either as a replacement variable for consumer expectations (Martilla and James, 1977) or as a weighting parameter for another variable being studied in the same decision context (Barksy, 1992; Barsky and Labagh, 1992; Carman, 1990; Cronin and Taylor, 1992; Kivela, 1998; Teas, 1993). One of the fundamental reasons for favoring attribute importance over the expectations is that customers expect uniformly high levels of service (Brown, Churchill and Peter, 1993) and customer expectations can be manipulated externally (Davidow and Uttal, 1989), whereas the importance attached to product /service attributes are based on deep-seated cultural norms and personal values (Barsky, 1992).

The original Importance-Performance analysis, proposed by Martilla and James (1977), maintains that satisfaction is a function of customer perceptions of performance and the importance of the attribute. Valuable information can be gained from this method (Hemmasi et al 1995). The importance and performance items can be mapped through an importance performance analysis. It does not involve subtraction or any other type of computation. The importance performance model has been found to be conceptually valid and a powerful technique for identifying service areas requiring remedial strategic actions (Hemmasi et al 1995). The importance performance analysis seems to provide a clear direction for action, as it is able to identify areas where limited sources should be focused. Consequently, practitioners lacking sophisticated computer knowledge can use importance performance mapping. Until recently, the performance importance grid analysis was considered to be an affective management tool but it lost favor where more quantitative methods became practical with computerization (Duke and Persia, 1995). Recently, multiplication of the importance score on an attribute with the evaluative score given to the same attribute in order to create a new weighted variable has gained a substantial popularity.

Weighted Importance-Performance technique has been employed to assess customer satisfaction in a number of tourism and hospitality studies (Barksy, 1992; Barsky and Labagh, 1992; Kivela, 1998). Researchers of this tact assert that the weighting of attribute performance by importance is a powerful technique in determining customer satisfaction, however, they do not supply any empirical evidence that shows that the importance-weighted variable performs better than the original variable, which is not weighted or not multiplied with its corresponding importance. Therefore, whether the weighting attribute importance contributes to the model's diagnostic power needs to be investigated thoroughly.

THE ATTRIBUTION THEORY

Research of the Attribution Theory is primarily developed from the Weiner, Frieze and Kukla's (1971) work. It is important to note that the Attribution theory has been mostly used in dissatisfaction/ complaining behavior models than in satisfaction models per se. According to this model, consumers are regarded as rational processors of information who seek out reasons to explain why a purchase outcome, for example dissatisfaction, has occurred (Folkes, 1984). This model argues that when the delivery of a service does not match customers' prior expectations or other standards, customers engage in an attributional process in order to make sense of what has occurred (Bitner, 1990). More specifically, this model assumes that consumers tend to look for causes for product successes or failures and usually attribute these successes or failures using a three dimensional schema (Folkes, 1989; Oliver and DeSarbo, 1988; Pearce and Moscardo, 1984; Weiner et al 1971)

Locus of Causality (internal or external): This means that the purchase outcome, for example, is cause of dissatisfaction and can be attributed either to the consumer (internal) or to the marketer or something in the environment or situation (external).

Stability (stable/ permanent or unstable/ temporary): Stable causes are thought not to vary over time, while unstable causes are thought to fluctuate and vary over time.

Controllability (volitional/ controllable or non volitional/uncontrollable): Both consumers and firms can either have volitional control over an outcome or be under certain controllable constraints.

It is argued that under some conditions, for example, when a number of consumers find themselves in agreement about the cause of their dissatisfaction, when the same establishment repeats their mistake over and over again (consistency), and when only this establishment commits error (distinctiveness of the behavior is high), external attribution process takes place. On the other hand, when the agreement is low, consistency is low and distinctiveness is low, consumers are assumed to relate their negative reactions (dissatisfaction) to themselves (i.e., just having an "off" day) (Pearce and Moscardo, 1984)

In his study, Folkes (1984) asked subjects to remember the last time they went to a restaurant, ordered something and did not like it. The subjects were further asked who had to be responsible for this (locus), whether this type of incident happens at this restaurant (stability), and whether the restaurant could prevent the problem (control). The subjects were then asked whether they would prefer a refund, exchange, or an apology. Folkes found that the subjects who felt that the problem was restaurant related (external) stated that they deserved a refund, exchange, or an apology. Subjects who felt the cause as stable were more likely to prefer a refund rather than an exchange, while subjects who thought that the company could have prevented the problem demonstrated high levels of anger, and showed their behavioral intentions to hurt the restaurant's business. Such feelings of anger toward the company were heightened when the responsiveness of the firm to the problem was considered less than adequate and hence resulted in negative word-of-mouth recommendations. In addition, under conditions where the consumer perceived the company to be non-responsive, they were less likely to complain to the company and more likely to use negative word-of-mouth recommendations to express their dissatisfaction. Similarly company-related (external) attributions elicited greater feelings of anger and desire to hurt the company than internal attributions (Folkes, 1984; Richins, 1985).

In the past, attribution models have been more useful in predicting consumers' reactions when they are dissatisfied than in explaining the satisfaction process itself (Huang and Smith, 1996). However Folkes (1984) and Richins (1985) have obtained some evidence that supports a relationship between locus of causality (internal and external attributions) and satisfaction judgments. The results, especially those of Folkes', demonstrate that the locus of causality dominates satisfaction judgments and satisfaction is associated more with internal than with external factors. Oliver and Desarbo (1988) who compared the effects of five determinants of satisfaction (expectancy, performance, disconfirmation, equity and attribution) have reported similar findings that the attribution dimension was the least significant of all effects in the situation tested.

Some researchers suggest the Attribution theory as an alternative model to explain customer satisfaction, however, it seems rather like an extension of the Expectancy-Disconfirmation paradigm because the attribution process is triggered off primarily by the negative disconfirmation of expectations. The attribution theory further appears to be more useful to apply in ascertaining customer dissatisfaction and complaining behavior.

THE EQUITY THEORY

According to the Equity Theory, satisfaction exists when consumers perceive their output/input ratio as being fair (Swan and Oliver, 1989). Equity models are derived from the Equity Theory (Adams, 1963), and are based on the notion of input-output ratio, which plays a key role in satisfaction (Oliver and Swan, 1989). According to this theory, parties to an exchange will feel equitably treated (thus, satisfied), if in their minds, the ratio of their outcomes to inputs is fair (Oliver and DeSarbo, 1988). Whether a person feels equitably treated or not may depend on various factors including the price paid, the benefits received, the time and effort expended during the transaction and the experience of previous transactions (Woodruff et al 1983). This implies that comparative baseline may take many different forms. This theory shares similarities with the Comparison Level Theory which posits that bases of comparison used by consumers in satisfaction judgments may be more than just expectations.

Equity models of consumer satisfaction appear to be different from the other models, in that satisfaction is evaluated relative to other parties (people) in an exchange and the outcomes of all parties sharing the same experience are taken into consideration. Erevvels and Leavitt (1992) argue that equity models can provide a much richer picture of consumer satisfaction in situations that may not be captured using traditional satisfaction models. For example, they may be especially useful in modeling situations where satisfaction with the other party is considered to be an important element of the transaction

Translated into a tourism context, the Equity theory suggests that tourists compare perceived input-output (gains) in a social exchange: if the tourist's gain is less than their input (time, money, and other costs), dissatisfaction results (Reisinger and Turner, 1997). Satisfaction is therefore, "a mental state of being adequately or inadequately rewarded" (Moutinho, 1987, p. 34). The comparison may take other forms. The output/input ratio for a service experience may be compared to the perceived net gain of some others (such as friends) who have experienced a similar offer (Meyer and Westerbarkey, 1996). According to this theory, satisfaction is seen as a relative judgment that takes into consideration both the qualities and benefits obtained through a purchase as well as the costs and efforts borne by a consumer to obtain that purchase. Fisk and Coney (1982), for instance, found that consumers were less satisfied and had a less positive attitude toward a company when they heard that other customers received a better price deal and better service than them. In other words, their perceptions of equitable treatment by the company translated into satisfaction judgments and even affected their future expectations and purchase intentions.

Equity theory applied to customer satisfaction/dissatisfaction has become accepted as an alternative way to conceptualise how comparisons work (Oliver and Desarbo, 1988). Equity disconfirmation has been supported empirically, though it applies primarily to social interactions (Oliver and Swan, 1989). The equity theory as well as the attribution theory has been proposed as satisfaction determinants, however "they have not generated the same level of interest in customer satisfaction/dissatisfaction research (as the EDP did)" (Oliver, 1993, p. 419).

THE EVALUATIVE CONGRUITY THEORY

According to Sirgy's (1984) Evaluative Congruity Model (or the Social Cognition Model), satisfaction is a function of evaluative congruity, which is a cognitive matching process in which a perception is compared to an evoked referent cognition in order to evaluate a stimulus or action. The result of this cognitive process is assumed to produce either a motivational or an emotional state. Customer satisfaction/ dissatisfaction is regarded as an emotional state because it prompts the consumer to evaluate alternative course of action to reduce an existing dissatisfaction state and /or obtain a future satisfaction state (Sirgy, 1984).

This model argues that there are three congruity states; negative incongruity, congruity, and positive incongruity. Similar to the confirmation/disconfirmation concept, negative incongruity is a cognitive state that results from a negative discrepancy between the valence levels of a perception and an evoked referent cognition, which induces dissatisfaction. Congruity is a cognitive state that leads to a non-significant or negligible discrepancy between a perception and an evoked referent cognition, which results in a neutral evaluation state or a satisfaction state. Finally, positive incongruity-state results from a positive discrepancy between a perception and an evoked referent cognition, which generates satisfaction. Unlike the EDP, Sirgy's model views the customer satisfaction/dissatisfaction as a function of one or more congruities between perceptual and evoked referent states and states that the occurrence of multiple comparison processes could explain consumer satisfaction better. More specifically, the original Evaluative Congruity Model assumes that satisfaction may be determined by one or more cognitive congruities, such as between (1) new product performance after usage and expected product performance before use, (2) new product performance after use and old product performance before use, (3) expected product performance after purchase and ideal product performance before purchase, (4) expected product performance after purchase and deserved product performance after use. Such discrepancies are argued to independently influence consumer's overall satisfaction with a given product (Sirgy, 1984).

One of the most important features of the Evaluative Congruity Theory seems to be its ability in explaining the different states of satisfaction/dissatisfaction resulting from different combinations of expectations and performance outcome (Chon, 1992; Chon, Christianson and Cin-Lin, 1998). Recall that the traditional Expectancy-Disconfirmation paradigm holds the view that the level of resulting satisfaction will be the same in both cases where low expectations are met by low performance and high expectations are met by high performance. According to the Evaluative Congruity Theory, however, different expectation-performance combinations (high expectation/high performance; low expectation/low performance) would result in different satisfaction states (Chon and Olsen, 1991; Chon, 1992; Chon et al 1998; Sirgy, 1994).

For instance, Chon (1992) and Chon et al (1998), based on the Evaluative Congruity Theory, postulated that under a positive incongruity condition, in which the tourist expectation of a given service performance is negative but his/her perceived outcome is positive, the tourist would be most satisfied. Indeed, their results revealed that when the tourist's expectation of a destination was negative but the perceptions were positive the tourist was most satisfied, whereas when the tourist's expectations were positive and perceptions were positive, the level of satisfaction was moderate. In addition, when the tourist's expectations were negative and perceptions were negative, the satisfaction was lower than the first two congruity conditions, and when the tourist expectations were positive but the perceptions were negative, the tourist was least satisfied. These findings provides some degree of support for the underlying assumption of the Evaluative Congruity Theory which suggests that different states of satisfaction may result from different combinations of expectations and performance perceptions.

In addition, Sirgy further postulated that product images should be classified as being functional (i.e. physical benefits associated with the product) and symbolic (i.e., self image) and argues that customer satisfaction/dissatisfaction is not only an evaluative function of the consumer's expectations and performance, but it is also an evaluative function of the consumer's self image and product image congruity. Chon and Olsen (1991) in their study on tourist satisfaction with destinations found some evidence supporting the view that the consumer decision making process involves the evaluation of not only the functional attributes of a product (the availability of suitable accommodation) but also personality related attributes. They found that functional congruity explained customer satisfaction better than symbolic congruity.

It is important to note that although Evaluative Congruity model has been offered as an alternative way to explain satisfaction process, its methodological mechanism is analogous to that of the Expectancy-Disconfirmation paradigm (Oh and Parks, 1997). That is, both the Evaluative Congruity and Expectation-Disconfirmation models are based on the disconfirmation concept which presupposes that customers form expectations about the product prior to purchase and compare these expectations against perceived performance after the product is used. Both models, however, may not be suitable to apply in consumption situations where customers do not have prior expectations such as with unfamiliar products.

THE PERSON-SITUATION-FIT CONCEPT

It has been also noted that tourist satisfaction can be explained by the Person-Situation Fit concept (Pearce and Moscardo, 1984). This concept argues that people deliberately seek situations, which they feel match their personalities and orientations. The implication of this idea may become particularly appropriate to tourist settings where individuals make a conscious choice to visit a specific tourist destination (Reisinger and Turner, 1997). This principle states that the optimal fit between tourists and their environment occurs when the attributes of their environment are congruent with their beliefs, attitudes, and values as in the case of Value-Percept Disparity model. When the activities available in the environment fit the activities sought and valued by the tourists the satisfaction occurs. Where values and value orientations do not fit, mismatch can lead to feelings of stress, anxiety, uncertainty and result in dissatisfaction (Pearce and Moscardo, 1984). As the degree of fit increases, tourist satisfaction also increases. This concept has been applied generally in the tourist motivation studies.

SUMMARY

This chapter presents and discusses a number of frameworks developed to explain customer satisfaction in the literature. The theories explicated in this chapter include the Dissonance Theory, the Contrast Theory, the Expectancy-Disconfirmation Theory, the Comparison Level Theory, the Value-Percept Theory, the Attribution Theory, The Equity theory, the Person-Situation Fit concept, and the Importance-Performance model. There is widespread consensus among these satisfaction theories that satisfaction is an evaluative judgment, which results from a comparison of product performance to some forms of evaluation standard. The majority of these theories, for example the Expectancy Disconfirmation Paradigm, the Comparison Level Theory, and the Evaluative Congruity Theory concur that product performance exceeding prior expectations or some form of standards signifies satisfaction, whereas dissatisfaction is the outcome when product performance falls short of that standard. Thus, the disparity concept between the actual outcome and the expected constitutes the core of the majority of the satisfaction theories.

Early theories of the satisfaction concept assume that consumers may either exaggerate (the Contrast Theory) or adjust (the Dissonance Theory) the perceived disparity between the product performance and the initial expectations or the norm. As these early theories have not been applied in tourism and hospitality settings, the validity of their assumptions remains unclear. Based on the logic of the Dissonance Theory, some researchers suggest that in order to have a higher product evaluation, companies should raise customer expectations substantially above the product performance. This assumption is criticized on the grounds that it does not take into account of the concept of tolerance levels. Drawing on these two early satisfaction theories, Oliver developed the Expectancy-Disconfirmation paradigm which postulates that if the outcome of a product is judged to be better than or equal to the expected, the consumer will feel satisfied. If, on the other hand, actual outcome is judged not to be better than expected, the consumer will be satisfied. The EDP has gained growing support from researchers and it has become the most widely applied framework in studies assessing customer satisfaction with tourism and hospitality services.

Last decades also saw the development of other models to explain customer satisfaction. In contrast to EDP which assumes satisfaction resulting from disconfirmation of predictive expectations, LaTour and Peat's (1979) Comparison Level Theory views satisfaction as a function of comparison between product performance and consumers' past experiences and experiences of other consumers. Westbrook and Riley (1983) introduced the Value-Percept Theory which proposes that satisfaction is an emotional response that is triggered by a cognitive evaluative process in which the perceptions of an offer are compared to one's values, needs, wants or desires, in contrast to expectations suggested in Oliver's EDP model. Sirgy's Evaluative Congruity Model views satisfaction as a function of evaluative congruity, which is a cognitive matching process in which a perception is compared to an evoked referent cognition for the purpose of evaluating a stimulus object/action. The Importance-Performance model, borrowed from Fishbein and Ajzen's consumer behavior model, and adapted to hospitality services by Barsky, assumes that consumer satisfaction is a function of beliefs about an object's attributes (that is a product possesses a particular attribute) and the strength of these belief (that is, the relative importance of each attribute to the customer's overall satisfaction with the product or service). As stated earlier, majority of these theories suggest that customer satisfaction is a relative concept and judged in relation to a standard. While several comparison standards have been proposed in the literature, no consensus exists concerning which standard might be the most appropriate (which standard best predicts customer satisfaction) (Cote, Foxman and Cutler, 1989; Erevelles and Leavitt, 1992).

REFERENCES

Adams, S. J. (1963). Toward and Understanding of Inequity. *Journal of Abnormal and Social Psychology*, 67: 422-436.

Anderson, E. R. (1973). Consumer dissatisfaction: the effect of disconfirmed expectancy on perceived product performance. *Journal of Marketing Research*, 10, 38-44.

Babakus, E. and Boller, W. G. (1992). An Empirical Assessment of the Servqual Scale. *Journal of Business Research*, 24: 253-268.

Barsky, J. D. (1992). Customer Satisfaction in Hotel Industry: Meaning and Measurement. *Hospitality Research Journal*, 16, 51-73.

Barsky, J. D., and Labagh, R. (1992). A Strategy for Customer Satisfaction. *The Cornell Hotel and Restaurant Administration Quarterly*, October, 32-40.

Bearden, W.O., and Teel, E.J. (1983). Selected Determinants of Consumer Satisfaction and Complaint Reports. *Journal of Marketing Research*, 20, 21-28.

Bitner, M. J. (1990). Evaluating Service Encounters: The Effect of Physical Surrounding and Employee Responses. *Journal of Marketing*, 54, 69-82.

Bojanic, D., and Rosen, D. L. (1995). Measuring Service Quality in Restaurants: An Application of the Servqual Instrument. *Hospitality Research Journal*, 18, (1):3-14

Botterill, T. D. (1987). Dissatisfaction with a construction of Satisfaction. *Annals of Tourism Research*, 14: 139-141.

Boulding, W., Karla, A., Staelin, R., and Zeithaml, V.A. (1993) A Dynamic Process Model of service quality, From Expectations to Behavioural Intentions. *Journal of Marketing Research*, 30 February: 7-27.

Brown, J. T., Churchill, A. G., and Peter, P. L. 1993 Improving the Measurement of Service Quality. *Journal of Retailing*, 69 (1), 127-139.

Cadotte, E. R., Woodruff, R. B ., and Jenkins, R. J. (1987). Expectations and Norms in Models of Consumer Satisfaction. *Journal of Marketing Research*, 24, 305-14.

Cardozo, R. (1965). An experimental study of consumer effort, expectations and satisfaction. *Journal of Marketing Research*, 2, 244-9.

Carman, J. M. (1990). Consumer Perceptions of Service Quality: An Assessment of the SERVQUAL Dimensions. *Journal of Retailing*, 66, 35-55.

Cho, B.H. (1998). Assessing Tourist Satisfaction: an exploratory study of Korean youth tourists in Australia. *Tourism Recreation Research*, 23, (1), 47-54.

Chon, K. (1992). Self image/ destination image congruity. *Annals of Tourism Research*, 19 (2), 360-376.

Chon, K., and Olsen, M/ D. (1991). Functional and Symbolic congruity approaches to consumer satisfaction/ dissatisfaction in consumerism. *Journal of the International Academy of Marketing Research*, 1, 2-23.

Chon, K., Christianson, J. D., and Chin-Lin, L. (1998). Modeling Tourist satisfaction: Japanese Tourists' evaluation of hotel stay experience in Taiwan. *Australian Journal of Hospitality Management*, 2 (1), 1-6.

Churchill, G. R., and Surprenant, C. (1982). An Investigation into Determinants of Customer Satisfaction. *Journal of Marketing Research*, 19, 491-504.

Cote, J. A., Foxman, E. R., and Cutler, B. D. (1989). Selecting an appropriate standard of comparison for post-purchase evaluations. *Advances in Consumer Research*, 16, 502-506.

Crompton, L. J., and Love, L. L. (1995). The Predictive Validity of Alternative Approaches to Evaluating Quality of a Festival. *Journal of Travel Research*, 34 (1) Summer: 11-25.

Cronin, J .J. Jr., and Taylor, S. A. (1992). Measuring Service Quality: A Re-examination and Extension. *Journal of Marketing*, 56, 55-68.

Danaher, P. J., and Haddrell, V. (1996). A comparison of question scales used for measuring customer satisfaction. *International Journal of Service Industry Management*, 17 (4): 4-26.

Danaher, P. J., and Mattsson, J. (1994). Customer Satisfaction during the Service Delivery Process. *European Journal of Marketing*, 28 (5): 5-16.

Danaher, P. J., and Arweiler, W. (1996). Customer satisfaction in the tourism industry, a case study of visitors to New Zealand. *Journal of Travel Research*, 89-93.

Davidow, H. W., and Uttal, B. (1990). *Total Customer service: the Ultimate Weapon.* Harpercollins, New York, USA.

Day, R. (1977). *Consumer satisfaction, dissatisfaction and complaining behaviour.* In Symposium Proceedings, School of Business, University of Indiana.

Dorfman, P. W. (1979). Measurement and Meaning of Recreation Satisfaction: A Case study in camping. *Environment and Behaviour*, 11 (4):483-510.

Duke, C. R., and Persia, A. M. (1996), "Performance-Importance Analysis of Escorted Tour Evaluations". *Journal of Travel and Tourism Marketing*, Vol. 5 No. 3, pp. 207-223.

Festinger, L. (1957). *A theory of Cognitive Dissonance*. Stanford, CA, USA: Stanford University

Engel, J. F., Kollat, T. D., and Blackwell, R. D. (1968). *Consumer Behaviour*. New York, USA: Holt, Rineheart and Winston.

Ennew, T. C., Reed, V. G., and Binks, R. M. (1993) Importance-performance analysis and the Measurement of service quality. *European Journal of Marketing*, 27, (2): 59-70.

Erevelles, S., and Leavitt, C. (1992). A Comparison of Current Models of Consumer Satisfaction / Dissatisfaction. *Journal of Consumer Satisfaction /Dissatisfaction and Complaining Behavior*, 5, 104-114.

Fishbein, M., and Ajzen, I. (1975). *Belief, attitude, intention, and behavior: an introduction to theory and research*. MA, USA: Addison-Wesley Publishing Company Press.

Fick, G. R., and Ritchie, B. J. R. (1991). "Measuring Service Quality in the Travel and Tourism Industry". *Journal of Travel Research*, Fall, pp. 2-9.

Fisk, R. P., and Coney, A. K. (1982). *Postchoice evaluation: an equity theory analysis of consumer satisfaction and dissatisfaction with service choices*. In Hunt, H.K., and Day, L. R. (Eds). Conceptual and Empirical Contributions to Consumer Satisfaction and Dissatisfaction and Complaining Behavior, Bloomington, IN, USA: Indiana University School of Business, 9-16.

Folkes, V. A. (1988). Recent Attribution Research in Consumer Behavior: A review and New Directions. *Journal of Consumer Research*, 14, March, 548-565.

Folkes, V. A. (1984). Consumer reactions to product failure, an attributional approach. *Journal of Consumer Research*, 10, 398-409.

Getty, M. J., and Thomson, N. K. (1994). The Relationship between quality, satisfaction, and Recommending Behaviour in Lodging Decisions. *Journal of Hospitality and Leisure Marketing*, 2, (3), 3-22.

Gronroos, C. (1993). *Toward a third phase in service quality research: challenges and directions*. in Swart, et al. (Eds.). Advances in Service Marketing and Management, 2, JAI Press, Greenwich, CT, 49-64.

Halstead, D. (1993). Exploring the concept of retrieved expectations. *Journal of Consumer Satisfaction, Dissatisfaction and Complaining Behaviour*, 6, 56-62.

Halstead, D., Hartman, D., and Schmidt, L. S. (1994). Multi source Effects on the Satisfaction Formation Process. *Journal of the Academy of Marketing Science*, 22 (2), 114-129.

Helson, H. (1964). *Adaptation-level theory*. New York, USA: Harper and Row.

Hemmasi, M., Strong, C. K., and Taylor, A. S. (1996). Measuring service quality for strategic planning and analysis in service firms. *Journal of Applied Business Research*, 10 (4), 24-35.

Howard, A. J., and Sheth, N. J. (1969). *The theory of buyer behaviour*. Wiley, New York, USA: 147

Hughes, K. (1991). Tourist satisfaction: A Guided Tour in North Queensland. *Australian Psychologist*, 26 (3): 166-171

Huang, C. H., and Smith, K. (1996). Complaint Management: Customers' Attributions Regarding Service Disconfirmation in Restaurants. *Journal of Restaurant and Foodservice Marketing*, 1 (3/4), 121-134.

Iacobucci, D., Grayson, A. K., and Ostrom, A. L. (1994). *The Calculus of Service Quality and Customer Satisfaction: Theoretical and Empirical Differentiation and Integration*. In Advances in Service Marketing and Management, Swarts et al (eds) 3 JAI Press Greenwich, CT: 1-67

Jayanti, K. R., and Ghosh, K. A. (1996). Service Value Determination: An Integrative Perspective. *Journal of Hospitality and Leisure Marketing*, 3, (4): 5-25.

Jayanti, R., and Jackson, A. (1991). Service Satisfaction: An Explatory Investigation of Three Models. *Advances in Consumer Research*, 18, 603-610.

Johns, N., and Tyas, P. (1996). Use of Service Quality Gap Theory to Differentiate between Foodservice Outlets. *The Service Industries Journal*, 16 (3): 321-346.

Kivela, J. (1998). Dining satisfaction and its impact on return patronage in Hong-Kong, *Third Annual Conference on Graduate Eductaion and Graduate Student Research*.

LaTour, S. T., and Peat, N. C. (1979). Conceptual and Methodological issues in consumer satisfaction research. *Advances in Consumer Research*, 6, 431-437.

Lewis, R.C., and Chambers, E.R. (1989). *Marketing leadership in hospitality*. Van Nostrad, New York, USA.

Lewis, R.C., and Chambers, E.R. (1989). *Marketing leadership in hospitality*. Van Nostrad, New York, USA.

Lounsburry, L. W., and Hoopes, L. L. (1985). An Investigation of factors Associated with Vacation Satisfaction. *Journal of Leisure Research,* 17, 1-13.

Martilla, J., and James, J. (1978). Importance-performance analysis. *Journal of Marketing*, 41, 77-79.

Mazursky, D. (1989). Past Experience and Future Tourism Decisions, Annals of Tourism Research, 16: 333-344.Mautinho, L. (1987) Consumer Behaviour in tourism. *European Journal of Marketing*, 21 (10): 5-44.

McGill, L. A., and Iacobucci, D. (1992). The Role of Post-Experience Comparison Standards in the Evaluation of Unfamiliar Services. *Advances in Consumer Research*, 19, 570-578.

Meyer, A., and Westerbarkey, P. (1996). Measuring and Managing Hotel Guest Satisfaction., in Olsen, D. M., Teare, R., and Gummesson, E. (Eds.) *Service Quality in Hospitality Organisations*. Cassell, New York, NY, 185-204.

Oh, H., and Parks, C. S. (1997). Customer Satisfaction and Service Quality: A critical Review of the Literature and Research Implications for the Hospitality Industry. *Hospitality Research Journal*, 20 (3), 36-64.

Olander, F. (1979). *Consumer Satisfaction: A Sceptic's view*. Aarhus Denmark.

Oliver, L. R. (1997). *Satisfaction a behavioral perspective on the consumer*. The McGraw-Hill Companies, Inc. New York.

Oliver, R. L. (1993). A Conceptual Model of Service Quality and Service Satisfaction: Compatible Goals and Different Concepts, In Swart, T. A., Bowen, D. E., and Brown, S. W. (eds.) *Advances in Service Marketing and Management*, 3, JAI Press, Greenwich, CT, 65-86.

Oliver, L. R., and Swan, E. J. (1989). Consumer perceptions of interpersonal equity and satisfaction in transactions: a field survey approach. *Journal of Marketing*, 53, 21-35

Oliver. R. L. (1980). A Cognitive Model of the Antecedents of Satisfaction Decisions, Journal of Marketing Research, 17, 46-49.

Oliver, L. R. (1977). Effect of expectation and disconfirmation on post exposure product evaluations: an alternative interpretation. *Journal of Applied Psychology*, 62 (4), 480-486.

Oliver R. L., and DeSarbo, W. S. (1988). Response Determinants in Satisfaction Judgment. *Journal of Consumer Research*, 14, 495- 507.

Olshavsky, R., and Miller, J. (1972). Consumer expectations, product performance and perceived product quality. *Journal of Marketing Research*, 9, 19-21.

Parasuraman, A., Zeithaml, A. V., and Berry, L. L. (1988). Servqual: a Multiple Item Scale for Measuring Consumer Perceptions of Service Quality. *Journal of Retailing*, 64, Spring, 12-40

Pearce, P. L. (1980). A Favorability-satisfaction model of tourists' evaluations. *Journal of Travel Research*, Summer,13-17.

Pearce, P. L. (1991). Introduction, The Tourism Psychology. *Australian Psychologist*, 26 (3):145-46.

Pearce, L. P., and Moscardo, M. G. (1984). Making Sense of Tourists' Complaints. *Tourism Management*, 20-23.

Pizam, A., and Milman, A. (1993). Predicting Satisfaction Among First Time Visitors to a Destination by Using the Expectancy Disconfirmation Theory. *International Journal of Hospitality Management*, 12, 197-209.

Prakash, V., and Lounsbury, W. J. (1992). A Reliability Problem in the Measurement of Disconfirmation of Expectations, In Bagozzi, P. R., and Tybout , M. A. (Eds.). *Advances in Consumer Research*, 10, 244-249.

Reisineger, Y., and Turner, L. (1997). Tourist Satisfaction with Hosts: A Cultural Approach Comparing Thai tourists and Australian Hosts. *Pacific Tourism Review*, 1, 147-159.

Reisinger, Y., and Waryszak, Z. R. (1994). Tourists' perceptions of service in shops. *International Journal of Retail and Distribution Management*, 22 (5): 20-28.

Richins, M. L. (1985). *Factors affceting the level of consumer initiated complaints to marketing organizations*. In Hunt, K. H., and Day, L. R. (Eds) Consumer Satisfaction, Dissatisfaction and Complaining Behavior, Bloomington, IN, USA: Indiana University School of Business, 2-8.

Saleh, F., and Ryan, C. (1991). Analysing Service Quality in the Hospitality Industry Using the Servqual Model. *Service Industries Journal*, 11, (3), 324-345.

Sherif, M., and Hovland, C. I. (1961). Social judgements: Assimilation and contrast effects in communication and attitude change, New Haven, Yale University Press.

Sirgy, J. M. (1984). *A social cognition model of CS/D: an experiment, Psychology, and Marketing*. 1, 27-44.

Smith, M. A. (1995). Measuring service quality: is Servqual now redundant. *Journal of Marketing Management*, 11: 257-276.

Spreng, R. A., Mackenzie, S. B., and Olshavsky, R. W. (1996). A reexamination of the determinants of consumer satisfaction. *Journal of Marketing*, 60, 15-32.

Swan, J. E., and Martin, S. (1981). Testing comparison level and predictiveexpectations model of satisfaction, In Kenth, B. (Ed) Advances in Consumer Research, Ann Arbor, MI: Association for Consumer Research, 77-82

Swan, J., and Oliver, R.L. (1989). Consumers Perception of Interpersonal Equity and Satisfaction in Transaction: A Field Survey Approach. *Journal of Marketing*, 53, 21-35.

Swan J. E., and Trawick, I. F. (1981). Disconfirmation of expectations and satisfaction with a retail service. *Journal of Retailing*, 57, 49-7.

Teas, R. K. (1993a). Consumer Expectations and The Measurement of Perceived Service Quality. *Journal of Professional Services Marketing*, 8 (2), 35-54.

Teas, R. K. (1994). Expectations as a comparison standard in measuring service quality: an assessment of a reassessment. *Journal of Marketing*, 58, 132-139.

Thibaut, J. W., and Kelly, K. H. (1959). *The social psychology of groups*. New York, USA: John Wiley and Sons, Inc.

Tribe, J., and Snaith, T. (1998). From Servqual to Holsat: holiday satisfaction in Varadero, Cuba. *Tourism Management,* 19, 125-34.

Tse, D. K., and Wilton, C. P. (1988). Models Of Customer Satisfaction Formation: An Extension. *Journal of Marketing Research*, 25, 204-212.

Weber, K. (1997). Assessment of Tourist Satisfaction, Using the Expectancy disconfirmation theory, a study of German Travel Market in Australia. *Pacific Tourism Review*, 1, 35-45.

Weiner, B., Frieze, I., Kukla, A., and Reed, L. (1971). *Perceiving the causes success and failure*. Morristown, NJ, USA: General Learning Press.

Westerbrook, R. A., and Newman, W. (1978). An Analysis of Shopper Dissatisfaction for Major Household Appliances. *Journal of Marketing Research*, Vol. 15, (August), 456-66.

Westbrook, R. A., and Reilly, M. D., (1983). *Value-Percept disparity: an alternative to the disconfirmation of expectations theory of customer satisfaction.* in Bogozzi, P. R., and Tybouts, A. (eds). Advances in Consumer Research, Association for Consumer Research, 10, Ann Arbor, MI: 256-61.

Williams, C. (1998). Is the Servqual model an appropriate management tool for measuring service delivery quality in the UK leisure industry. *Managing Leisure*, 3: 98-110.

Whipple, W. T., and Thach, V. S. (1988). Group Tour Management: Does Good Service Produce Satisfied Customers. *Journal of Travel Research*, 16-21.

Woodruff, R. B., Ernest, R. C., Jenkins, R. L. (1983). Modeling Consumer Satisfaction Processes Using Experience-Based Norms. *Journal of Marketing Research*, 20, 296-304.

Yüksel, A., and Rimmington, M. (1998). Customer Satisfaction Measurement: Performance Counts. *The Cornell Hotel and Restaurant Administration Quarterly*, December.

Yi. Y. (1990). *A Critical Review of Consumer Satisfaction*. in V. A. Zeithaml (Ed.), Review of Marketing, Chicago, USA: American Marketing Association, 68-123.

Zeithaml, V. A. (1981). How consumer evaluation process differ between goods and services. *Advances in Consumer Research*, 186-190.

In: Tourist Satisfaction and Complaining Behavior
Editor: Atila Yüksel

ISBN 978-1-60456-002-2
© 2008 Nova Science Publishers, Inc.

Chapter 5

COMPARISON STANDARDS IN CUSTOMER SATISFACTION/DISSATISFACTION RESEARCH

Atila Yüksel and Fisun Yüksel

Adnan Menderes University, Turkey

INTRODUCTION

The measurement of satisfaction in the most realistic way is a prerequisite for accurate prediction of consumer behavior and development of a robust management strategy. Previous chapters sought to define customer satisfaction and attempted to explain the concept further. Chapter Three presented different competing approaches that have been developed to explain customer satisfaction/ dissatisfaction. Review of literature undertaken in the previous chapter highlighted that although the consumer satisfaction measurement literature is in a state of debates, one of the few aspects of customer satisfaction on which there is widespread agreement is that the state of satisfaction or dissatisfaction is a reaction to a comparison (Oliver, 1989) (i.e., a perceived experience is compared against a standard or standards). Several standards have been proposed in the literature, for example, predictive expectations, norms, past experience, experiences of others, desires and ideals, however, no consensus exists concerning which standard might be most appropriate (which standard best predicts customer satisfaction).

Theoretically, the comparative standard issue is extremely important because different types of standards may yield different levels against which perceived experience is compared (Woodruff, Cleanop, Schumm, Godial and Burns, 1991). It is important to note that respondents are likely to be sensitive to the type of the standard used in a customer satisfaction/dissatisfaction research which in turn might impact on the resultant level of customer satisfaction obtained by the researcher. Olander (1979) observed this and suggested that responses to measures will be sensitive to the type of disconfirmation standard being used and that it was artificial to apply a common yardstick when people use their own criteria for evaluation. In order to illustrate how the use of different type of standards might impact on satisfaction, Woodruff et al provide a very interesting example. In this case, a company has changed the wording of a disconfirmation question by asking respondents to rate perceived brand performance relative to that of a competitor instead of relative to expected performance and got different results (i.e., satisfaction score obtained from averaging comparison of performance against competitors was different from that of expectations). Strictly speaking, if satisfaction ratings are contingent on which standard is used, "then historical commitment to expectancy disconfirmation by the academics and practitioners may be detrimental to advancing knowledge critical to understanding customer satisfaction/dissatisfaction" (Woodruff et al 1991). To this end, the following section presents current discussions pertaining to expectations and other alternative comparative baselines that have been used to explain the formation of satisfaction judgment.

EXPECTATIONS

Almost every model of satisfaction formation process, for example, the Expectancy-Disconfirmation Paradigm, the Comparison Level Theory, and the Evaluative Congruity Theory, maintains that feeling of satisfaction arise when consumers compare their perceptions of a product performance to their expectations. A variety of conceptualizations of expectation exist in the literature (Woodruff et al 1991). In general, the term expectation is used to mean pre-consumption beliefs about the overall performance of the product created by manufacturer's claims or product information, while others view it differently. Customer expectations represent a norm against which performance is compared and they take many forms varying from some minimum tolerable level of performance through to some concept of the ideal or perfect service (Ennew, Reed and Binks, 1993). As understanding of comparison standards is imperative in the development of the research, the following section presents different conceptual definitions and use of expectations in research studies. The comparative standards being discussed are the predictive, deserved, desired, minimum tolerable, ideal, excellence, best product norm, product based norm, and zone of indifference.

THE EXPECTATIONS AS PREDICTIONS STANDARD

Customer expectations have been investigated in a number of research fields but have received the most thorough treatment in the customer satisfaction/ dissatisfaction and service quality literature (Zeithaml, Berry and Parasuraman, 1993). In these literatures, the concept of expectations has been viewed as a baseline against which subsequent experiences are compared and result in the evaluation of satisfaction or quality. Expectations involve the consumer's estimate at the time of purchase or prior to usage of how well or poorly the product will supply the benefits that are of interest to the consumer (Day, 1977; Olson and Dover, 1979). Expectations are "consumer-defined probabilities of occurrence of positive and negative events if the consumer engages in some behavior" (Oliver, 1981, p. 33).

Some researchers consider expectations as primary perceptions of the likelihood (or probability of occurrence), while others maintain that expectations consist of an estimate of the likelihood of an event plus an evaluation of goodness and badness of that event (Spreng,

Mackenzie and Olshavsky, 1996). Oliver (1981, p. 33), for instance, states that "expectations have two components: a probability of occurrence (for example, the likelihood that the staff will be available to wait on customers in the restaurant) and an evaluation of occurrence (for example, the degree to which staff are attentive)". In contrast, Spreng and Dixon (1992) argue that expectations should be conceptualized as beliefs and not as evaluations. Applications in which expectations are regarded as predictions made by customers about what is likely to happen during an impending transaction or exchange has become dominant in the customer satisfaction/dissatisfaction literature.

In his classification of expectations, Miller (1977) called this standard the expected standard, which he defined as an objective calculation of probability of performance, and which he contrasted with three other types of expectations; deserved, ideal and minimum acceptable. Others termed this standard predictive expectation, which may be described as estimates of anticipated performance (Prakash, 1984; Swan and Trawick, 1980). Predictive expectations have been found to have a direct positive effect on satisfaction (Oliver, 1980, 1981; Tse and Wilton, 1988) and an indirect effect through disconfirmation. Expectations have a direct positive effect of on satisfaction because "without observing the performance, expectations may have already predisposed the consumer to respond to the product in a certain way (the higher the expectations, the higher the satisfaction or vice versa)" (Oliver, 1997, p. 89). Recall that a similar notion is held by the Dissonance Theory discussed in Chapter Two.

Expectations-as-prediction standards have been employed as a form of comparison baseline in a number of tourism and hospitality research studies. For instance, Pizam and Milman (1993) asked first-time travelers' predictive expectations about Spain. Weber (1997) used predictive expectations as a comparison standard in her study on German tourists in Australia, while Hughes (1991) and Whipple and Thach (1989) measured respondents' predictive expectations in their research on tourist satisfaction with organized tours. Similarly, Duke and Persia (1996) and Tribe and Snaith (1998), in their studies on tourist satisfaction with organized tour industry, used predictive expectations (for example, I expect we will see as much as possible) as the comparison standard.

A number of researchers in the marketing and consumer behavior literature adopt a different notion of expectations that equate standards with levels of performance different from that expected from the focal object. Prakash (1984), for instance, proposed normative expectations, i.e., how a brand should perform in order for the consumer to be completely satisfied. Miller (1977) suggested different expectation categories, such as ideal expectations, minimum tolerable and deserved that would clearly lead to different comparative standard levels. The following section explicates each of these alternate comparative standards.

THE EXPECTATIONS AS DESERVED LEVEL STANDARD

The deserved level has been viewed as a type of equity that involves an evaluation of the consumer's input and outputs without any other comparison. Deserved level conveys "what the individual, in the light of his investments, feels performance ought to be or should be" (Miller, 1977, p. 76). Recall that the Equity Theory bases its conceptualization of customer satisfaction on this comparison standard. The Equity Theory proposes that a consumer evaluates the benefits received from a brand in relation to its cost (price and effort) and then compares this ratio with the corresponding cost/benefit ratio realized by some other relevant person (for example, the seller, a friend). The basis for comparison, in this case, becomes the degree of equity which consumers perceive between what they achieved and what the other person achieved.

Results concerning the ability of this comparison standard in explaining customer satisfaction are contradictory. Investigating the relationship between the deserved level standard and dependent variables such as satisfaction, Oliver and DeSarbo (1988) found that equity influences satisfaction. Fisk and Coney (1982) and Tse and Wilton (1988), however, did not find any relation between this standard and the dependent variables, and consequently drew the conclusion that the deserved level standard (equity) is not a good operationalisation of comparison standard (in Randal and Senior, 1996).

THE EXPECTATIONS AS MINIMUM TOLERABLE LEVEL

Another form of expectations is the minimum tolerable level (Miller, 1977). That is, the least acceptable level, for example "it is better than nothing". This level reflects the minimum level that the respondent feels the performance must be. The use of minimum tolerable level as a comparison standard is, however, challenged. According to Linjander and Strandvick (1993), the consumer will not be satisfied just because the performance is above the minimum tolerance level. If performance is above the minimum tolerance level but below the predicted level, the consumer will feel dissatisfied. Consumers can be expected to have minimum requirements for certain attributes, for example that there has to be a parking space beside a restaurant (Nightingale, 1986). However, consumers are not likely to consider (and certainly not buy) a product which is perceived as below the minimum acceptable level (Oliver, 1980b). This suggests that unless a product is grossly overestimated or was a cost-free acquisition, the must be (minimum acceptable) criterion may not be a consideration (ibid.).

THE EXPECTATIONS-AS-DESIRED STANDARDS

A number of satisfaction frameworks explicated in Chapter Three (for example, the Value-Percept Disparity Theory and the Evaluative Congruity Theory) suggest that customer satisfaction/dissatisfaction is more likely to be determined by how well a brand performance fulfils the innate needs, wants, or desires of the consumer, rather than the extent to which the brand's performance compares with pre-purchase predictions, as held by the Expectancy Disconfirmation theory. Recall that the main argument of these theories was that what is expected from a product may not correspond to what is desired or valued in a product (Westbrook and Reilly, 1983).

The desired and predicted expectations are seen different from one another. Desires are present-oriented and stable whereas expectations are future-oriented and relatively malleable (Spreng et al 1996). The predictive expectations are "the consumer's pre-usage estimate of the performance level that the product is anticipated to achieve on specific attributes" (Swan, Trawick and Carrol, 1982, p. 15). In contrast, desired expectations are seen as the consumer's pre-usage specification of the level of product performance that would be necessary in order to satisfy or please the consumer (ibid.).

In essence, this class of standard deals with the performance that is desired or wanted and is not necessarily constrained by past performance (Spreng and Dixon, 1992). Empirical tests on desires as a standard have been somewhat limited and contradictory. The results of Swan and Trawick's (1979) research suggest that only confirmation of desired expectations would lead to satisfaction while the confirmation of predictive expectations would lead to indifference. In a recent study, Swan et al (1991) measured both expectations and desires and found that when the performance of the product was greater than or equal to desires, satisfaction was higher. In a study of student satisfaction with a course, Barbeau (1984) found desires disconfirmation to have the strongest effect (B= .46), past experience disconfirmation the next strongest (B= .34) and expectation disconfirmation was non significant (B= .005)

In their Value-Percept Disparity theory, Westbrook and Reilly (1983) proposed that consumers' desires or values might influence the appraisal of perceived performance. Their theoretical argument seems compelling, but the empirical results of the study did not support their argument. They found that the expectation congruency had a stronger effect on satisfaction than did the desire congruency. The results of Spreng's and Olshavsky's (1993) recent study suggest that the extent to which product/service performance in congruent with desires is a powerful antecedent to satisfaction, while the effect of disconfirmation of expectations is non-significant. Myers (1991) tested expected versus wanted disconfirmation with car buyers and found that though both had a significant effect on satisfaction, the impact of wanted disconfirmation was stronger. Meyer concluded that what consumers want makes a better standard (i.e. more useful in predictions) than their expectations. Investigating the effect of these two on consumer satisfaction Spreng et al (1996) have recently concluded that desires and expectations need to be integrated into a single framework because both are found to influence satisfaction.

THE EXPECTATIONS AS IDEAL STANDARDS

A second standard that can be included in the desires category is the ideal performance standard. This standard often deals with the performance that is the best imaginable or relates to an abstract ideal (Spreng and Dixon, 1992). Ideal expectations are defined as the wished for level of performance (Miller, 1977). The ideal performance standard may correspond to perfection, or it could represent "my most desired combination of attributes" (Iacobucci et al 1994). Overly demanding consumers might be the ones who compare their experiences to ideal standards, and practically speaking, in such situations, a manager has no hope of exceeding such standards (ibid.).

In an early study, Liechty and Churchill (1979) compared Miller's (1977) four conceptualizations of expectations (predictive, ideal, deserved, and minimum acceptable) as to their applicability to services. They argue that the minimum tolerable and deserved expectations are best suited for services, while the ideal expectations are only "weakly appropriate for services because services are not easily quantified or averaged" (p.10). Tse and Wilton (1988) found that ideal performance did not have a direct effect on satisfaction. Rather it indirectly affected performance and this had a negative effect on satisfaction. In fact, whether this standard is actually used by consumers remains unclear (Spreng and Dixon, 1992).

THE EXPECTATIONS AS EXPERIENCE BASED STANDARDS

Some researchers argue that while expectations may be quite helpful in making a purchase choice, they may have much less impact on a post-use appraisal of a product or a service (Woodruff et al 1991). As consumers often have experiences with more than the focal object, experiences with other brands, other products, and services are also likely to play a role in the dis/confirmation comparison. As predicted by the Comparison Level Theory, the typical or last received performance of a brand may set the standard for appraising perceived performance of the focal brand.

Consumers with extensive experience with the product category might use one of the experience-based norms, such as average performance, favorite or last used, as a standard, while those who have little experience may use what others have received, what is promised or their expectations (Spreng and Dixon, 1992). Prior experience is probably the most important determinant of consumer satisfaction because personal experience is more vivid and salient (LaTour and Peat, 1980). In a similar line, Van Raaij and Francken (1984) comment that one's own earlier experience or the experience of others, serves as the baseline for social comparison that determines levels of satisfaction. Using a similar line of thought, Mazursky (1989, p.335) argues that in the context of tourism "the assessment of performance may be more profound and could cause a retrieval of memories from past experiences and norms which may function as comparison baselines". "Our experiences and resultant generalizations from them can be weighted more heavily than any information received. This is due, in part, to the fact that as our decision criteria strengthened, our need for information is weakened" (Mill and Morrison, 1984, p. 11] cf. Mazursky 1989). These arguments imply that past experience might be a significant comparison baseline against which customers compare their current experiences.

Applying Thibaut's and Kelley's (1959) Comparison Level Theory to the confirmation / disconfirmation process, LaTour and Peat found that experience based standards or norms play a role as a baseline for comparisons in consumers' satisfaction judgments. In their study, LaTour and Peat (1979) conceptualized satisfaction as an additive function of positive and/or negative disconfirmations of perceived attribute levels obtained from a brand and the corresponding levels of those attributes. LaTour and Peat proposed that the comparison level could be influenced "by perceived capabilities of brands other than the one purchased and used". Thus, it is possible to consider that the bases of comparison used by consumer may be "more than just expectations" (Woodruff et al 1983, p. 297). That is, satisfaction may not be totally dependent on whether a brand performance meets or exceeds predicted performance. Standards in the form of experience based norms, along with predictive expectations, may also have a role in the formation of satisfaction judgments. Reviewed literature suggests that there are at least two different types of experience based norms: brand based and product based (Cadotte et al 1987, Woodruff et al 1983). The following section explains these standards in turn.

THE EXPECTATIONS AS BRAND BASED STANDARD

Brand-based norms are those operating when one brand dominates a consumer's set of brand experiences. This norm might be "the typical performance of a particular brand, for example a consumer's most preferred brand, a popular brand, or last purchased brand" (Cadotte et al 1987, p. 306). For example, when appraising the dining experience in a new restaurant, a consumer may apply a norm that is the typical performance of another, favorite restaurant. Cadotte and his colleagues maintain that focal brand expectations may correspond to this norm, but only if the focal brand is also the brand, from which the standard is derived, such as when a consumer dines in his or her favorite restaurant. In all other cases, Cadotte et al (1987) claim that the norm is necessarily different from expectations because the norm is derived from an experience with a different brand. That is, these experiences "form a distribution along an overall performance dimension" (Woodruff et al 1983, p. 298). The actual norm is then drawn from this distribution and is represented by the most likely performance of a brand or the most frequent performance of a brand (ibid.).

THE EXPECTATIONS AS PRODUCT BASED STANDARDS

Another kind of norm suggested is the product based norm which is supposed to be operative when a consumer has had experiences with several brands of a product type within a product class but has no desired reference brand because all brands in that product category are similar. Here the norm performance might develop from a pooling of experience across the similar product brands. The reference norm is assumed to be some level of performance drawn from this distribution such as the most likely or the most frequent level of performance. Woodruff et al argue that because an individual's brand experiences can vary so much, different norms are likely to be used by different people in similar situations. For instance, one kind of norm may be used to determine satisfaction with a restaurant visited for a special occasion, whereas another might be applied when the family goes out for a meal (ibid). Another interesting assumption made by these authors is that for some consumers and in some situations, more than one norm may influence confirmation/disconfirmation. Multiple norms, according to these authors, are most likely to emerge during important events such as driving a recently purchased automobile, visiting a restaurant on an anniversary, or taking a long awaited vacation. In these situations the consumer is consciously and extensively assessing the brand use experience (ibid.).

THE EXPERIENCE-BASED NORMS: IS THIS THE WAY FORWARD?

Experience based norms are another type of comparison standard proposed in the literature. This standard recognizes that consumers have often experiences with more than the focal object, such as those with other brands, other products and or other services. These broad experiences are likely to play a role in disconfirmation comparisons. For example, the typical or last received performance of a favorite brand (a favorite restaurant) may set the standard for appraising the perceived performance of the focal brand (for example, a dining experience in a new restaurant). In general there can be several different norm standards (brand-based, product-based) against which perceived performance may be compared to, and depending on the situation consumers may use one or a combination of these norms in their comparisons.

The concept of experience-based norms is relatively new. A few studies have tested its validity and these revealed contradicting results. For example, Thirkell and Vredenburg (1982) found no significant relationships between prior experience and new product choice satisfaction. In contrast, Westbrook and Newman (1987) pointed out that people with previous experience developed more moderate expectations and rated greater satisfaction than did people without previous experience. Similarly, LaTour and Peat (1980) reported that confirmation of past experience standard was a stronger predictor of satisfaction than that of predictive expectations. In an earlier study carried out by Cadotte, Woodruff and Jenkins (1982), experience based evaluations of a comparison brand were better predictors of satisfaction than evaluations using focal brand expectations. Similarly, in a subsequent study, Cadotte et al (1987, p.313) reported that the product norm model and best brand norm model are "consistently better than the brand expectation model at explaining variation in satisfaction feelings and total model fit".

One of the strengths of incorporating experience-based standards into the assessment of satisfaction is its ability in capturing the relative performance of the company in comparison to other companies in the same product/service category. Surprisingly, there has been no attempt made to incorporate experience-based standards into tourist satisfaction assessments. Such comparative approach could be of significance in the long-term success of tourism and hospitality services, as it serves to identify relative strengths and weaknesses. It might be possible that experience of competing destinations may influence the standards against which the current destination is being judged. This implies that when assessing tourist satisfaction the performance relative to rivals should also be taken into account. From a managerial point of view, the information derived from the use of experience-based standards may be crucial, as what counts for the short and long term success is not only the product performance attained by the company/destination but also its performance relative to its competitors.

THE EXPECTATIONS AS EXCELLENCE STANDARD

In addition to its use in customer satisfaction literature, the expectations construct has also been viewed as playing a central role in consumer evaluations of service quality (Gronroos, 1984; Lehtinen and Lehtinen, 1991; Parasuraman et al. 1985; Brown and Swartz, 1989), which, as already explained in the second chapter, adds to the confusion between customer satisfaction and service quality constructs. Its meaning in the service quality literature is similar to the ideal standard in the customer satisfaction literature (Zeithaml et al 1993). Service quality researchers regard expectations as desires or wants of customers, i.e., what they feel a service provider should offer rather than would offer (Parasuraman et al 1988). Recall that both the desires and wants are also used in the assessment of customer satisfaction (for example, the Value-Percept Disparity theory). In an attempt to differentiate service quality from satisfaction, Parasuraman et al later changed the wording of their standards to excellent companies. Excellence, however, is not markedly different from several other standards used in customer satisfaction literature. Zeithaml et al (1993), for instance, employed excellence as the comparison standard in identifying service quality, and defined it in terms of what the consumers want or need. However from their usage, it is not clear whether this anchored to consumer values or to past experience, for example if a consumer defines it as what the best firm provides, "then this is clearly an experience based norm" (Spreng and Dixon, 1992, p. 88), and not different from best-brand norm used in the customer satisfaction literature.

THE EXPECTATIONS AS ZONES OF INDIFFERENCE

A recent development in research of customer satisfaction and service quality is to consider expectations and evaluations as "zones of tolerance" (Randall and Senior, 1996). Anderson (1973) introduced this concept into the consumer satisfaction literature arguing that purchasers are willing to accept a range of performance around a point estimate as long as the range could be reasonably expected (in Oliver, 1997) (for example a 30-minute pizza delivery in a realistic range of 20 to 45 minutes). Blomer and Poiesz (1991) suggest that expectations and evaluations should be expressed as zones and not as discrete points on a scale. They argue that customers might not be capable of giving precise point estimates. In line with Poiesz and Bloemer (1991), Woodruff et al (1983) argue that perceptual limitations of people can cause some imprecision when the confirmation-disconfirmation cognition is made. An alternative rationale is derived from the Assimilation (Contrast) Theory. Perceptions of a brand performance, which are close to the norm, are within latitude of acceptable performance, and may even be assimilated toward the norm. That is, perceived performance within some interval around a performance norm is likely to be considered equivalent to the norm. However, when the distance from the norm is great enough (perceived performance is outside the latitude of acceptance) brand performance is perceived as different from the norm. Perceived performance that is below or above the norm but within the indifference zone leads to confirmation, and difference causes disconfirmation. Positive and negative disconfirmation is argued to result when perceived performance is outside the zone and is different enough from the norm to be noticed.

Perceived brand performance within the zone of indifference probably does not cause much attention to be directed toward the evaluation process. Moreover, brand performance, which is close to the norm, is likely to be usual occurrence. In contrast, perceived brand performance, outside the zone of indifference is unusual and attention getting. When this condition occurs, "the satisfaction process is more likely to be raised to a conscious level and thus evoke a positive or negative emotional response" (Woodruff et al 1983, p. 300). Parasuraman et al (1991) attempted to measure the "zone of tolerance" by computing the difference between desired level and adequate level of expectations. The desired expectations refer to what they hope to receive, a blend of what can and should be, which is a function of past experience (Lewis, 1990). The adequate level refers to what is acceptable which is based on an assessment of what the service will be (the predicted service), and depends on the alternatives which are available. Although it seems intuitively appealing, the operationalisation of zone of difference was found to be practically difficult.

SINGLE VERSUS MULTIPLE STANDARDS

So far, this discussion suggests that no single model or unique comparison process fully explains consumer satisfaction/dissatisfaction judgments. Some researchers suggest that a better description of consumer satisfaction/dissatisfaction should include the occurrence of multiple processes and multiple standards of comparison (Erevelles and Leavitt, 1992). Indeed, recent conceptualizations of customer satisfaction (Tse and Wilton, 1988) have considered that customer satisfaction is a post-choice process involving complex, and simultaneous interactions with which may involve more than one comparison standard.

Cadotte et al (1987), for instance, developed and examined alternative customer satisfaction models involving different standards of comparison. Their Product Norm model and Best Brand Norm model were consistently better than the brand expectation (prediction) model at explaining the variation in explaining satisfaction feelings and total model fit. These different norms (best brand, product based and predictive expectations) were, however, moderately correlated, suggesting that "they share a common core but that each also has a unique component" (Zeithaml, 1993, p. 2). Using path analysis, Tse and Wilton (1988) quantified the influence of both predicted and ideal expectations. They concluded "more than one comparison standard may be involved in customer satisfaction formation because both expectations (prediction) and ideal relate individually to satisfaction. Expectations and ideal appear to represent different constructs contributing separately to the customer satisfaction/dissatisfaction formation process. The single standard models fail to represent the underlying process adequately in comparison with a multiple standard paradigm" (p, p. 209-10). Oliver and Desarbo (1988) observed the combined effects of various variables in the satisfaction/ dissatisfaction formation process. They suggested that disconfirmation though objective may be subjected to psychological interpretations that may dominate under certain conditions. These findings suggest the occurrence of a multiple comparison process including complex interactions, which may take place either sequentially or simultaneously.

Similarly, Sirgy's Evaluative Congruity model (1984) suggests the occurrence of multiple comparison processes could explain consumer satisfaction, and gathered empirical evidence, which demonstrated that consumers might use multiple standards to arrive at satisfaction judgments. In his model, Sirgy (1984) argues that (in) congruities may take place between different perceptual and evoked referent states. Such (in) congruities may take place between (1) new product performance after usage and expected product performance before use, (2) new product performance after use and old product performance before use, (3) expected product performance after purchase and ideal product performance before purchase, (4) expected product performance after purchase and deserved product performance after use. In his empirical test, Sirgy (1984) found that each of these congruities significantly influenced customer satisfaction separately and jointly. Similar observations have been reported by Cadotte et al (1987), suggesting that comparison standards are multidimensional, as consumers use a standard that is a weighted composite of various other standards. This multidimensional standard may be formed from past experience including experience with the focal brand and with competing brands.

Boulding, Karla, Staelin and Zeithaml (1993) have recently proposed two types of prior expectations that might have a combined and a separate impact on satisfaction. These are will and should expectations. They defined will expectations as those characteristics of the service that consumers consider likely to occur. Thus, these researchers define will expectations as predictive, as referred to by Tse and Wilton (1988) who defined expectations as the most likely performance, affected both by the average product performance and by advertising. Boulding et al (1993) define should expectations as those characteristics of service that consumers "would consider to be reasonable". Thus they define the should expectation as a consumer's judgment of a more realistic norm. Their study suggests that a firm should increase the will expectations and decrease the should expectations in order to raise the quality perceptions.

MULTIPLE STANDARDS: IS THIS THE WAY FORWARD?

Although some studies suggest that multiple standards be used in the formation of customer satisfaction judgments, the measurement of multiple standards seems to be problematic. The use of multiple standards requires researchers to design multiple scales, one for each type of standard (Woodruff et al 1991). This might make the task of answering the questions rather tedious for respondents not to mention risking response bias across the questions. There is, for example, a great probability that respondents bored by rating three identical set of questions may tend to choose the same rating for all questions. Such evidence is found in Parasuraman, Zeihaml and Berry's (1994) recent study. The authors acknowledge that despite the three-column format questionnaire's (two comparison standards and perceived performance) superior diagnostic value, the administration of the whole questionnaire may pose practical difficulties. Childress and Crompton (1997) report that any approach, which incorporates the assessment of two or more standards and involves performance perception measurement, has response error problems. The questionnaires may appear long and repetitive to the respondents since they are required to complete the same set of items three times at one sitting. William (1998) emphasizes that people became anxious when confronted with the length of such questionnaires, their anxiety towards keeping the rest of their party waiting and wasting their leisure times. The expansion of the instrument to three columns (two standards and performance measures) to allow for the " zone of tolerance" data to be collected appears to exacerbate this problem.

SOURCES OF EXPECTATIONS

Although expectation has been the dominant comparison baseline in assessments of customer satisfaction, the source(s) of consumer expectations has been relatively unexplored (Zeithaml et al 1993). Very little research has focused on how consumers form expectations, on the variables that impact upon customer expectations, and the extent to which the variables influence expectations (Clow, Kurtz and Ozment, 1996).

Cadotte et al (1987) suggest that experience is a source of the expectation norm. They suggest that the norm may be derived from the typical performance of a particular brand (the favorite brand, the last purchased and the most popular brand). Also the norm might be based on perceptions of an average performance that is believed to be typical of a group of similar brands (a product-type norm). Based on results of a series of focus group interviews, Zeithaml and her colleagues (1990, p. 19-20) found five different sources influencing customers' expectation formation. First, what customers hear from other customers and word-of-mouth communication, was found to be a potential determinant of expectations. Second, respondents' expectations appeared to vary somewhat depending on customers' individual characteristics and circumstances, suggesting that the personal needs of customers might moderate their expectations to a certain degree. Third, it was found that the extent of past experience with using a service could also influence customers' expectation levels. Fourth, external communications from service providers, for example advertising, was found to play a key role in shaping customer expectations. Another factor influencing customer expectations was the price, whose influence on expectations could be grouped under the general influence of company's external communications. In their study on restaurants, Clow et al (1996) state that primary antecedents of customer expectations of a restaurant are the image consumers have of the restaurant, satisfaction with the last service experience, word-of-mouth, tangible characteristics of the restaurant, price structure of the menu, the availability and accessibility of restaurant to customers, advertising and situational factors such as overcrowding and noise.

However, little is known about whether different sources lead to development of different kinds of standards (i.e., what source of expectations is used under which conditions and what the relative performance of each source is in forming overall expectations) (Clow et al 1996). LaTour and Peat (1979) undertook a field experiment to investigate the effect of prior experience, situationally induced expectations, and other consumers' experiences on customer satisfaction. They found that situationally induced expectations had little effect on satisfaction, whereas expectations based on prior experiences were the major determinants of customer satisfaction. This finding suggests that consumers may attach less importance to manufacturer-provided information when they have personal experience and relevant information about other consumers' experiences (Yi, 1990). In contrast, Spreng and Dixon (1992) argue that persuasion based expectations which are the explicit statements from the seller regarding the performance of the product (i.e., a marketer dominated stimuli like advertising) appear to develop very strong expectations.

SUMMARY

The concept of customer satisfaction is integral to marketing thought. Various theoretical frameworks, based on various standards, have been developed to explain this important concept. Researchers have not converged on the exact conceptualization of the comparison standard and disconfirmation constructs (Tse and Wilton, 1988). Several researchers concur that consumers may use expectations but other kinds of baselines may be operative in the formation of satisfaction judgments. As early as 1977, Miller, for instance, developed a classification scheme by using four different kinds of comparisons: expected, deserved, ideal and minimum tolerable performance.

Predictive expectations have been widely adopted as the comparison standard in many tourism and hospitality research investigations. However, the marketing literature is replete with evidence demonstrating that expectations-based dis/confirmation measures, at best, have yielded only modest correlations with satisfaction measures. As a result, the validity of using expectations as the sole pre-consumption antecedent of the dis/confirmation process and as the basis for predicting its outcomes has become disputable. Expectations have been elevated to some grand conceptual status "but there is no compelling theoretical or empirical reason that expectations per se must be the comparison for judgment" (Iacobucci et al 1994, p. 25). Past research may have attached " unwarranted importance to expectations as the standard of performance influencing feelings of satisfaction" (Cadotte et al 1987, p. 306). There is a very little justification for consumers using only focal brand expectations to judge performance after purchase (Westbrook and Reilly, 1983).

Research in consumer behavior has suggested that some standards of comparison may be better than others at explaining satisfaction and that the relationship between disconfirmation, performance, and satisfaction may change depending on the standards used to measure them. However, at present there is no consensus of an appropriate standard, and some researchers have suggested that the standard that is used is contingent upon a number of consumer and situational factors (Spreng and Dixon, 1992). The comparison standard, for example, has been conceptualized as expected (Oliver, 1980), ideal (Sirgy, 1984), or normative performance (Woodruff et al 1983).

Some researchers have suggested that consumers may not only use a single standard but may also engage in multiple comparisons in customer satisfaction/dissatisfaction formation. Although there seems to be an agreement as to the fact that customer satisfaction can be a function of multiple standards, it is not clear, however, which combination of standards is more applicable to different consumption situations, and to different products and services. It is important to note that in spite of the emphasis placed on the different types of standards, only a few have received much empirical attention. For instance, predictive expectation as a standard has been studied extensively in marketing literature in general and in tourism and hospitality literature in particular. Other standards have not been examined as well in the tourism and hospitality literature.

A review of customer satisfaction literature clearly manifests that researchers in marketing and consumer behavior in general and hospitality and tourism in particular have favored the use of Expectancy-Disconfirmation paradigm , which employs predictive expectations as the comparative standard. Despite the fact that no model or theory is complete, limited research has been carried out whether the dominant Expectancy-Disconfirmation paradigm possesses any theoretical and/or methodological shortcomings and whether it could be possible to apply the model in every situation.

REFERENCES

Anderson, E. R. (1973). Consumer dissatisfaction: the effect of disconfirmed expectancy on perceived product performance. *Journal of Marketing Research*, 10, 38-44.

Barbeau, B. J. (1985). Predictive and Normative Expectations in consumer satisfaction, a utilisation of adaptation and comparison levels in a unified framework, in Hunth, K. H., and Day, L. R. (Eds) *Conceptual and Empirical contributions to Consumer Satisfaction and Complaining Behaviour*, 27-32.

Bloemer, J. M. M., and Poiesz, T. B. C. (1989).The Illusion of Customer Satisfaction. *Journal of Consumer Satisfaction, Dissatisfaction and Complaining Behaviour*, (2): 43-48.

Boulding, W., Karla, A., Staelin, R., and Zeithaml, V.A. (1993). A Dynamic Process Model of service quality, From Expectations to Behavioural Intentions. *Journal of Marketing Research,* 30 (February), 7-27.

Brown, W. S., and Swartz, T. A. (1989). Consumer and Provider Expectations and experiences in evaluating professional service quality. *Journal of the Academy of Marketing Science,* 17, (2), 189-195.

Cadotte, E. R., Woodruff, R. B., Jenkins, R. J. (1987). Expectations and Norms in Models of Consumer Satisfaction. *Journal of Marketing Research,* 24 , 305-14.

Childress, D. R., and Crompton, L. J. (1997). A comparison of alternative direct and discrepancy approaches to measuring quality of performance at a festival. *Journal of Travel Research,* 43-57.

Clow, E. K., Kurtz, L. D., and Ozment, J. (1996). Managing Customer Expectations of Restaurants: An Empirical Study. *Journal of Restaurant and Foodservice Marketing,* 1 (3/4), 135-159

Day, R. (1977). *Consumer satisfaction, dissatisfaction and complaining behavior.* In Symposium Proceedings, School of Business, University of Indiana.

Duke, R. C., and Persia, M. A. (1996). Consumer defined dimensions for the escorted tour industry segment, expectations, satisfaction and importance. *Journal of Travel and Tourism Marketing,* 5, (2), 77-99

Ennew, T. C., Reed, V. G., and Binks, R. M. (1993). Importance-performance analysis and the Measurement of service quality. *European Journal of Marketing,* 27, (2), 59-70.

Fisk, R. P., and Coney, A. K. (1982). *Post choice evaluation: an equity theory analysis of consumer satisfaction and dissatisfaction with service choices.* In Hunt, H.K., and Day, L. R. (Eds). Conceptual and Empirical Contributions to Consumer Satisfaction and Dissatisfaction and Complaining Behavior, Bloomington, IN, USA: Indiana University School of Business, 9-16.

Erevelles, S., and Leavitt, C. (1992). A Comparison of Current Models of Consumer Satisfaction / Dissatisfaction. *Journal of Consumer Satisfaction /Dissatisfaction and Complaining Behavior,* 5, 104-114.

Gronroos, C. (1984). A Service quality model and its marketing implications. European *Journal of Marketing,* 18, 36-44.

Hughes, K. (1991). Tourist satisfaction: A Guided Tour in North Queensland. *Australian Psychologist,* 26 (3), 166-171.

Iacobucci, D., Grayson, A. K., Ostrom, A. L. (1994). *The Calculus of Service Quality and Customer Satisfaction: Theoretical and Empirical Differentiation and Integration.* in Advances in Service Marketing and Management, Swarts et al (eds) 3 JAI Press Greenwich, CT, 1-67.

LaTour, S .A., and Peat, N. (1980). The Role of Situationally Produced Expectations, Others' Experiences and Prior Experience in Determining Customer Satisfaction. in Olson, C. J. (ed). *Advances in Consumer Research,* 588- 592.

Lehtinen, U., and Lehtinen, R. J. (1991). Two approaches to service quality dimensions. *The Service Industries Journal,* 3, 287-303.

Lewis, R. B. (1991). *Measuring customer expectations and satisfaction.* 1-19.

Liechy, M., and Churchill G. A. (1979). *Conceptual insights into consumer satisfaction with services.* In Niel Beckwith (ed). Educators Conference Proceedings, 509-515.

Liljander, V., and Strandivk, T. (1993). Estimating zones of tolerance in perceived service quality and perceived service value. *International Journal of Service Industry Management*, 4, (2).

Mazursky, D. (1989). Past Experience and Future Tourism Decisions. *Annals of Tourism Research*, 16, 333-344.

Miller, J. A. (1977). Studying *satisfaction, modifying models, eliciting expectations, posing problems, and making meaningful measurements*. 72-92. In Hunt, H. K (Ed) Conceptualisation and measurement of consumer satisfaction and dissatisfaction, Cambridge, MA, USA: Marketing Science Institute.

Myers, J. H. (1991). Measuring Customer Satisfaction: Is Meeting Expectations Enough?. *Marketing Research,* 3 (4), 35-43.

Nightingale, M. (1985). The Hospitality Industry: Defining Quality for a Quality Assurance Programme- A Study of Perceptions. *Service Industries Journal*, 5, (1), 9-24.

Olander, F. (1979). *Consumer Satisfaction: A Sceptic's view*. Aarhus Denmark.

Oliver, L. R. (1997). *Satisfaction a behavioural perspective on the consumer*, The McGraw-Hill Companies, Inc. New York, USA.

Oliver, R. L. (1989). Processing of the Satisfaction Response in Consumption: A Suggested framework and Research Propositions. *Journal of Consumer Satisfaction, Dissatisfaction and Complaining Behavior,* 2, 1-16.

Oliver R. L., and DeSarbo, W. S.(1988). Response Determinants in Satisfaction Judgment. *Journal of Consumer Research*, 14, 495- 507.Oliver, R. L. (1981), Measurement and Evaluation of satisfaction process in retail setting. *Journal of Retailing*, 57, 25-48.

Oliver. R. L. (1980). A Cognitive Model of the Antecedents of Satisfaction Decisions. *Journal of Marketing Research*, 17, 46-49.

Parasuraman, A., Zeithaml, A. V., and Berry, L. L. (1985). A Conceptual Model of Service quality and Its Implications for Future Research. *Journal of Marketing*, 49, 41-50.

Parasuraman, A., Zeithaml, A. V., and Berry, L. L. (1988). Servqual: a Multiple Item Scale for Measuring Consumer Perceptions of Service Quality. *Journal of Retailing*, 64, Spring, 12-40.

Pizam, A., and Milman, A. (1993). Predicting Satisfaction Among First Time Visitors to a Destination by Using the Expectancy Disconfirmation Theory. *International Journal of Hospitality Management*, 12, 197-209.

Prakash, V. (1984). Validity and Reliability of the Confirmation of Expectations Paradigm as a Determinant of Consumer Satisfaction. *Journal of the Academy of Marketing Science*, 12, (4), 63-77.

Sirgy, J. M. (1984). *A social cognition model of CS/D: an experiment, Psychology, and Marketing*. 1, 27-44.

Spreng, R. A., Mackenzie, S. B., and Olshavsky, R. W. (1996). A reexamination of the determinants of consumer satisfaction. *Journal of Marketing,* 60, 15-32.

Spreng, R. A., and Olshavsky, R. W. (1993). A desires congruency model of consumer satisfaction. *Journal of the Academy of Marketing Science*, 21 (3), 169-177.

Spreng, R. A., and Dixon, A. L. (1992). *Alternative Comparison Standards in the Formation of Satisfaction/Dissatisfaction*. in Enhancing Knowledge Development, In Leone and Kumar (eds) Marketing, Chicago, LL, USA: American Marketing Association, 85-91.

Swan J. E., Trawick, I. F., and Carroll, G. M. (1982). Satisfaction related to predictive, desired expectations. a field study, In Day, L. R., and Hunt, K. (Eds). *New findings on Consumer satisfaction and complaining*, 15-19.

Swan, J., and Travick, F. I. (1980). Satisfaction related to the predictive vs. desired expectations, in Hunt, H. K., and Day, R. (eds). *Refining concepts and measures of consumer satisfaction and complaining behavior*. Indiana University, 7-12.

Thibaut, J. W., and Kelly, K. H. (1959). The social psychology of groups, New York, USA: John Wiley and Sons, Inc.

Thirkell, P., and Vredenburg, H. (1982). Prepurchase Information Search and Postpurcahse Product Satisfaction: The Effects of Different Sources. in Bruce L. W. (ed) *Assessment of Marketing Thought and Practice*, Chicago, American Marketing Association.

Tribe, J., and Snaith, T. (1998). From Servqual to Holsat: holiday satisfaction in Varadero, Cuba. *Tourism Management* 19. 125-34.

Tse, D. K., and Wilton, C. P. (1988). Models Of Customer Satisfaction Formation: An Extension. *Journal of Marketing Research*, 25, 204-212.

Van Raaij, W. F., and Francken, D. A. (1984). Vacation Decisions, Activities and Satisfactions. *Annals of Tourism Research*, 11, 101-112.

Weber, K. (1997). Assessment of Tourist Satisfaction, Using the Expectancy disconfirmation theory, a study of German Travel Market in Australia. *Pacific Tourism Review*, 1, 35-45.

Westerbrook, R. A., and Newman, W. (1978) An Analysis of Shopper Dissatisfaction for Major Household Appliances. *Journal of Marketing Research*, Vol. 15, (August), 456-66.

Westbrook, R. A., and Reilly, M. D., (1983). *Value-Percept disparity: an alternative to the disconfirmation of expectations theory of customer satisfaction*. in Bogozzi, P. R., and Tybouts, A. (eds). Advances in Consumer Research, Association for Consumer Research, 10, Ann Arbor, MI, 256-61.

Whipple, W. T., and Thach, V. S. (1988). Group Tour Management: Does Good Service Produce Satisfied Customers. *Journal of Travel Research*, Fall,16-21.

Williams, C. (1998). Is the Servqual model an appropriate management tool for measuring service delivery quality in the UK leisure industry. *Managing Leisure*, 3: 98-110.

Woodruff, R. B., Cleanop, D. S., Schumn, D. W., Godial, S. F., and Burns, M. J. (1991). The standards issue in CS/D research: Historical perspective. *Journal of Consumer Satisfaction/ Dissatisfaction and Complaining Behavior*.

Yi. Y. (1990). *A Critical Review of Consumer Satisfaction*. in V. A. Zeithaml (Ed.), *Review of Marketing*. Chicago, USA: American Marketing Association, 68-123.

Zeithaml, V. A., Berry, L. L., and Parasuraman, A. (1993). The nature and determinants of customer expectations of service. *Journal of the Academy of the Marketing Science*, 21, (1), 1-12.

In: Tourist Satisfaction and Complaining Behavior
Editor: Atila Yüksel

ISBN 978-1-60456-002-2
© 2008 Nova Science Publishers, Inc.

Chapter 6

IMAGE AND MULTIPLE COMPARISON STANDARDS IN TOURIST SERVICE SATISFACTION

Héctor San Martín Gutiérrez, Jesús Collado Agudo and Ignacio Rodríguez del Bosque Rodríguez

Department of Business Administration, Faculty of Economics
Cantabria University

INTRODUCTION

Knowledge of the customer satisfaction process, a psychological process which the individual goes through during the pre-encounter and post-encounter stages with services, is a critical issue in tourism research. In this sense, it is necessary to explore in depth the interrelationships between several psychological concepts of individuals in relation to their service experiences such as attitudes, prior beliefs, service assessments and behavioural intentions. In this field, new findings will allow researchers and practitioners to manage the customer satisfaction with tourist services and their main antecedents and consequences more effectively (i.e. it will facilitate a wider knowledge of tourist service satisfaction).

Many unresolved questions come up when a revision of earlier findings about tourist service satisfaction is carried out. One of the most important and unexplored trends is the move away from a single comparison standard (expectations) towards multiple standards in the consumer satisfaction process. In tourism; how many standards of comparison are employed by individuals to form their satisfaction judgments with tourist services? If they used several types of standards during the tourist service encounter; would these standards play the same role in the customer satisfaction process? Finally, it is generally accepted that perceived image influences the individual's choice process. However; might the different stages of the customer satisfaction process be significantly influenced by perceived image of the tourist service provider too?

With these important questions in mind, empirical research was carried out in the travel agency sector to enhance the body of knowledge on tourist service satisfaction in several ways: (1) by exploring in depth the effect of multiple comparison standards on customer satisfaction; and (2) by examining how the different stages of the customer satisfaction process are influenced by perceived image of the tourist service provider (these stages are closely related to the service encounter phases). In turn, these objectives will guide the literature review and theoretical model.

THEORETICAL FRAMEWORK

The customer satisfaction process is formed by the state of satisfaction with a service, the psychological variables that contribute to its formation, as well as by the outcome of this mental state of the individual. As established, the different stages of the customer satisfaction process are closely related to the service encounter phases. Service encounter can be defined as a "period of time during which a consumer directly interacts with a service" (Shostack, 1985). Thus, a service encounter is based on the interaction between individuals and different elements of the service provider such as its physical facilities or its employees (Bitner, Booms, and Stanfield, 1990). Following the model of service encounter evaluation from Bitner (1990), three main phases can be distinguished through time: pre, during and after the encounter. Firstly, each individual is supposed to have expectations of the service performance. Secondly, customers will express some psychological reactions during the service encounter in terms of, for example, satisfaction. Finally, behavioural intentions towards the service provider will take place after the service encounter.

In this context, satisfaction research has been focused on the nature of consumer satisfaction, as well as on its antecedents and consequences (Singh, 1991). Recently, consumer satisfaction has been defined as a cognitive-affective state derived from the experience with a product or service (Bowen and Clarke, 2002; Jun, Hyun, Gentry, and Song, 2001; Van Dolen, De Ruyter, and Lemmink, 2004). In relation to the antecedents and consequences of consumer satisfaction, the expectancy disconfirmation model is the most applied in earlier studies (Erevelles and Leavitt, 1992; Wirtz, Mattila, and Tan, 2000). Under this approach, predictive expectations, performance and disconfirmation are the most important judgments or cognitions contributing to consumer satisfaction (Oliver, 1997). Finally, customer loyalty towards the service provider is generally considered the main consequence of satisfaction (Selnes, 1993; Yu and Dean, 2001).

EXPECTATIONS AND THE CUSTOMER SATISFACTION PROCESS

In literature, satisfaction is traditionally conceived as the individual's response to an evaluation between what was received and what was expected (Liljander and Strandvik, 1997). According to this, the product's performance is evaluated by consumers in relation to a standard or basis for comparison, generally called expectations. Despite the importance of expectations in satisfaction research, there is no consensus about the type of standard (expectations) that consumers use to form their satisfaction judgments (Tse and Wilton, 1988). Predictive expectations, which can be conceptualised as the individual's beliefs about how a product is likely to perform in the future (Oliver, 1987; Prakash and Lounsbury, 1984), are the most used standard in previous studies. However, several alternative standards have been suggested in literature on satisfaction: ideal expectations (Spreng and Dixon, 1992), experience-based norms (Woodruff, Cadotte, and Jenkins, 1983), or desires (Spreng, Mackenzie, and Olshavsky, 1996).

With regard to the role of expectations in the customer satisfaction process, expectations are not only analyzed as a standard for evaluating product performance (a function proposed in the traditional disconfirmation paradigm), but also as a direct antecedent of consumer satisfaction (Szymanski and Henard, 2001). The direct effect of expectations on consumer satisfaction can be explained by the Assimilation Theory (Sherif and Hovland, 1961). Consumers suffer a psychological conflict when they recognize discrepancies between perceived performance and prior expectations. Then, consumers tend to adjust the product's perception to their expectations in order to reduce or remove that tension. In other words, individuals may mediate in the consumption process to justify their predictions (Oliver, 1997). Under this assumption, consumer satisfaction would be positively led by expectations (Andreassen, 2000; Churchill and Surprenant, 1982; Oliver and Burke, 1999; Pieters, Koelemeijer, and Roest, 1995; Yi, 1993). The more favourable the prior expectations of individuals, the higher their levels of satisfaction during the service encounters.

MULTIPLE COMPARISON STANDARDS AND THE DYNAMIC NATURE OF EXPECTATIONS

Two phenomenon associated with consumer expectations are explored in this section: multiple comparison standards and dynamic expectations. Firstly, it is necessary to emphasize that most previous studies propose a single comparison standard in the satisfaction process, usually in the form of predictive expectations. However, it has been suggested that consumer evaluations are processes involving complex, simultaneous interactions which may imply several comparison standards (Forbes, Tse, and Taylor, 1986). In satisfaction literature, Tse and Wilton (1988) demonstrated that predictive expectations (direct effect) and ideal expectations (indirect effect) influence consumer satisfaction. On the other hand, Spreng, Mackenzie, and Olshavsky (1996) found that expectations and desires operate simultaneously in the consumer satisfaction process. More recently, Santos and Boote (2003) proposed a hierarchy of expectations, which can range from the ideal standard to the minimum tolerable level, influencing affective states of individuals (e.g. states of satisfaction or dissatisfaction). These models, which incorporate several comparison standards into evaluations, may explain the customer satisfaction process more effectively (Oliver, 1997). Nevertheless, a bigger effort is needed to understand to a greater degree the phenomenon of multiple standards.

Secondly, consumer expectations may be dynamic, changing over time (Boulding, Kalra, Staelin, and Zeithaml, 1993). Expectations may be revised and updated by consumers during the service encounter (Oliver, 1997). Some empirical evidence is recently provided by Tam (2005), where expectations are updated (adjusted upwards) following a positive experience. However, they seem to remain stable after a negative experience. In line with Oliver (1997), this updated expectations level may be used by individuals in their satisfaction judgements. In a similar way, Ngobo (1997) establishes that individuals are likely to build ad hoc standards when their prior beliefs aren't well articulated and/or are difficult to retrieve. These standards would be strongly affected by the service experience. Finally, some standards really different to the pre-encounter expectations may emerge during the consumption process (Yüksel and Yüksel, 2001). For example, individuals may use as a reference for service evaluations the performance received by other customers (Gardial, Woodruff, Burns, Schumann, and Clemons, 1993), the service level provided by other brands (Woodruff, Cadotte, and Jenkins, 1983), or even the "need for emotional arousal" (Cote, Foxman, and Cutler, 1989).

THE ROLE OF IMAGE IN THE CUSTOMER SATISFACTION PROCESS

Image can be conceptualised as the individual's overall attitude towards a company (Andreassen and Lindestad, 1998) or, more concretely, the set of impressions, beliefs and feelings of individuals about an organisation (Barich and Kotler, 1991). In a similar way, the service provider image may be considered as a representation of the provider in the individual's mind, and where three perception components can be identified: holistic (impressions); cognitive (beliefs); and affective (feelings towards the provider). Next, several findings from previous studies on consumer satisfaction are indicated to justify the role of provider image during the different stages of the customer satisfaction process (i.e. pre, during and after the service encounter).

Firstly, image has been defined as an expectations communicator in service contexts (Grönroos, 1990). In particular, perceived image is considered by individuals as a real sign of the provider's capabilities (Weigelt and Camerer, 1988). Consequently, image helps individuals to anticipate the product performance at some moment in the future (the more favourable the image of a provider, the more favourable the individual's expectations of the service). A significant and positive relationship between image and expectations is found in previous studies on service satisfaction (Clow, Kurt, Ozment, and Ong 1997; Devlin, Gwynne, and Ennew, 2002).

Secondly, a service evaluation is complex due to its intangibility (Bebko, 2000). Under these circumstances, individuals may have more confidence in their prior images of the provider than in their service evaluations. Therefore, satisfaction would be significantly guided by the prior image that individuals have of the service provider in their minds (Andreassen and Lindestad, 1998; Kristensen, Martensen, and Gronholdt, 1999). Finally, it has been established that image positively influences loyalty (Andreassen and Lindestad, 1998; ECSI Technical Committee, 1998; Kristensen, Martensen, and Gronholdt, 1999). Based on this assumption, individuals with a positive image of the provider will continue their relationship with this provider regardless of the level of satisfaction during a particular service encounter, and vice versa.

A MODEL OF TOURIST SERVICE SATISFACTION

A new satisfaction approach is adopted in this chapter of the book. More concretely, a model is proposed which simultaneously incorporates: (1) the individual's psychological variables pertaining to different phases of the tourist service encounter, i.e. pre, during and after the encounter; (2) multiple comparison standards in the customer's evaluation; and (3) the influence of perceived image of the provider on the customer satisfaction process (figure 1). This new and more complex approach to satisfaction can be extremely useful in building up a broad theoretical perspective on satisfaction in the tourism industry. In turn, the conceptual model is developed on the basis of the reasons established in the previous section and several findings from tourism research (such as some antecedents and consequences of tourist satisfaction or some evidence for the influence of image on the tourist satisfaction process).

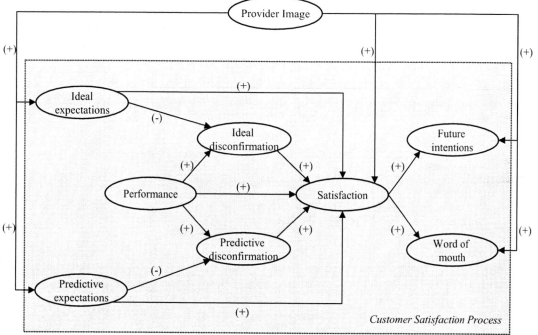

Figure 1. Theoretical model

Firstly, psychological variables involved in the complete disconfirmation model –i.e. expectations, performance and disconfirmation– represent the basis for this tourist satisfaction model. According to Yi (1990), expectations and disconfirmation (judgment that reflects if the product performed better or worse than expected) can be considered key variables influencing consumer evaluation. Additionally, two individual dimensions of customer loyalty –i.e. intention to continue the relationship with the service provider and word-of-mouth– are conceived as the main consequences of satisfaction judgement (Dabholkar and Thorpe, 1994; Sivadas and Baker-Prewitt, 2000; Söderlund, 2002). In tourism research, disconfirmation has also been proposed as a direct antecedent of satisfaction (Bigné and Andreu, 2004; Chon and Olsen 1991), whereas future intentions and word-of-mouth have been defended as the most important consequences of tourist satisfaction in several contexts, e.g. accommodation or holiday destinations (Bigné, Sánchez, and Sánchez, 2001; Danaher and Haddrell, 1996; Kozak and Rimmington, 2000).

Secondly, multiple comparison standards are proposed in the customer satisfaction process with tourist services. Service evaluation is a process which may involve several comparison standards in the customer's mind. On the basis of Ngobo (1997), a list with the standards which individuals might potentially use to evaluate tourist services is proposed

(Table 1). In this study, predictive expectations and ideal standard are chosen to take part in the tourist satisfaction process. Predictive expectations are the most used standard in past research on satisfaction (Santos and Boote, 2003). Nevertheless, individuals may not have much motivation to process or generate those expectations (Yüksel and Yüksel, 2001). Under these circumstances, ideal expectations might play a significant role in tourist service evaluations since this standard requires a minor mental effort for individuals.

However, the contribution of expectations to customer satisfaction has received little attention in tourism research. An exception is the study completed by Rodríguez Del Bosque, San Martín and Collado (2006) in the travel agency sector, which found that the user's satisfaction is positively influenced by predictive expectations. In this new satisfaction approach (see figure 1), both kinds of expectations are proposed to operate simultaneously as: (1) standards for evaluating the performance of the tourist service during the encounter; and (2) direct antecedents of customer satisfaction with the tourist service (more concretely, it is assumed that the user's satisfaction is dominated by the so-called phenomenon of assimilation).

Table 1. Comparison standards in tourist service satisfaction

Comparison Standards	Definition
Predictive expectations	Prior beliefs about the salient attributes (or performance) of a tourist service at some moment in the future
Ideal expectations	Performance of a tourist service that is the best that individuals can imagine
Experience-based norms	Performance that individuals believe the typical for a particular brand (or a group of brands) of a tourist service category
Schema	Performance that individuals believe should come from a tourist service (or brand) on the basis of the result from a typical member of the category
Equity	Performance that individuals deserve given what they put into the tourist service encounter
Desires	Performance of a tourist service that individuals consider will lead to their higher-level values

Finally, the importance of image is universally acknowledged since it affects the tourist's choice process (Gallarza, Gil, and Calderón, 2002). Unfortunately, little research has been done on the influence of image on the tourist satisfaction process. In this study, it is established that expectations, satisfaction and loyalty are influenced by the image that users have of the provider before the service encounter (see figure 1). Perceived image, considered a mental representation of the provider's capabilities, "moulds" the user's expectations of a tourist service (Bigné, Sánchez, and Sánchez, 2001). In other words, the user will anticipate the service's performance on the basis of his/her attitude towards the provider. In the travel agency context, Rodríguez Del Bosque, San Martín and Collado (2006) empirically proved that image is an expectations-generating factor of users (image → comparison standard).

On the other hand, intangibility and risk are two characteristics frequently associated with services, and particularly, tourism (Bowen and Clarke, 2002). In this context, users might have difficulties in evaluating their service experiences in a reliable way. These difficulties, as well as the user's confidence in his/her own mental representation of the provider, would justify the role of image as an important conductor of tourist service satisfaction (image → satisfaction). In past research, tourist satisfaction was found to be positively influenced by image (Bigné, Sánchez, and Sánchez, 2001). Lastly, a positive relationship between image and loyalty has been established in tourism research too (Bigné, Sánchez, and Sánchez, 2001; Court and Lupton, 1997). In the present study, it is defended that users with a positive image of the tourist service provider will continue their interactions with this provider regardless of the level of satisfaction during a particular encounter (image ➜ loyalty). Therefore, image should be considered by the provider as a powerful instrument for generating user loyalty, one of the main challenges of organizations today.

METHODOLOGY

Qualitative and quantitative research was developed in order to fully explore interrelationships among variables in the proposed model. In the qualitative phase, four in-depth interviews were carried out with travel agency managers. Additionally, one focus group was set up with travellers of a different age, gender and occupation. This qualitative research helped to define the quantitative phase, i.e. survey design and data collection, in a more reliable way.

DATA COLLECTION

Empirical research was carried out in several urban areas in the north of Spain. The target population was constituted of users of travel agencies. The sample was selected by a quota method, considering the urban areas in the north of Spain and market share of the travel agencies. A questionnaire was personally administered to each subject after they had completed their visit to the travel agency. The interviewed customers were selected on the basis of a convenience method. Consequently, participants were not conscious of their participation in the research until they had finished their visit to the travel agency. In addition, the interviews were not observed by another potential participant. As a result, independence between observations is assured. The final sample was 380 valid responses, representing a sampling error in the case of an infinite population (the size of the population is not available) of 5.13% for a confidence level of 95.5% ($p=q=0.5$). The data was gathered during 2003.

MEASURES

The measurement of the variables that were included in the model is detailed in the appendix. Predictive and ideal expectations are defined on the basis of the study completed by Ngobo (1997). Respondents were asked to indicate their levels of expectations on a 7-point scale (1= very low; 7= very high). Performance reflects the customer's overall service evaluation after the visit to the travel agency. This approximation is used in past research on service satisfaction (Yi and La, 2003). Predictive disconfirmation and ideal disconfirmation were captured by asking the following question: "Did you feel the travel agency was (much) better / (much) worse overall compared with your expectations (predictive or ideal standard)?" (Westbrook and Oliver, 1991; Yi and La, 2003). Disconfirmation was measured with a 7-point Likert scale (1= much worse than expected; 7= much better than expected).

On the other hand, satisfaction was measured with four items. The cognitive and affective components of customer satisfaction are captured through this measurement scale. Following the recommendations of Oliver (1997), a satisfaction anchor was included in the scale too. This measurement of customer satisfaction is applied in a similar way in previous studies on satisfaction (Brady and Robertson, 2001; Van Dolen, De Ruyter, and Lemmink, 2004). Future intentions and word-of-mouth, i.e. two loyalty dimensions, were constructed by items based on measures commonly used in past research (Dabholkar and Thorpe, 1994; Oliver and Swan, 1989; Patterson, Johnson, and Spreng, 1997). Each scale was operationalized on three 7-point bipolar adjective scales. Finally, provider image was measured with a 7-point Likert scale by asking respondents: 'How would you describe the image that you have of this travel agency?' (1= highly unfavourable; 7= highly favourable). According to Bigné, Sánchez, and Sánchez (2001), a single measure is adequate when the aim is to explore the relationship between image and other concepts and not the nature of this psychological variable.

MEASURE VALIDATION

The multi-item scales i.e. satisfaction, future intentions and word-of-mouth– were validated through a confirmatory factorial analysis (CFA) with EQS for Windows 6.1, one of the most widely used Structural Equation Modelling programs. The Cronbach's Alpha and the composite reliability coefficient are higher than the recommended value of 0.7 (Bagozzi and Yi, 1988), thus confirming the reliability of the scales. With regard to the convergent validity, all indicators are significant and their standardized lambda coefficients exceed 0.5, justifying the convergent validity of the scales (Steenkamp and Van Trijp, 1991). Finally, discriminant validity is checked by constructing the confidence interval for the correlation coefficient between pairs of latent variables (Anderson and Gerbing, 1988). None of the intervals includes unity, thus confirming the discriminant validity of the measurement scales. These results demonstrate empirically the correct definition of the measures proposed for satisfaction, future intentions and word-of-mouth.

RESULTS

Estimation of the proposed model was made through a path analysis with EQS for Windows 6.1[1]. Results are shown in table 2. The goodness-of-fit statistics exceed or stand very close to recommended values. Therefore, these results demonstrate an adequate fit of the proposed factorial structure.

---

[1] Previously, satisfaction, future intentions and word of mouth were calculated as the average response to the items confirmed in the CFA.

Table 2. Results of the estimated model

		Ideal expect.	Predictive expect.	Ideal disconf.	Predictive disconf.	Satisfaction	Future intentions	Word-of-mouth
Independent Variables	Provider image	-0.04 [a]	0.32***			0.39***	0.60***	0.53***
	Ideal expectations			0.13***		-0.03		
	Predictive expectations				0.30***	0.11***		
	Performance			0.15***	0.50***	0.30***		
	Ideal disconfirmation					-0.08**		
	Predictive disconfirmation					0.13***		
	Satisfaction					-	0.28***	0.34***
		R^2=0.00	R^2=0.10	R^2=0.13	R^2=0.42	R^2=0.60	R^2=0.69	R^2=0.65
		$\chi^2(18)$=172.07 (P=0.000) BBNFI=0.92 BBNNFI=0.86 GFI=0.93 AGFI=0.88 SRMR=0.07						

[a] Standardized estimations; *** $p<0.01$; ** $p<0.05$

Firstly, the relationships between variables of the customer satisfaction process are explained. With regard to the ideal disconfirmation, both ideal expectations (0.13; p<0.01) and performance (0.15; p<0.01) have a positive impact on this variable. On the other hand, the effects of predictive expectations (0.30; p<0.01) and performance (0.50; p<0.01) on predictive disconfirmation are also significant and positive. In both cases, the influence of expectations on disconfirmation is contrary to the hypothesized effect. This may be due to the retrospective measurement of expectations (after the tourist service encounter), a result also found by Oliver and Burke (1999). As a result, service experience may affect expectations (not only disconfirmation), causing a positive correlation between both judgments.

Satisfaction is extensively explained in the model (R2=0.60). As hypothesized, predictive expectations (0.11; p<0.01), performance (0.30; p<0.01) and predictive disconfirmation (0.30; p<0.01) have a positive impact on customer satisfaction. On the contrary, the relationship between ideal expectations and satisfaction is not significant (-0.03; p>0.10) and the influence of ideal disconfirmation is contrary to the hypothesized effect (-0.08; p<0.05). However, ideal expectations have an indirect negative effect on customer satisfaction through the ideal disconfirmation. Finally, satisfaction has a positive effect on loyalty dimensions, future intentions (0.28; p<0.01) and word-of-mouth (0.34; p<0.01).

Finally, the influence of provider image on the customer satisfaction process is also analyzed in the proposed model. Provider image has a significant and positive influence on predictive expectations (0.32; p<0.01), satisfaction (0.39; p<0.01), future intentions (0.60; p<0.01) and word-of-mouth (0.53; p<0.01). Consequently, it is empirically demonstrated in this research that provider image plays an important role in all the stages of the customer satisfaction process, i.e. formation of expectations, satisfaction and customer loyalty

CONCLUSIONS AND MANAGERIAL IMPLICATIONS

Predictive expectations and ideal standard are simultaneously employed by users in the evaluations of tourist services. However, the effects of these comparison standards on customer satisfaction are very different. The influence of predictive expectations on satisfaction is direct and indirect, whereas the effect of ideal expectations on satisfaction is only through disconfirmation judgment. Therefore, the function of expectations in satisfaction formation may depend on the type of standard. For predictive expectations, the customer's satisfaction with a tourist service is guided by two effects, assimilation and contrast; for ideal, it is dominated by the contrast phenomenon (expectations act only as a basis for comparison). Finally, an interesting effect is the negative influence of ideal disconfirmation on customer satisfaction. It can be explained on the basis of the ideal point concept, which is similar to the ideal expectations. According to Ngobo (1997), the ideal point represents the "ideal or optimal" amount of an attribute. When a performance is greater or lower that the ideal point, users will be disappointed. In line with it, the greater the ideal disconfirmation (more discrepancy between performance and ideal expectations), the lower the level of customer satisfaction.

Image plays a significant role in all stages of the customer satisfaction process. On the one hand, a favourable image of the service provider will positively influence the individual's beliefs (or predictive expectations) of a future encounter. However, ideal standard is not influenced by provider image. This is reasonable since the ideal standard is associated with the wants of individuals (Zeithaml, Berry, and Parasuraman, 1993) and predictive expectations with the signals of service quality –e.g. perceived image of a provider–. On the other hand, it is extremely interesting that provider image is the main determinant of both satisfaction and customer loyalty. For building their satisfaction judgments, users have more confidence in perceived image of the provider than in their service evaluations. The high levels of intangibility and risk associated with the evaluations of tourist services would justify the strong confidence of individuals in their prior attitudes (or images) towards the provider. In addition, it is demonstrated that a positive image of the service provider will reinforce the individual's commitment to return in the future and recommend the provider to others, regardless of the level of satisfaction during a specific encounter.

With regard to the managerial implications, it is necessary to emphasize that knowledge of the customer satisfaction process will help in the management of service encounters. First, tourist service managers should not only make a great effort to provide a quality service (high performance), but also to appropriately deal with customer expectations. Given that ideal expectations are not controllable by the provider, the provider will have to control the predictive expectations of users. More concretely, providers should communicate expectations consistent with high performance. In this context, image should be considered as a key factor in order to communicate favourable expectations of the service provider. If this is achieved by the provider, first, this provider will have a privileged position compared with the alternatives evoked by users in their choice processes, and next, expectations will positively contribute to user satisfaction.

Given the role of provider image as a factor contributing to generate satisfaction and customer loyalty, service providers should be appropriately communicated and positioned in the target markets in order to project a positive image of the organization and their tourist services. An identification of the provider's capabilities, as well as an accurate definition of the target groups will be necessary to achieve this purpose. In particular, a positive image of the provider would add value to the service experience, and therefore, would contribute to customer satisfaction with the tourist service. In addition, it is recognized that customer retention is the main challenge in today's competitive landscape. A positive image of the provider is the basis for achieving the user's commitment, which will be constituted not only of the intention to continue the relationship with the provider, but also of the word-of-mouth communication.

Finally, some limitations and additional directions for further research are mentioned. The main limitation of this study is the use of a cognitive approach to explore customer satisfaction with tourist services. A cognitive-affective approach, which would incorporate cognitions and emotions derived from a service experience, may help to explain the customer satisfaction process more effectively. In relation to further research, it is extremely interesting to examine the role of other comparison standards in the satisfaction process, e.g. desires, equity or experience-based norms. Additionally, it would be necessary to study how relevance of the comparison standards in service evaluations is affected by individual factors –e.g. past experience or customer involvement– and/or contextual factors –e.g. product intangibility–. Lastly, it is required an additional effort to explore the phenomenon of dynamic expectations in the customer satisfaction process.

REFERENCES

Anderson, J.C., and Gerbing, D.W. (1988). Structural Equation Modelling in Practice: A Review and Recommended Two–Step Approach. *Psychological Bulletin*, 103 (3), 411-423.

Andreassen, T.W. (2000). Antecedents to Satisfaction with Service Recovery. *European Journal of Marketing*, 34 (1/2), 156-175.

Andreassen, T.W., and Lindestad, B. (1998). Customer Loyalty and Complex Services. The Impact of Corporate Image on Quality, Customer Satisfaction and Loyalty for Customers with Varying Degrees of Service Expertise. *International Journal of Service Industry Management*, 9 (1), 7-23.

Bagozzi, R.P., and Yi, Y. (1988). On the Evaluation of Structural of Equation Models. *Journal of the Academy of Marketing Science*, 16 (1), 74-94.

Barich, H., and Kotler, P. (1991). A Framework for Marketing Image Management. *Sloan Management Review*, 32 (2), 94-109.

Bebko, C. P. (2000). Service Intangibility and Its Impact on Consumer Expectations of Service Quality. *Journal of Services Marketing*, 14 (1), 9-26.

Bigné, E., and Andreu, L. (2004). Modelo Cognitivo-Afectivo de la Satisfacción en Servicios de Ocio y Turismo. *Cuadernos de Economía y Dirección de la Empresa*, 21, 89-120.

Bigné, J.E., Sánchez, M.I., and Sánchez, J. (2001). Tourism Image, Evaluation Variables and After Purchase Behaviour: Inter-Relationship. *Tourism Management*, 22, 607-616.

Bitner, M.J. (1990). Evaluating Service Encounters: The Effects of Physical Surroundings and Employee Responses. *Journal of Marketing Research*, 54, 69-82.

Bitner, M.J., Booms, B.H., and Stanfield, M. (1990). The Service Encounter: Diagnosing Favorable and Unfavorable Incidents. *Journal of Marketing*, 54, 71-84.

Boulding, W., Kalra, A., Staelin, R., and Zeithaml, V.A. (1993). A Dynamic Process Model of Service Quality: From Expectations to Behavioral Intentions. *Journal of Marketing Research*, 30, 7-27.

Bowen, D., and Clarke, J. (2002). Reflections on Tourist Satisfaction Research: Past, Present and Future. *Journal of Vacation Marketing*, 8 (4), 297-308.

Brady, M.K., and Robertson, C.J. (2001). Searching for a Consensus on the Antecedent Role of Service Quality and Satisfaction: An Exploratory Cross-National Study. *Journal of Business Research*, 51 (1), 53-60.

Chon, K-S. and Olsen, M.D. (1991). Functional and Symbolic Congruity Approaches to Consumer Satisfaction/Dissatisfaction in Tourism. *Journal of the International Academy of Hospitality Research*, 3, 1-25.

Churchill, G. A., and Surprenant, C. (1982). An Investigation into the Determinants of Customer Satisfaction. *Journal of Marketing Research*, 19, 491-504.

Clow, K.E., Kurtz, D.L., Ozment, J., and Ong, B.S. (1997). The Antecedents of Consumer Expectations of Services: An Empirical Study across Four Industries. *Journal of Services Marketing*, 11 (4), 230-248.

Cote, J.A., Foxman, E.R., and Cutler, B.D. (1989). Selecting an Appropriate Standard of Comparison for Post–Purchase Evaluations. *Advances in Consumer Research*, 16, 502-506.

Court, B., and Lupton, R.A. (1997). Customer Portfolio Development: Modeling Destination Adopters, Inactives, and Rejecters. *Journal of Travel Research*, 36 (1), 35-43.

Dabholkar, P.A., and Thorpe, D.I. (1994). Does Customer Satisfaction Predict Shopper Intentions?. *Journal of Consumer Satisfaction, Dissatisfaction and Complaining Behavior*, 7, 161-171.

Danaher, P.J., and Haddrell, V. (1996). A Comparison of Question Scales Used for Measuring Customer Satisfaction. *International Journal of Service Industry Management*, 7 (4), 4-26.

Devlin, J.F., Gwynne, A.L. and Ennew, C.T. (2002). The Antecedents of Service Expectations. *The Service Industries Journal*, 22 (4), 117-136.

ECSI Technical Committee (1998). European Customer Satisfaction Index: Foundation and Structure for Harmonized National Pilot Projects. *Report prepared for the ECSI Steering Committee*, October.

Erevelles, S., and Leavitt, C. (1992). A Comparison of Current Models of Consumer Satisfaction/Dissatisfaction. *Journal of Consumer Satisfaction, Dissatisfaction and Complaining Behavior*, 5, 104-114.

Forbes, J.D., Tse, D.K., and Taylor, S. (1986). Toward a Model of Consumer Post-Choice Response in Behavior. In R.L. Lutz (Ed.). *Advances in Consumer Research,* 658-661. Ann Arbor, MI, USA: Association for Consumer Research.

Gallarza, M.G., Gil, I., and Calderón, H. (2002). Destination Image: Towards a Conceptual Framework. *Annals of Tourism Research*, 29 (1), 56-78.

Gardial, S.F., Woodruff, R.B., Burns, M.J., Schumann, D.W., and Clemons, S. (1993). Comparison Standards: Exploring Their Variety and the Circumstances Surrounding Their Use. *Journal of Consumer Satisfaction, Dissatisfaction and Complaining Behavior*, 6, 63-73.

Grönroos, C. (1990). *Service Management and Marketing: Managing the Moments of Truth in Service Competition*. Lexington, USA: Lexington Books.

Jun, S., Hyun, Y.J., Gentry, J.W., and Song, C-S. (2001). The Relative Influence of Affective Experience on Consumer Satisfaction under Positive versus Negative Discrepancies. *Journal of Consumer Satisfaction, Dissatisfaction and Complaining Behavior*, 14, 141-153.

Kozak, M., and Rimmington, M. (2000). Tourist Satisfaction with Mallorca, Spain, as an Off-Season Holiday Destination. *Journal of Travel Research*, 38 (3), 260-269.

Kristensen, K., Martensen, A., and Gronholdt, L. (1999). Measuring the Impact of Buying Behaviour on Customer Satisfaction. *Total Quality Management*, 10 (4/5), 602-614.

Liljander, V., and Strandvik, T. (1997). Emotions in Service Satisfaction. *International Journal of Service Industry Management*, 8 (2), 148-169.

Ngobo, P.V. (1997). The Standards Issue: An Accessibility-Diagnosticity Perspective. *Journal of Consumer Satisfaction, Dissatisfaction and Complaining Behavior*, 10, 61-79.

Oliver, R.L. (1987). An Investigation of the Interrelationship between Consumer (Dis)satisfaction and Complaint Reports. *Advances in Consumer Research*, 14, 218-222.

Oliver, R.L. (1997). *Satisfaction: A Behavioral Perspective on the Consumer*. New York, USA: McGraw–Hill.

Oliver, R.L., and Burke, R.R. (1999). Expectation Processes in Satisfaction Formation. *Journal of Service Research*, 1 (3), 196-214.

Oliver, R.L., and Swan, J.E. (1989). Consumer Perceptions of Interpersonal Equity and Satisfaction in Transactions: A Field Survey Approach. *Journal of Marketing*, 53, 21-35.

Patterson, P.G., Johnson, L.W., and Spreng, R.A. (1997). Modelling the Determinants of Customer Satisfaction for Business-to-Business Professional Services. *Journal of the Academy of Marketing Science*, 25 (1), 4-17.

Pieters, R., Koelemeijer, K., and Roest, H. (1995). Assimilation Processes in Service Satisfaction Formation. *International Journal of Service Industry Management*, 6 (3), 17-33.

Prakash, V. and Lounsbury, J.W. (1984). The Role of Expectations in the Determination of Consumer Satisfaction. *Journal of the Academy of Marketing Science*, 12 (3), 1-17.

Rodríguez del Bosque, I., San Martín, H., and Collado, J. (2006). The Role of Expectations in the Consumer Satisfaction Formation Process: Empirical Evidence in the Travel Agency Sector. *Tourism Management*, 27, 410-419.

Santos, J., and Boote, J. (2003). A Theoretical Exploration and Model of Consumer Expectations, Post-Purchase Affective States and Affective Behaviour. *Journal of Consumer Behaviour*, 3 (2), 142-156.

Selnes, F. (1993). An Examination of the Effect of Product Performance on Brand Reputation, Satisfaction and Loyalty. *European Journal of Marketing*, 27 (9), 19-35.

Sherif, M., and Hovland, C.I. (1961). *Social Judgment: Assimilation and Contrast Effects in Communication and Attitude Change*. New Have, CT, USA: Yale University Express.

Shostack, G.L. (1985). Planning the Service Encounter, In J.A. Czepiel, M.R. Solomon and C.F. Surprenant (Eds.), *The Service Encounter* (243-254). New York: Lexington Books.

Singh, J. (1991). Understanding the Structure of Consumers´ Satisfaction Evaluations of Service Delivery. *Journal of the Academy of Marketing Science*, 19 (3), 223-245.

Sivadas, E., and Baker-Prewitt, J.L. (2000). An Examination of the Relationship between Service Quality, Customer Satisfaction, and Store Loyalty. *International Journal of Retail and Distribution Management*, 28 (2), 73-82.

Söderlund, M. (2002). Customer Familiarity and Its Effects on Satisfaction and Behavioral Intentions. *Psychology and Marketing*, 19 (10), 861-879.

Spreng, R.A., and Dixon, A.L. (1992). Alternative Comparison Standards in the Formation of Consumer Satisfaction/Dissatisfaction. In R.P. Leone and V. Kumar (Eds.), *Enhancing Knowledge Development in Marketing* (85-91). Chicago, IL: American Marketing Association.

Spreng, R.A., Mackenzie, S.B., and Olshavsky, R.W. (1996). A Reexamination of the Determinants of Consumer Satisfaction. *Journal of Marketing*, 60, 15-32.

Steenkamp, J.B., and Van Trijp, H.C.M. (1991). The Use of LISREL in Validating Marketing Constructs. *International Journal of Research in Marketing*, 8, 283-299.

Szymanski, D.M., and Henard, D.H. (2001). Customer Satisfaction: A Meta-Analysis of the Empirical Evidence. *Journal of the Academy of Marketing Science*, 29 (1), 16-35.

Tam, J. L. M. (2005). Examining the Dynamics of Consumer Expectations in a Chinese Context. *Journal of Business Research*, 58 (6), 777-786.

Tse, D.K., and Wilton, P.C. (1988). Models of Consumer Satisfaction Formation: An Extension. *Journal of Marketing Research*, 25, 204-212.

Van Dolen, W., De Ruyter, K., and Lemmink, J. (2004). An Empirical Assessment of the Influence of Customer Emotions and Contact Employee Performance on Encounter and Relationship Satisfaction. *Journal of Business Research*, 57 (4), 437-444.

Weigelt, K., and Camerer, C. (1988). Reputation and Corporate Strategy: A Review of Recent Theory and Applications. *Strategic Management Journal*, 9, 443-454.

Westbrook, R.A., and Oliver, R.L. (1991). The Dimensionality of Consumption Emotion Patterns and Consumer Satisfaction. *Journal of Consumer Research*, 18, 84-91.

Wirtz, J., Mattila, A.S., and Tan, R.L. (2000). The Moderating Role of Target-Arousal on the Impact of Affect in Satisfaction – An Examination in the Context of Service Experiences. *Journal of Retailing*, 76 (3), 347-365.

Woodruff, R.B., Cadotte, E.R., and Jenkins, R.L. (1983). Modeling Consumer Satisfaction Processes Using Experience–Based Norms. *Journal of Marketing Research*, 20, 296-304.

Yi, Y. (1990). A Critical Review of Consumer Satisfaction. In V.A. Zeithaml (Ed.), *Review of Marketing* (68-123). Chicago, IL: American Marketing Association.

Yi, Y. (1993). The Determinants of Consumer Satisfaction: The Moderating Role of Ambiguity. *Advances in Consumer Research*, 20, 502-506.

Yi, Y., and La, S. (2003). The Moderating Role of Confidence in Expectations and the Asymmetric Influence of Disconfirmation on Consumer Satisfaction. *The Service Industries Journal*, 23 (5), 20-47.

Yu, Y-T., and Dean, A. (2001). The Contribution of Emotional Satisfaction to Consumer Loyalty. *International Journal of Service Industry Management*, 12 (3), 234-250.

Yüksel, A., and Yüksel, F. (2001). Comparative Performance Analysis: Tourists´ Perceptions of Turkey Relative to Other Tourist Destinations. *Journal of Vacation Marketing*, 7 (4), 333-355.

Zeithaml, V.A., Berry, L.L., and Parasuraman, A. (1993). The Nature and Determinants of Customer Expectations of Service. *Journal of the Academy of Marketing Science*, 21 (1), 1-12.

APPENDIX: MEASURES

Predictive expectations (1= very low; 7= very high)
Given your experience and information of this travel agency, What level of service expects to receive?

Ideal expectations (1= very low; 7= very high)
Given the best service performance that could be imagined, What level of service expects to receive?

Performance (1= very bad; 7= very good)
After your visit, How good did you feel the travel agency was overall?

Predictive disconfirmation (1= much worse than expected; 7= much better than expected)
Given your experience and information of this travel agency, Did you feel the travel agency was (much) better / (much) worse overall compared with your expectations?

Ideal disconfirmation (1= much worse than expected; 7= much better than expected)
Given the best service performance that could be imagined, Did you feel the travel agency was (much) better / (much) worse overall compared with your ideal expectations?

Satisfaction (1=strongly dissagree; 7=strongly agree)	
SAT1	I'm very satisfied with the service of this travel agency
SAT2	This travel agency exceeded my expectations
SAT3	I think I did the right thing when I decided to use this travel agency
SAT4	I'm really pleased with my choice of this travel agency

FUTURE INTENTIONS									
If you require the service of a travel agency in the near future, would you select the same travel agency?									
FUT1	Not probable	-3	-2	-1	0	1	2	3	Very probable
FUT2	Impossible	-3	-2	-1	0	1	2	3	Very possible
FUT3	No chance	-3	-2	-1	0	1	2	3	Certain

WORD-OF-MOUTH									
Would you recommend this travel agency to other people?									
WOM1	Not probable	-3	-2	-1	0	1	2	3	Very probable
WOM2	Impossible	-3	-2	-1	0	1	2	3	Very possible
WOM3	No chance	-3	-2	-1	0	1	2	3	Certain

Provider image (1= highly unfavourable; 7= highly favourable)
How would you describe the image that you have of this travel agency?

In: Tourist Satisfaction and Complaining Behavior
Editor: Atila Yüksel

ISBN 978-1-60456-002-2
© 2008 Nova Science Publishers, Inc.

Chapter 7

WHO DETERMINES SATISFACTION: RESEARCHER OR THE RESEARCHED?

Fisun Yüksel and Atila Yüksel
Adnan Menderes University, Turkey

INTRODUCTION

Customer satisfaction is an important topic both for researchers and managers. It is likely that a high level of customer satisfaction can lead to increases in repeat patronage among current customers and aid customer recruitment by enhancing an organisation's market reputation (Augustyn and Ho, 1998; Weber, 1997). Successfully being able to judge customers' satisfaction levels and to apply that knowledge is imperative to establish and maintain a long-term relationship with customers and long-term competitiveness (Henning-Thurau and Klee, 1997). Recent studies have shown that a dissatisfied customer never returns, and repeated purchase is directly related to company cash flows, as getting a new customer costs more than to keep an existing one.

Given its vital role in the profitability of hospitality and tourism organizations, one should not be surprised that a great deal of research has been devoted to investigating the process by which customers form judgments about a service experience (Yuksel and Rimmington, 1998). There is constant debate on how one can and ought to measure customer satisfaction. In an attempt to provide theoretical explanations of customer satisfaction, the majority of previous researchers seem to have focused largely on the conceptual issues and underlying processes of satisfaction. As a consequence, several frameworks have been developed to gauge the concept, however, no consensus has been reached on which framework is best suited to assess customer satisfaction. Some of these frameworks specify one or more standards for respondents to consider when forming a response (e.g., the Servqual, the Expectancy-Disconfirmation Paradigm, the Value-Percept model, the Congruity model, the Desires Congruency, the Experience-Based Norms model), while others do not include measurement of any particular comparison standard (the Performance only model). These frameworks have been widely utilised in researching consumer satisfaction within numerous tourism and hospitality contexts. Duke and Persia (1996), Tribe and Snaith (1998), Fick and Ritchie (1991), and Saleh and Ryan (1992) used the gap or the Servqual model, developed by Parasuraman et al. (1988), while Pizam and Milman (1993), Whipple and Thach (1988), Reisinger and Waryszack (1996), and Weber (1997) applied Oliver's (1980, 1997) expectancy-disconfirmation model or its variants.

Self-complete survey instruments (questionnaires) in which respondents are asked to fill in a pre-determined set of questions are probably the most popular among scholars studying customer satisfaction (Peterson and Wilson, 1992). The popularity of self-complete questionnaire derives from its directness, ease of administration and interpretation, and standardization and statistical generality (Peterson and Wilson, 1992). While it is the most popular tool in measuring satisfaction, the use of self-complete questionnaires has a number of limitations (Orams and Page, 2001). Respondents may be forced to rate or rank questions to which they may not know the answer and some respondents may not understand a question in the way it is intended by the researcher (Tease, 1993). Question wording, format and context can profoundly influence participants' reports (Schwarz and Oyserman, 2001). Responses to a survey item may depend on its position and neighbouring items in the questionnaire (Drew and Bolton, 1991; Schwarz and Oyserman, 2001). The number of response positions in any question scale may influence respondents from different cultures differently (Pizam and Ellis, 1999).

The questionnaire length is another issue. The research instruments should be as short and unimposing as possible due to the special circumstances and nature of tourist populations under study. Lengthy questionnaires, which ask everything that might turn out to be interesting, should be avoided, as they are demoralizing for both respondents and researchers (Moser and Kalton, 1989). Orams and Page (2000) note that it may be difficult to recruit tourists, whose main motivations are enjoyment and relaxation, into working on a lengthy questionnaire.

Last but not least, self-complete questionnaires are incapable of capturing the consumer voice (Bowen, 2001). In self-complete questionnaires, overall satisfaction process is constructed in large part by the researcher and it may not capture customers' real expectations, preferences or attitudes (Swan and Bowers, 1998). It is possible that attributes included in a research instrument may be unimportant or irrelevant to customers (Pizam and Ellis, 1999). Different customers may have different perceptions about what contributes to a satisfactory experience, and thus measurement of customer satisfaction would be most valid when based on the customer perception of personally selected attributes (Kreck, 1998).

Measuring tourist satisfaction is not an option but an essential part of destination management information system. Tourism and hospitality managers who measure satisfaction against what customer really want would seem to receive far more powerful data to act upon than do present surveys where things are checked off from a list that may or may not have relevant items on them (Dillman, 1997, cf. Kreck, 1998). This study uses a modified version of the research instrument originally developed by Kreck (1998) in order to (1) identify critical service attributes that are important to customers, (2) assess their current performance, and (3) benchmark how Turkey performs on these attributes compared to one of its competitors – Spain - in the Mediterranean Rim. Compared to over-theorized, complex and costly measurement tools, this modified research instrument appears to be tractable and it does not require sophisticated knowledge of statistical techniques.

This chapter is organized into three sections. The first section presents some of the problems inherent in developing and administering questionnaires. It should be noted that the chapter does not seek to be a comprehensive review of diverse issues relating to survey-based research. It rather aims to raise some of the practical and methodological issues. The research instrument is introduced next and data collection is explained. The findings of the study are presented and recommendations are provided.

MEASUREMENT TOOLS: LIMITATIONS

The majority of previous satisfaction studies, with few exceptions (e.g., Bowen, 2001), have employed quantitative approach, in which close-ended questions in relation to destination attributes are rated or ranked. These fixed-format devices are receiving criticism since they might not capture attributes that are really important to customer satisfaction. Dann (1996) argues that since the researcher rather than the researched usually generates the checklist of items in a visitor survey, there is a corresponding likelihood that subjective definitions of participants may be overlooked and replaced by so called objective measures: "Yet, while the latter can yield statistical reliability, they may do so at the expense of validity, given that the way situations are defined ultimately associated with the perceived reality of effect" (Dann, 1996, p. 43).

Dann, Nash and Pearce (1988) point out that tourism researchers may be sometimes insufficiently aware of the possibility of collecting invalid data: "Nowhere is the likelihood of gathering invalid data greater than in tourism motivational studies. Yet cliché replies, while usually masking deeper realities, are often taken to form the basis for the entire marketing of a destination" (Dann et al. 1988, p. 16). Similarly, destination image researchers argue that unless considerable effort is expended in the initial design stages, attribute lists may be incomplete by failing to incorporate all of the relevant functional and psychological characteristics (Pearce, 1988; Echtner and Ritchie, 1993). This may result from differences between the sample of subjects involved in attribute elicitation research phase and the sample involved in actual research. The question in point is that whether attributes considered relevant by a sample involved in the attribute elicitation phase would be considered relevant by, and applicable to, a wider sample of people, probably with different personality, culture, situational constraints and so on. Krippendorf (1987) argues that many things remain hidden sub-consciousness and cannot be brought into light by simple questions. Nisbett and Wilson (1977) report that people are often able to provide answers to questions about their cognitive processes, but researchers should treat these answers as socially acceptable account, not reliable indicators of their mental functioning. According to the cognitive psychology perspective, people may not reliably report on the processes, which lie behind the content of their thoughts (e.g. what mixtures of factors motivated them to come, what combination of circumstances lead them to a particular decision).

Researchers are advised to follow and document the process of scale development to assure that the scale accurately measures what it is supposed to measure and the scale can be used confidently by researchers in future studies and by practitioners as a real-world measure (Hensley, 1999). Researchers have proposed various frameworks for detailing scale development processes. These frameworks appear to have several strengths, as well as, limitations.

SCALE DEVELOPMENT

Several factors must be given special attention in developing and evaluating scales: response bias, ease of use and administration, respondent interpretation and understanding, and actionability of results (Devlin, Dong and Brown, 1992). Above all, however, a good scale is one that is reliable and valid. Churchill (1979) suggested an eight-step procedure that needs to be followed when developing measures of reliable and valid marketing constructs. This procedure has gained a growing approval predominantly from researchers in the marketing literature (Getty and Thomson, 1994).

The first step in these procedures involves specifying the domain of the construct. That is, "the researcher must be exacting in delineating what is included in the definition and what is excluded" (Churchill, 1979, p. 67). The use of different definitions makes it difficult to compare and accumulate findings (Smith, 1999). The second step is to generate items, which capture the domain as specified. The item generation stage is to ensure that questionnaire items have content validity and they capture the specific domain of interest yet contain no extraneous content (Hensley, 1999; Hinkin, Tracey and Enz 1997). Techniques such as literature searches, experience surveys, and insight stimulating examples are exercised at this stage (Churchill, 1979). After the data are gathered, the stability of the scales should be measured. Reliability measures and factor analysis are frequently recommended as part of this process (Hinkin et al. 1997). At this stage, the researcher needs to scrutinise the internal consistency of the set of items developed in the previous stage. The main objective of this stage is to retain (or drop) the items that are effective (ineffective) in capturing the construct under investigation. The scale should then be evaluated for its content validity, construct validity and predictive validity (Churchill, 1979). Following the reduction of the scale and the assurance of its internal consistency (reliability), the next stage involves collecting new data in order to assess the reliability and validity of the refined scale.

A recent study questions Churchill's scale development model and provides empirical evidence in relation to limitations in development of measures utilising such processes (Smith, 1999, p. 109): "There are, however, many problems involved in the adoption of Churchill's framework. Some are endemic to the paradigm itself; whereas, others arise through researchers' adaptations of the recommended stages". Smith's research shows that the criteria for establishing reliability and validity may be more indicative of measurement error than of evidence that the scale is an effective measure of the underlying construct. The first set of problems relates to the statistical manipulation of data and the reliability and validity of the measure (Smith, 1999). According to Smith, important items may be deleted in scale purification and high alpha values may indicate deficiencies rather than superior qualities of a scale (Smith, 1999, p. 117): "These deficiencies may include problems of scale content, such as duplicative items or problems of data attenuation". High internal consistency for the total scale brings up the question of why there should be identifiable factors within it (Smith, 1999). The procedure for the deletion of items can also have implications on the scale integrity. The concern for high alpha values in scale purification process, which emphasise internal consistency, may result in deleting items that are important to customers (Smith, 1999). Smith further argues that different items would be dropped from the scale according to the measurement scale adopted (see Smith, 1999 for more details).

A MORE CUSTOMER-FOCUSED APPROACH

These and other limitations suggest that measurement of satisfaction may be less than precise, possibly confounded with other variables, subject to considerable methodological contamination, and likely to be reflective of numerous factors other than those explicitly incorporated into measuring devices (Peterson andWilson, 1992). Customer satisfaction is simply what the customer says it is. Different customers may have different perceptions about what contributes to a satisfactory experience, and thus measurement of customer satisfaction would be most valid when based on the consumer's perception of personally selected attributes (Kreck, 1998). There is a need for measuring customer satisfaction that includes exclusively respondent-generated attributes, which would be individualized for each particular context and this instrument should have limited number of attributes in order to reduce the pressure of completing questionnaires (Kreck, 1998). Yuksel and Yuksel (2001a) criticise that the trustworthiness of customer satisfaction research results is generally attributed to the complexity of the measurement techniques used in a research: "However, transforming customer satisfaction information from mere numbers to actionable data will not be achieved by increasing the sophistication of the measurement technique and using elegant statistical analyses. A more pragmatic strategy by using simple research techniques, containing a limited number of questions in order to reduce the pressure of completing questionnaires, and establishing the goal of the company from measuring to managing customer satisfaction should be adopted" (p. 106).

Kreck has recently proposed a research instrument that includes two categories of questions; (1) statement and ranking of the three most important service attributes to the respondent and (2) assessment of performance delivered on these attributes. A major strength of this approach is that it allows respondents to freely state service attributes significant to them instead of being restricted to answer to a pre-established set of attribute questions determined by the researcher. Managerial usefulness of this instrument could be improved by inclusion of an additional question that elicits the respondent's evaluation of current performance relative to other organizations that are directly or indirectly in competition (Yuksel and Yuksel, 2001b). Inclusion of this question is practical, as the tourist is likely to interact with various components of the destination products, weight up these experiences, and form an overall impression of the entire experience (Pizam, Neumann and Reichel, 1978). It is also likely that in their evaluation, they will make implicit or explicit comparisons between the facilities, attractions, and service standards of alternative destinations, as the majority of tourists have experiences with other destinations (Laws, 1995). Hence, it is possible that the extent and nature of tourists' past/recent experiences with similar or different destination(s) may set the standard against which the present experience is judged (Cadotte, Woodruff and Jenkins, 1987; Mazursky, 1989; Woodruff, Cleanop, Schumn, Godial and Burns, 1991). A negative (positive) discrepancy between what other destination(s) offered and what the current destination was able to render may lead to the feeling of dissatisfaction

(satisfaction). It may influence future travel decisions, as well as the image held for the destination.

RESEARCH INSTRUMENT AND DATA COLLECTION

A modified version of the measurement tool, originally developed by Kreck, was used in this study in order to identify destination attributes that tourists consider important, explore how their current destination, in this case Turkey, perform on these attributes and benchmark how Turkey's performance compares to that of Spain - one of Turkey's main competitors in the Mediterranean Rim. Three questions were included in the questionnaire. The first question read: "Based on your experience as a traveller, what are the three most important attributes that come to your mind immediately when visiting a summer holiday destination abroad? Most important attribute…Second…Third…". The second question was: "Based on your present visit, how would you rate Turkey's performance based on the three attributes that are important to you? A seven-point Likert type scale, with poor to excellent boundaries, followed the First, Second and Third most important attributes. The last question read: "How would you compare current performance to that of Spain?". First, Second and Third attributes were followed by a three point better/similar to/worse than scale. Only respondents who visited Spain in the past two years were required to fill in this section. The questionnaire was one-page in length and it was written in German and English. It was self administered to conveniently selected 400 tourists departing from an international airport in Turkey. In sum, this short questionnaire fulfilled four objectives: (1) it is particular to the individual respondent, (2) it expresses respondent's individual importance of items, (3) it is short and evaluates recent experience, and (4) it provides managerially useful comparative information (Kreck, 1998).

RESULTS AND DISCUSSION

A total 400 questionnaires were distributed and 45 of them returned incomplete. Most of the respondents participated in this study were on a two-week package holiday (90%) and hotels were their principal accommodation type (70%). The study sample was consisted of British (61%), Germans (16%), Benelux (10.7%), Scandinavian (4.8%) and others. More than half of the respondents (54%) were first-time visitors. 165 (46%) respondents were male and 190 were female. Respondents represented all age groups (27% were between 25-34, 22% 35-44, 30% 45-54, and 15% were over 55). 162 of the respondents stated that they had visited Spain in the past two years. The analysis identified 39 important attributes (Table 1). The researcher combined 39 attributes into eleven factors. After completing this task, an independent judge then sorted attributes based on eleven categories provided by the researcher. The agreement rate was 92 percent, which provided evidence for reliability for the categories established in the initial sorting process. Those cases on which consensus was not achieved initially, the researchers reread and recategorised the attributes. Consistent with Kreck's (1998) approach, "Most Important" was assigned three points each, "Second Important" two points each and "Third Important" one point each (Table 2).

Table 1. Destination attributes – verbatim details

Environment, Beaches and Climate: natural environment, scenic beauty, uncongested beaches, seawater quality, beach safety, hot weather, suitable temperature

Activities and Entertainment: entertainment, quality of tours and excursions, water sports, interesting places to visit, activities of interest

Hospitality: local hospitality and friendliness, non-exploitative attitude, authentic culture

Accommodation: location, ease of access to nearby restaurants and beaches, water and power supply, accommodation services

Services: staff responsiveness, timeliness and efficiency, consistent quality, check in checkout at the airport

Transportation Quality and Traffic Safety: quality of roads, quality of public transport, traffic safety

Hygiene: cleanliness of public facilities, staff hygiene, food hygiene

Food: variety of restaurants, local food, familiar dishes, interesting food

Prices: reasonable prices, value for money

Safety: destination safety

Shopping: shopping facilities, hassle free shopping, quality purchases

IMPORTANT ATTRIBUTES

Respondents in this study frequently named pleasant environment, beaches and climate as the most important attribute that they seek when visiting a summer holiday destination (Table 2). Consistent with findings of previous studies (see Pizam, Neuman and Reichel (1978), Lounsburry and Hoopes (1985)), this finding suggests that travelers are likely to spend their holiday time and money in environments that prompt a feeling of pleasure and that they will avoid unpleasant environments.

Table 2. Most important attributes and their frequency of mention

Rank	Attributes	Most important	2nd important	3rd important	Total points
1	Environment, Beaches and Climate	52	41	23	261
2	Activities and Entertainment	46	28	34	228
3	Hospitality	40	32	30	214

Table 2. Most important attributes and their frequency of mention (continued)

Rank	Attributes	Most important	2nd important	3rd important	Total points
4	Accommodation:	44	22	30	206
5	Services	38	18	41	191
6	Hygiene	29	33	33	186
7	Food	34	28	22	180
8	Transportation Quality	24	29	37	167
9	Safety	21	31	33	158
10	Prices	15	24	39	132
11	Shopping	12	11	29	87

An interesting verbatim detail to notice under environment and beaches is "the crowd". Perhaps tourists participated in this study experienced difficulties in finding available space and they felt uncomfortable with the noise as a result of the crowd. Proper management of tourists' beach experience is essential, as beaches are the places where summer tourists spend much of their vacation. Lawson and Thyne (2001), in a study on how destination sets are defined, particularly with respect to the reason for choosing not to visit a destination, found crowd as one of the most important reasons for avoidance. Another interesting attribute to notice under environment, beaches and climate is "beach safety". Perhaps respondents who became subjects of petty crimes named this attribute most. Destination management has to ensure that security measures are put on beaches in order to increase safety perceptions of visitors. Another frequently sought attribute, "seawater quality" (Table 2), appearing under environment, beaches and climate, sends an important message to resort managers that it should be assessed periodically. Measures to maintain and improve the seawater quality should be strictly observed and relevant information should be provided for users. Pleasant weather was another much sought attribute. As in the case of seawater quality, provision of information about high and low temperatures, expected changes in weather conditions and pollen times will help tourists to prepare themselves (Kreck, 1998).

Activities and entertainment received the second highest ranking (Table 2). This is not a surprising finding considering that escaping from home environment and visiting new and exciting places are the two main motivators of pleasure travelers (Iso–Ahola, 1982) and that the majority of respondents in this study were relatively young. Activities and entertainment are considered essential to release the tension arising from constraints and the monologue of daily routines. Hospitality was another much sought attribute by the respondents in this study (Table 2). This is a consistent finding with that of other tourist satisfaction studies. Friendliness toward travelers was reported to be an important criterion in destination selection (Ross and Iso-Ahola, 1991, 1992; Ryan, 1995). Hu and Ritchie (1993) identified local people's attitude as one of the factors, which could significantly contribute to the attractiveness of a tourism destination. Tourist satisfaction studies reported that holiday satisfaction did not only come from beautiful sights but also from the behavior one encounters (Ohja, 1982). Authentic local culture is another important attribute that shapes tourists' experiences. Authentic local culture and customs can provide a rich experimental tapestry for the visiting tourists (Cohen, 1988). The respondents' concern about "non-exploitative attitude" under hospitality sends an important message to resort managers. 34 tourists specifically named commercialization out of 355 total participants as an important consideration. Some written comments indicated double pricing exercised by vendors (i.e., different pricing for tourists and for locals). Commercialisation may be considered as a typical consequence of tourism development, however it holds the potential to mar enjoyment of the holiday and curb future business.

Perhaps not surprisingly, accommodation was another attribute that was considered very important by the respondents in this study. The high ranking of accommodation quality in this study and in other satisfaction studies suggests that physically and psychologically comforting accommodation facilities are instrumental in summer holidays. Emergence of situational factors (e.g., location and access to nearby restaurants, bars, and beaches) among the most often sought attributes sends a clear message to managers. Tourists want "comfort" (Kreck, 1998). The service quality delivered in accommodation facilities, responsiveness of service personnel, accurate billing, safety, cleanliness and facilities for children are frequently mentioned by the respondents as other important qualities sought in accommodation. Emergence of responsiveness of accommodation personnel as an important attribute shows that personnel and customer contact is relatively high in resort hotels. Tourists expect timely solutions to their complaints and problems. This conveys important implications for human resources management in lodging facilities: not only personnel in high-customer contact areas (e.g., reception, restaurants, etc) should have communication skills but also they should be empowered to address customer problems when they occur. Another interesting attribute to notice in the verbatim detail under "accommodation" is "water and power supply". Infrastructure in a destination is part of the destination tourist product that can factor into the visitors' trip experience (Choy, 1992). It may be that respondents in this study might have had power cuts during their stay and this factor became important in their evaluation. Delivery failures on water and power supply may cause dissatisfaction but performing more than adequate may not be noticed and thus rewarded by tourists.

Consistent with previous tourist satisfaction research, service quality appeared among the attributes that are highly important. Different from previous studies, a number of tourists (n. 18) in this study frequently mentioned consistency of quality as an important attribute. Perhaps, tourists in this study experienced inconsistencies in the quality or quantity of the same service/product at different times (e.g., dishes are not prepared consistently over time). The same quality should be offered each time the establishment is visited. Efficiency of services is another most often named attribute under the "services" dimension. Time spent at tourist facilities (e.g., restaurants) is an important issue for tourists. One of the explanations for this may be that tourists are on holiday and they want to use the time effectively to fulfill as many holiday aspirations as possible within the constraints of their holiday time. Tourists in this study often wanted efficiency in airport services. The airport service encounter may play part in tourist holiday evaluations, as it is generally the initial and the last experience the tourist has with the destination (Laws, 1995).

Emergence of restaurants among the most often mentioned attributes shows that tourists want enjoyable and memorable restaurant experiences. An interesting verbatim detail to notice under food and beverage is "local food" and "familiar food". This may suggest that there might be tourists who have a desire for familiar food, and at the opposite end of the continuum, there might be the tourist who wants to try different cuisine. Another moderately sought attribute by the respondents in this study was transportation quality and traffic safety at destination. The tourist participates in daily domestic traffic as a pedestrian and sometimes as a driver (e.g., sightseeing with a rent-car, jeep tours, etc). The quality of roads and traffic safety thus become two important considerations for tourists while visiting a different destination from their own.

Travel to unfamiliar destinations can increase the risk of health and safety issues. Interestingly, respondents in this study did not rank destination safety among the three much sought destination attributes. Similarly, in another study, safety and security considerations ranked as the least important factor in making a destination choice decision (Norton, 1987). The moderately low ranking of safety in importance appeared in this study should be interpreted with caution. Its rank would have been different had the study been undertaken following an international crisis (e.g., 11 September terrorist attack). The fact that the majority of tourists have already been to Turkey before might have altered their responses.

Visitors to Turkey were reported to be package holidaymakers with relatively low propensity to spend while on holiday (Travel and Tourism Intelligence, 1997). While current tourists in this study mentioned price fairly often, its relative importance suggests that the price was important but it was not the determinant variable (Table 2). Shopping facilities and staff attitude toward shoppers was another attribute that received relatively low importance by the respondents in this study. The verbatim detail under shopping: "hassle free shopping" sends a clear message to resort managers. Tourists expect shopping to be free of staff pestering them to buy things. Harassment is one of the most frequently identified negative experiences reported by travellers in other studies (Albuquerque and McElroy, 2001). For example, when those visiting the island of Barbados were asked in exit surveys what they liked least about their vacation, harassment on the beaches and in the streets, particularly by vendors, consistently topped the list (Albuquerque and McElroy, 2001).

Table 3. Comparison of destination attributes with other studies

Current study	Ministry of Tourism Survey	Kreck (1998)
Environment, beaches, and climate	Lodging	Lodging
Activities and entertainment	Restaurants	Transportation
Hospitality	Internal transport	Activity and
Accommodation	Sanitary conditions	entertainment
Services	Security	Food and beverage
Hygiene	Health services	Friendliness
Food	Service staff	Crime and safety
Transportation quality	General price levels	Information
Safety		Location
Prices		Cleanliness
Shopping		Price
		Surrounding beauty
		Weather

A comparison was made between the attributes mentioned by recent tourists in the present study and two previous studies (Kreck's 1998 and the satisfaction survey used by the Ministry of Tourism (MoT) in Turkey) in order to check if there are any differences (Table 3). It can be noticed that a number of attributes appear on the MoT survey were also mentioned by current tourists and by tourists in Kreck's study: lodging, restaurants, transport, security, cleanliness and price levels. It can also be observed that four attributes are absent from the survey instrument that Turkish Ministry of Tourism (MoT) used in gathering tourist satisfaction information: "environment, beaches and climate" (1st position) in Table 2, "activities and entertainment", "hospitality" and "shopping". The difference between the set of considerations and their order in Kreck's and the present study may be attributed to the subject-related differences (e.g., domestic tourists vs. international tourists). Nevertheless, the difference suggests that managers and researchers need to be cautious in adopting fixed-format research findings to the design of satisfaction improvement programmes.

PERFORMANCE RELATIVE TO OTHER DESTINATIONS

The third question asked respondents to compare the performance of Turkey to that of Spain. 162 respondents, who stated that they had been to Spain for a summer holiday in the past two years, completed this section. Respondents were required to indicate whether the level of performance delivered on the stated attributes that are important to them was better, similar to, or worse than that of Spain. Table 4 presents factor-mean scores and the perceived performance scores relative to Spain. Only two of the eleven attributes – hospitality and prices - were considered to be noticeably better than that of Spain. Similarly, in a study comparing U.S. international pleasure travelers' images of four Mediterranean countries, Baloglu and McCleary (1999) reported hospitality and prices as two of the major strengths of Turkey against two other Mediterranean-based competitors- Italy and Greece.

Table 4. Factor mean scores and their perceived superiority-inferiority

Factors	Grand Mean*	Better	Similar	Worse
Environment, Beaches and Climate	5.66	41	22	15
Activities and Entertainment	5.10	18	34	16
Hospitality	5.75	44	20	7
Accommodation	5.71	14	36	24
Service standards	5.43	34	26	18
Hygiene	5.24	15	25	48
Food	5.63	14	52	32
Transportation and traffic	4.73	14	25	41
Safety	5.96	28	44	26
Prices	5.63	32	15	14
Shopping	4.55	25	25	13

*Based on 7 point poor to excellent scale

A relatively high number of respondents reported that the current level of performance of the remaining attributes was not superior to that of Spain (Table 4). In fact, they were perceived as being similar or inferior. This finding sends an important message to resort managers in Turkey. A high number of tourists perceiving no performance differences between Turkey and one of its main competitors suggest that if Turkey wants to increase its market share and become competitive, she has to improve and differentiate its services. Managers need to ensure that not only the service/product is designed differently to that of competitors, but is perceived to be different as well. It is argued in the literature that there are only a handful of destinations in customer's consideration set (Woodside and Ronkainen, 1980). The tourist will choose the best alternative after subjecting alternative destinations to mental weight evaluation. Unless a differentiation from competitors is achieved, Turkey may find itself in "inert set" of the tourist, which consists of alternatives that the tourist is indifferent toward because they are not perceived as having any particular advantage.

A comparison of figures in Table 4 suggests that just looking at high performance scores may lead to wrong conclusions. For example, the mean scores for accommodation in this study are fairly high (Table 4). The comparative information however shows that a moderately high number of visitors find the current performance to be inferior to that of Spain. Hence, unless competitors' performance is taken on board, high performance scores may lead to management complacency. This finding also sends an important message to Turkish hoteliers. Considering that accommodation ranked third in much sought attribute list and that the majority of these facilities in Turkey are relatively old, it is high time that Turkey upgraded its accommodation facilities to remain competitive.

The majority of respondents found activities and entertainment to be inferior to those in Spain (Table 4). In another study, good nightlife and entertainment appeared as an area on which Turkey was perceived as inferior to both Italy and Greece (Baloglu and McCleary, 1999). Another attribute that received one of the most noticeable "worse than" ratings is the traffic safety and transportation. Poor road conditions, news about frequent domestic traffic accidents and reckless driving on busy touring routes might have contributed to this result. The cleanliness dimension appears to perform relatively poorly in comparison to that of Spain. This finding corresponds with that of Baloglu and McCleary (1999) in which Turkey was found to be inferior to both Greece and Italy on standard hygiene and cleanliness. Table 2 and 4 suggests that not all attributes are viewed as equally important and some of these attributes are found superior, while others are inferior to another main holiday destination. This has important implications for destination management in terms of whether all weaknesses should be corrected or all strengths should be emphasized in marketing messages (Kotler et al, 1993). As not all attributes are viewed equally important, marketers may need to focus on those attribute strengths and weaknesses most likely to affect the perceptions and behaviors of its target market.

CONCLUSION

The credibility of a customer satisfaction measurement tool should not be associated with the complexity of the measurement techniques or number of items that it includes. As Weber (1992: 4) notes, regardless of the degree of a study's sophistication, "the key to its success is in the interpretability of research results and in their use as a pointer for the creation, execution, and evaluation of an appropriate marketing strategy". Increasing the sophistication of the measurement technique and using elaborate statistical analyses may not achieve transforming customer satisfaction information from mere numbers to actionable data. A more pragmatic strategy is to use a simpler research technique, which reduces the pressure of completing questionnaires, and which does not require sophisticated knowledge for data analysis. Easy to use instruments are essential tools for managers in examining tourist satisfaction (Ryan, 1995), as it may be difficult to recruit tourists, whose main motivations are enjoyment and relaxation, into working on a lengthy questionnaire (Orams and Page, 2001). The research instrument presented here is a tool to assists managers accomplish this goal.

This study used the approach, originally proposed by Kreck (1998), which suggests that service quality is perceived when the individual customer determines that make up service quality. Kreck's methodology was modified by inclusion of benchmarking against a competitor in order to provide information for managers to act upon. Thus, the modified instrument fulfils three objectives. It enables understanding of attributes critical to customers, provides managers with information on current performance, and enables them to benchmark their operations against competitors. Findings of this study will be of primary interest to Turkish tourism authorities, and tangentially to other destination authorities. Managers can gather further useful information by examining whether the level of attribute importance attached to the factors differs among tourists from different countries. This instrument will benefit from further tests in different tourism and hospitality areas.

REFERENCES

Albuquerque, K., and McElroy, L. J. (2001). Tourist harassment Barbados survey results. *Annals of Tourism Research*, 28 (2), 477-492.

Augustyn, M., and Ho, K. S. (1998). 'Service quality and tourism'. *Journal of Travel Research*, 37, 71-75.

Baloglu, S., and McCleary, W. K. (1999). U.S. International pleasure travellers' images of four Mediterranean destinations: A comparison of visitors and non-visitors. *Journal of Travel Research*, 38, 144-152.

Bowen, D. (2001). Research on tourist satisfaction and dissatisfaction: Overcoming the limitations of positivist and quantitative approach. *Journal of Vacation Marketing*, 7 (1),31-30.

Cadotte, E. R., Woodruff, R. B., and Jenkins, R. J. (1987). Expectations and norms in models of consumer satisfaction. *Journal of Marketing Research*, 24, 305-314.

Choy, D. J. L. (1992). Life cycle models for Pacific island destinations. *Journal of Travel Research*, 30, 26-31.

Churchill, A. G. Jr. (1979). A paradigm for developing better measures of marketing constructs. *Journal of Marketing Research*, 16, 64-73.

Cohen, E. (1988). Authenticity and commodification in tourism. *Annals of Tourism Research*, 18 (2), 371-386.

Dann, G. D. (1996). Tourists' images of a destination- an alternative analysis. *Journal of Travel and Tourism Marketing*, 15 (1/2), 41-55.

Dann, G., D., Nash., and Pearce, P. (1988). Methodology in tourism research. *Annals of Tourism Research*, 15, 1-28.

Devlin, J.S., Dong, K. H., and Brown, M. (1993). Selecting a scale for measuring quality. *Marketing Research: A magazine of Management and Applications*, 5 (3), 12-17.

Drew, J. H., and Bolton, N. R. (1991). 'The structure of consumer satisfaction, effects of survey measurement'. *Journal of Consumer Satisfaction, Dissatisfaction, and Complaining Behaviour*, 4, 21-31.

Duke, R. C., and Persia, M. A. (1996). Consumer defined dimensions for the escorted tour industry segment, expectations, satisfaction and importance. *Journal of Travel and Tourism Marketing*, 5 (2), 77-99.

Echtner, C. M., and Ritchie, J. R. (1993). The measurement of destination image: An empirical assessment. *Journal of Travel Research*, 31, 3-13.

Fick, G. R., and Ritchie, B. J. R. (1991). Measuring service quality in the travel and tourism industry. *Journal of Travel Research*, 2-9.

Getty, M. J., and Thomson, N. K. (1994). The Relationship between quality, satisfaction, and Recommending Behaviour in Lodging Decisions. *Journal of Hospitality and Leisure Marketing*, 2 (3), 3-22.

Henning-Thurau, T., and Klee, A. (1997). 'The impact of customer satisfaction and relationship quality on customer retention: a critical reassessment and model development'. *Psychology and Marketing*, 14 (8), 737-764.

Hensley, L. R. (1999). A review of operations management studies using scale development techniques. *Journal of Operations Management*, 17, 343-358.

Hinkin, R. T., Tracey, B. J., and Enz, A.C. (1997). Scale construction: developing reliable and valid measurement instruments. *Hospitality Research Journal*, 21 (1), 100-120.

Kotler, P., Haider, D., and Rein, I. (1993). *Marketing Places: Attracting investment, industry, and tourism to cities, states and nations*. New York, USA: The Free Press.

Kreck, A. L. (1998). Service quality: who should determine it? Research and practice. *Journal of International Hospitality, Leisure and Tourism Management*, 1(4), 63-77.

Krippendorf, J. (1987). *The holiday makers; understanding the impact of leisure and travel*. Heinemann: London.

Laws, E. (1995). *Tourist destination management issues, analysis and policies*. Routhledge: London.

Lawson, R., and Thyne, M. (2001). Destination avoidance and inept destination sets. *Journal of Vacation Marketing*, 7 (3), 199-208.

Lounsburry, L. W., and Hoopes, L. L. (1985). An Investigation of factors Associated with Vacation Satisfaction. *Journal of Leisure Research*, 17, 1-13.

Mazursky, D. (1989). Past Experience and Future Tourism Decisions. *Annals of Tourism Research*, 16, 333-344.

Moser, C.A., and Kalton, G. (1989). *Survey methods in social investigations*. Gower Publishing: Aldershot.

Nisbett, R. E., and Wilson, T. D. (1977). Telling more than we know: Verbal reports on mental processes, *Psychological Review*, 84, 231-259.

Norton, G. (1987). Tourism and terrorism. *World Today*, 44.

Ohja, J. M. (1982). Selling Benign Tourism: Case references from Indian scene. *Tourism Recreation Research*, 23-24.

Oliver, L. R. (1997). *Satisfaction a behavioural perspective on the consumer*. The McGraw-Hill Companies, Inc. New York, USA.

Oliver. R. L. (1980). A Cognitive Model of the Antecedents of Satisfaction Decisions. *Journal of Marketing Research*, 17: 46-49.

Orams, B. M., and Page, J. S. (2000). Designing self-reply questionnaires to survey tourists: issues and guidelines for researchers, *Anatolia: An international Journal of Tourism and Hospitality Research*, 11(3), 125-139.

Parasuraman, A., Zeithaml, A. V., and Berry, L. L. (1988). 'Servqual: A Multiple Item Scale for Measuring Consumer Perceptions of Service Quality'. *Journal of Retailing*, 64, 12-40.

Pearce, P. L. (1988). *The Ulysses factor: Evaluating visitors in tourist settings*, Springer-Verlag: New York.

Peterson, A. R., and Wilson, R. W. (1992). 'Measuring customer satisfaction: Fact and artefact'. *Journal of the Academy of Marketing Science*, 20 (1), 61-71.

Pizam, A., and Ellis, T. (1999). 'Customer satisfaction and its measurement in hospitality enterprises'. *International Journal of Contemporary Hospitality Management,* 11 (7), 326-339.

Pizam, A., and Milman, A. (1993). Predicting satisfaction among first time visitors to a destination by using the Expectancy Disconfirmation theory. *International Journal of Hospitality Management*, 12, 197-209.

Pizam, A., Neumann, Y., and Reichel, A. (1978). Dimensions of tourist satisfaction with a destination area. *Annals of Tourism Research*, July/September, 314-322.

Reisinger, Y., and Waryszak, R. (1996). Catering to Japanese tourists: What service do they expect from food and drinking establishments in Australia?. *Journal of Restaurant and Foodservice Marketing*, 1 (3/4), 53-71.

Ross, D. L. E., and Iso-Ahola, S. E. (1991). Sightseeing tourists' motivation and satisfaction, *Annals of Tourism Research*, 18, 226-237.

Ryan, C. (1995). *Researching Tourist Satisfaction: Issues. Concepts, Problems*. New York: Routledge.

Saleh, F., and Ryan, C. (1991). Analysing Service Quality in the Hospitality Industry Using the Servqual Model. *Service Industries Journal*, 11(3), 324-345.

Schwarz, N., and Oyserman, D. (2001). Asking questions about behaviour: Cognition, communication, and questionnaire construction. *American Journal of Evaluation,* 22 (2), 127-160.

Smith, M. A. (1999). Some problems when adopting Churchill's paradigm for the development of service quality measurement scales. *Journal of Business Research*, 46, 109-120.

Teas, R. K (1993). Expectations, performance evaluation, and consumers' perception of quality. *Journal of Marketing*, 57, 18-34.

Travel and Tourism Intelligence (1997*). International Tourism Reports*, 59-70.

Tribe, J., and Snaith, T. (1998). From Servqual to Holsat: holiday satisfaction in Varadero, Cuba. *Tourism Management*, 19, 125-34.

Weber, K. (1997). Assessment of tourist satisfaction, using the Expectancy disconfirmation theory, a study of German travel market in Australia. *Pacific Tourism Review*, 1, 35-45.

Weber, S. (1992). Trends in tourism segmentation search. *Marketing and Research Today*, 20 (2), 116-223.

Whipple, W. T., and Thach, V. S. (1988). Group tour management: Does good service produce satisfied customers. *Journal of Travel Research*, 16-21.

Woodruff, R. B., Cleanop, D. S., Schumn, D. W; Godial, S. F., and Burns, M. J. (1991). The standards issue in CS/D research: Historical perspective. *Journal of Consumer Satisfaction/ Dissatisfaction and Complaining Behaviour,* 4, 103-109.

Woodside, A., and Ronkainen, I. (1980). Vacation travel planning segments: self-planning vs. user of motor clubs and travel agents. *Annals of Tourism Research,* 7 (3), 385-394.

Yuksel, A., and Yuksel, F. (2001a). Measurement and Management issues in customer satisfaction research: review, critique and research agenda: part 2. *Journal of Travel and Tourism Marketing,* 10 (4), 81-112.

(2001b). Comparative performance analysis: tourists' perceptions of Turkey relative to other tourist destinations. *Journal of Vacation Marketing,* 7 (4), 333-355.

Yuksel, A., and Rimmington, M. (1998). Customer Satisfaction Measurement: Performance Counts. *The Cornell Hotel and Restaurant Administration Quarterly,* 39 (6), 60-70.

In: Tourist Satisfaction and Complaining Behavior
Editor: Atila Yüksel

ISBN 978-1-60456-002-2
© 2008 Nova Science Publishers, Inc.

Chapter 8

CROSS-CULTURAL COMPARISONS OF TOURIST SATISFACTION: ASSESSING ANALYTICAL ROBUSTNESS

Sara Dolnicar, Bettina Grün and Huong Le*

University of Wollongong, *Vienna University of Technology

INTRODUCTION

The construct of tourist satisfaction has been studied extensively in the past. Yet, very little research has been undertaken to assess how tourist satisfaction can most validly be measured or which measures may be prone to bias. One of the few studies investigating such effects was published by Sirakaya, Petrick and Choi (2004). The authors find that the mood of respondents affects satisfaction rating. Yet, mood can be claimed to be a variable which is likely to be randomly distributed across the sample. As such the bias of mood is likely to even out across all respondents in the sample. Factors of real concern, however, are those that are systematically associated with certain respondents, such as age, gender and education level, and that are also of interest in the analysis. One such variable has been repeatedly identified as causing systematic bias in survey responses: the cultural background of respondents. Pizam and Ellis (1999) discuss these "global issues" in consumer satisfaction measurement in detail. They identify a large number of potential biases that can distort satisfaction data collected from respondents from different cultural backgrounds. The particular aspect that will be discussed in this book chapter is referred to as "scalar equivalence" with the key question Pizam and Ellis recommend satisfaction researchers should ask being "Do corporate chosen scales function similarly in different cultures?" (p. 336).

The aim of this chapter is to raise awareness for the problem of scalar equivalence in satisfaction measurement among tourism and hospitality researchers, to empirically demonstrate the problem and to illustrate a simple method that can help researchers assess how robust their findings regarding the identified cross-cultural differences are.

RESPONSE STYLES

Throughout this chapter the term response bias will be understood to be "a systematic tendency to respond to a range of questionnaire items on some basis other than the specific item content (i.e., what the items were designed to measure)". Furthermore, the term response style will refer to response bias that "an individual displays [...] consistently across time and situations" (Paulhus, 1991, p.17). The two main forms of response styles are Extreme Response Style (ERS) and Acquiescence Response Style (ARS). Respondents with an ERS tend to use the endpoints of an answer scale. Respondents with an ARS tend to give a positive answer.

Substantial empirical evidence exists for the fact that the cultural background of respondents heavily affects the way in which they use answer formats in questionnaires. Zax and Takahashi (1967) conducted one of the earliest empirical studies on cross-cultural response styles concluding that Japanese female students exhibit ERS to a higher extent than their American counterparts. Chun, Campbell and Yoo (1974) conclude that American respondents demonstrate higher ERS scores than Korean participants in surveys, whereas Marshall and Lee (1998) find that in a comparison of seven Asian and Western countries the Asian respondents have a higher level of ERS. Differences in responses styles have also been empirically demonstrated to exist between respondents from different European countries (van Herk, Poortinga, and Verhallen, 2004; Welkenhuysen-Gybels, Billiet and Cambre, 2003) and between Hispanic and Non-Hispanic respondents (Hui and Triandis, 1989; Marin, Gamba, and Marin 1992) generally concluding that Hispanic respondents are to a higher extent susceptible to ERS.

It should be noted at this point that most empirical studies demonstrating response styles have used multi-category answer formats, such as five or seven point scales which currently dominate empirical social science research. As early as in 1950 Cronbach (1950) – aware of the serious problem of response styles for the validity of survey findings – recommended to use binary scales with only two answer options to avoid the contamination of data with not content related systematic error. Clarke III (2000, 2001) provides some empirical support for Cronbach's early recommendation. He finds that using a higher number of scale options is more susceptible to culturally determined response styles.

Although – to the authors' knowledge – no empirical work has been done to better understand why respondents from different cultural backgrounds use answer formats in a different manner, a few of the authors of the above cited empirical studies propose some explanations: Hui and Triandis (1989) propose that the difference between cultures lies in how they match the continuous construct that is being examined by the questions with the limited number of answer categories available in a questionnaire. The argument made by Stening and Everett (1984) is based on difference in value systems. In Asia modesty is an important trait. Using extreme response options is not modest. This may be a reason that Asian respondents are known to tend to use the middle answer options. Contrarily, Hispanic respondents believe that questions must be answered honestly. Honesty is expressed by taking strong positions and using the endpoints on an answer scale more frequently. More generally, Pizam and Ellis (1999, p. 335) state that "Differing languages, levels of literacy, interpretations of constructs and cultural behaviour must all be taken into account when creating a foreign customer satisfaction survey."

The best way of addressing the problem clearly is to collect data in a way that is not susceptible to capturing response styles. This leads back to Cronbach's recommendation of considering to use binary answer formats. In addition new answer formats such as best-worst scaling can be used for certain kinds of questions. Lee, Soutar, Louviere and Daly (2006) used best-worst scaling and could not detect any cross-cultural response styles in their data. This is, however, not always possible. If data sets have already been collected or if the researcher only has limited influence on the questionnaire development it may be necessary to work with data that is likely to be contaminated by response styles. A number of authors have made recommendations how to detect and correct for response styles before conducting the analysis (Fischer, 2004; Byrne and Campbell, 1999; Cheung and Rensvold, 2000; Greenleaf, 1992a and b; Van de Vijver and Poortinga, 2002; Welkenhuysen-Gybels, Billiet and Cambre, 2003). The proposed methods range from simple counting procedures to modelling approaches to extract ERS and ARS. All of the correction approaches proposed, however, have one major disadvantage: they assume that they have detected the true nature of the response style which they subsequently eliminate. Any data transformation is endangered by being either incorrect or introducing new biases into the data. The method proposed by Dolnicar and Grün (2007) is illustrated in this chapter avoids this problem. It is a diagnostic tool that informs researchers about the robustness of their results and therefore protects them from drawing wrong conclusions without manipulating the original data set.

RESPONSE STYLES IN TOURISM SATISFACTION RESEARCH

To assess the extent to which satisfaction research in the field of tourism is affected by the problem of response styles, a descriptive bibliography study [1] was conducted.

The following journals were used as sources for publications on tourism satisfaction: Journal of Travel Research, Annals of Tourism Research, Tourism Management, International Journal of Hospitality Management, Cornell Hotel and Restaurant Administration Quarterly, and the Journal of Tourism Studies. These journals were selected because they are ranked among the top 10 journals in tourism research according to the tourism journal ranking published by the Journal of Travel Research in 2004 and because they are readily available through online databases.

Articles to be included in the review were selected by searching for the keyword "satisfaction". Only original articles based on empirical satisfaction data and published between 2000 and 2007 were included. This selection algorithm led to a total of 45 articles used for the review. The full list of references is provided in the Appendix. The distribution of papers across publication outlets is provided in Table 1. Table 1 shows that Tourism Management published the largest number of empirical satisfaction studies, more than half of all studies undertaken in the listed journals since 2000. The Journal of Travel Research published the second largest number of satisfaction studies, followed by Annals of Tourism Research. Counting the total number of articles published in the top three tourism journals and the number of articles which investigate satisfaction, it becomes evident that a substantial

---

[1] Bibliographic study (also called bibliographical study) is a systematic description and history of printed material (Center for Bibliographical Studies and Research, 2006).

amount of satisfaction research is published in tourism. In Tourism Management, 11% of all articles published from 2000 study satisfaction, the respective proportions for the Journal of Travel Research and Annals of Tourism Research are 8% and 6%.

The review of articles was undertaken by coding each article with respect to a set of predefined variables. Twenty six such variables were used. Variables were divided into three groups: (1) aims of the research and general aspects of articles such as authors; years of publication; names of the journals; (2) aspects of methodology such as sample size determination; if the sample involved people from one country or from different countries, if the authors correct for cross-cultural response styles, number of attributes, data format, number of answer options, statistical analysis; (3) measurement aspects such as how and when levels of tourists' satisfaction were measured, if importance of attributes was measured, measurement of behavioural intentions as consequences of satisfaction; and (4) the main results of the research and managerial recommendations or managerial notes.

Table 1. Distribution of empirical satisfaction studies across journals

Journal of publication	Total number	%
Tourism Management	24.0	53.3
Journal of Travel Research	10.0	22.2
Annals of Tourism Research	7.0	15.6
International Journal of Hospitality Management	2.0	4.4
Cornell Hotel and Restaurant Administration uarterly	1.0	2.2
Journal of Tourism Studies	1.0	2.2
Total	45.0	100.0

Table 2 contains the results of the review for the main variables of interest. As can be seen, more than half of all satisfaction studies conducted in tourism research use data sets that contain respondents from more than one country. This is not surprising because frequently guest surveys are used to study satisfaction. Yet, it highlights the importance of addressing the issue of potential data contamination by response styles. The risk of data contamination by response styles has to be assessed as high given that 93 percent of all studies use multi-category scales to measure satisfaction: nearly half of the studies chose five-point scales, almost a third of studies use seven-point scales. None of the studies that include respondents from different countries of origin have corrected for cross-cultural response styles. In fact, none of them even mention that cross-cultural response styles could potentially bias the results.

Given the concerning statistics presented in Table 2, a more detailed analysis of those articles that used respondents from various countries of origin was undertaken, leading to the conclusion that 7 out of 45 of the reviewed studies (18%) actually examined cross-cultural differences in satisfaction levels. Nield, Kozak and LeGrys (2000), in their study on satisfaction of tourists with food use five point scales to measure satisfaction and compare Western European with Eastern Europeans. Chaudhary (2000) compares satisfaction ratings on five point scales for British, German and Dutch tourists. Results are insignificant, the authors blame small sample sizes, and response styles problems are not mentioned. Kozak (2001) compares the satisfaction statements of British and German tourists using a seven point scale. Joppe, Martin and Waalen (2001) use four and five point scales and compare

Canadian, US and overseas tourist satisfaction levels. Wong and Law (2003) compare satisfaction levels across countries of origin using a five point scale to measure satisfaction. Yu and Goulden (2006) test differences in satisfaction of European, US, Japanese and other Asia Pacific Countries using satisfaction statements measured on a 5 point multicategory scale. Hui, Wan and Ho (in press) compare satisfaction levels for respondents from different regions of the world. The bases for the analysis are responses provided on a seven point scale.

Table 2. Characteristics of satisfaction studies in tourism research

	Frequency	Percent
Respondents		
Only from 1 country	14	31.1
From more than 1 country	24	53.3
Not stated	7	15.6
Total	45	100.0
Correction for cross-cultural response styles		
No	45	100.0
Yes	0	0.0
Total	45	100.0
Data format		
Multi-category	42	93.3
Not stated	1	2.2
Not applicable (qualitative studies)	2	4.4
Total	45	100.0
Number of answer options		
Not specified	2	4.4
4 point scale	1	2.2
5 point scale	19	42.2
6 point scale	1	2.2
7 point scale	13	28.9
9 point scale	1	2.2
10 point scale	4	8.9
Others / combination of formats	2	4.4
Not applicable (qualitative studies)	2	4.4
Total	45	100.0

With the exception of Chaudhary (2000) all studies report significant differences across countries. In many cases these differences are not only significant, they are obviously highly systematic with respondents from certain cultural backgrounds producing higher satisfaction scores consistently over a large number of attributes for which satisfaction was measured. Not a single one of these studies mentions the potential danger of cross-cultural responses styles.

The results from this bibliographic study demonstrate very clearly that tourism researchers are in need of a tool that will enable them to discriminate between response style artefacts and true cross-cultural differences. We illustrate the problem of cross-cultural response style contamination and a simple method to assess the danger of data contamination in the following section.

AN EMPIRICAL ILLUSTRATION

The data set used for the empirical illustration is from the most recent wave (1999-2002) of the World Values Study (Inglehart, Basanez, Diez-Medrano, Halman and Luijkx, 2004), a data set collected by a network of social scientists since 1980. Random sampling techniques are used in all countries and only respondents of the age of 18 and above are included.

The analysis is restricted only to a subset containing the respondents of three different countries (n=3771): United States of America (1200 respondents, 32% of the sample), Spain (1209 respondents, 32%) and Japan (1362 respondents, 36%). These three countries are chosen because cross-cultural analyses of response styles have often been made between Americans and Hispanic as well as Asian respondents and have shown significant differences in response styles. Consequently, it is reasonable to assume that respondents from these countries will differ in the way they respond to multi-category survey questions.

Sixty-seven questions from the World Values Survey form the basis of the analysis, 47 of which respondents answered by using a four point scale. Respondents answered the remaining 20 questions on a ten point scale. The core variables for analysis are four questions which investigate the satisfaction of respondents. More specifically, the following aspects of satisfaction: (1) satisfaction with life (four point scale), (2) satisfaction with the financial situation of the household (four point scale), (3) satisfaction with democracy developing in their country of residence (ten point scale) and (4) satisfaction with the people in the national office (ten point scale).

The answer options for the first questions were "Very satisfied", "Rather satisfied", "Not very satisfied", and "Not at all satisfied"; for the second question "Very satisfied", "Fairly satisfied", "Fairly dissatisfied" and "Very dissatisfied". Both ten point scale questions required respondents to use a numerical scale with the endpoints anchored verbally as "Dissatisfied" and "Satisfied".

The satisfaction questions in the World Values Data represent very well the nature of questions typically asked when satisfaction is measured in a tourism context. The typical approach to testing whether respondents from different countries of origin have different satisfaction levels is to conduct ANOVAs and establish whether the mean values differ. In this case the ANOVA for each of the four satisfaction question indicates a significant difference (all p-values < 0.001). In the next step pair-wise comparisons are made using Tukey's honest significant different (HSD) method to correct for multiple testing in order to assess which countries differ significantly. Each one of these pair-wise tests has three possible outcomes: (1) respondents from country A are more satisfied (A>B), (2) there is no difference in the satisfaction of respondents from countries A and B (A=B), and (3) respondents from country B are more satisfied (A<B). Ignoring the problem of cross-cultural response styles these results (see Table 3 providing the mean differences and p-values for all pair-wise comparisons of the three countries along all four satisfaction variables) would be interpreted as follows: Japanese respondents are for the least satisfied (across all items), and Americans are the most satisfied (across all items except the questions regarding democracy). However, the possibility that these differences are systematic and that we may in fact be interpreting response styles rather than actual content has not been taken into account by this analysis, consequently putting the results at risk of being invalid.

Table 3. Analysis of the Raw Data

Answer Scale	Question	Spain vs. Japan (p-value)	USA vs. Japan (p-value)	USA vs. Spain (p-value)
Ten point	Life	0.109 A>B (<0.001)	0.261 A>B (<0.001)	0.153 A>B (<0.001)
	Financial situation of household	0.020 A=B (0.56)	0.075 A>B (<0.001)	0.055 A>B (0.02)
Four point	Democracy developing in country	0.253 A>B (<0.001)	0.206 A>B (<0.001)	-0.047 A<B (0.03)
	People in the national office	0.370 A>B (<0.001)	0.541 A>B (<0.001)	0.171 A>B (<0.001)

In order to address this problem the presence of cross-cultural response styles is investigated. Individual means and standard deviations are the recommended measures for assessing ARS and ERS respectively. For instance, if a respondent has high agreement levels for all satisfaction questions, states to have engaged in many vacation activities and states that most travel motivations apply to him or her (including resting, relaxing and doing nothing), the validity of his or her responses is in question, as an observed general tendency of using only the positive range of the scale over several different constructs is more likely to be a sign of ARS than of actual content information. As a consequence his or her mean value over all questions will be rather high and hence reflect the degree of susceptibility to ARS of the respondent. Similar, the observed individual standard deviation over several questions from unrelated constructs is used as a measure for susceptibility to ERS of the respondent.

For the present illustration individual mean values and standard deviations are determined separately for each answer format because previous research demonstrated that the susceptibility of answer formats to culture-specific response styles is associated with the number of answer categories (Hui and Triandis, 1989; Clarke III, 2000, 2001). In order to determine if the individual means and standard deviations are valid measures for response styles the interdependence between the different questions in the questionnaire is analyzed. Low correlations between the answers suggest that they are unrelated and systematic differences in use of the scale between the respondents are likely to be due to response styles. Given that the correlations have a mean of 0.07 (standard deviation 0.13) for the four point scale and a mean of 0.06 (standard deviation 0.19) for the ten point scale it can be assumed that the individual means and standard deviations can be used as measures for ARS and ERS.

In order to assess cross-cultural differences in response styles ANOVAs are performed which show that the countries differ significantly in the individual means and standard deviations (four point scale: F-value=124, df_1=2, df_2=3768, p-value < 0.001 (means), F-value=106, df_1=2, df_2=3768, p-value < 0.001 (standard deviations); ten point scale: F-value=84, df_1=2, df_2=3763, p-value < 0.001 (means); F-value=61.1, df_1=2, df_2=3763, p-value < 0.001 (standard deviations)). A pair-wise comparison using Tukey's HSD method at a significance level of 95% indicates that the Americans have the highest means and the Japanese the lowest means and standard deviations, while the difference in standard deviations are not significant between Americans and Spanish for the four point scale. For the ten point scale the Japanese have again the lowest means and standard deviations, while the differences in means are not significant between Americans and Spanish. However, the Americans have higher standard deviations than the Spanish. These results suggest that analyzing uncorrected raw data might be distorted by the presence of culture-specific response styles.

The seemingly logical consequence from the above results is that the raw data needs to be corrected; that the scores for each of the three cultural groups have to be somehow modified to reduce the amount of bias. Unfortunately this is a dangerous approach. By correcting the raw data additional or different bias could be introduced to the data. The approach we are illustrating in this book chapter therefore does not take a correction approach. Instead we present a simple way to assess how reliable each of the differences are that we originally found between respondents from the three countries. We refer to this as a robustness comparison. A detailed explanation of the procedure is provided in Dolnicar and Grün (2007). The underlying idea is that we apply a number of alternative, theoretically suitable corrections to the data, re-compute the original test to compare the three countries and then assess whether the results from the different correction methods as well as the raw data lead to the same or different results. If all of them lead to the same result (either that the countries differ or that they do not in their satisfaction) we can safely assume that this is the correct result, despite the response style contamination. If, however, there is no agreement on the results, findings with respect to such a variable have to be reported with great care, as it cannot be firmly established if a satisfaction difference or a response style difference is captured.

For the robustness comparison of the World Values Data we use seven different correction methods: the raw data, the data corrected for ARS using individual means as well as using country-specific means, the data corrected for ERS using individual standard deviations as well as using country-specific standard deviations and the data corrected for both ARS and ERS using either the individual measures as well as the country-specific ones.

The ANOVA indicates that country-specific differences indeed do exist for each of the questions (all p-values < 0.001 for each corrected data set and question). This preliminary result is very encouraging, as it confirms that the identified differences are not merely based on response styles. However, pair wise comparisons are needed to be able to draw final conclusions about possible cross-cultural differences. For this purpose Tukey's HSD method was used (significance level of 95%). Because the test is computed seven times (once for each of the corrected data sets and once for the raw data) each of the three cases can occur between 0 and 7 times. The higher the agreement across the seven computations are the more robust the finding. Optimally the resulting values will mainly be 0s and 7s. In the worst case most of them will be 3s and 4s, indicating high levels of correction dependence of results.

Table 4 contains the results of these pair-wise tests for the World Values Data. The respective country pair is stated in the column heading. Each row contains the frequency of the three outcomes as outlined above (A>B, A=B, A<B) for each satisfaction item under study. The robust test results are highlighted in a light grey shade. As can be seen five of six comparisons on the four point scale are highly robust, but only two of six on the ten point scale.

Table 4. Robustness of Cross-Cultural Findings

Answer Scale	Question	Spain vs. Japan	USA vs. Japan	USA vs. Spain
Ten point	Life	A<B 0 A=B 4 A>B 3	A<B 0 A=B 0 A>B 7	A<B 0 A=B 0 A>B 7
	Financial situation of household	A<B 4 A=B 3 A>B 0	A<B 0 A=B 4 A>B 3	A<B 0 A=B 3 A>B 4
Four point	Democracy developing in country	A<B 0 A=B 0 A>B 7	A<B 0 A=B 0 A>B 7	A<B 6 A=B 1 A>B 0
	People in the national office	*A<B 0* *A=B 0* *A>B 7*	*A<B 0* *A=B 0* *A>B 7*	*A<B 0* *A=B 0* *A>B 7*

None of the pair wise comparisons indicates unambiguously insignificant differences between two countries. The comparisons indicate that the Japanese are the least satisfied with respect to the democracy developing in their country. No safe conclusion for this question can be drawn for the comparison of Americans and Spanish respondents, as the data set corrected for individual standard deviations indicates no significant differences between these two countries (p-value=0.45). With respect to satisfaction with the people in the national office the Japanese are again the least satisfied and the Americans are the most satisfied. With respect to satisfaction with their life the Americans are the most satisfied and with respect to satisfaction with the financial situation of the household no safe conclusions can be drawn for any of the comparisons. A majority vote of the corrected data sets would indicate lower levels for Spanish than Japanese and Americans while insignificant differences are suggested between the Americans and the Japanese. The majority vote would therefore agree with the raw data analysis only for one out of four comparisons which are assessed as not robust for the ten point scale. However, these conclusions would also not seem to be very reliable as the majority vote is always only based on 4 out of 7 corrected data sets.

The analysis of satisfaction questions from the World Values Data illustrates that response styles can have a major distorting effect on cross-cultural studies. In the worst case response styles can lead to wrong conclusions. It is consequently very important for researchers who are interested in comparing satisfaction ratings from respondents from different countries of origin to assess the degree to which their results are based on differences in satisfaction (actual content) or differences in using answer formats (response styles).

CONCLUSIONS

Satisfaction research is very popular among tourism researchers. Satisfaction is assumed to play a central role in tourists' intentions to revisit a destination and to lead to positive word of mouth. The majority of satisfaction studies use multi-category answer formats to measure satisfaction, either directly or through the measurement of both expectations / importance and performance independently. A large proportion of satisfaction studies is based on data sets which include respondents from different cultural backgrounds who are known to use multi-category response scales in systematically different ways. Such systematic differences can affect the validity of conclusions drawn from empirical satisfaction research, particularly if respondents from different cultural backgrounds are directly compared. In the worst case – if researchers are comparing countries with very strong response styles – the statistically significant differences in satisfaction as determined by an analysis of variance or t-test may be entirely due to differences in response styles. This would mean that tourists from different countries do not at all differ in their satisfaction. In addition true differences in satisfaction can also be masked by response styles and hence might not be detected.

Because of the danger of interpreting methodological artefacts it is particularly important in the context of empirical tourism research to assess the extent of the potential contamination of data with response styles. One way of doing this was presented in this chapter: first the raw data is corrected for various possible response styles. The derived data set and the raw data set are used independently to undertake significance testing. For each variable, the test results of all (raw and corrected) data sets are compared. The higher the level of agreement between those computations, the more reliable the finding that countries do or do not significantly differ with respect to that particular aspect of satisfaction.

Tourism research may also want to consider alternative answer formats, such as best-worst scaling or binary answer formats in cases where these answer formats are viable ways of collecting the required data. Best-worst scales and binary scales are less susceptible to capturing response styles than the typically used multi-category answer formats.

Within the group of multi-category answer formats and their susceptibility to response styles, future empirical studies are needed. Particularly to assess whether lower number of answer options are generally more robust to culture-specific response styles than ten point scales (as suggested by our empirical analysis where four point scales appeared to be less in danger than ten point scales). In addition the effect of labeling of answer formats on cross-cultural response style susceptibility needs to be assessed empirically.

ACKNOWLEDGEMENTS

This research was supported by the Australian Research Council (through grants DP0557257 and LX0559628) and the Austrian Academy of Sciences (ÖAW) through a DOC-FFORTE scholarship for Bettina Grün.

REFERENCES

Byrne, B. M., and Campbell, T. L. (1999). Cross-cultural comparisons and the presumption of equivalent measurement and theoretical structure - A look beneath the surface. *Journal of Cross-Cultural Psychology, 30* (5), 555-574.

Center for Bibliographical Studies and Research (2006). *Website of the Center for Bibliographical Studies and Research (CBSR)*. Retrieved 2 January, 2007 from http://www.cbsr.ucr.edu/

Cheung, G. W., and Rensvold, R. B. (2000). Assessing extreme and acquiescence response sets in cross-cultural research using structural equations modelling. *Journal of Cross-Cultural Psychology, 31* (2), 187-212.

Chaudhary, M. (2000). India's image as a tourist destination -- A perspective of foreign tourists. *Tourism Management, 21* (3), 293-297.

Chun, K. T., Campbell, J. B., and Yoo, J. H. (1974). Extreme response style in cross-cultural research – Reminder. *Journal of Cross-Cultural Psychology, 5* (4), 465-480.

Clarke III, I. (2000). Extreme response style in cross cultural research: An empirical investigation. *Journal of Social Behaviour and Personality, 15* (1), 137-152.

Clarke III, I. (2001). Extreme response style in cross-cultural research. *International Marketing Review, 18* (3), 301-324.

Cronbach, L. (1950). Further evidence on response sets and test design. *Educational and Psychological Measurement, 10* (1), 3-31.

Dolnicar, S. and Grün, B. (2007). Cross-cultural comparisons: Assessing analytical robustness. *International Journal of Culture, Tourism and Hospitality Research.*

Fischer, R. (2004). Standardization to account for cross-cultural response bias: A classification of score adjustment procedures and review of research in JCCP. *Journal of Cross-Cultural Psychology, 35* (3), 263-282.

Greenleaf, E. A. (1992a). Improving rating-scale measures by detecting and correcting bias components in some response styles. *Journal of Marketing Research, 29* (2), 176-188.

Greenleaf, E. A. (1992b). Measuring extreme response style. *Public Opinion Quarterly, 56* (3), 328-351.

Hui, C. H., and Triandis, H. C. (1989). Effects of culture and response format on extreme response style. *Journal of Cross-Cultural Psychology, 20* (3), 296-309.

Hui, T. K., Wan, D., and Ho, A. (in press). Tourists' satisfaction, recommendation and revisiting Singapore. *Tourism Management, In Press, Corrected Proof.*

Inglehart R., Basanez M., Diez-Medrano J., Halman L., Luijkx R. (2004). *Human Beliefs and Values: A Cross-Cultural Sourcebook Based on the 1999-2002 Values Surveys*. Mexico: Siglo XXI Editores.

Joppe, M., Martin, D. W., and Waalen, J. (2001). Toronto's image as a destination: A comparative importance-satisfaction analysis by origin of visitor. *Journal of Travel Research, 39* (3), 252-260.

Kozak, M. (2001). Comparative assessment of tourist satisfaction with destinations across two nationalities. *Tourism Management, 22* (4), 391-401.

Lee, J. A., Soutar, G. N., Louviere, J., and Daly, T. M. (2006). *An Examination of the Relationship between Values and Holiday Benefits Across Cultures Using Ratings Scales and Best-Worst Scaling*. ANZMAC CD Proceedings.

Marin, G., Gamba, R. J., and Marin, B. V. (1992). Extreme response style and acquiescence among Hispanics - The role of acculturation and education. *Journal of Cross-Cultural Psychology, 23* (4), 498-509.

Marshall, R., and Lee, C. (1998). A cross-cultural, between-gender study of extreme response style. *European Advances in Consumer Research, 3,* 90-95.

Nield, K., Kozak, M., and LeGrys, G. (2000). The role of food service in tourist satisfaction. *International Journal of Hospitality Management, 19* (4), 375-384.

Paulhus, D.L. (1991), Measurement and control of response bias, In J.P. Robinson, P.R. Shaver and L.S. Wrightsman (eds.), *Measures of Personality and Social Psychological Attitudes*, San Diego: Academic Press, 17-59.

Pizam, A., and Ellis, T. (1999). Customer satisfaction and its measurement in hospitality enterprises. *International Journal of Contemporary Hospitality Management, 11* (7), 326-339.

Sirakaya, E., Petrick, J., and Choi, H. S. (2004). The role of mood on tourism product evaluations. *Annals of Tourism Research, 31* (3), 517-539.

Stening, B. W., and Everett, J. E. (1984). Response styles in a cross-cultural managerial study. *Journal of Social Psychology, 122* (2), 151-156.

van de Vijver, F. J. R., and Poortinga, Y. H. (2002). Structural equivalence in multilevel research. *Journal of Cross-Cultural Psychology, 33* (2), 141-156.

van Herk, H., Poortinga, Y. H., and Verhallen, T. M. M. (2004). Response styles in rating scales - Evidence of method bias in data from six EU countries. *Journal of Cross-Cultural Psychology, 35* (3), 346-360.

Welkenhuysen-Gybels, J., Billiet, J., and Cambre, B. (2003). Adjustment for acquiescence in the assessment of the construct equivalence of Likert-type score items. *Journal of Cross-Cultural Psychology*, 34 (6), 702-722.

Wong, J., and Law, R. (2003). Difference in shopping satisfaction levels: A study of tourists in Hong Kong. *Tourism Management, 24* (4), 401-410.

Yu, L., and Goulden, M. (2006). A comparative analysis of international tourists' satisfaction in Mongolia. *Tourism Management, 27* (6), 1331-1342.

Zax, M., and Takahashi, S. (1967), Cultural influences on response style: Comparison of Japanese and American college students. *Journal of Social Psychology, 71* (1), 3-10.

Reviewed literature

Akama, J. S., and Kieti, D. M. (2003). Measuring tourist satisfaction with Kenya's wildlife safari: a case study of Tsavo West National Park. *Tourism Management, 24* (1), 73-81.

Alegre, J., and Cladera, M. (2006). Repeat visitation in mature sun and sand holiday destinations. *Journal of Travel Research, 44* (3), 288-297.

Baker, D. A., and Crompton, J. L. (2000). Quality, satisfaction and behavioural intentions. *Annals of Tourism Research, 27* (3), 785-804.

Bigne, J. E., and Andreu, L. (2004). Emotions in segmentation: An empirical study. *Annals of Tourism Research, 31* (3), 682-696.

Bigne, J. E., Andreu, L., and Gnoth, J. (2005). The theme park experience: An analysis of pleasure, arousal and satisfaction. *Tourism Management, 26* (6), 833-844.

Bigne, J. E., Sanchez, M. I., and Sanchez, J. (2001). Tourism image, evaluation variables and after purchase behaviour: Inter-relationship. *Tourism Management, 22* (6), 607-616.

Bowen, D. (2001). Antecedents of consumer satisfaction and dis-satisfaction (CS/D) on long-haul inclusive tours -- A reality check on theoretical considerations. *Tourism Management, 22* (1), 49-61.

Bowen, D. (2002). Research through participant observation in tourism: A creative solution to the measurement of consumer satisfaction/dissatisfaction (CS/D) among tourists. *Journal of Travel Research, 41* (1), 4-14.

Chang, J., Yang, B.-T., and Yu, C.-G. (2006). The moderating effect of salespersons' selling behaviour on shopping motivation and satisfaction: Taiwan tourists in China. *Tourism Management, 27* (5), 934-942.

Chaudhary, M. (2000). India's image as a tourist destination -- A perspective of foreign tourists. *Tourism Management, 21* (3), 293-297.

Chen, C.-F., and Tsai, D. (in press). How destination image and evaluative factors affect behavioural intentions? *Tourism Management, In Press, Corrected Proof.*

Deng, W. (in press). Using a revised importance-performance analysis approach: The case of Taiwanese hot springs tourism. *Tourism Management, In Press, Corrected Proof.*

Duman, T., and Mattila, A. S. (2005). The role of affective factors on perceived cruise vacation value. *Tourism Management, 26* (3), 311-323.

Ekinci, Y., Prokopaki, P., and Cobanoglu, C. (2003). Service quality in Cretan accommodations: Marketing strategies for the UK holiday market. *International Journal of Hospitality Management, 22* (1), 47-66.

Fuchs, M., and Weiermair, K. (2004). Destination benchmarking: An indicator-system's potential for exploring guest satisfaction. *Journal of Travel Research, 42* (3), 212-225.

Gallarza, M. G., and Gil Saura, I. (2006). Value dimensions, perceived value, satisfaction and loyalty: An investigation of university students' travel behaviour. *Tourism Management, 27* (3), 437-452.

Heung, V. C. S., and Cheng, E. (2000). Assessing tourists' satisfaction with shopping in the Hong Kong special administrative regions of China. *Journal of Travel Research, 38* (4), 396-404.

Hui, T. K., Wan, D., and Ho, A. (in press). Tourists' satisfaction, recommendation and revisiting Singapore. *Tourism Management, In Press, Corrected Proof.*

Jang, S., and Feng, R. (2007). Temporal destination revisit intention: The effects of novelty seeking and satisfaction. *Tourism Management, 28* (2), 580-590.

Joppe, M., Martin, D. W., and Waalen, J. (2001). Toronto's Image as a destination: A comparative importance-satisfaction analysis by origin of visitor. *Journal of Travel Research, 39* (3), 252-260.

Kozak, M. (2001). Comparative assessment of tourist satisfaction with destinations across two nationalities. *Tourism Management, 22* (4), 391-401.

Kozak, M. (2001). Repeaters' behaviour at two distinct destinations. *Annals of Tourism Research, 28* (3), 784-807.

Kozak, M. (2002). Destination benchmarking. *Annals of Tourism Research, 29* (2), 497-519.

Kozak, M., and Rimmington, M. (2000). Tourist satisfaction with Mallorca, Spain, as an off-season holiday destination. *Journal of Travel Research, 38* (3), 260-269.

Lee, C.-K., Yoon, Y.-S., and Lee, S.-K. (2007). Investigating the relationships among perceived value, satisfaction, and recommendations: The case of the Korean DMZ. *Tourism Management, 28* (1), 204-214.

Millan, A., and Esteban, A. (2004). Development of a multiple-item scale for measuring customer satisfaction in travel agencies services. *Tourism Management, 25* (5), 533-546.

Nash, R., Thyne, M., and Davies, S. (2006). An investigation into customer satisfaction levels in the budget accommodation sector in Scotland: A case study of backpacker tourists and the Scottish Youth Hostels Association. *Tourism Management, 27* (3), 525-532.

Nield, K., Kozak, M., and LeGrys, G. (2000). The role of food service in tourist satisfaction. *International Journal of Hospitality Management, 19* (4), 375-384.

Petrick, J. F. (2004). The roles of quality, value, and satisfaction in predicting cruise passengers' behavioural intentions. *Journal of Travel Research, 42* (4), 397-407.

Petrick, J. F., and Backman, S. J. (2002). An examination of the determinants of golf travelers' satisfaction. *Journal of Travel Research, 40* (3), 252-258.

Pizam, A., Uriely, N., and Reichel, A. (2000). The intensity of tourist-host social relationship and its effects on satisfaction and change of attitudes: The case of working tourists in Israel. *Tourism Management, 21* (4), 395-406.

Reisinger, Y., and Turner, L. W. (2002a). Cultural differences between Asian tourist markets and Australian hosts: Part 1. *Journal of Travel Research, 40* (3), 295-315.

Reisinger, Y., and Turner, L. W. (2002b). Cultural differences between Asian tourist markets and Australian hosts: Part 2. *Journal of Travel Research, 40* (4), 374-384.

Reisinger, Y., and Turner, L. W. (2002c). The determination of shopping satisfaction of Japanese tourists visiting Hawaii and the Gold Coast compared. *Journal of Travel Research, 41* (2), 167-176.

Rodriguez del Bosque, I. A., San Martin, H., and Collado, J. (2006). The role of expectations in the consumer satisfaction formation process: Empirical evidence in the travel agency sector. *Tourism Management, 27* (3), 410-419.

Sirakaya, E., Petrick, J., and Choi, H.-S. (2004). The role of mood on tourism product evaluations. *Annals of Tourism Research, 31* (3), 517-539.

Skogland, I., and Siguaw, J. A. (2004). Are your satisfied customers loyal? *Cornell Hotel and Restaurant Administration Quarterly, 45* (3), 221-234.

Spinks, W., Lawley, M., and Richins, H. (2005). Satisfaction with Sunshine Coast tourist attractions: The influence of individual visitor characteristics. *Journal of Tourism Studies, 16* (1), 12-23.

Tonge, J., and Moore, S. A. (in press). Importance-satisfaction analysis for marine-park hinterlands: A Western Australian case study. *Tourism Management,* In Press, Corrected Proof.

Truong, T. H., and Foster, D. (2006). Using HOLSAT to evaluate tourist satisfaction at destinations: The case of Australian holidaymakers in Vietnam. *Tourism Management, 27* (5), 842-855.

Um, S., Chon, K., and Ro, Y. (2006). Antecedents of revisit intention. *Annals of Tourism Research, 33* (4), 1141-1158.

Vitterso, J., Vorkinn, M., Vistad, O. I., and Vaagland, J. (2000). Tourist experiences and attractions. *Annals of Tourism Research, 27* (2), 432-450.

Wong, J., and Law, R. (2003). Difference in shopping satisfaction levels: A study of tourists in Hong Kong. *Tourism Management, 24* (4), 401-410.

Yoon, Y., and Uysal, M. (2005). An examination of the effects of motivation and satisfaction on destination loyalty: A structural model. *Tourism Management, 26* (1), 45-56.

Yu, L., and Goulden, M. (2006). A comparative analysis of international tourists' satisfaction in Mongolia. *Tourism Management, 27* (6), 1331-1342.

Yuksel, A., and Yuksel, F. (2007). Shopping risk perceptions: Effects on tourists' emotions, satisfaction and expressed loyalty intentions. *Tourism Management, 28* (3), 703-713.

In: Tourist Satisfaction and Complaining Behavior
Editor: Atila Yüksel

ISBN 978-1-60456-002-2
© 2008 Nova Science Publishers, Inc.

Chapter 9

DIVERS' EXPERIENCES AND THEIR LEVEL OF SATISFACTION IN THE MALDIVES – EMPIRICAL RESEARCH

Ahmed Salih and Alison McIntosh*

Hong Kong Polytechnic University, *University of Waikato

INTRODUCTION

Tourism is dynamic, multifaceted and is regarded as the largest and fastest growing industry. According to United Nations World Tourism Organisation (UNWTO), (2006), 2006 would be the third consecutive year of healthy growth in international tourist arrivals. Their reports shows a 10.1 per cent growth in tourist arrivals in 2004 over 2003, 5.5 per cent growth in 2005 over 2004 and up to October 2006, a 4.5 per cent growth over the same period in 2005. In 2006, the tourism industry is expected to generate US$ 6,477.2 billion of economic activity, contributing to 10.3 per cent of global Gross Domestic Product (GDP) and about 234,305,000 jobs, approximately 8.7 per cent of total world employment (WTTC, 2006). Small island nations like the Maldives want to share the benefits generated from this mega industry, including foreign exchange earnings, employment, and the multiplier effect arising from tourism for the development of the nation.

Tourist arrivals became evident in the Maldives in 1972. More of the country being under water, it has the perfect ingredients to make it one of the best diving destinations: good visibility, the sheer number and variety of fish, and thriving coral reefs (Camerapix, 1992; Hassan, et al, 1994). Hence, Scuba Diving is the main recreational activity offered in the resorts. It is estimated that 35 per cent of the tourists visiting the Maldives participate in diving (source). It is thus important that the divers' needs and expectations are met in the pursuit of satisfaction and positive word of mouth recommendation and potential repeat visiting (do repeat visit patterns of divers match with those of say hotel customers?).

This chapter provides the results of an empirical research on tourist satisfaction with a focus on diving in the Maldives. The aim of the chapter is to analyse the level of satisfaction of divers related to their diving experiences during their holiday in the Maldives.

TOURIST SATISFACTION

Research in customer satisfaction and dissatisfaction began in the 1960s and 1970s in the United States of America in goods marketing, and in the 1980s and 1990s it widened to include services marketing (Bowen, 2001). Customer satisfaction has been examined widely, especially in marketing literature (see Andrson, 1993; Anderson and Fornell, 1993; Cronin and Taylor, 1992; Iacobucci, Grayson and Ostrom, 1994; Gronroos, 1990; Oliver, 1980; Parasuraman, Zeithaml and Berry, 1985; Westbrook, 1980). There has been an increase in the number of articles related to customer satisfaction in the published tourism and hospitality literature. For example, Saleh and Ryan (1992), Barsky (1992), Bojanic (1996), Chon, Christianson and Lin (1998), Heung (2000) and Meyer and Wesetbarkey (1996) studied guest satisfaction with hotels, Hu and Richie (1993), Hughes (1991) Kozak (2001), Kozak and Remmington (2001) and Pizam, Neumann and Reichel (1978) assessed tourists' satisfaction with destinations and Pearce (1980) examined visitor satisfaction with the behaviour of the locals. Authors tend to agree that the confirmation or disconfirmation of preconceived service standards and the quality of experience is the essential determinant of the satisfaction levels among consumers (Oliver, 1996).

Two schools of thoughts exist in the marketing literature on undertaking research in customer satisfaction. According to Parasurman, Zeitham, and Berry (1985), customer satisfaction should be considered as a positive or negative outcome from comparing the initial expectations of the consumer and what the consumer's perception of the performance of the product or service. The second school of thought is referred to as the Nordic school, proposed by Gronroos (1990) whereby customer satisfaction is only an outcome of the actual quality of performance and its perception by consumers. According to Oh and Parks (1997), there is no consensus on which method is the best in measuring customer satisfaction and which factors determine customer satisfaction in the marketing literature. This is mainly due to shortfalls in using expectation and perception approaches in customer satisfaction research. Some of the drawbacks include continuous updating of customer expectation with time via numerous sources of information, the wide and complex array of factors that influence consumer expectations, and difficulty faced by consumers in distinguishing between expectations and perceived performances (Meyer and Westerbarkey, 1996). Irrespective of these drawbacks, both of these approaches have been applied in conducting research on customer satisfaction in the tourism and hospitality literature.

The concept of leisure experience has been emphasised in academic discourse (Kelly, 1982; Lee, Dattilo and Howard, 1994; Murphy, 1974; Pieper, 1963; Wearing and Wearing, 1988), and it could be stated that the services provided for divers would contribute substantially to their satisfaction. However, it could be argued that the quality of service, which was studied extensively in the 1980s, only represents the cognitive aspect of customer satisfaction (Oliver, 1993). To fully capture the essence of diver satisfaction, psychological responses such as those factors that motivate divers and their emotions during the actual diving should be considered (e.g. Dunn Ross and Iso-Ahola, 1991; Otto and Ritchie, 1996).

Diving is a recreational activity and it offers a natural environment that is designed to take the divers away from their normal life to an adventurous and an unknown world. However, the number of activities involved in experiencing a dive in a particular destination is large and all these activities would influence the level of satisfaction among divers. Starting from the initial selection of a location to dive, travel to the location, interaction with service providers at different levels such as tour operators, travel agents, employees of the dive school, employees of the lodging facilities, quality of food and accommodation, and many other variables would dictate the levels of satisfaction among divers. Therefore, satisfaction among divers could be conceptualized in terms of a series of interactions rather than a single transaction; thus, from an experience perspective. This difference between tourism products and other consumer products potentially make it more difficult to measure customer satisfaction in the tourism and hospitality industry (Kozak and Rimmington, 2000).

Indeed, the complex and subjective nature of the tourism experience has been widely acknowledged (see for example, Beeho and Prentice, 1997). Hence, it is important to identify and measure divers' satisfaction with each component of diving for the reason that divers' satisfaction or dissatisfaction with anyone of the components leads to divers' overall satisfaction or dissatisfaction with their diving in the Maldives (Pizam, Neumann and Reichel, 1978). The overall satisfaction of divers influences their future behaviour. A significant relationship exists between tourist satisfaction, intention to visit the destination in the future, and positive word-of-mouth communication (Berkman and Gilson, 1986). Likewise, if the tourists are dissatisfied, they will look for another destination and would share their frustration with others (Pizam, 1994). This highlights the importance of tourist satisfaction in obtaining a competitive advantage over rivals.

There are different prepositions on the most suitable time for evaluating tourist satisfaction during the tourism experience. Some scholars suggest comparison of preholiday expectations and postholiday perceptions (Pizam and Milman, 1993), whilst others propose evaluating satisfaction during the holiday period (Gyte and Phelps, 1989), just prior to holiday ending (Goodrich, 1978), or on completion of the overall holiday experience (Pearce, 1980). In this study, diver satisfaction was evaluated while tourists were still staying in their resorts as they are experiencing their holiday and problems associated with memory recall can be avoided. Thus, this chapter presents the results of an empirical study of divers' satisfaction during their dive experiences in the Maldives. Although a diverse range of variables will affect the level of satisfaction among divers, and the overall diver satisfaction or dissatisfaction is the result of evaluating various positive and negative experiences, the findings focused primarily on the services provided at the residing resorts and dive schools of divers and the attributes of the underwater world of the Maldives.

The findings could be utilised in formulating policies, introduction of new regulations, revision of current regulations, product development and as a measure of service standards. Primarily, these actions should be aimed at increasing the satisfaction level among divers. In order to understand the level of satisfaction among divers, it is important to understand the perception held by divers regarding the quality of their diving experience in the Maldives because it is important to understand the divers' response to tourism activities and its application in advertising or consumer persuasion (Bealer and Willits, 1989). As the perception of the quality of experience differs depending on socio-demographic variables (Crompton, 1979; Goodrich, 1978, and Reilly, 1990), a demographic profile of the divers is compiled. Divers consume a variety of products and utilises a diverse range of services as part and parcel of their diving experience, their satisfaction level from the actual diving itself could be affected by some of these products and services. Hence, how divers receive these products and services is examined. In addition, divers' views on some of the existing regulations such as the controversial limitations of a dive depth to 30 metres by Ministry of

Tourism, level of damage to corals, cost of diving in the Maldives and the opportunities available to experience the local culture and way of life are also investigated. These aspects are examined as they potentially impact on the level of diver satisfaction.

MALDIVES AS A DIVE DESTINATION

The Maldives contains thousands of submerged reefs with rainbow-coloured fish, corals and critters. The warm tropical temperature with an average of 24 degrees celsius, visibility at more than 30 meters and easy access to a large number of coral reefs attracts divers from different parts of the world each year. Hans Hass stated that "The Maldives are certainly one of the great wonders of the world. Here more than anywhere else on the planet, perhaps, one can savour the beauty of undersea fauna" (as cited in Hassan and Azeez, 1994, p. 1).

The marine species living on the reefs are diverse and varies among different location. While some reefs in the Maldives are homes for sharks, some for turtles, others have all the attractions like Maya Thila in North Ari Atoll. This submerged reef is "…. one of the most exciting and vibrant reef systems in the world. One of those that underwater adventurers dream about and die to see" (Aw, 1999).

The first divers to the Maldives were Italians but contrary to today' divers who visit the Maldives to experience and enjoy the underwater world, their main purpose was underwater hunting. They arrived in the Maldives, equipped with spear guns and other hunting gear. They used spear guns daily in and killed sharks, manta rays and eels. In fact, the first brochures on Maldives were developed to promote the Maldives as a good place for spear fishing. However, German tourists who visited the country in the same year raised their voice against spear fishing and use of guns in the water. So the resort operators banned spear fishing and even today spear fishing is banned in the Maldives (Ministry of Tourism, 1998). These actions have helped keep the fragile environment relatively intact so that divers can today enjoy the natural wonder.

STUDIES ON SCUBA DIVING

International organisations such as Diving Equipment and Marketing Association, (DEMA), Professional Association of Diving Instructors (PADI) and others compile data on the demographics of divers. These reports present the significance and the high level of interest shown by people on diving. However, as mentioned above, little empirical research is evident on divers' satisfaction in the academic literature. DEMA reveals that close to half of adult Americans are interested in scuba diving and the significance of this report was stressed by Executive Director of DEMA when he stated that, "This study is significant because in addition to the 16 million Americans who considered themselves as active divers, there are more than 75 million Americans who want to know more about our sport" (http://www.dema.org). It also revealed that the attractive demographic features of the dive fraternity; 40 per cent of the potential American dive market has an annual household income of more than US$ 50,000. Out of the total surveyed, 77 per cent are under 45 years old and 67 percent are college educated.

According to Professional Association of Diving Instructors (PADI), there are 8.5 million certified scuba divers in the United States. PADI alone has certified between 8 to 8.5 million divers worldwide. Diving is dominated by male gender (72 per cent), however the gap is gradually reducing. There is an increase in the number of females following diving. For example, out of the total membership of the British Sub Aqua Club, 35 per cent are women. The average age is 36 years and 58 per cent of divers are married (http://www.padi.com).

When these figures are compared with studies done by Skin Divers in 1987 and in 1989, there are not many variations. They also found that divers are well educated, young, financially secure, and dominated by male. The average age increased from 30.8 in 1987 to 35.3 in 1989. In the study conducted by PADI, they found that the average age has gone up to 36. This increase in age could be due to highly advanced and state of the art equipment and training required (http://www.divernet.com). An empirical study undertaken by Musa, Kadir and Lee in 2004 on scuba divers' satisfaction among divers visiting Layang Layang island similarly reveals that divers are older, experienced and have completed high education. The overall satisfaction visiting the island is high and the main contributors include underwater attributes, and the comfort and ease of access to dive sites. Due to the similarities in the Maldivian marine environment with Malayisa, it is believed that some similarities would be observed between these two studies.

TOURIST SATISFACTION - EMPIRICAL STUDY

In this chapter, an attempt is made to assess the level of satisfaction among tourists visiting the Maldives for scuba diving. As secondary data on the topic is not available, primary data on several aspects of the diving holiday experience related to their overall satisfaction was collected. A research process to gain an understanding of divers' perceptions of quality of services and their respective sources of satisfaction/dissatisfaction with diving experience in the Maldives was applied (Bryant et al, 1998).

Diving in the Maldives is mainly limited to 10 atolls out of the 20 atolls comprising the archipelago. The name of the atolls are North Male and South Male Atoll (K), North Ari Atoll (NA), South Ari Atoll (SA), Baa Atoll (B), Raa Atoll (R), Lhaviyani Atoll (LH), Vaavu Atoll (V), Faafu Atoll (F), Dhaal Atoll (DH), Meemu Atoll (M) and Addu Atoll (S). Tourist resorts from each of the above atolls were used in the study to cover the dive sites in all the atolls (Table 1)

A structured questionnaire containing behavioural, demographic, and attitudinal questions was used as a data collection instrument. The objective was to obtain accurate information from respondents and to provide a structure and format as well as to facilitate data analysis. The questionnaire comprised of three sections: a) a diver profile, b) visitor satisfaction, and c) a general socio-demographic section. A pilot test was undertaken and the necessary changes were made to improve the study instrument based on the findings from the pilot test.

The questionnaires were mailed to the dive schools in participating resorts. The actual number of questionnaires for each resort was pre-determined based on the assumption that 35 per cent of the in-house guests of any resort at any given time would be divers. A convenient

Table 1. Resorts

No.	Atoll	Resort
1	B	COCO PALM RESORT
2	B	REETHI BEACH RESORT
3	DH	VILU REEF RESORT
4	K	BANDOS ISLAND RESORT
5	K	DHIGUFINOLHU ISLAND RESORT
6	K	EMBUDU VILLAGE
7	K	ERIYADU ISLAND RESORT
8	K	FIHAALHOHI TOURIST RESORT
9	K	FULL MOON BEACH RESORT
10	K	FUN ISLAND RESORT
11	K	GIRAVARU ISLAND RESORT
12	K	HELENGELI TOURIST VILLAGE
13	K	IHURU TOURIST RESORT
14	K	LAGOONA BEACH RESORT
15	K	LOHIFUSHI ISLAND RESORT
16	K	MEERU ISLAND RESORT
17	K	PARADISE ISLAND RESORT
18	K	REETHI RAH RESORT
19	K	RIHIVELI BEACH RESORT
20	K	THULHAGIRI ISLAND RESORT
21	K	VILLIVARU ISLAND RESORT
22	LH.	KUREDU ISLAND RESORT
23	LH.	PALM BEACH ISLAND
24	N.A	ELLAIDHOO TOURIST RESORT
25	N.A	FESDU FUN ISLAND
26	N.A	HALAVELI HOLIDAY VILLAGE
27	N.A	MADOOGALI TOURIST RESORT
28	N.A	NIKA ISLAND RESORT
35	S	EQUATOR VILLAGE - GAN
29	S.A	ARI BEACH RESORT
30	S.A	HILTON MALDIVES ON RANGALI ISLAND
31	S.A	HOLIDAY ISLAND
32	S.A	LILY BEACH RESORT
33	S.A	THUNDUFUSHI ISLAND RESORT
34	S.A	VAKARUFALHI ISLAND RESORT
36	V	ALIMATHA AQUATIC RESORT

sample of divers from each resort were included in the survey as the questionnaires were conducted only in English. So, only those divers who were English speaking were included in the sample. A total of 1430 questionnaires were administered in those selected resorts between February 15, 2000 and March, 15, 2000. On completion, questionnaires were returned to the dive school or to the resort reception in a sealed envelope which were delivered to the authors. Out of the 1430 questionnaires distributed, 287 (20%) were returned. Out of the 36 resorts, 24 resorts sent back completed questionnaires.

RESULTS AND DISCUSSION

Demographic Profile

Respondents to the survey were from 10 different nationalities and highest number of questionnaires were completed by Germans followed by Italians, British, Swiss, French, Japanese, Austrian, Dutch, Americans and Singaporean divers.

While some tourist generating markets of the Maldives have been over-represented, others are under-represented in the study. For example, Switzerland, France and Austria are over-represented while the Netherlands, and Japan are under-represented. However, the main generating markets; Italy and Germany are well represented among the participants. The result also indicates that divers from various nationalities residing in countries like Turkey, New Caledonia, United Arab Emirates, Cyprus, and Vanuatu are visiting the Maldives.

The age structure of the sample is similar to the studies carried by Professional Association of Divers [(PADI) (http://www.padi.com)] and Diving Equipment and Marketing Association [(DEMA) (http://www.dema.org)]. The study by DEMA revealed that 77 per cent of the divers are less than 45 years old while the average age was 36 years of age in the research project conducted by PADI. In this study 48 per cent of the divers are between 30-39 years. This age structure seems to be consistent with the studies done by Skin Divers in 1987 and in 1989, which found that the average age increased from 30.8 in 1987 to 35.3 in 1989 and by Musa (2002).

According to Kozak and Rimmington (2000), those tourists with lesser income, low level of education, older and in the low socioeconomic groups tend to have lower expectations. It is important to understand these characteristics because differences in attitudes, behaviour and social class can influence perceptions and expectation (Lewis, 1991; Mayo and Jarvis, 1981). Hence, most of the studies on divers aim to understand these aspects regarding divers.

Several studies on socio-demographics of diving fraternity have indicated that divers are highly educated (Skin Diver, 1987 and 1989; http://www.dema.org; http://www.padi.com; Musa, 2002) and this study demonstrates similar characteristics. About 49 per cent of the respondents have attended university education with either at Under Graduate or Post Graduate level. Sixty per cent of the respondents hold full-time employment. The socio-demographic profile of the divers visiting the Maldives could be summarised as mature, highly educated and financially sound.

With regard to the diving experience, the respondents have extensively travelled with vast experience in diving and the results support the notion that divers are novelty seekers and will not revisit a place they have visited in the past unless new experiences are expected. Their past experiences in other destinations will be used in comparing facilities, attractions, and services standard in the Maldives, which would influence their perception about the Maldives (Laws, 1995). The reason for the high percentage of the divers (27.08 per cent) indicating that they had their first diving experience in the Maldives could be visitors who begin diving in the Maldives during this trip or on a previous trip. The second highest number of divers had their first experience in Italy (12.5 per cent), followed by Germany (7.64 per cent). This may be due to the highest representation of these nationalities in the sample as well as the ease of access to diving training facilities in these countries.

Most of the divers participated in the survey hold Open Water Diver Certificate (34.9 per cent) while 23.3 per cent holds Advanced/Advanced Plus level Certification. It is also important to highlight that 26.17 per cent have been diving for more than eight years. On average, most of them (65 per cent) dive more than 30 times in a year and most of them have travelled quite extensively (31 per cent of the respondents have travelled to more than 4 countries. Egypt is the country commonly mentioned by the divers. This result could be a pointer that Egypt could be regarded as a competitor to the Maldives in the context of diving. Egypt is also noted by the respondents as the destination with the most satisfying diving experience followed by Australia, Mexico and Philippines. However, it is important to highlight even though 22 per cent of the respondents are first time visitors to the Maldives, 78 per cent visited the Maldives more than once. The highest number of visits by an individual diver is 25. This high percentage of repeat visits could be due to the high level of satisfaction among divers with their dive experience in the Maldives.

The divers visiting the Maldives are widely travelled and experienced in diving in other parts of the world; they thus have referral points by which to compare their experience in the Maldives. They can comprehend the favourable and the less favourable features of their experience in the Maldives.

The continuous updating of information about the destination, facilities and services will influence the divers' expectations as divers might update their expectations once they receive the updates on the destination (Boulding, William, Kalra, Staeling and. Zeithaml, 1993). Divers were found to use magazines, books and brochures (29 per cent), friends and relatives (23 per cent), tour operators (13 per cent), travel agents (14 per cent), and Internet (11 per cent) as sources of information. Not one respondent referred to tourism promotional fairs but 11 per cent referred to the Internet; almost equal to those referring to travel agents and tour operators. Information is vital in creating divers' expectations.

The average length of stay among divers is 13 nights which reflects the holiday characteristics of the European market. The national average of duration of stay in 1999 was 8.07 (Ministry of Tourism, personal communication, February, 27, 1999). So majority of the divers are staying longer than the national average, making the dive market very attractive for developers. The primary purpose for respondents to visit the Maldives is for diving (80 per cent) while 15 per cent indicated that their visit was for general holidaying including diving. So divers seem to arrange their trip for a specific purpose and it is important that the services provided to them enhance their satisfaction from the time of arrival to the time of departure.

DIVER SATISFACTION

According to Laws (1995), the majority of tourists have traveled widely, be it within their home country or international, gaining experiences with other destinations and they compare among facilities, attractions, and service standards, which influences their perceptions. Their satisfaction is affected by all the activities, services, facilities as well as natural factors they experience during their holiday. Hence, these factors should be measured separately (Danher and Arewieler, 1996; Gnoth, 1990). In other words, tourist satisfaction across as many aspects as possible should be examined as their motivation is a multiple and tourists look for satisfaction across all the products, services and interactions they experience during their holiday experience (Musa, 2002). As the divers' experience would be affected by the services and facilities offered in the resorts and interaction between employees working in the resorts, it is important to examine these aspects as part of evaluating their level of satisfactions. In this respect, respondents were asked to rank specific facilities, services and attributes that are not directly related to diving but which would impact their experience using a five points likert-scale (1 = Very Good and 5 = Very Poor).

With regard to the overall satisfaction of their holiday trip to the Maldives, 65 per cent of respondents indicated that they are very satisfied with their trip and 29 per cent of respondents indicated that they are satisfied. The highest level of satisfaction is further shown by the high percentage of respondents (94 per cent) willing to recommend Maldives to their dive buddies. However, four percent of respondents were unable to make a decision and one percent said that they are dissatisfied and in particular one percent of respondents indicated that they are very dissatisfied with their trip to the Maldives.

ARRIVAL AND TRANSFER

In the Maldives, tourists who have prior bookings for tourist resorts are received by the representatives of the respective facilities and transfers to and from resorts to the airport are arranged by tourist resorts. Hence, services provided at the airport and their travel to the holiday destination is the beginning of their experiences in the Maldives. These services are well received by the divers as the results show that divers are satisfied with the travel arrangements between respective resorts and the airport (mean = 2.21). First impression of the resorts would impact on the perception of the divers about the tourist resorts. Divers' evaluation of the first impression of the resorts are positive (mean = 0.52) and employees of the resorts is seen as friendly and hospitable (mean = 1.66). Resorts are believed to provide a peaceful and tranquil environment (mean = 1.64). Respondents tend to agree that they received value for money they spend for their holidays (mean = 2.5).

DIVE SCHOOL AND FEATURES

Services at dive school play a key role in ensuring an enjoyable diving experience. Hence, the facilities and services as well as the interaction of the dive school staff with the divers need to be understood to understand the diver's level of satisfaction. The results show that divers agree that the dive school are well located in the resorts (mean = 1.39) meaning easy access to and from the sea as well as from their rooms, and are happy with the information provided about the dive school in the resort (mean = 1.59). Similarly respondents agree that the dive school staff act professionally in dealing with the divers (mean = 1. 26), the diving equipments are of high standard (mean = 1.57), and safety procedures are well followed (mean = 1.36). They are happy with the size of the dive boats (mean = 1.55), pre and post dive briefing (mean = 1.38) and respondents do not feel that that dive boats are too crowded (mean = 1.69). With regard to variety of services of available at the dive school they rank this aspect also good (mean = 1.59).

ENVIRONMENTAL FEATURES

As the most important component of divers experience occurs below the surface the some of the important attributes related to underwater experience were measured using the same scale. The results are presented in Table 2.

Table 2. Ratings of selected attributes related to diving

Attribute	Mean Score
Visibility	1.99
Diversity of Marine Species	1.52
Variety of Corals	2.72
Underwater Geology	2.21
Artificial Reefs	2.90
Access to Dive Sites from Resorts	1.68

1= Very Good, 2 = Good, 3 = Neutral, 4 = Poor, 5= V. Poor

As shown in Table 2, the mean scores for these attributes vary from good to very good. The lowest ranked attribute is artificial reefs (shipwrecks). As there are very few artificial reefs and shipwrecks accessible to tourists, this rating is understandable. As a policy of the government, it is not encouraged to create artificial shipwrecks by sinking old vessels or by other means as there are numerous natural reefs in the country. As diving is based on the marine environment, it is important to seek their views on some of the management aspects of this vital resource. In this regard, divers believe that night fishing, which is a common practice in most of the resorts except a few, should be stopped. It is of no surprise that the respondents agree to stop night fishing which is quite detrimental to the house reefs as fishing line, lead and hooks stuck onto the reefs damage the reefs. Although diving in the Maldives has been undertaken for more than 30 years, there is no proper dive site management regime except declaring some dive sites as marine protected sites. However, more is expected than declaring marine protected sites. Divers agree that some dive sites should be closed for rejuvenation. Although, it might expected that divers would enjoy going to deeper depths, the results are inconclusive on allowing diving deeper than 30 meters and whether professional divers should be allowed to dive without supervision and divers.

LEVEL OF SATISFACTION WITH DIVING EXPERIENCE

In relation to their diving experience, 48.41 per cent of respondents stated that they were very satisfied with their diving experience and 38.16 per cent of respondents reported that they were satisfied with their diving experience. However, 2.47 per cent of respondents were very dissatisfied with their experience, and 3.50 per cent of respondents were dissatisfied while 7.42 per cent of respondents did not indicate a response.

When divers were asked to describe in their own words about the three most exciting moments of their diving experience in the Maldives, most of the respondents stated that they were impressed with the diversity and richness of marine species in the Maldives. "Many Sharks", "Mantas", "Many Fish", "Whale Sharks", "Corals", "Eagle Ray", "Soft Corals, were mostly mentioned by the respondents.

Similarly, respondents were asked to list the three most disappointing aspects of their visit to the Maldives. Respondents were mainly disappointed with "Coral Bleaching", "Destruction of Corals", and the "high Prices". When asked about the sites they visited, respondents have named 86 different sites and the the five highest ranked sites are Manta Point (6.13 %), Maaya Thila (4.25 %), Alimata DC (3.77 %), Embudu Experess (3.77 %) and Kuredu Caves. The last question in this section relates to post behaviour of respondents and the responses will be effected by their level of satisfaction. It inquired whether the respondents would recommend Maldives to friends and dive buddies. The responses indicated a high level of satisfaction among respondents. Indeed, 94 per cent of the respondents said that they would recommend the Maldives to friends and dive buddies.

The last question in the survey gave the opportunity for respondents to give any additional comments. These remarks can be categorised into "compliments", "concerns" and "disappointments". 11.58 per cent of the comments stressed their concern for protection and preservation including statements such as "I come back to Maldives every year, but I am afraid of future crowding". Ten percent of the comments complimented the Maldives and one diver commented that "I cannot imagine a nicer place to dive than the Maldives! We will keep coming back" and another diver stated that "My best holiday ever! Wish I had come earlier. It is more expensive than some others, but worth it". About 7.37 per cent of the comments praised the high standard of services offered at the dive schools. One diver commented, "Every visit seems to get better and the dive school is run with a more efficient and professional awareness".

Some of the dissatisfied divers have expressed their frustration in words as well. About 9.47 per cent were very unhappy with price of diving and drinks. 5.26 per cent expressed that the services offered in the resorts are not satisfactory. One diver commented that, "Too expensive for all drinks. Should be able to bring in own alcohol for personal consumption. This one reason I would not visit again" and another diver commented on the price, "The dives are too expensive! Drinks are too expensive!" A comment from diver expressing his/her dissatisfaction with the services said "5 start prices + 10% service charge without 5 star accommodation and services. Please rather have 3 start prices + 10% service."

IMPLICATIONS

This empirical study focused on satisfaction among divers from different parts of the world visiting the Maldives to enjoy the world-famous reef systems of the Maldives. The results of the study confirmed that the divers are highly satisfied with the diving experience in the Maldives irrespective of their level of experience and qualification in diving. The high level of satisfaction appears mainly due to the diversity and variety of marine species, professionalism of the staff at dive schools and the friendliness of the staff in the resorts. Only a few divers expressed their unhappiness about the prices of the resorts and the prices of soft drinks and alcoholic beverages, but on the whole, these sources of dissatisfaction were relatively minor.

Further research is needed to understand satisfaction among tourists who travel to participate in specific recreational activities such as diving, skiing etc. With regard to this study, in-depth analysis is needed of the causal factors that contribute to satisfaction. One area, which needs urgent attention, is the high level of discontent among the divers regarding the prices of drinks and diving. Consideration need to be given to changes in satisfaction levels and tourist arrivals because these two are complimentary.

This chapter would advance the understanding of readers on measurement and evaluation of tourist satisfaction involved with diving which embodies many experiential characteristics which is minimal in the literature on tourist satisfaction. Implications drawn from this study could be of great value to other destinations offering similar diving related products and services in the international tourism market (Thailand, Philippines, Fiji, Caribbean nations, Malaysia). This could enable these countries to compare and contrast their services with the Maldives and identify gaps and restructure their products if necessary to suit the diver's needs.

Conclusions drawn from the study are subject to some limitations. First, this empirical research on tourist satisfaction encompassed only English speaking divers staying in tourist resorts. From a research perspective, future research should consider how to broaden and capture all the elements in the diving market; especially divers staying on safari boats, guest houses and cruise ships and non-English speaking divers. Therefore, a replication is needed among those divers who cannot speak English, representing larger populations. Secondly, motivations affecting divers' decision to visit the Maldives could have been taken into account in evaluating diver satisfaction.

However, it is hoped that this chapter will be valuable to resort operators, dive operators, in drawing attention to aspects of satisfaction that can be used in evaluating the existing their current performance levels and in future planning of their products and services. In particular, the quality and perception of the marine environment, quality of the dive experience and professionalism of the dive schools are vital components in assessing divers' satisfaction levels.

REFERENCES

Anderson, E.W., and Fornell, C. (1993). A customer satisfaction research prospectus. In R.L. Oliver and R.T. Rust (Eds.), *Service quality: new directions in theory and practice* (239-266). Newbury Park: Sage.

Anderson, E. R. (1973). Consumer dissatisfaction: The effect of disconfirmed expectancy on perceived product performance. *Journal of Marketing Research,* 10, 38-44.

Aw, M. (1999). *24-hours beneath a rainbow sea: Maldives: the pictorial almanac.* Carlingford, NSW, Australia: OceanNEnvironemnt Australia.

Barsky, J. D. (1992). Customer satisfaction in hotel industry: Meaning and measurement. *Hospitality Research Journal, 16,* 51-73.

Bealer, R., and Willits, F. (1989). *The rural mystique in American culture: some musings.* Staff Paper No. 157, Pennsylvania State University, Agricultural Economics and Rural Sociology Department.

Beeho, A. J., and Prentice, R., C. (1997). Conceptualizing the experiences of heritage tourists: a case study of New Lanark World Heritage Village. *Tourism Management, 18* (2), 75-87.

Berkman, H.W. and Gilson, C. (1986), *Consumer behaviour: concepts and strategies* (3rd ed.). Kent, Boston.

Bojanic, D., C. (1996). Consumer perceptions of price, value, and satisfaction in the hotel industry: an exploratory study. *Journal of Hospitality and Leisure Marketing, 14* (1), 5-22.

Boulding, W., Kalra, A., Staeling, R., and Zeithaml, V. A. (1993). a dynamic process model of service quality: from expectations to behavioural intentions. *Journal of Marketing Research*, 30, 7-27.

Bowen, D. (2001). Research on tourist satisfaction and dissatisfaction: overcoming the limitations of a positivist and quantitative approach. *Journal of Vacation Marketing, 7* (1), 31-40

Bryant, C., Kent, B., Lindengeger, J., Schreigher, J. M., carnight, M. W., Cole, S., Uccellani, V., Brown, A. C., Blari, R. C., and Bustillo-Hernandes, M. M. (1998). Increasing consumer satisfaction. *Marketing health services.* 18 (4), 4-17.

Camerapix. (1993). *Spectrum guide to Maldives.* Nairobi: Camerapix Publishers International.

Chon, K., Christianson, J. D., and Chin-Lin, L. (1998). Modelling tourist satisfaction: Japanese tourists' evaluation of hotel stay experience in Taiwan. *Australian Journal of Hospitality Management, 2* (1), 1-6.

Crompton, J. L. (1979). Motivations fro pleasure vacation. *Annals of Tourism Research, 6*(4), 408-424.

Cronin, J. J., and Taylor, S. A. (1992). Measuring service quality: a re-examination an extension. *Journal of Marketing, 56* (3), 55-68

Danaher, P. J., and Arweiler, N. (1996). Customer satisfaction in the tourist industry: a case study of visitors to New Zealand. *Journal of Travel Research, 34* (Summer), 89-93

Gnoth, J. (1990). *Expectation and satisfaction in tourism: an exploratory study into measuring satisfaction.* Centre for Tourism, University of Otago, Dunedin, New Zealand: PhD thesis

Goodrich, J. N. (1978). The relationship between preferences for and perceptions of vacation destinations: application of a choice model. *Journal of Travel Research, 17* (Fall), 8-13.

Iacobucci, D., Grayson, K. A., and Ostrom, A. L. (1994), The calculus of service quality and satisfaction: theoretical and empirical differentiation and integration", In T. A. Swartz, D. E. Bowen, and S.W. Brown (Eds.), *Advances in Services Marketing and Management: Research and Practice* (1-67), Greenwich: JAI Press,

Gronroos, C. (1990). Service Management and marketing: managing the moments of truth in service competition. Lexington: Lexington Books.

Gyte, D. M., and Phelps, A. (1989). Patterns of Destination Repeat Business: British Tourists in Mallorca, Spain. *Journal of Travel Research, 28* (Summer), 24-28.

Hassan, K. and Azeez, N. D. (1994). *Maldives.* Torino: Tipografia Canale.

Heung, V. C. S. (2000). Satisfaction levels of mainland Chinese travellers with Hong Kong hotel services. *International Journal of Contemporary Hospitality Management, 12* (5), 308-315

http://www.dema.org

http://www.divernet.com

http://www.padi.com

Hu, Y., and Ritchie, J. R. B. (1993). Measuring destination attractiveness: a contextual approach. *Journal of Travel Research, 32* (2), 25-34

Hughes, K. (1991). Tourist satisfaction: A guided tour in North Queensland. *Australian Psychologist, 26*(3), 166-171.

Kelly, J. R. (1982). *Leisure.* Englewood Cliffs, NJ: Prentice-Hall.

Kozak, M. (2001). Comparative assessment of tourist satisfaction with destinations across two nationalities. *Tourism Management, 22* (4), 391-401

Kozak, M., and Rimmington, M. (2000). Tourist satisfaction with Mallorca, Spain as an off-season holiday destination. Journal of Travel Research, 38 (3), 260-269.

Laws, E. (1995). Tourist destination management: issues, analysis and policies. New York: Routledge

Lewis, B. R. (1991). Service quality: an international comparison of bank customers' expectations and perceptions. *Journal of Marketing Management, 7* (1), 47-62.

Mayo, E. J., and Jarvis, L. P. (1981). *The psychology of leisure travel: effective marketing and selling of travel services.* MA: CBI Publishing Company.

Meyer, A., and Westerbarkey, P. (1996). Measuring and managing hotel guest satisfaction. In D. M. Olsen, R. Teare, and E. Gummesson (Eds.), *Service quality in hospitality organisations* (185-204). London: Cassell.

Ministry of Tourism. (1998). *Maldivian tourism: 25 years of sustainable tourism development.* Malé: Novelty Printers and Publishers.

Murphy, J. (1974). *Concepts of Leisure: Philosophical Implications.* Englewood Cliffs, NJ: Prentice-Hall.

Musa, G. (2002). Sipadan: an over-exploited scuba-diving paradise? An analysis of tourism impact, diver satisfaction and management peiorities, *Tourism Geography,* 4, 195-209.

Musa, G., Kadir, S. L. and Lee, L. (2006). Layang Layang: an empirical study on scuba divers' satisfaction. *Tourism in marine environment, 2* (2), 89-102.

Oh, H., and Parks, S. C. (1997). Customer satisfaction and service quality: a critical review of the literature and research implications for the hospitality industry. *Hospitality Research Journal, 20* (3), 35-64.

Oliver, R. L. (1980). A cognitive model for the antecedents and consequences of satisfaction decisions. *Journal of marketing research, 27*, 460-469.

Oliver, R. L. (1993). Cognitive, affective, and attribute bases of the satisfaction response. *Journal of Consumer Research, 20* (3), 418-430.

Oliver, R.L. (1996). *Satisfaction: A behavioural perspective on the consumer.* New York: McGraw-Hill.

Otto, J. E., and Ritchie, J. R. B. (1996). The service experience in tourism. *Tourism Management, 17* (3), 165-174.

Parasuraman, A., Zeithaml, V. A., and Berry, L. L. (1985). Conceptual model of service quality and its implications for future research. *Journal of Marketing, 49* (4), 41-50

Pearce, P. L. (1980). A favourability-satisfaction model of tourists' evaluations. *Journal of Travel Research, 19* (1), 13-17.

Pieper, J. (1963). *Leisure: the Basis of Culture.* New York: Random House.

Pizam, A. (1994). Monitoring customer satisfaction. In B.E. Davis, and A.J. Lockwood, (Eds.), *Food and Beverage Management: A Selection of Readings* (231-247). London: Butterworth Heinemann.

Pizam, A. and Milman, A. (1993). Predicting satisfaction among first time visitors to a destination by using the expectancy disconfirmation theory. *International Journal of Hospitality Management, 12* (2), 197-209.

Pizam, A., Neumann, Y., and Reichel, A. (1978). Dimentions of tourist satisfaction with a destination area. *Annals of tourism Research, 5* (3), 314-322.

Reilly, M. D. (1990). Fee elicitation of descriptive adjectives for tourism image assessment. *Journal of Travel Research, 28* (4), 21-26

Ross, E. L. D., and Iso-Ahola, S. E. (1991). Sightseeing tourists' motivation and satisfaction. *Annals of Tourism Research, 18,* 226-237.

Saleh F., and Ryan, C. (1992). Client perceptions of hotels: a multi-attribute approach. *Tourism Management, 13* (2), 163-168.

Skin Diver. (1987). *Subscriber Survey.* Los Angels: Peterson Publishing.

Skin Diver. (1989). *Subscriber Survey.* Los Angels: Peterson Publishing.

U United Nations World Tourism Organisation (UNWTO). (2006). Third year of sustained growth [electronic version]. UNWTO World Tourism Barometer, 4 (3).

Wearing, B., and Wearing, S. (1988). 'All in a day's leisure': gender and the concept of leisure. *Leisure Studies,* 7, 11-123.

Westbrook, R. A. (1980). A rating scale for measuring product/service satisfaction. *Journal of Marketing, 44* (4), 68-72.

World Travel and Tourism Council (WTTC). (2006). Executive summary: Travel and tourism climbing to new heights. The 2006 Travel and tourism economic research. Retrieved December, 15, 2006, from http://www.wttc.org/2006TSA/pdf/ Executive% 20Summary %202006.pd

In: Tourist Satisfaction and Complaining Behavior
Editor: Atila Yüksel

ISBN 978-1-60456-002-2
© 2008 Nova Science Publishers, Inc.

Chapter 10

DIFFERENT NATIONALITIES, DIFFERENT HOLIDAY MOTIVATIONS AND ATTRIBUTE-SEEKING PATTERNS

Atila Yüksel and Fisun Yüksel
Adnan Menderes University, Turkey

INTRODUCTION

The need to analyze "what makes people from different countries to take overseas pleasure travels" and "what destination attributes they desire most" can be hardly debated (Baloglu and Uysal, 1996; Muller, 1989, 1991; Mok and Armstrong, 1998; Reisinger and Turner, 1998; Sussmann and Raschovsky, 1997; You, O'Leary, Morrison, and Hong, 2000). In the context of today's competitive and challenging international business environment, products in tourism should be designed, promoted and delivered, to fulfill needs, expectations and interests of actual and prospective customers (Mattila, 2000; Middleton, 1994; Reid and Reid, 1997; Uysal and Hagan, 1993). Middleton (1994, p. 71) stresses that "the more an organization knows about its customers and prospective customers-their needs and desires, their attitudes and behavior, the better it will be able to design and implement the marketing efforts required to stimulate their purchasing decisions". Delineating travel motivations and attribute–seeking patterns of travelers offers useful insights into understanding of their decision-making (Uysal and Hagan, 1993). It helps in designing effective promotional campaigns, as well as, in assessing what clientele is appropriate for a particular country, or destination, given its physical and cultural limitations.

Examining differences of motivations for taking holidays among travelers and understanding their attribute-seeking patterns are strategically important to stimulate purchasing decisions of prospective travelers. However, along with differences, investigation into similarities may have important implications for marketers of organizations operating across national and continental boundaries (McCleary et al. 1998). Given their position among the world's major tourist originating countries (Cope, 2000; Poon, 2000), surprisingly there has been little research focusing upon travelers from Germany and the UK (with few recent exceptions, e.g., Weber, 1997; Kozak, 2002). At present, the literature offers little help to marketers aiming to increase their share of foreign visitors from these two origin countries. Previous cross-national studies explored motivational differences among travelers mainly from Asian and Western countries. Most of these studies treated travelers originating from a nation as one single segment. Potential variations within travelers from the same country were however rarely analyzed. The motives that push people from one country to take holidays might be quite different from those of other nationalities. At the same time, travelers from the same country are likely to vary in their motivations and in the importance they attach to destination attributes. As Dann (1993) notes, not all people who have the same nationality will have identical cultures. Within a culture are several sub-segments. These segments may show greater variation on some variables than comparisons across nationalities can demonstrate. That is, within variations may sometimes be greater than between variations (Dann, 1993).

This chapter sought to explore British and German travelers' motivations for taking overseas holidays and their attribute-seeking patterns. The chapter further examined variations within British and German travelers (due to space limitations, only the results relating to British group will be discussed here). Based on its ease of administration and relatively few costs (Veal, 1997), a two-page self-reply survey instrument was administered to a total of 905 German and British travelers. The results suggested that push and pull factors were nationality-sensitive. The two prime reasons for taking overseas summer holidays for British and German travelers were desire for escape/relaxation and visiting new and exciting places. Additionally, cluster analysis showed that there were three segments within British travelers with significant differences in terms of importance attached to push and pull forces. This suggests that effective tourism marketing will be maximized when industry practitioners understand not only what travelers from different countries want from their vacation, but also how existing sub-segments within those particular countries make their travel decisions. Treating travelers from the same country as one single segment may not produce appropriate marketing/management solutions for individuals belonging to a distinct-subculture.

TRAVEL MOTIVATIONS

The key question of "what makes people travel?" has attracted considerable attention from academics. The answer to this question is not a simple one. Depending on the individual and his/her cultural conditioning, there may be many answers (Mayo and Jarvis, 1981). Travel is basically need-related (Cooper, Fletcher, Gilbert and Wanhill, 1993) and the inner urges, which initiate travel demand, are called travel motivations. Motivation refers to a state of need that exerts a push on the individual toward certain types of action that are likely to bring satisfaction (Moutinho, 1986). Travel is often stated to be a complex form of behavior through which the traveler seeks to satisfy not one single motivation but several distinct needs simultaneously (Baloglu and Uysal, 1996). According to Mannel and Iso-Ahola (1987), the desire to change from one's daily routine (i.e., escaping) and the desire to gain intrinsic personal and interpersonal rewards (i.e., seeking) operate simultaneously to bring about travel behavior. Some theories stress the need for balance and harmony, considering the traveler to be satisfied with the expected, and to be uncomfortable with the unexpected. Others suggest that the unexpected is satisfying and the individual will seek for complexity, not the sameness (Moutinho, 1986).

In his attempt to bring an answer to "why people travel", Dann (1977) proposed pull and push factors. The push factors are those socio-psychological factors that are internal to the individual and which explain the desire to go on holiday. Most of the push factors are intangible desires of the individual travelers such as the desire for escape, rest and relaxation, health and fitness, adventure, and social interaction (Baloglu and Uysal, 1996; Crompton, 1979). Pull factors are those, which affect the consumers' destination choice (Pearce, 1982). They represent the specific attractions of the destination, which induce the traveler to go there once the prior decision to travel was made (Dann, 1981). They both respond and reinforce push factor motivation (Dann, 1981). Pull factors include scenic attractions, beaches, historical sights, cultural characteristics (culinary), hospitality/friendliness, receptiveness, cost, climate, tourist activities, nightlife/entertainment, sports facilities and other destination characteristics (Bello and Etzel, 1985; Reisinger and Turner, 2000). Combination of these attributes determines a destination's attractiveness (Gearing, Swart and War, 1974).

Crompton (1979) identified nine motivations influencing the selection of vacation destination. These motivations were escape from a perceived mundane environment, exploration and evaluation of self, relaxation, prestige, regression, enhancement of kinship relationships, and facilitation of social interaction, novelty and education. Mayo and Jarvis (1981) developed a four-category travel motivation. Physical motivators included physical rest and participation in sports. The desire for knowledge of other countries, folklore, religion, and culinary constituted cultural motivators. The desire to meet new people and to visit friends was labeled as interpersonal motivators. The desire for recognition, attention, appreciation and good reputation were called status and prestige motivators. Similarly, Ragheb and Beard (1982) proposed a four-category motivation scale. The intellectual component-learning, exploring, discovering, or imagining, the social component-the need for friendship and interpersonal relationships, and the need for the esteem of others, the competence-mystery component-master, challenge, and compete, and the stimulus-avoidance component-the drive to escape and get away from over-stimulating life situations. A perusal of other studies suggests that the adjectives and the categories of tourist motivations may differ in number, but similar themes recur (Ryan 1997). In general, holidays are seen to arise from the need to escape from everyday surroundings for purposes of relaxation and discovering new things, places and people, and may be periods of self-discovery (Ryan, 1997). A holiday could be for recuperation and regeneration, compensation and social integration, escape, communication, freedom and self-determination, self-relation, happiness and to broaden the mind (Krippendorf, 1987).

NATIONALITY AND TRAVEL MOTIVATIONS

While there are critics against its use (Dann, 1993), previous studies showed that nationality might determine a tourist's choice of a vacation destination, other economic behavior related to foreign travel for pleasure, information search, and expectations for tourism services (Muller, 1991; Pizam, 1999). Travelers with different country origins have shown evidence of differences in destination behavior patterns such as trip arrangement, recreation activities, expenditure, etc. Yuan and McDonald (1990) examined motivations of travelers from Japan, France, Germany and France. They identified five push factors from 29 motivational items. These include escape, novelty, prestige, enhancement of kinship relationships, and relaxation/hobbies. Seven pull factors were identified from 53 attraction items. These include: budget, culture and history, wilderness, ease of travel, cosmopolitan environment, facilities and hunting.

Using national household surveys conducted by the Canadian Tourism Commission and U.S. Tourism Industries for a cross-cultural comparison between British and Japanese travelers, You et al. (2000) found different travel motives and benefit-seeking patterns among the travelers from the UK and Japan. They specifically stated that the motives (push factors) that cause people from one country to make long haul pleasure travel trips might be quite different from those of other nationalities. At the same time, international travelers from different countries are likely to vary significantly in the importance they attach to specific destination attributes (pull factors). For the travelers from the UK, socialization with other people was very important travel motivation. For the Japanese, physical motivators of getting physical rest, relaxing from work, and having fun and being entertained were of greater relative importance. Travelers from the UK and Japan attached different levels of importance to pull factors such as people-interactive activities, prices of restaurants and culture and heritage activities and outdoor activities.

McClellan and Foushee (1983) found that level of importance attached to selected vacation attributes varies between respondents from different countries. In a similar tradition, Kim and Lee (2000) examined cultural differences between Japanese and American travelers with respect to cultural attitudes that reflect individualism and collectivism and travel motivation. They found that two cultures differ with regard to specific attitudes. They differed in prestige/status family togetherness and novelty while they were insignificantly different in knowledge and escape. Japanese travelers showed more collectivism in expressing their travel motivation, while Anglos exhibited individualist characteristics. Summers and McColl-Kennedy (1998) compared the decision process as well as the influence of motivations, perceived risk and cultural values in destination choice used by a convenient sample of young Americans and Chinese-Malaysian business major students in terms of Australia as a holiday destination. They found considerable cultural variation in terms of the value systems of each group, the factors influencing the process, and the specific destination choice criteria used to make a destination choice. They concluded that while the decision making process may be universal; the factors that influence the process may not.

Research of Mok and Armstrong (1998) points out that travelers from different countries, in this case from the UK, USA, Australia, Japan and Taiwan, do have dissimilarity in their expectations for hotel services. In their study, two of the service quality dimensions, tangibles and empathy, were significantly different among the five tourist groups. They suggest that special arrangements may be needed to cater for the specific needs of customers from different cultures. The study of Armstrong et al. (1997) reached a similar conclusion that customer expectations for hotels might be culture-bound rather than culture-free. McCleary et al. (1998) identified many significant differences between Korean and U.S. business travelers in the importance placed on specific hotel characteristics. Mattila's (2000) recent study in the hospitality area provides support that customers' evaluations of service encounters might be culturally bound. Mattila (2000) found that Asian traveler gave lower ratings to the service provider. The managerial implication of such divergence is of great importance. Hospitality and tourism organizations might benefit from providing cultural training for their customer-contact employees (Mattila, 2000).

Several other studies highlighted the variations in the travel characteristics and behaviors of visitors from different countries. Pizam and Sussmann's (1995), Pizam and Jeong's (1996), and Pizam et al's (1997) studies reinforce the existence of a culture-vacation travel relationship. Pizam et al (1997) identified significant differences between Japan, France, Italy and the U.S. visitors in the behavioral characteristics researched. They found perceived differences in eighteen of the twenty behavioral characteristics. The greatest difference by nationality was socializing with other travelers. Japanese travelers were found to stay mostly with their own group and avoid socializing with other travelers. The French behaved in a similar way as the Japanese, while Italian travelers and American travelers had higher levels of interaction and socializing with others. Another study on cross-cultural analysis of vacation travel patterns revealed that there were significant differences between French and English Canadians. They differed in numbers of vacation trips taken, number of sources consulted before traveling, importance assigned to several accommodation attributes and importance assigned to several destination attributes (Sussmann and Rashchovsky, 1997). French Canadians were found to prefer organized activities more than their English counterparts. They placed greater importance on outdoor activities and the sun, while English Canadians placed greater importance on visiting friends and relative and trying local food.

As was stated earlier, rarely has been a research conducted to explore differences and similarities between German and British travelers. Weber (1997) studied German travelers to Australia. She found that seeing spectacular landscapes, experiencing the expanse of the country and watching the unique fauna were the highest in terms of expectations. This finding corresponds with that of another study, which showed that an unspoiled environment was crucial to whether or not Germans were satisfied with the holiday (Lettl-Schoreder, 1998). A growing number of German travelers are now interested in holidays providing direct nature experience (Lettl-Schoreder, 1998). Respect for the customs and tradition of local people is a very important issue for Germans (Lettl-Schoreder, 1998). There is an increasing segment within the German travelers who want to get to know the tourists sights, but is also interested in the country and the people, seeking social contacts with the local population (Lettl-Schoreder, 1998). It was forecasted that tourism for relaxation would not disappear completely, but diminish in importance for German travelers (Lettl-Schoreder, 1998). Baloglu and Uysal (1996) investigated German travelers and looked into the relationship between push and pull factors. Experiencing new and different lifestyles, being free, and seeing and experiencing a foreign destination were the three most important travel motivations. Outstanding scenery, warm welcome for tourists, standard of hygiene, personal safety and different culture were identified as the five most important pull items for Germans. A recent research into holiday motivations of German and British travelers to two different destinations, Turkey and Mallorca, identified significant differences (Kozak, 2002). Germans traveling Turkey were found to travel for relaxation and physical reasons, whereas British were more concerned with pleasure and fantasy. Another striking difference was found on cultural motivations. Germans gave higher importance to cultural motivations than British travelers did. Travelers from the two countries were found to vary in the range of desired destination attributes.

RESEARCH INSTRUMENT AND DATA COLLECTION

Previous studies have made substantial contribution to our understanding about motivations and specific destination attributes sought by travelers from different countries. Despite the significance of outbound travel from both Germany and the UK to major European and other tourist destinations, German and British travelers' holiday motivations, and potential variations between the two, have seldom been studied. Additionally, most studies treated travelers originating from a nation as one segment and explored differences mostly between two or more Asian and Western nationalities. Potential variations within travelers from the same country were rarely analyzed. The motives that push people from one country to take holidays might be quite different from those of other nationalities. At the same time, travelers from the same country are likely to vary in their motivations and in the importance they attach to destination attributes.

The main aim of this research was to explore differences and similarities in push and pull variables between British and German travelers. The study also examined variations within British travelers. To fulfill the research objectives, in this study a two-page self-completed questionnaire was developed. Self-completed questionnaires are popular among researchers (Orams and Page, 2001; Veal, 1997). The push and pull items were derived primarily from the literature search and unstructured interviews with prospective travelers (n= 20). Additionally, a free-response survey carried out with 120 German and British travelers departing from an international airport in Turkey to elicit their holiday motives, and compliments and complaints about destination service attributes. The prime reason for eliciting respondents' complaints and compliments was that these aspects do highlight important dimensions of holiday experience, which travelers really care about. A pilot test was conducted (n =35) in order to check and fine-tune the item list. Revisions were made based on the recommendations. Eleven holiday motivations and 28 destination attributes were retained after this process.

The final questionnaire consisted of two sections. In the first section, general information about the respondents was obtained. The second section was structured to identify travelers' holiday motivations and destination service attributes sought from overseas summer holiday destination. For the push items, respondents were asked to rate how important each reason was when considering an overseas summer holiday. For pull items, respondents were asked to rate how important each item was when choosing an overseas summer holiday destination. Specifically, respondents were required to give a rating between 1=not important and 7=very important for each of the attribute variables included in the questionnaire. The researcher adopted the use of seven-point labeled Likert scales, as these scales have been reported to create variance that is necessary for examining the relationships among variables and create adequate reliability estimates (Hinkin, Tracey and Enz, 1997). The questionnaire was translated and back translated from English to German.

The research was conducted at the passenger departure lounge of an international airport situated in southwest of Turkey. A total of 905 travelers departing from Dalaman Airport during a three-week period in September 1999 were surveyed. Intercept survey design was adopted (Denstadli, 2000). Depending on the numbers of departure, every nth respondent passing from immigration services was approached and invited to the study. 25 travelers refused to participate because of their flight time. 30 respondents returned incomplete questionnaires

DATA ANALYSIS

A series of chi-square tests was conducted to determine whether significant difference existed in the demographic profile of respondents between the two groups. These tests showed that there were no such significant differences in terms of age and gender. It was therefore concluded that the two groups were homogeneous in terms of these two characteristics. This finding suggests that measured differences were due to research design effects rather than differing characteristics of the two samples. As a second step in the analysis, the Principal Components and Orthogonal (Varimax) rotation methods were employed in the factor analysis so as to summaries most of the original information to a minimum number of factors. The criteria for the number of factors to be extracted were based on the Eigenvalue (≥ 1) and the significance of factor loading ($\geq .5$). A series of independent t-tests were employed based on the factor and attribute means in order to test whether British and German travelers differed in their reasons for taking overseas summer holiday and destination attributes that they seek when selecting an overseas summer holiday destination. Finally, Cluster analysis was employed to identify segments within British travelers group. One-way ANOVA tests were used to understand whether differences in importance attached to both push and pull forces were statistically significant.

RESULTS AND DISCUSSION

All respondents were on package tours. 442 respondents (52%) were British and 408 (48%) were German. 55% of the British and 56% of the German travelers were female. The age distribution of both German and British travelers was similar. The majority of respondents (44% and 42% respectively) were young to middle-age travelers (between 25-44 years old). The majority of German and British travelers were on two weeks package holiday (51% and 49% respectively). Hotels were the principal accommodation type used by both German and British travelers.

THE PUSH FORCES

The appropriateness of the factor analysis was examined by correlation, measures of sampling adequacy (MSA) and reliability alpha to ensure that the data set was appropriate for factor analysis. A visual inspection of correlation matrix revealed that the majority of correlation values were significant at 0.01 level. This suggests that there was an adequate basis to proceed on to the next level of examination of adequacy for factor analysis. The overall significance of the correlation matrix was examined by the Bartlett test of Spherity. The test revealed that the overall significance of the correlation matrix was 0.000 with a Bartlett test of Spherity value of 5996. It indicated that the data matrix had sufficient correlation to the factor analysis. The Kaiser-Meyer-Olkin overall measure of sampling adequacy was 0.91, which was meritorious, suggesting that data were appropriate to factor analysis. The total scale reliability was 0.75. From the Orthogonal (Varimax) rotated factor matrix, 3 factors, which explained 63% of the variance, were identified (Table 1). The communality of each variable was relatively high, ranging from 0.57 to 0.82.

Table 1. Comparison of travel motivations

	Novelty and Culture	Escape and Relaxation	Socializa-tion	Mean (British)	Mean (German)	t-value	2-tail sig.
To relax mentally		.741		6.3150	6.2911	-.191	.849
To rest physically		.781		6.1167	6.083	-.109	.919
To get away from everyday life		.805		6.0959	5.7869	-1.845	.066
To be away from crowds of people		.621		5.4116	4.5974	-4.273	.000
To experience something entirely different	.564			5.5101	5.0132	-2.887	.004
To visit new and exciting places	.767			4.0261	4.8312	3.406	.001
To see beautiful scenery	.821			5.8406	5.7375	-.738	.461
To see and do new things	.835			5.8290	6.0886	1.689	.092
To get to know local culture and the way of life	.705			5.3878	5.7179	2.055	.040
To have fun, being entertained			.859	5.6812	5.9367	1.719	.086
To make new friends			.686	4.3130	5.0000	3.185	.002
Variance explained (%)	32.8	17.9	12.3				

Each factor was named based on the common characteristics of the variables it included (Table 1). The first factor explained 33% of the variance. It was labeled novelty/culture. This factor contained experiencing something entirely different, visiting new and exciting places, seeing beautiful scenery, doing new things, and getting to know local culture and the way of life. The second factor was labeled as escape/relaxation and it consisted of mental and physical relaxation, getting away from everyday life and being away from crowds of people. It accounted for 18% of the variance. Socialization was chosen to identify the final factor, as it contained having fun, being entertained and making new friends. This final factor explained 12% of the variance (Table 1).

The structure of the motivation dimensions appeared in this study corresponded with the results of other studies. For example, the relaxation, novelty/culture and socialization dimensions are similar to physical motivators, cultural motivators and interpersonal motivators classification of Mayo and Jarvis (1981). The top five push forces reflect some interesting information on what motivate travelers from these two countries (Table 1). For

British travelers, the top five motivations are: relaxation, getting away from everyday life, visiting new and interesting places, seeing beautiful scenery and to get to know local culture and the way of life. For Germans, the top five are, relaxation, seeing beautiful scenery, getting to know local culture and the way of life, getting away from everyday life and visiting new and exciting places. British and German travelers did not differ significantly in their importance ratings for "relaxation" and "visiting new and exciting places". This may suggest that escaping from home environment and visiting new and exciting places are the two main motivators of pleasure travelers, no matter where they are from (Iso–Ahola, 1982). This finding supports Ryan's (1997) statement: "holidays are seen to arise from the need to escape from everyday surroundings for purposes of relaxation and discovering new things, places and people".

Independent t-tests showed significant differences between British and German travelers in eight of the eleven travel motivations (Table 2). British travelers viewed "being away from crowds of people" as being more important than did Germans. They also rated "experiencing entirely different things", as being more important than Germans. "Getting away from everyday life" was another moderately important motivation for them, but slightly less so for Germans. They attached less importance to "getting to know local culture and the way of life". Comparatively high desire of this group for escaping routine or some particular source of stress may indicate that British travelers may be more escape-minded. Compared to Germans, British travelers were less for cultural interactions with local people or other travelers. "To experience something entirely different" was another important holiday motivation to British travelers. This may indicate that the sample British travelers are adventuresome. While the data does not enable, it may be speculated that rather than to choose the destination which has previously proven satisfactory, British travelers may seek a different destination brand with which they had no previous experience. Novelty oriented British travelers might anticipate that re-experiencing a known stimuli would not contribute as much as experiencing new stimuli (Crompton, 1979). Destination authorities should offer new and exciting experiences to British travelers each time in order to gain their repeat business. British travelers may however choose the same destination for a series of other reasons. The mean age of the respondents in this study however should be acknowledged. Young British travelers may have different holiday motivations from other age groups.

"Having fun, being entertained" was a more important travel motivation for Germans than it was for British travelers. Germans rated "seeing and doing new things" as being more important than British travelers did. "Making new friends" was another more important holiday motivation for Germans than it was for British travelers. Germans also attached more importance to "getting to know local culture and the way of life" than British travelers did. Interactions with unknown people of host culture and other travelers contain elements of risks and adventure. It may be speculated that German travelers have more tolerance for cultural differences, and appreciation for the unique aspects of the host culture. They might be socially motivated travelers, viewing the vacation as an opportunity to interact with other people.

THE PULL FACTORS

The scale was first subjected to a reliability analysis. The total scale reliability was 0.91 (Table 2).

Table 2. Pull Factors

	Service quality	Hospitality	Variety/Prices	Entertainment	Pleasant Environment
Standard of services	.620				
High quality food and drink	.573				
Food hygiene	.793				
Ease/safety of traffic	.721				
Quality of accommodation	.552				
Consistent quality of services	.545				
Friendly and courteous services	.654				
Efficient immigration services	.560				
Welcoming attitudes of local people		.635			
Welcoming attitudes of vendors		.701			
Transportation efficiency			.540		
Price levels			.589		
Availability/accessibility of information			.620		
Variety of interesting places to visit			.660		
Availability/quality of water sports				.665	
Day time entertainment				.725	
Night time entertainment				.674	
Ease of communication				.511	
Clean/pleasant environment					.519
Peaceful/ quiet area					.613
Uncrowded beaches					.655
Variance explained (%)	**33.3**	**8.2**	**5.3**	**4.3**	**3.7**

Principal Factor analysis was employed with Varimax rotation to identify dimensions of pull factors. The analysis reduced the attributes to five factors that accounted for 55% of the total variance. These factors were labeled according to the variables that carried higher factor loadings on a certain factor (Table 2). The first factor was labeled as "Service Quality", and the remaining were Hospitality, Variety and Prices, Entertainment and Pleasant Environment. The structure of pull factors shares similarities with that of other destination choice and attractiveness studies. Mok and Amstrong (1995) found that the top five destination choice criteria were safety, scenic beauty, price of trip, service in hotels and restaurants and friendliness of local people. In a study on criteria for judging destination attractiveness, Var, Beck, and Loftus (1977) identified natural factors, social factors, historical factors, recreational and shopping facilities, and infrastructure and food and shelter as significant. Before discussing the pull factors that play important role in travelers' destination choice based on country of origin, it is worth taking a look at the overall importance score distribution. Table 3 highlights the five attributes that received the highest scores.

Table 3. Comparison of importance (destination attributes)

	British	German	t-value	2-tail sig.
Availability/quality of water sports	2.9265	4.0506	4.900	.000
High quality food and drink	5.9827	5.4103	-3.886	.000
Price levels	6.0029	5.4487	-4.420	.000
Convenient location of facilities	5.8285	5.4000	-3.388	.001
Traffic ease/safety	5.2616	4.6667	-2.889	.004
Standard of services	5.9043	5.5500	-2.571	.010
Uncrowded beaches	5.7500	6.1392	2.473	.014
Transportation efficiency	5.1130	4.7125	-2.078	.038
Ease of communication	4.3198	3.8861	-2.040	.042
Safety and security	5.9507	5.6154	-1.952	.052
Food and drink variety	5.6667	5.9367	1.940	.053
Accommodation quality	6.0116	5.7792	-1.828	.068
Shopping facilities	4.7572	5.0886	1.700	.090
Sunny climate	6.1590	5.9494	-1.644	.101
Food hygiene	6.4220	6.5375	.999	.318
Day time entertainment	3.8924	3.7308	-.785	.433
Welcoming attitudes of local people	6.1214	5.9494	-1.515	.130
Availability of information	4.9333	4.9873	.283	.777
Pleasant environment	6.2580	6.2000	-.468	.640
Peaceful and quiet area	5.9391	5.9125	-.172	.864
Night time entertainment	3.5598	3.6329	.311	.756
Consistent quality of services	5.4058	5.3462	-.372	.710
Convenient operating hours of facilities	5.1192	5.1026	-.099	.922
Efficient immigration services	5.4913	5.4557	-.194	.846
Efficient services at tourist facilities	5.2471	5.1333	-.683	.495
Friendly and courteous services	5.6696	5.7436	.530	.597
Welcoming attitudes/behaviors of vendors	5.7681	5.7564	-.089	.929
Variety of interesting places to visit	5.4855	5.5584	.478	.633

The variable received the highest score from both German and British travelers is "food hygiene". Obviously, sanitation should be a priority for destination authorities. Food safety reputation of a destination may affect German and British travelers' visit decisions. Clean and pleasant environment was the second highest rated item. Travelers are likely to spend their holiday time and money in environments that prompt a feeling of pleasure, whereas they will avoid unpleasant environments (Wakefield and Blodgett, 1994). The welcoming attitudes/friendliness of local people was the next highly rated variable. This is consistent with results of some previous studies. Friendliness toward travelers was reported to be an important criterion in destination selection (Ryan, 1995). Friendliness was among the motivations most likely to influence travelers to visit northern Australia (Ross, 1992). Hu and Ritchie (1993) identified local people's attitude as one of the factors, which could significantly contribute to the attractiveness of a tourism destination. Tourist satisfaction studies reported that holiday satisfaction did not only come from beautiful sights but also from the behavior one encounters, from the information one gets, and from the efficiency with which needs are served (Ohja, 1982). Tourist impressions of tourist-host interaction may become a significant element in holiday satisfaction because hosts (or service providers) are the first contact point for travelers and remain in direct contact through an entire holiday (Krippendorf, 1987). Authentic interpersonal experiences between hosts and travelers may lead to psychological comfort in satisfying travelers' needs. Consistent with the push factors, the opportunities for visiting new places while on vacation was of great importance to both British and German travelers. This finding is consistent with that of Weber. Weber (1997) found that Germans rated visiting new places and beautiful scenery high. The peacefulness of the destination was another attribute highly rated by Germans.

Independent t-tests indicated that Germans were far less concerned with standard of services than British travelers were. "Quality of food and drink" received greater importance rating from British travelers. Availability/quality of water sports appeared to be important to Germans more than it was to British travelers. This is consistent with the trend of German travelers favoring more activity holidays (Weber, 1997). You et al. (2000) reported a similar finding. Sports activities appeared to be important for German travelers, but this was not the case for both UK and Japanese travelers.

Ease/safety of traffic was an attribute to which British travelers attached higher ratings than Germans did. The price levels of services and goods in the area were more important to British travelers, but far less important to German travelers. British travelers attached more importance to location of accommodation than did Germans. The crowd level on beaches was a very important attribute for German travelers than it was for British travelers. Being able to communicate in one's own language was more important to British travelers than it was to German travelers. This is another finding consistent with that of previous studies. The ease/difficulty of communication influences destination selection. It may affect enjoyment of the host environment and their future destination selection decisions (Reisinger and Waryszak, 1996). Ease of communication may foster empathy and a feeling of safety.

The difference in destination safety issue between German and British travelers is interesting (Table 3). British travelers were more safety concerned than Germans. Destination safety however did not rank among the top five destination attributes sought. Similarly, in another study, safety and security considerations ranked as the least important factor in making destination choice decisions (Norton, 1987). The low ranking of safety in importance appeared in this study should not be misleading. Travelers' safety-related attitudes are bound to change as a result of social unrests, terrorist attacks, and so on. Hence, had the study been undertaken following an international crisis (e.g., 11 September attack) safety and security consideration would have been among the top important factors. Reputation of shopkeepers attitude/behavior toward travelers was another moderately important pull variable. Harassment is one of the most frequently identified negative experiences reported by travelers (Albuquerque and McElroy, 2001). Moderately high mean ratings of both German and British travelers suggest that attitudes and behavior of vendors/shopkeepers should not be annoying. British travelers had a slightly higher importance on accommodation quality. This difference however was not statistically significant. Their high ratings for accommodation quality may suggest that physically and psychologically comforting accommodation facilities are instrumental in selection. British and German travelers did not differ in their importance ratings for the remaining attributes (Table 3).

VARIATIONS WITHIN BRITISH TRAVELERS

A combination of hierarchical and non-hierarchical cluster analysis was employed to segregate British travelers into mutually exclusive groups based on their motivation ratings. Using both approaches was proven to be more reliable than using only one method (Hair et al., 1995). In this study, a hierarchical technique (Complete Linkage with squared Euclidean Distance) was conducted on a randomly selected sub-sample to obtain some idea about the number of clusters using the dendogram. This process suggested that three clusters were appropriate. Subsequently, a non-hierarchical cluster analysis was conducted to generate three clusters. The number of sample decreased to 395 due to missing values. The first Cluster accounted for 40% of the respondents, the second Cluster represented 28%, and the third Cluster included 32% of the respondents (Table 4).

Table 4. Segments within British Travelers

	N	Cluster 1	Cluster 2	Cluster 3	F	Sig.
Novelty /Culture	159	.63357	-1.13659	.01134	153.869	.000
Escape/Relaxation	110	.42160	-.19192	-.25770	21.202	.000
Socialization	126	.28431	.68290	-1.13031	197.671	.000

A one way ANOVA test showed the relative importance of push forces differed significantly among the three clusters (Table 5). Travelers in cluster one and three attached significantly higher importance to experiencing something entirely different. This was a less travel motivation for cluster two. Having fun, being entertained was a more important travel motivation for cluster two than it was for cluster three and one. Visiting new and exciting places was another important holiday motivation for cluster one. This holiday motivation received moderate importance ratings from cluster two. Getting away from crowds of people was relatively more important holiday motivation for Cluster one than for cluster three. Clusters also differed significantly on getting to know local culture and the way of life.

As for pull variables, there were significant differences among clusters (Table 6). Cluster one attached higher ratings to food hygiene, clean and pleasant environment, welcoming attitude of local people, high quality food/drink, sunny climate, quality of accommodation, level of prices, peaceful and quite area. Cluster two gave higher importance to sunny climate, food hygiene, clean and pleasant environment, quality of accommodation, price levels, high quality food and drink, welcoming attitudes of shopkeepers, standard of services.

Clean and pleasant environment, food hygiene, peaceful and quite area, sunny climate, welcoming attitudes of local people, accommodation quality, uncrowded beaches received higher importance ratings from cluster three. This cluster did not attach high importance to price levels. Different from the other two clusters, travelers in this cluster did not highly concern with standard of services.

Table 5. Comparison of importance within segments (motivations)

	Cluster 1	Cluster 2	Cluster 3	F	Sig.
To relax mentally	6.6174	5.9767	6.1415	14.248	.000
To relax physically	6.3087	5.9651	5.4623	13.711	.000
To get away from everyday life	6.6040	5.8023	5.6226	29.256	.000
To be away from crowds of people	5.7517	4.3488	5.7925	33.384	.000
To experience something entirely different	6.1946	4.7442	5.1698	49.925	.000
To have fun, being entertained	4.6174	5.1860	2.3019	106.456	.000
To visit new and exciting places	6.4631	5.0000	5.6698	64.514	.000
To see beautiful scenery	6.4765	4.3953	6.0755	125.386	.000
To see-do new things	6.2013	4.3837	5.0566	81.189	.000
To get to know local culture-the way of life	6.3020	4.6512	5.6604	71.251	.000
To make new friends	5.0268	4.8488	2.8491	73.416	.000

Table 6. Comparison of importance within segments (destination attributes)

	Mean (Cluster 1)	Mean (Cluster 2)	Mean (Cluster 3)	F	Sig.
Standard of services	6.2432	5.7326	5.5472	15.032	.000
Availability/quality of water sports	3.2808	2.9767	2.3846	7.996	.000
High quality food and drink	6.2953	5.8372	5.6321	12.886	.000
Sunny climate	6.2349	6.4302	5.8396	9.500	.000
Food hygiene	6.6846	6.3256	6.1321	11.439	.000
Traffic ease/safety	5.7919	4.8140	4.8571	16.144	.000
Day time entertainment	4.3378	4.2093	3.0283	26.031	.000
Transportation efficiency	5.6689	5.0000	4.4057	25.793	.000
Accommodation quality	6.2215	5.9186	5.7714	7.197	.001
Welcoming attitudes of local people	6.4228	5.9651	5.8302	18.079	.000
Price levels	6.2752	5.8837	5.7264	12.766	.000
Convenient location of facilities	6.0946	5.8721	5.4381	15.317	.000
Safety and security	6.3087	5.9551	5.4623	13.711	.000
Availability of information	5.4662	4.7558	4.3208	20.947	.000
Clean /pleasant environment	6.5068	6.1047	6.0660	8.356	.000
Peaceful/ quiet area	6.2365	5.1628	6.1321	23.744	.000
Availability of night time activities	3.8311	4.8140	2.1429	69.039	.000
Ease of communication	4.6622	4.8140	3.4057	26.406	.000
Consistent quality of services	5.8176	5.3721	4.8491	18.674	.000
Convenient operating hours of facilities	5.5203	5.2558	4.4245	24.280	.000
Efficient immigration services	5.9392	5.3605	4.9434	16.577	.000
Shopping facilities	5.3490	4.7674	3.8774	30.957	.000
Variety of food and drink	6.0872	5.5882	5.1415	25.326	.000
Uncrowded beaches	6.1544	5.2824	5.5849	15.244	.000
Efficient services at tourist facilities	5.7785	4.9059	4.7925	26.922	.000
Friendly and courteous services	6.1342	5.3529	5.2830	26.149	.000
Welcoming attitudes of vendors	6.1678	5.5647	5.3962	22.873	.000
Variety of interesting places to visit	5.9463	4.8605	5.3774	26.811	.000

CONCLUSION AND IMPLICATIONS

This paper has used empirical data from a recent cross-national research on British and German travelers to explore their personal motivations for taking overseas holidays and their attribute-seeking patterns. Results of the study suggested that travelers had multiple travel motives and the push and pull factors were nationality-sensitive. Multiple motives suggest that travelers seek different types of rewards or satisfactions when they travel (Mayo and Jarvis, 1981). Destination marketers must therefore view each country differently and adjust the messages by taking into account of cultural differences. Marketing messages emphasizing the provision of opportunities for relaxation (a sensory reward) would be of great interest to both German and British travelers. Messages stressing provision of opportunities for socializing, friendliness and getting to know other cultures (a social reward) would be of greater appeal to Germans than it would be for British travelers. Messages that stress availability of opportunities that enable travelers to be away from crowd of people would appeal to British travelers more than it would to German travelers.

In order to pull travelers, it is imperative to understand their attribute seeking patterns. Results of the study suggested that in additional to such universal factors as climate, pleasant environment and trip cost, other variables, including destination reputation for food safety, ease/safety of traffic, ease of communication, etc., would play role in traveler's selection decisions. The importance attached to destination attributes differed between German and British travelers. This has important marketing implications. Marketing messages emphasizing availability of sport activities would appeal more to Germans. British travelers would be more responsive to messages emphasizing ease/safety of traffic, food quality and convenient location of facilities.

It is important to comprehend push and pull factor differences and similarities among travelers from different countries and to develop tourism products and services in response to these differences and similarities. Effective tourism marketing will however be maximized when industry practitioners understand not only what travelers from a particular country want from their vacation, but also how existing sub-segments within that culture make decisions. The study identified three clusters within British travelers. They differed in their importance attached to both push and pull factors. While the same analysis was not run for the German respondents, as other studies show (Lettl-Schoreder, 1998), it is possible that different consumer groups may exist within German travelers. A German consumer group may like to lying around on the beach and swimming, barely interested at all in the destination country. Another group of German travelers may seek social interaction with local people. These differences require differentiated marketing focus. For example, to attract more British travelers from cluster one, tourism marketers should emphasize opportunities for experiencing something entirely different, visiting new places, and physical and mental relaxation.

While this study adds to our understanding of differences and similarities between German and British travelers, certain limitations of the present study should be noted and serve to guide future research. The generalisability of the findings is limited due to sample and methodological considerations. It would be useful to have a larger sample with a wider variety of points of departure and times of the season. Not all possible dimensions of motivation were empirically investigated in this study. Future studies should include motivations dealing with self-actualization. Respondents' answers regarding the importance of pull and push factors were not for a specific destination, but for overseas pleasure travel. Their importance ratings were gathered following the end of their holiday at an airport departure lounge. The importance ratings might be biased by respondents' highly positive or negative experiences in Turkey. The use of attribute importance may have further limitations, as respondents may have different interpretations of the importance question. The study identified three clusters. It however did not make further analysis to establish viability, actionability, and reachability of segments to declare them as feasible market segments. This study did not examine the correspondence between travelers' holiday motivations and destination attributes desired. Finally, the need for a careful choice of segmentation variables can hardly be debated, as follow-up management decisions will rely on the information based on the selected variables. This study used nationality for segmentation. However, several other factors may affect travelers' motivation and attribute seeking patterns. Future studies may employ different segmentation bases, including personal values. The results of this study will hopefully serve as a base for more comparative research.

REFERENCES

Albuquerque, K., and McElroy, L. J. (2001). Tourist harassment Barbados survey results. *Annals of Tourism Research*, 28 (2), 477-492.

Armstrong, W. R., Mok, C., Go, M. F., and Chan. A. (1997). The importance of cross-cultural expectations in the measurement of service quality perceptions in the hotel industry. *International Journal of Hospitality Management,* 162, 181-190

Baloglu, S., and Uysal, M. (1996). Market segments of push and pull motivations: a canonical correlation approach. *International Journal of Contemporary Hospitality Management*, 8(3), 32-38.

Bello, D.C., and Etzel, M. J. (1985). The role of novelty in the pleasure travel experience. *Journal of Travel Research*, 24, 20-26.

Cooper, C., Fletcher, J., Gilbert, D., and Wanhill, S. (1993). Tourism: Principles and practices, London, UK: Pitman Publishing.

Cope, R. (2000). *UK outbound. Travel and Tourism Analyst*, 1, 19-39.

Crompton, J. L. (1979). An assessment of the image of Mexico as a vacation destination and the influence of geographical location upon that image. *Journal of Travel Research, 17*(4), 18-24.

Dann, G. (1977). Anomie, ego-enhancement and tourism. *Annals of Tourism Research*, 4 (4), 184-194.

Dann, G. (1981). Tourist motivation: an appraisal. *Annals of Tourism Research*, 8, 187-219.

Dann, G. (1993). Limitations in the use of nationality and country of residence variables. *In Tourism Research: Critique and Challenges,* D. Pearce and R, Butler. (Eds). London, UK Routlege, 88-112.

Destadli, M. J. (2001). Analysing air travel. A comparison of different survey methods and data collection procedures. *Journal of Travel Research*, 39, 4-10.

Dillman, D.A. (1978). *Mail and telephone surveys. The total design method.* New York, USA.

Gearing, E.C., Swart, W.C., and Var, T. (1974). Establishing a measure of touristic attractiveness. *Journal of Travel Research*, 12, 1-8.

Hair, J. F., Anderson, R., and Black, W. C. (1995). *Multivariate Data Analysis with Readings*, New Jersey, USA, Prentice Hall Inc.

Hinkin, R.T., Tracey, B. J., and Enz, A.C. (1997). Scale construction: developing reliable and valid measurement instruments, *Hospitality Research Journal*, 21 (1), 100-120.

Hu, Y., and Ritchie, B. R. J. (1993). Measuring destination attractiveness: a contextual approach. *Journal of Travel Research*, Fall, 25-34.

Iso-Ahola, S.E. (1982). Toward a social psychological theory of tourism motivation: a rejoinder. *Annals of Tourism Research*, 12 (1), 256-262.

Kim, C., and S. Lee.(2000). Understanding the cultural differences in tourist motivation between Anglo-American and Japanese tourist. *Journal of Travel and Tourism Marketing*, 9(2), 153-170.

Krippendorf, J. (1987). *The holiday makers*; Understanding the impact of leisure and travel, Heinemann.

Kozak, M. (2002). Comparative analysis of tourist motivations by nationality and destination. *Tourism Management*, 23, 221-232.

Mannel, R.C., and Iso-Ahola, S.E. (1987). Psychological nature of leisure and tourism experience, *Annals of Tourism Research*, 14 (3), 314-329.

Mattila, S.A. (2000). The impact of culture and gender on customer evaluations of service encounters. *Journal of Hospitality and Tourism Research*, 242, 263-273.

Mayo, E., and Jarvis, L. P. (1981). *The psychology of Leisure Travel, Boston*, USA, CBI Publishing.

McCleary, W. K., Choi, M. B., and A. P. Weaver. (1998). A comparison of hotel selection criteria between U.S. and Korean business travelers. *Journal of Hospitality and Tourism Research*, 221, 25-38.

McCLellan, J., and Foushee, K. D. (1983). Negative images of the United States as expressed by tour operators. *Journal of Travel Research*, 221, 2-5.

Middleton, T. C. V. (1994). *Marketing in travel and tourism*, 2nd edition, London, UK: Butterworth-Heinemann.

Mok, C., and Armstrong, W. R. (1998). Expectations for hotel service quality: Do they differ from culture to culture? *Journal of Vacation Marketing*, 44, 381-391.

Mok, C., and De Franco, L. A. (1999). Chinese cultural values: their implications for travel and tourism marketing. *Journal of Travel and Tourism Marketing*, 82, 99-114.

Moutinho, L. (1986). Consumer Behavior in tourism, *Management Bibliographies and Reviews, 12 (3)*.

Muller, T. E. (1991). Using personal values to define segments in an international tourism market. *International Marketing Review*, 81, 57-70.

Muller, T.E. (1989). The two nations of Canada vs. the nine nations of North America: a cross cultural analysis of consumers' personal values. *Journal of International Consumer Marketing*, 14, 57-79.

Norton, G. (1987). Tourism and terrorism, *World Today*, 44.

Ohja, J. M. (1982). Selling Benign Tourism: Case references from Indian scene. *Tourism Recreation Research*, 23-24;

Orams, B. M., and Page, J. S. (2000). Designing self-reply questionnaires to survey tourists: issues and guidelines for researchers. *Anatolia: An international Journal of Tourism and Hospitality Research*, 11 (3), 125-139.

Pearce, L. P. (1982). *The social psychology of tourist behavior*, Oxford, UK, Pergamon.

Pizam, A., and Jeong, H. (1996). Cross-cultural tourist behavior: Perceptions of Korean tour-guides international. *Tourism Management,* 17(4), 277-86.

Pizam, A., and Sussmann, S. (1995). Does nationality affect tourist behavior. *Annals of Tourism Research*, 224, 901-917.

Pizam, A. (1999). The American group travelers as viewed by British, Israeli, Korean, and Dutch tour guides. *Journal of Travel Research*, 38, 119-126.

Pizam, A., Tarlow, E. P., and Bloom, J. (1999). Making Tourists feel safe, whoops responsibility is it? *Journal of Travel Research*, Summer, 23-28.

Pizam, A., Jansen-Verbeke, M., and Steel, L. (1997). Are all travelers alike, regardless of nationality? The perceptions of Dutch tour-guides. *Journal of International Hospitality, Leisure and Tourism Management, 11*,19-39.

Pizam, A., Pine, R., Mok, C., and Shin, J. Y. (1997). Nationality vs. industry cultures: which has a greater effect on managerial behavior. *International Journal of Hospitality Management*, 162, 127-145.

Poon, A. (2000). Germany outbound. *Travel and Tourism Analyst*, 4, 17-36.

Ragheb, M. G., and Beard, J. G. (1982). Measuring leisure attitudes. *Journal of Leisure Research*, 14, 155-162.

Reid, J. L., and Reid, D.S. (1997). Traveler geographic origin and market segmentation for small island nations: the Barbados case. *Journal of Travel and Tourism Marketing*, 6 (4), 5-22.

Reisinger, Y., and Turner, L. (2000). Japanese tourism satisfaction: Gold Coast versus Hawaii. *Journal of Vacation Marketing,* 64, 299-311.

Reisinger, Y., and Turner, L. (1998). Cross-cultural differences in tourism: a strategy for tourism marketers, *Journal of Travel and Tourism Marketing*, 74, 79-106.

Reisinger, Y., and Turner, L. (1997). Tourist satisfaction with hosts: A cultural approach comparing Thai travelers and Australian hosts. *Pacific Tourism Review*, 1, 147-159.

Reisinger, Y., and Waryszak, R. (1996). Catering to Japanese tourists: What service do they expect from food and drinking establishments in Australia?. *Journal of Restaurant and Foodservice Marketing*, 1 (3-4), 53-71.

Ross, G. (1992). Tourist motivation among backpacker visitors to the Wet tropics of Northern Australia. *Journal of Travel and Tourism Marketing*, 1(3), 43-59.

Ryan, C. (1995). *Researching Tourist Satisfaction: Issues, Concepts, Problems*, Routledge, New York, USA.

Ryan, C. (1997). The Tourist Experience: The New Introduction, London, UK: Cassell, 25-47.

Summers, J., and McColl-Kennedy, R. J. (1998). Australia as a holiday destination: Young Americans' vs. young Chinese Malaysians' decision-making. *Journal of Hospitality and Leisure Marketing,* 54, 33-55.

Sussmann, S., and Rashcovsky, C. (1997). A cross cultural analysis of English and French Canadians' vacation travel patterns, *Int. Journal of Hospitality Management*, 16 (), 191-208.

Uysal, M., and Hagan, L. A. R. (1993). Motivation of pleasure travel and tourism, in Khan, M., Olsen, M, and T. Var (Eds), *Encyclopaedia or Hospitality and Tourism*, 798-810.

Veal, A. J. (1997). *Research Methods for Leisure and Tourism: A Practical Guide*, 2nd Edition, Pitman Publishing.

Var, T., Beck, A. D., and Loftus, P. (1977). Determination of touristic attractiveness of the touristic areas in British Columbia, *Journal of Travel Research*, 15 (3), 23-29.

Weber, K. (1997). Assessment of tourist satisfaction, using the Expectancy disconfirmation theory, a study of German travel market in Australia. *Pacific Tourism Review*, 1, 35-45.

You, X., O'Leary, J., Morrison, A., and Hong, G. (2000). A cross-cultural comparison of travel push and pull factors: United Kingdom versus Japan. *International Journal of Hospitality and Tourism Administration*, 12, 1-25.

Yuan, S., and McDoanld, C. (1990). Motivational determinants of international pleasure time. *Journal of Travel Research*, 24 (1), 42-44.

In: Tourist Satisfaction and Complaining Behavior
Editor: Atila Yüksel

ISBN 978-1-60456-002-2
© 2008 Nova Science Publishers, Inc.

Chapter 11

SEGMENTING TOURISTS BASED ON SATISFACTION AND SATISFACTION PATTERNS

Sara Dolnicar and Huong Le

University of Wollongong

INTRODUCTION

While consumer satisfaction is one of the most heavily researched constructs in tourism research, market segmentation is one of the most widely used methods to gain understanding of the market structure in tourist markets. This is not surprising given that each of these two streams of research is based on assumptions which are fundamental to the successful operation of the tourism industry: (1) different people have different tourism needs and (2) if tourists are satisfied with their experience they will return. The latter assumption has been investigated many times in tourism research, most recently by Jang and Feng (2007) who find a significant association between stated overall satisfaction and the intention to revisit a destination within the next 12 months.

The fact that tourists are heterogeneous makes it possible for tourism destinations and service provides at destinations to select a particularly suitable market segment and provide the best possible service for this target segment. Such a segmentation approach provides some protection as destinations / tourism providers no longer compete with the entire global tourism market but compete only with destinations / providers who cater for the same target segment. Consequently, market segmentation has been used in tourism research for a very long time. In its simplest form market segmentation (a priori or commonsense market segmentation, Dolnicar, 2004; Mazanec, 2000) refers to the profiling of certain groups of tourists where the groups are defined in advance. For instance, the most typical commonsense segmentation approach used by national tourism organisations around the world is to group tourists or potential tourists into groups on the basis of their country of origin.

The concept of a posteriori or data-driven market segmentation (Dolnicar, 2004; Mazanec, 2000) has been adopted by tourism researchers (Calantone, Schewe and Allen, 1980; Crask, 1981; Goodrich, 1980; Mazanec, 1984) from the marketing literature (Haley,

1968). In data-driven segmentation – as opposed to commonsense segmentation – it is not clear in advance which respondent will become a member of which market segment. For instance, one may want to identify segments based on tourists' statements whether or not each of 20 travel motivations applies to them. In this case, these 20 motivation variables become the basis of the grouping. Only in the second stage of the process are the resulting groups (segments) described. A comparison of the two basic approaches to segmentation is provided in Figure 1.

Note that data-driven segmentation is an exploratory technique which leads to a different result each time a segmentation solution is computed. Consequently data-structure has to be thoroughly examined before naturally existing segments can be claimed. Whether or not the data is structured can best be determined by assessing the stability with which segments occur if a number of independent segmentation studies is conducted. Naturally existing segments can be assumed to exist if segments can be identified with a high level of stability, meaning that a large number of replications with different algorithms and even different number of clusters leads to the identification of one or more segments repeatedly. This is, however, not typically the case in empirical data sets from surveys. If stable segments cannot be identified, segments are artificially constructed (constructive clustering, Dolnicar and Leisch, 2001). Constructive clustering still has all advantages of market segmentation, but it is important to know that the resulting segments represent managerially useful groupings rather than obvious natural segments in the marketplace.

Although tourism researchers sometimes still refer to data-driven segmentation studies as the "more sophisticated" approach to market segmentation, it is the segmentation approach that is of most managerial benefit that represents the most suitable solution. For instance, a data-driven segmentation based on tourism motives may lead to very interesting segments, yet destination management may choose that segmenting by country of origin is the more suitable approach given the practicalities of such an a prior technique (each country of origin has a different language and a unique media landscape). The quality of a segmentation solution can ultimately only be judged by its value to destination management. Any segmentation approach that produces a valuable grouping of tourists is a legitimate segmentation approach.

Satisfaction is one possible base for market segmentation. One way to use commonsense segmentation with satisfaction as the segmentation criterion is to profile highly satisfied tourists and compare them with dissatisfied tourists. Such a simple segmentation approach could provide valuable insight into the differences between these groups and inform destination managers of managers of service providers whether any of the discriminating factors are under their control. If this is the case, improvements could be made. If this is not the case, the segment of satisfied tourists may simply be the more suitable segment to target in future. Similarly, identifying market segments based on patterns of satisfaction (data-driven segmentation) could be very insightful. For this purpose a number of satisfaction questions could be used where respondents indicate their satisfaction with different aspects of their tourism experience. Resulting segments would then represent groups of tourists who require specific improvements or who may not be suitable segments given the strengths and weaknesses of the destination or service provides. Yuksel and Yuksel (2002a and b) propose this approach in the context of tourism. They also confirm that "Surprisingly [...] examination of segment-based satisfaction has attracted only limited attention from researchers."

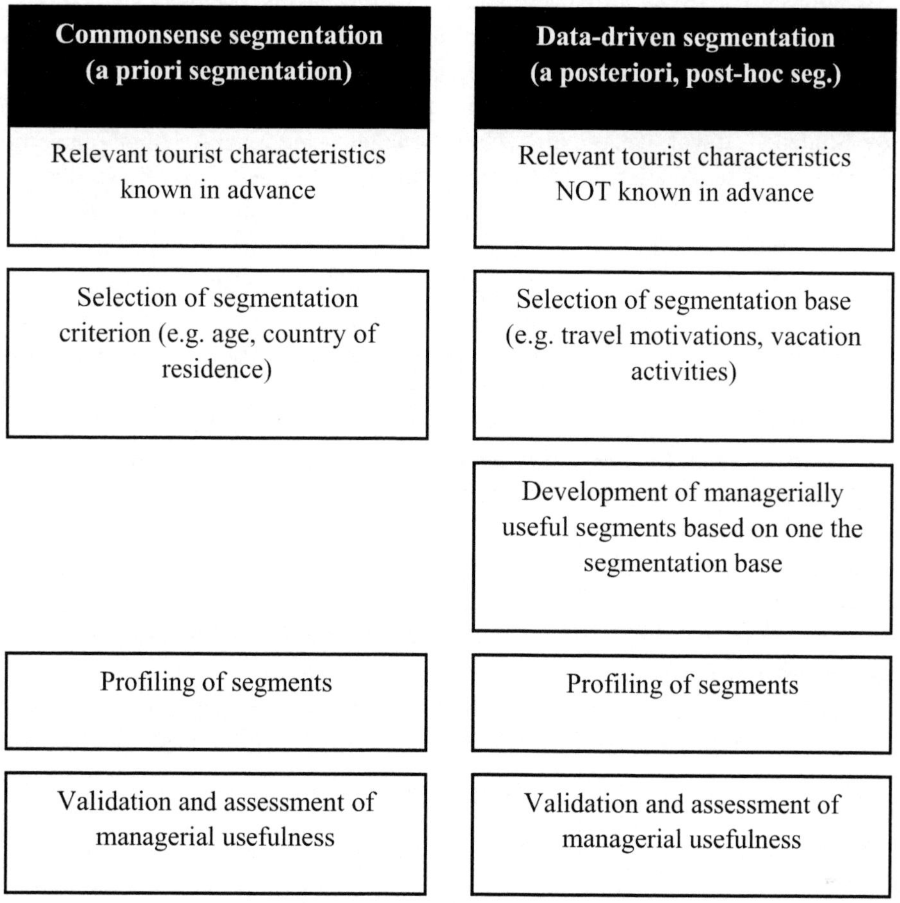

Commonsense segmentation (a priori segmentation)	Data-driven segmentation (a posteriori, post-hoc seg.)
Relevant tourist characteristics known in advance	Relevant tourist characteristics NOT known in advance
Selection of segmentation criterion (e.g. age, country of residence)	Selection of segmentation base (e.g. travel motivations, vacation activities)
	Development of managerially useful segments based on one the segmentation base
Profiling of segments	Profiling of segments
Validation and assessment of managerial usefulness	Validation and assessment of managerial usefulness

Figure 1. A comparison of commonsense and data-driven segmentation

It should be noted that satisfaction ratings are generally skewed towards the higher end and that not all dissatisfied customers voice their dissatisfaction. Such potential distortion effects on findings have to be taken into consideration when resulting segments are interpreted.

Despite the potential to gain additional useful insight about the tourism market from both commonsense and data-driven segmentation studies based on satisfaction data, very few such studies have been conducted in the past. Most satisfaction research in tourism, travel and hospitality conducted in the recent past focused on empirically determining tourist satisfaction with different aspects of the vacation, such as the destination itself, shopping, service quality, attractions and accommodation. The most popular topic of investigation appears to be the study of satisfaction with destinations with more than 30 percent of all studies published between 2000 and 2007[1] focusing on this particular aspect. A typical example is provided by Kozak and Rimmington (2000) who assess British tourists' satisfaction with off-season holiday in Mallorca, Spain. Other studies focus on investigating

---

[1] See details on methodology on the precise selection of reviewers articles

the interrelationship between satisfaction and its antecedents (such as perceived service quality) or consequences (such as behavioural intentions to revisitation, loyalty and word of mouth). A typical example is provided by Gallarza and Gil Saura (2006) who investigate the relationship between quality, perceived value, satisfaction, and loyalty in a study of Spanish university students' travel behaviours. They conclude that quality is an antecedent of perceived value and satisfaction is the behavioural consequence of perceived value, and in turn, loyalty attitude is the final outcome of this chain. Evaluations of effectiveness or limitations of satisfaction models and recommendations for improvements have also been presented by a number of authors. Deng (in press), for instance, proposes a revised importance-performance analysis and illustrates the usefulness for the context of Taiwanese hot spring tourism. Market segmentation studies based on satisfaction are very rare; those few studies that have combined market segmentation and satisfaction research have typically not used satisfaction as the segmentation criterion / base, as will be discussed below. Outside of the field of tourism, Hahn, Johnson, Herrmann, and Huber (2002) conducted a study in which they use different aspects of satisfaction with convenience stored to identify segments of consumers which differ in the way in which each of these aspect influences their overall satisfaction with the store. This study demonstrates the potential of segmentation studies based on satisfaction statements in tourism industry.

The aim of this chapter is (1) to review prior studies that have used tourist satisfaction as a segmentation basis, (2) to analyse which managerial insights were derived from these studies in order to assess the value of segmentation studies based on satisfaction, and (3) to provide empirical examples of a commonsense and a data-driven satisfaction-based segmentation.

BIBLIOGRAPHIC STUDY

Data and methodology

To gain insight into prior studies that combined satisfaction and segmentation research and to evaluate the managerial recommendations that were derived by the authors of these studies, a descriptive bibliography study 2 was conducted.

The following sources were used: Journal of Travel Research, Annals of Tourism Research, Tourism Management, International Journal of Hospitality Management, Cornell Hotel and Restaurant Administration Quarterly, and the Journal of Tourism Studies. The criterion for including those sources was that the Journals had to be listed as being among the top ten journal in the field of tourism and that they had to be readily available online to the researchers. All empirical articles published since 2000 were included. Although there is a large number of publications in these journals on the topic of satisfaction, pure review articles and articles measuring other forms of satisfaction (e.g. job satisfaction) were excluded. Forty five articles (see Appendix) were used for the review. Each article was coded as one case into an SPSS file; each variable represented an aspect of interest for the present review.

---

[2] Bibliographic study (also called bibliographical study) is a systematic description and history of printed material (Center for Bibliographical Studies and Research, 2006).

Results

We report on two dimensions of prior satisfaction studies. First we review the theoretical foundation that they are based on. Second we investigate some of the methodological characteristics of past empirical studies.

While 12 of the reviewed studies did not explicitly mention which theoretical model they based their satisfaction measurement on, the majority of studies did explicitly declare the theoretical model upon which the measurement was based. As can be seen from Table 1, the most common approach taken was to build on the expectation disconfirmation model as proposed by Oliver (1980). More than fifteen percent of all empirical studies choose the expectation disconfirmation model as the basis of their study. The expectation-perception / performance gap model (SERVQUAL) as proposed by Parasuraman, Zeithaml and Berry (1985) was used by nearly nine percent of all studies, followed by the importance-performance model. Performance only models in which respondents are asked directly and only about their satisfaction without requesting them to define a reference point are rarely used.

Table 1. Theoretical approached to measuring satisfaction

Underlying theory / model	Frequency	Percent
Expectancy disconfirmation theory	7	15.6
Importance-performance	4	8.9
Expectation-perception/performance gap model (SERVQUAL)	4	8.9
Performance-only model (SERVPERF)	2	4.4
Congruity model	1	2.2
HOLSAT model	1	2.2
Other or combined models	12	26.7
Not stated	12	26.7
Not applicable (qualitative studies)	2	4.4
Total	45	100.0

Table 2 reports on some of the methodological characteristics of the reviewed satisfaction studies. As can be seen no single best way to measure tourist satisfaction appears to have developed. Eleven percent of the studies measure overall satisfaction rather than satisfaction with various aspects of the vacation, 15 percent measure satisfaction at attribute level, meaning that various aspects of the vacation are studied separately and 17 percent include both overall and attribute-based measures. It should be noted, however, that many of the studies that measure only overall satisfaction choose to use more than one item to do so.

All satisfaction studies, without exception, use multi-category (ordinal) scales as answer formats. Five and seven-point scales are most popular. The dominance of multi-category answer formats is surprising given that they are most susceptible to response styles and given that data analytic technique that require metric data (factor analysis, correlation analysis, regression analysis) are used in a high proportion of satisfaction studies (Dolnicar, 2006).

Table 2. Analysis of recent satisfaction studies

Level of satisfaction measurement			
		Frequency	Percent
	based on attributes	15	33.3
	overall evaluation	11	24.4
	Both	17	37.8
	Not applicable (qualitative studies)	2	4.4
	Total	45	100.0
Segmentation component			
	No	30	66.7
	Yes	15	33.3
	Total	45	100.0
Data format			
	Ordinal	42	93.3
	not stated	1	2.2
	Total	43	95.6
	Not applicable (qualitative studies)	2	4.4
	Total	45	100.0
Number of answer options			
	not specified	2	4.4
	4 point scale	1	2.2
	5 point scale	19	42.2
	6 point scale	1	2.2
	7 point scale	13	28.9
	9 point scale	1	2.2
	10 point scale	4	8.9
	Others	2	4.4
	Total	43	95.6
	Not applicable (qualitative studies)	2	4.4
	Total	45	100.0
Which type of analysis / test was conducted?			
	factor analysis	13	28.9
	correlation analysis	4	8.9
	regression analysis	2	4.4
	Mix	11	24.4
	chi square	1	2.2
	Others	14	31.1
	Total	45	100.0

Finally, the review also indicates that a third of all studies contain a segmentation component. Not that any kind of profiling was coded as containing a segmentation component. Detailed review of these articles reveals, however, that satisfaction is never used as the segmentation criterion or segmentation base. Most of the studies combining satisfaction research with market segmentation use a commonsense approach and use the country of origin of tourists as the segmentation criterion: Kozak (2001) compares the satisfaction statements of British and German tourists. Hui, Wan and Ho (in press) compare satisfaction levels (at factor level) for respondents from different regions of the world. Nield, Kozak and

LeGrys (2000) study satisfaction with food in particular and use data that contains respondents from 17 nationalities which are grouped in 2 segments (Western European, Eastern European and Romanian) for comparison. Yu and Goulden (2006) test differences in satisfaction of European, US, Japanese and other Asia Pacific Countries. Joppe, Martin and Waalen (2001) measure 14 attribute level and one global level satisfaction items and compare Canadian, US and overseas tourist satisfaction levels. Chaudhary (2000) compares satisfaction ratings on 5 point scales for British, German and Dutch tourists. Finally, Wong and Law (2003) compare expectations and satisfaction levels across countries of origin (US, Australia, Asia). The only segmentation study that does not use country of origin as the segmentation criterion was conducted by Pizam, Uriely and Reichel (2000) who compared differences between 3 segments of working tourists in Israel, finding that those working in a Kibbutz have the highest satisfaction levels. It can be consequently concluded that segmentation studies using satisfaction as the basis are rare in tourism research. It can also be concluded that the vast majority of satisfaction studied that use a commonsense segmentation approach are based on cross-cultural comparisons. The results of such analyses have to be interpreted with great case given the high probability of cross-cultural response style contamination of data. For more details see Chapter 7 in this book.

The main conclusions drawn from satisfaction studies which authors state are of practical value to destination management are (1) that customers should be kept satisfied by improving areas in which tourists express dissatisfaction (Ekinci, Prokopaki and Cobanoglu, 2003; Kozak and Remmington 2000), (2) that areas of satisfaction and dissatisfaction can be used as a benchmarking tool in competition analyses with other destinations (Kozak and Remmington, 2000; Kozak, 2002), (3) that resources for improvement are invested into service improvements which have the strongest effect on intentions to repurchase (Petrick, 2004), and, representing the recommendation most in line with the dominant expectation disconfirmation paradigm, to provide accurate information to tourists in advance of their vacation to ensure that realistic expectations are developed (Petrick and Backman, 2002; Rodriguez del Bosque, San Martin and Collado, 2006) and negative disconfirmation can be avoided. All these recommendations, are, however, based on the assumption of homogeneity of consumers. It is therefore implicitly assumed that all destinations should aim to be perfect in all respects. This may not be necessary. Only areas which are of relevance to the target segment for which the destination is catering may be critical in terms of avoiding dissatisfaction and achieving positive disconfirmation. The exceptions mainly include authors of studies that use countries of origin as segments. They conclude that segment-specific satisfaction needs to be optimized (Nield et al, 2000). This recommendation, however, is questionable given that cross-cultural differences detected are likely to be – at least partially - due to cross-cultural response styles rather than actual differences. Rodriguez del Bosque et al. (2006) explicitly point to the need to manage the expectations of different target groups differently, although no segmentation was performed in the empirical study.

ILLUSTRATION OF SEGMENTATION STUDIES

Data and Methodology

Data from the Austrian National Guest Survey3 collected during the winter season of 1997 was used. The sample contains 3599 respondents. Quota sampling was used to ensure representativity of the data set. However, it should be noted that representativity is not essential for segmentation studies if the aim is to profile segments. If, however, it is important to know which proportion of the total tourist population a segment represents, it is essential that the data set is representative of the respective tourist population.

The Austrian National Guest Survey contains a set of questions where respondents are asked to state whether their expectations have been exceeded, met or not met with respect to various aspects of their trip, such as the landscape, the entertainment opportunities, shopping opportunities, cultural offers etc. The question formulation assumes an expectation-disconfirmation model of satisfaction. As opposed to typically used satisfaction scales it does not request respondents to directly state the extent of satisfaction or directly state both the expected level and the perceived performance level. Instead it integrates both the expectation and performance dimension into the same question and asks the respondents to assess the difference. It should be noted at this point that response styles, especially cross-cultural response styles pose a serious danger to empirical tourism studies (see Chapter XXX for details). Consequently, satisfaction studies asking respondents from a large variety of countries of origin for an absolute evaluation of their satisfaction on a multi-category scale are in danger of response style contamination. The data set we have chosen for this illustration is less prone to such biases because no absolute assessment was requested and only three answer options were provided. Prior studies on response styles have concluded that answer formats with fewer response options are less susceptible to bias (Clarke III, 2000, 2001; Cronbach, 1950).

For the commonsense segmentation (Case 1 segmentation according to the classification by Dolnicar, 2004) one of these items is selected: stated satisfaction with entertainment opportunities at the destination. This variable is chosen because it represents part of the tourism experience that destination management or the service providers at the destination could improve should the segmentation analysis demonstrate that improvement is required in order to secure satisfaction of a market segment that is essential to the destination. In a first step commonsense segments were constructed by assigning all respondents who stated that their expectations have been exceeded to one and all respondents who stated that their expectations have not been met to another group. The sample sizes for these commonsense satisfaction segments were 374 and 355, respectively. Next, the characteristics of these two segments were compared using the following additional information about the respondents: age, gender, number of children, country of origin, occupation, travel motivations, travel party, type of vacation and vacation activities. These additional variables were analysed using descriptive statistics (chi-square tests for nominal and ordinal variables and analyses of variance for metric variables) to explore the profiles of the resulting segments. A binary

---

[3] This data has been kindly provided to us for scientific use by the Austrian National Tourism Organisation, the Oesterreich Werbung.

logistic regression was computed to assess the predictive ability of these additional variables on segment membership.

For the data-driven segmentation, a set of 10 satisfaction variables was used in its binary form (a 1 indicated exceeded or met expectations, a 0 indicated unmet expectations). This binarization was undertaken because the primary aim of the data-driven segmentation based on respondents' statements of satisfaction is to gain insight into patterns of unmet expectations putting the emphasis on dissatisfaction rather than satisfaction, as negative deviation from expected outcomes is known to have a stronger impact on behaviour than positive deviations (prospect theory, Kahneman and Tversky, 1979). As a consequence, it can be expected that one large segment will result which will contain all the respondents whose expectations have been met. Any additional segments resulting from the data-driven segmentation will be used to learn about dissatisfaction patterns and the individuals expressing these patterns of dissatisfaction.

Only respondents who visited one of two provinces in Austria (Tirol and Vorarberg) were included this subset was chosen as Tirol and Vorarlberg are similar winter tourism destinations offering tourist an extensive range of skiing opportunities. Consequently this analysis represents a Case 5 segmentation according to the classification by Dolnicar (2004). Including all destinations would have created a too heterogeneous sample. For instance, tourists visiting Vienna would be expected to evaluate their satisfaction along different dimensions than tourist visiting ski resorts. The final sample size amounted to 949 respondents for the data-driven segmentation analysis.

A topology representing network analysis (Martinetz and Schulten, 1994) was conducted to explore segments. This analysis is very similar to the commonly used k-means algorithm, but has performed better in Monte Carlo simulations on artificial data sets (Buchta et al., 1997). In order to determine how many segments best describe the data set, 50 repetitions of segmentation analyses were computed for segment number from 2 to 7 and the stability of pair-wise assignments of individuals to the same segment was assessed comparatively. The 3 and 7 segment solutions emerged as the most stable. The 7 segment solution was chosen because it provided more detailed profiles of dissatisfaction segments. A brief profile of the results segments is provided based on descriptive statistics.

ILLUSTRATION OF A COMMONSENSE SEGMENTATION STUDY BASED ON EXPRESSED TOURIST SATISFACTION (CASE 1 SEGMENTATION)

A number of characteristics of satisfied and dissatisfied respondents were found to be significantly associated with the level to which they stated that their expectation of entertainment opportunities were met.

A number of differences emerged in psychographic variables such as travel motives. Respondents who sought excitement, adventures and a challenge (Pearson Chi-square 33.0 , 1 df, p < 0.001), opportunities to be creative (Pearson Chi-square 5.8 , 1 df, p < 0.05), cultural offers (Pearson Chi-square 27.2 , 1 df, p < 0.001), nature (Pearson Chi-square 11.3 , 1 df, p < 0.01) and a sufficient amount of entertainment facilities (Pearson Chi-square 28.8, 1 df, p < 0.001) were better represented in the segments the expectations of which were met. These findings are supported by the fact that tourist on a culture trip (Pearson Chi-square 21.0 , 1 df, p < 0.001) or city trip (Pearson Chi-square 39.1, 1 df, p < 0.010) had a higher likelihood to be members of the satisfied segment, whereas tourists on a spa holiday (Pearson Chi-square 3.8 , 1 df, p < 0.05) or on holiday for relaxation (Pearson Chi-square 5.3 , 1 df, p < 0.05) were less likely to belong to the dissatisfied group. All the above results indicate that the tourists whose expectations were not met are more passive tourist and do not actively seek out entertainment opportunities. This interpretation is supported by the differences in the vacation activities the two segments have engaged in. Respondents to participated in organised excursions, went out in the evening, went shopping, visited concerts, museums, the theatre, musicals, operas or the traditional Austrian Heurigen (all p-values < 0.05) expressed that their expectations were exceeded, whereas respondents who stated that they were mainly relaxing criticized the entertainment opportunities.

With respect to socio-demographic characteristics segment members differed with respect to their occupation (Pearson Chi-square 20.3, 8 df, p < 0.01). The most noteworthy difference was the high proportion of pensioners in the dissatisfied segment (12 percent as opposed to only 7 percent in the satisfied segment). German tourist hold the highest proportion of members in both segments with Austrians being the second strongest country of origin within the dissatisfied groups and tourist from the US representing the second strongest group in the satisfied segment (Pearson Chi-square 71, 13 df, p < 0.001). Note that the two segments compared to not include respondents who stated that their expectations were met. This measure was taken to avoid misinterpretations of satisfaction ratings due to the fact that respondents who are familiar with the destination because they have visited it repeatedly typically state that their expectations were met. The reasons, however, is not excellent performance but calibrated expectations. Tourists on a family vacation were more frequently assigned to the dissatisfied group. The average number of children is significantly higher (2.5, F = 4.4, p < 0.05) among tourists in this segment than in the satisfied segment (1.7).

In terms of travel behaviour members of the dissatisfied segment undertake a higher number of vacation trips per year (2.3 as opposed to 2.0, F = 26.2, p < 0.001) and spent fewer night in Austria during the trip on which they were interviewed (7.5 nights as opposed to 6 nights, F= 26.2, p < 0.001).

Finally, and possibly most importantly, respondents were also asked about their intentions to return to this particular destination for a vacation. A Chi-square test assessing the association between the stated intention to visit this destination again and segment membership indicates that members of the dissatisfied segment indeed express more frequently that they will "probably not" or "certainly not" return to the destination (Pearson Chi-square 10.4 , 3 df, p < 0.05) . It should be noted, however, that this is an association test only. It cannot necessarily be concluded that dissatisfaction with entertainment facilities causes lower intentions to revisit.

The logistic regression (Cox and Snell R square = 0.283, Nagelkerke R square = 0.380) using the above variables leads to 73 percent of all segment memberships being predicted correctly. This is a good result given that the segments are approximately of equal size. 78 percent of the tourists whose expectations have not been met could be identified correctly using only the additional variables.

This illustration shows that destination managers and managers of tourism service providers can gain interesting insight from simple commonsense segmentation studies. The main conclusions from the above analysis are that unmet expectations with respect to entertainment facilities should to be taken seriously by management as there could be an effect on intentions to revisit. It appears, however, that two underlying patterns have been identified: inactive tourists express that their expectations have not been met, whereas tourists actively seeking out opportunities do not. This may indicate that there is in fact no need to increase the offers, but possibly strategies could be developed to better inform such inactive tourists of entertainment opportunities and make them easier to access for them. More concerning is the fact that families appear to suffer from a lack of entertainment opportunities. This finding may indicate that family-specific entertainment infrastructure may have to be improved. Additional qualitative fieldwork focusing on families should be conducted to assess the precise nature of the problem and possibilities of addressing it at the destination / service provide level.

ILLUSTRATION OF A DATA-DRIVEN SEGMENTATION STUDY BASED ON EXPRESSED TOURIST SATISFACTION (CASE 5 SEGMENTATION)

The seven segments that emerged as suitable data-driven segmentation solution based on stability comparisons is provided in Figure 2. All charts in Figure 2 depict the percentage of segment members expressing that their expectations have not been met in each of the listed areas using a black column. The sample average of unmet expectations is plotted as a grey shaded are in the background to enable quick comparisons between the sample and the segment.

As can bee seen from inspecting the charts for all segments, one segment emerges that has no complaints (Segment 6). However, no segment of "complainers" (tourists who seem to complain about a large number of aspects of their vacation) can be identified despite the large number of segments extracted. This is encouraging as is indicates that respondents who have experienced areas in which their expectations have not been met answered the questions in a very differentiated manner rather than adopting a response style in responding to the satisfaction items.

The resulting segment profiles highlight clear problem areas: all members of Segment 1 are disappointed by the quality of ski slopes, all members of Segment 2 are disappointed by the food, but also express unmet expectations regarding ski slopes, friendliness of personnel and offers for families and children. All members of Segment 3 perceive the destination as not peaceful and quiet enough. They also express their disappointment with the opening hours of shops and shopping in general as well as offers for families and children. The problem areas expressed by Segment 4 members centre around the accommodation. All members are disappointed by the accommodation quality, 40 percent express that the service at the accommodation is bad, one third is disappointed by the food and 11 percent perceive the staff as not being as friendly as expected. Segments 5 and 7 are disappointed with the shopping at the destination with Segment 5 expressing unmet expectations with respect to shopping in general and Segment 7 members expressing their frustration about too restrictive opening hours of shops.

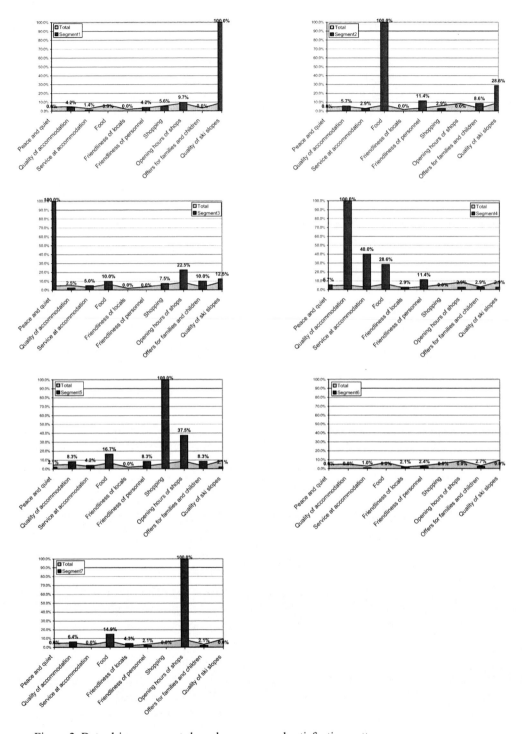

Figure 2: Data-driven segments based on expressed satisfaction patterns

The resulting segments differed significantly in a number of the additional variables that were used to describe the commonsense segments in detail. A few of the central findings include that tourist who classify their vacation as a relaxation holiday form the largest proportion of Segment 5 and 7, those unhappy with the shopping situation at the destination. Interestingly members of Segment 5 do not actually engage in shopping very frequently while a quarter of the members of Segment 7 state that they shop frequently. Tourists most heavily engaging in skiing are most represented by Segments 3 and 4. While each of the segments contains at least 25 percent families, the highest proportion can be found in Segment 1. This is interesting given that Segment 1 is mainly dissatisfied with the ski slopes and has no complaints about offers for families and children. Another interesting observation is that three quarters of Segment 4 members stay in hotels or pensions. This suggests the interpretation that members of this group have deliberately chosen more expensive accommodation options to ensure a high quality of accommodation which increases the level of disappointment if expectations are not met.

Results indicate that very specific patterns of dissatisfaction exist among tourists. These patterns are not obvious as it is not always the area of primary importance to tourists that causes disappointments. Data-driven segmentation analyses can help managers explore such patterns and investigate in detail the profiles of dissatisfaction segments of particular concern to them.

CONCLUSIONS

Although both satisfaction and segmentation research are seen to contribute significantly to tourism knowledge (as indicated by the large number of studies that has been published in both these areas over the past decades), only a small number of studies have made use of both concepts to gain insight into the marketplace. Those that have combined segmentation and satisfaction research have typically conducted cross-cultural comparisons to determine whether tourists from different countries of origin have systematically different satisfaction levels. None of the studies published since 2000 have used market segmentation to group tourist based on their satisfaction level and learn more about those tourists who are satisfied / dissatisfied or tourists with specific patterns of dissatisfaction. Such analyses could contribute to the understanding of the market and could consequently prove to be a valuable source of market information for tourism managers.

A commonsense and a data-driven segmentation were computed that illustrated how satisfaction data could be segmented. The managerial benefit that results from such studies is similar to the recommendations that are typically made by authors of satisfaction studies: areas of dissatisfaction should be improved. The segmentation based approach helps managers to learn precisely for which group of tourists which improvements are needed, thus making the most efficient use of resources needed to achieve improvement. It also enables tourism managers to manage expectations of specific market segments before the vacation with a particular emphasis on those aspects that concern the target market. As it is the case in all segmentation studies such an approach allows to make targeted improvements rather than trying to achieve 0% dissatisfaction in all areas, which is not necessary if only one or a limited number of market segments are actually targeted by a destination or a tourism service provider.

For all market segmentation studies based on satisfaction it is very important to take into consideration the data format. Whenever multi-category formats are used there is a danger of response styles occurring which can contaminate the data. We recommend the use of binary data, three-point formats or best-worst data (if only the relative satisfaction of various vacation aspects is of interest) to avoid response style contamination. If multi-category scales are used it is important to first assess the extent of response style contamination before data is segmented.

ACKNOWLEDGEMENTS

This research was supported by the Australian Research Council through Grants LP0453682 and DP0557769.

REFERENCES

Buchta, C., Dimitriadou, E., Dolnicar, S., Leisch, F., and Weingessel, A. (1997). A Comparison of Several Cluster Algorithms on Artificial Binary Data Scenarios from Travel Market Segmentation. Working Paper # 7, SFB 'Adaptive Information Systems and Modelling in Economics and Management Science', Viena, Austria.

Calantone, R., Schewe, C., and Allen, C. T. (1980). "Targeting Specific Advertising Messages at Tourist Segments", in *Tourism Marketing and Management* edited by Hawkins, D. E., Shafer, E. L., and J.M., Washington D.C, USA: George Washington University, 133-147.

Center for Bibliographical Studies and Research (2006).. Website of the Center for Bibliographical Studies and Research (CBSR). Retrieved 2 January, 2007 from http://www.cbsr.ucr.edu/

Chaudhary, M. (2000). India's image as a tourist destination - A perspective of foreign tourists. *Tourism Management*, 21 (3), 293-297.

Clarke III, I. (2000). Extreme response style in cross cultural research: An empirical investigation. *Journal of Social Behaviour and Personality*, 15 (1), 137-152.

Crask, M. (1981). Segmenting the vacationer market: Identifying the vacation preferences, demographics, and magazine readership of each group. *Journal of Travel Research*, 20 (2), 20-34.

Cronbach, L. (1950). Further evidence on response sets and test design. *Educational and Psychological Measurement*, 10 (1), 3-31.

Deng, W. (in press). Using a revised importance-performance analysis approach: The case of Taiwanese hot springs tourism. *Tourism Management*, In Press, Corrected Proof.

Dolnicar, S., and Leisch, F. (2001). Knowing what you get - A conceptual clustering framework for increased transparency of market segmentation studies. *Marketing Science*, Wiesbaden, Germany, 5 – 8 July.

Dolnicar, S. (2004). Beyond "commonsense segmentation" – A systematics of segmentation approaches in tourism. *Journal of Travel Research*, 42 (3), 244-250.

Dolnicar, S. (2006). Are we drawing the right conclusions? The dangers of response sets and scale assumptions in empirical tourism research. *Tourism Analysis*, 11 (3), 199-209.

Ekinci, Y., Prokopaki, P., and Cobanoglu, C. (2003). Service quality in Cretan accommodations: Marketing strategies for the UK holiday market. *International Journal of Hospitality Management*, 22 (1), 47-66.

Gallarza, M. G., and Gil Saura, I. (2006). Value dimensions, perceived value, satisfaction and loyalty: An investigation of university students' travel behaviour. *Tourism Management*, 27 (3), 437-452.

Goodrich, J. (1980). "Benefit Segmentation of US International Travelers: An Empirical Study with American Express", in *Tourism Marketing and Management* edited by D.E. Hawkins, E.L. Shafer, and J.M., Washington D.C, USA: George Washington University, 133-147.

Hahn, C., Johnson, M.D., Herrmann, A., and Huber, F. (2002). Capturing customer heterogeneity using a finite mixture PLS approach. *Schmalenbach's Business Review*, 54, 243-269.

Haley, R.J. (1968). Benefit segmentation: A decision-oriented research tool. *Journal of Marketing*, 32 (3), 30-35.

Hui, T. K., Wan, D., and Ho, A. (in press). Tourists' satisfaction, recommendation and revisiting Singapore. *Tourism Management*, In Press, Corrected Proof.

Jang, S., and Feng, R. (2007). Temporal destination revisit intention: The effects of novelty seeking and satisfaction. *Tourism Management*, 28 (2), 580-590.

Joppe, M., Martin, D. W., and Waalen, J. (2001). Toronto's image as a destination: A comparative importance-satisfaction analysis by origin of visitor. *Journal of Travel Research,* 39 (3), 252-260.

Kahneman, D., and Tversky, A. (1979). *Prospect theory – analysis of decision under risk.* *Econometrica*, 47 (2), 263-291.

Kozak, M. (2001). Comparative assessment of tourist satisfaction with destinations across two nationalities. *Tourism Management*, 22 (4), 391-401.

Kozak, M. (2002). Destination benchmarking. *Annals of Tourism Research*, 29 (2), 497-519.

Kozak, M., and Rimmington, M. (2000). Tourist satisfaction with Mallorca, Spain, as an off-season holiday destination. *Journal of Travel Research*, 38 (3), 260-269.

Martinetz, Thomas and Klaus Schulten (1994). Topology representing networks. *Neural Networks*, 7 (5), 507-522

Mazanec, J.A. (1984). How to detect travel market segments: A clustering approach. *Journal of Travel Research*, 23 (1), 17-21.

Mazanec, J.A. (2000). Market Segmentation, in J. Jafari (ed) *Encyclopaedia of Tourism*, Routledge, London, UK.

Nield, K., Kozak, M., and LeGrys, G. (2000). The role of food service in tourist satisfaction. *International Journal of Hospitality Management*, 19 (4), 375-384.

Oliver, R. L. (1980). A cognitive model of the antecedents and consequences of satisfaction decisions. *Journal of Marketing Research*, 17 (4), 460-469.

Parasuraman, A., Zeithaml, V. A., and Berry, L. L. (1985). A conceptual model of service quality and its implications for future research. *Journal of Marketing*, 49 (4), 41-50.

Petrick, J. F. (2004). The roles of quality, value, and satisfaction in predicting cruise passengers' behavioural intentions. *Journal of Travel Research*, 42 (4), 397-407.

Petrick, J. F., and Backman, S. J. (2002). An examination of the determinants of golf travelers' satisfaction. *Journal of Travel Research*, 40 (3), 252-258.

Pizam, A., Uriely, N., and Reichel, A. (2000). The intensity of tourist-host social relationship and its effects on satisfaction and change of attitudes: the case of working tourists in Israel. *Tourism Management*, 21 (4), 395-406.

Rodriguez del Bosque, I. A., San Martin, H., and Collado, J. (2006). The role of expectations in the consumer satisfaction formation process: Empirical evidence in the travel agency sector. *Tourism Management*, 27 (3), 410-419.

Wong, J., and Law, R. (2003). Difference in shopping satisfaction levels: A study of tourists in Hong Kong. *Tourism Management*, 24 (4), 401-410.

Yu, L., and Goulden, M. (2006). A comparative analysis of international tourists' satisfaction in Mongolia. *Tourism Management*, 27 (6), 1331-1342.

Yuksel, A., and Yuksel, F. (2002a). Measurement of tourist satisfaction with restaurant services: A segment based approach. *Journal of Vacation Marketing*, 9 (1), 52- 68

Yuksel, A., and Yuksel, F. (2002b). Market segmentation based on tourists' dining preferences. *Journal of Hospitality and Tourism Research*, 26 (4), 315-331.

APPENDIX: REVIEWED LITERATURE

Akama, J. S., and Kieti, D. M. (2003). Measuring tourist satisfaction with Kenya's wildlife safari: a case study of Tsavo West National Park. *Tourism Management*, 24(1), 73-81.

Alegre, J., and Cladera, M. (2006). Repeat visitation in mature sun and sand holiday destinations. *Journal of Travel Research*, 44(3), 288-297.

Baker, D. A., and Crompton, J. L. (2000). Quality, satisfaction and behavioural intentions. *Annals of Tourism Research*, 27(3), 785-804.

Bigne, J. E., and Andreu, L. (2004). Emotions in segmentation: An empirical study. *Annals of Tourism Research*, 31(3), 682-696.

Bigne, J. E., Andreu, L., and Gnoth, J. (2005). The theme park experience: An analysis of pleasure, arousal and satisfaction. *Tourism Management*, 26(6), 833-844.

Bigne, J. E., Sanchez, M. I., and Sanchez, J. (2001). Tourism image, evaluation variables and after purchase behaviour: Inter-relationship. *Tourism Management*, 22(6), 607-616.

Bowen, D. (2001). Antecedents of consumer satisfaction and dis-satisfaction (CS/D) on long-haul inclusive tours -- A reality check on theoretical considerations. *Tourism Management*, 22(1), 49-61.

Bowen, D. (2002). Research through participant observation in tourism: A creative solution to the measurement of consumer satisfaction/dissatisfaction (CS/D) among tourists. *Journal of Travel Research*, 41(1), 4-14.

Chang, J., Yang, B. T., and Yu, C. G. (2006). The moderating effect of salespersons' selling behaviour on shopping motivation and satisfaction: Taiwan tourists in China. *Tourism Management*, 27(5), 934-942.

Chaudhary, M. (2000). India's image as a tourist destination -- A perspective of foreign tourists. *Tourism Management*, 21(3), 293-297.

Chen, C. F., and Tsai, D. (in press). How destination image and evaluative factors affect behavioural intentions? *Tourism Management*, In Press, Corrected Proof.

Deng, W. (in press). Using a revised importance-performance analysis approach: The case of Taiwanese hot springs tourism. *Tourism Management*, In Press, Corrected Proof.

Duman, T., and Mattila, A. S. (2005). The role of affective factors on perceived cruise vacation value. *Tourism Management*, 26(3), 311-323.

Ekinci, Y., Prokopaki, P., and Cobanoglu, C. (2003). Service quality in Cretan accommodations: Marketing strategies for the UK holiday market. *International Journal of Hospitality Management*, 22(1), 47-66.

Fuchs, M., and Weiermair, K. (2004). Destination benchmarking: An indicator-system's potential for exploring guest satisfaction. *Journal of Travel Research*, 42(3), 212-225.

Gallarza, M. G., and Gil Saura, I. (2006). Value dimensions, perceived value, satisfaction and loyalty: An investigation of university students' travel behaviour. *Tourism Management*, 27(3), 437-452.

Heung, V. C. S., and Cheng, E. (2000). Assessing tourists' satisfaction with shopping in the Hong Kong special administrative regions of China. *Journal of Travel Research*, 38(4), 396-404.

Hui, T. K., Wan, D., and Ho, A. (in press). Tourists' satisfaction, recommendation and revisiting Singapore. *Tourism Management*, In Press, Corrected Proof.

Jang, S., and Feng, R. (2007). Temporal destination revisit intention: The effects of novelty seeking and satisfaction. *Tourism Management*, 28(2), 580-590.

Joppe, M., Martin, D. W., and Waalen, J. (2001). Toronto's Image as a destination: A comparative importance-satisfaction analysis by origin of visitor. *Journal of Travel Research*, 39(3), 252-260.

Kozak, M. (2001). Comparative assessment of tourist satisfaction with destinations across two nationalities. *Tourism Management*, 22(4), 391-401.

Kozak, M. (2001). Repeaters' behaviour at two distinct destinations. *Annals of Tourism Research*, 28(3), 784-807.

Kozak, M. (2002). Destination benchmarking. *Annals of Tourism Research*, 29(2), 497-519.

Kozak, M., and Rimmington, M. (2000). Tourist satisfaction with Mallorca, Spain, as an off-season holiday destination. *Journal of Travel Research*, 38(3), 260-269.

Lee, C. K., Yoon, Y. S., and Lee, S. K. (2007). Investigating the relationships among perceived value, satisfaction, and recommendations: The case of the Korean DMZ. *Tourism Management*, 28(1), 204-214.

Millan, A., and Esteban, A. (2004). Development of a multiple-item scale for measuring customer satisfaction in travel agencies services. *Tourism Management*, 25(5), 533-546.

Nash, R., Thyne, M., and Davies, S. (2006). An investigation into customer satisfaction levels in the budget accommodation sector in Scotland: A case study of backpacker tourists and the Scottish Youth Hostels Association. *Tourism Management*, 27(3), 525-532.

Nield, K., Kozak, M., and LeGrys, G. (2000). The role of food service in tourist satisfaction. *International Journal of Hospitality Management*, 19(4), 375-384.

Petrick, J. F. (2004). The roles of quality, value, and satisfaction in predicting cruise passengers' behavioural intentions. *Journal of Travel Research*, 42(4), 397-407.

Petrick, J. F., and Backman, S. J. (2002). An examination of the determinants of golf travelers' satisfaction. *Journal of Travel Research*, 40(3), 252-258.

Pizam, A., Uriely, N., and Reichel, A. (2000). The intensity of tourist-host social relationship and its effects on satisfaction and change of attitudes: The case of working tourists in Israel. *Tourism Management*, 21(4), 395-406.

Reisinger, Y., and Turner, L. W. (2002a). Cultural differences between Asian tourist markets and Australian hosts: Part 1. *Journal of Travel Research*, 40(3), 295-315.

Reisinger, Y., and Turner, L. W. (2002b). Cultural differences between Asian tourist markets and Australian hosts: Part 2. *Journal of Travel Research*, 40(4), 374-384.

Reisinger, Y., and Turner, L. W. (2002c). The determination of shopping satisfaction of Japanese tourists visiting Hawaii and the Gold Coast compared. *Journal of Travel Research*, 41(2), 167-176.

Rodriguez del Bosque, I. A., San Martin, H., and Collado, J. (2006). The role of expectations in the consumer satisfaction formation process: Empirical evidence in the travel agency sector. *Tourism Management*, 27(3), 410-419.

Sirakaya, E., Petrick, J., and Choi, H.-S. (2004). The role of mood on tourism product evaluations. *Annals of Tourism Research*, 31(3), 517-539.

Skogland, I., and Siguaw, J. A. (2004). Are your satisfied customers loyal? *Cornell Hotel and Restaurant Administration Quarterly*, 45(3), 221-234.

Spinks, W., Lawley, M., and Richins, H. (2005). Satisfaction with Sunshine Coast tourist attractions: The influence of individual visitor characteristics. *Journal of Tourism Studies*, 16(1), 12-23.

Tonge, J., and Moore, S. A. (in press). Importance-satisfaction analysis for marine-park hinterlands: A Western Australian case study. *Tourism Management*, In Press, Corrected Proof.

Truong, T. H., and Foster, D. (2006). Using HOLSAT to evaluate tourist satisfaction at destinations: The case of Australian holidaymakers in Vietnam. *Tourism Management*, 27(5), 842-855.

Um, S., Chon, K., and Ro, Y. (2006). Antecedents of revisit intention. *Annals of Tourism Research,* 33(4), 1141-1158.

Vitterso, J., Vorkinn, M., Vistad, O. I., and Vaagland, J. (2000). Tourist experiences and attractions. *Annals of Tourism Research*, 27(2), 432-450.

Wong, J., and Law, R. (2003). Difference in shopping satisfaction levels: A study of tourists in Hong Kong. *Tourism Management*, 24(4), 401-410.

Yoon, Y., and Uysal, M. (2005). An examination of the effects of motivation and satisfaction on destination loyalty: A structural model. *Tourism Management*, 26(1), 45-56.

Yu, L., and Goulden, M. (2006). A comparative analysis of international tourists' satisfaction in Mongolia. *Tourism Management*, 27(6), 1331-1342.

Yuksel, A., and Yuksel, F. (2007). Shopping risk perceptions: Effects on tourists' emotions, satisfaction and expressed loyalty intentions. *Tourism Management*, 28(3), 703-713.

In: Tourist Satisfaction and Complaining Behavior
Editor: Atila Yüksel

ISBN 978-1-60456-002-2
© 2008 Nova Science Publishers, Inc.

Chapter 12

A STUDY OF HOTEL SERVICE RECOVERY STRATEGY

John W. O'Neill and Anna S. Mattila

The Pennsylvania State University

INTRODUCTION

Many hospitality operators have developed service recovery policies to improve their relationship with dissatisfied guests (e.g., Cranage and Sujan 2004, Liu, Warden, Lee and Huang, 2001; Susskind, 2004) because service recovery is now recognized as a significant determinant of guest satisfaction and loyalty (Fornell and Wernerfelt, 1987; Smith and Bolton, 1998; Tax and Brown, 1998; Smith, Bolton and Wagner, 1999; Susskind, 2005). Most service operations, including hospitality organizations, are forced to pay attention to service recovery because dissatisfaction is not limited to the incident or customer at hand (Brown, 1997; Davidow, 2000). Previous research suggests that dissatisfied customers will tell approximately ten to twenty people about their bad experience with a service operation (Zemke, 1999). On the other hand, it is clear that a successful recovery can greatly enhance overall guest satisfaction with the service organization and increase repurchase intent (e.g., Smith and Bolton, 1998; McCollough, Berry and Yadav, 2000).

The primary goal of this chapter is to explore the role of hospitality employee explanations in mitigating the negative effects of service failures. More specifically, we investigate how hotel guests' stability attributions influence their post-recovery service perceptions and return intentions in a context of hotel overbooking. Our goal is to examine whether the way in which overbooking information is communicated to the guest influences his/her satisfaction. To that end, we manipulate the stability of service failure (i.e., the frequency of overbooking) and the stability of the service recovery (i.e., the likelihood of upgrading to a suite, should overbooking occur in the future) in a hypothetical consumption experience with actual hotel guests.

LITERATURE REVIEW AND HYPOTHESES DEVELOPMENT

Organizational justice theories are widely applied in the service recovery literature (Tax et al., 1998); because these frameworks enable us to better understand the dynamics of various service recovery efforts. Prior work has demonstrated that interactional justice strongly influences customer perceptions of service failures (Boshoff, 1997; Tax and Brown 2000; Goodwin and Ross 1992; Sparks and McColl-Kennedy 2001; Smith et al., 1999). These previous studies have mainly focused on understanding the role of politeness, courtesy and empathy in shaping consumers' fairness perceptions and post-recovery satisfaction judgments. However, research examining the power of explanations in mitigating the negative effects of service failures is scant. The lack of interest in this area is surprising because attribution theories suggest that people tend to seek causal explanations for an event that is either surprising and/or negative (Folkes, 1988; Weiner, 2000). In other words, when service problems occur, guests are concerned with explanations for the service failure (Collie, Sparks and Bradley, 2000).

Attribution theory assumes that people are rational information processors whose actions are influenced by causal inferences (Folkes, 1984). Wiener (1980) developed a categorization methodology that classifies causes for product failures by three dimensions: locus of control, stability, and controllability. Locus of control captures whether the failure was consumer-related or caused by external factors (Folkes, 1984). The stability dimension assesses the degree to which a cause is seen as relatively permanent (Folkes, 1988), while controllability refers to the degree to which a cause was under the firm's or the service provider's volitional control (Taylor, 1994).

The focus of the investigation presented in this chapter is on the stability of service failures and recovery efforts. Prior research has established that stability attributions are important in service failure situations (e.g., Smith and Bolton, 1988). In addition, Folkes' (1984) qualitative study with restaurant customers showed that 36 percent of the respondents attributed unpalatable food to stable causes. Moreover, the results from Folkes et al's (1987) field study of airline delays showed that passengers' stability inferences influence their repatronage intentions. In Smith and Bolton's (1998) study, the impact of stability attributions on cumulative satisfaction was limited to a restaurant (student) sample.

McCollough (2000) expanded on earlier research focusing on the restaurant industry and reported that hotel overbooking is a dangerous strategy because even superior recovery might not overcome the negative consequences of low harm failures. The author showed that for the recovery effect to occur, customers needed to feel confident that overbooking was unstable (i.e., not a company policy) and the recovery was stable (i.e., upgrading to a better room can be expected in the future, should the problem occur). However, a drawback of McCollough's work is that like much previous research, it used a student (convenience) sample.

Recent research in service recovery suggests that consumers have expectations not only for the initial service encounter but also for service recovery and service failures (e.g., Miller, Craighead, and Karwan, 2000). Consumer expertise or familiarity with a product category is directly linked to the concept of expectations (Oliver, 1997). Compared to novice consumers, frequent travelers have more accurate expectations for the frequency of overbooking in the hotel industry. Moreover, these experienced product users have realistic expectations for service recovery. In other words, their perceptions of service failures and recovery outcomes might be different from consumers with relatively low levels of familiarity with overbooking practices. For instance, forty percent of respondents (hotel guests) in Levesque and McDougall's (2000) study indicated that they had been victims of overbooking. Given the importance of product expertise in expectation formation processes, we argue that using student samples (as was the case with previous research in service recovery, e.g., Smith and Bolton, 1998; McCollough, 2000) may taint the results of such a study. Consequently, we put forth the following hypotheses:

Hypothesis 1: A hotel guest's overall satisfaction and service quality assessments will be higher (lower) when s/he believes that the service failure is unlikely (likely) to happen again.

Hypothesis 2: A hotel guest's overall satisfaction and service quality assessments will be higher (lower) when s/he believes that the service recovery is stable (unstable).

In addition to the robust satisfaction-behavioral intent link (e.g., Tam, 2000), prior research in consumer behavior shows that consumer attributions for product or service related problems influence their post-consumption behaviors (Richins, 1983). For example, Folkes et al. (1987) showed that travelers were less willing to repurchase an airline ticket when they attributed delays to stable causes. Accordingly, we hypothesize that stability attributions should influence the guest's return intentions. Therefore, we propose the following:

Hypothesis 3: A hotel guest's return intent will be higher (lower) when s/he believes that the service failure is unlikely (likely) to happen again.

Hypothesis 4: A hotel guest's return intent will be higher (lower) when s/he believes that the service recovery is stable (unstable).

Previous work in consumer behavior shows that attributions influence consumer preferences for redress (Folkes, Koletsky and Graham, 1987). In that study, consumers were more willing to accept product exchange as a compensation method when they attributed the failure to unstable causes. Conversely, stable attributions led to preference for refunds. We extend this line of reasoning to service recovery outcomes. Unlike in McCollough's (2000) study with undergraduate students, we argue that guest satisfaction with the recovery outcome (room upgrade) depends on the consumer's stability attributions. Knowing that the same compensation method will be available in the future should increase the guest's overall confidence in the hotel. As a result, satisfaction with the recovery outcome should be enhanced. Conversely, increased uncertainty about future outcomes associated with unstable recovery method (Weiner, 1980), should have a negative impact on guest perceptions. Feeling that the room upgrade was based on luck should reduce satisfaction with the compensation method. Hence, we hypothesize the following:

Hypothesis 5: A guest's satisfaction with the compensation method (an upgraded room) will be higher (lower) when s/he believes that the service recovery is stable (unstable).

RESEARCH METHODOLOGY

This study used scenarios to test our research hypotheses. The use of scenarios has been established as a valid methodology for investigating service quality and service failure/recovery in the hospitality literature (e.g., Mattila, 1999). Furthermore, service failures and recoveries are common in the lodging industry (Mount and Mattila, 2000). As a result, we expected real users (actual hotel guests) to find service failure (i.e., their reserved guest room not being available) and service recovery (i.e., being upgraded to a suite) to be both realistic and believable. Moreover, upgrading the guest to a superior guest room is a frequently encountered recovery technique in the lodging industry (McCollough, 2000).

Our study involved a 2 x 2 between-subjects design, with stable and unstable failure attributions, and stable and unstable recovery attributions. All four scenarios presented a failure in which a guest's reserved room, which was a basic, economy room, was not available due to the hotel being overbooked. In all four scenarios, the recovery technique of the hotel front office was kept constant (i.e., upgrading the guest to an available suite). In the two stable failure scenarios, the failure was depicted as common due to the hotel's policy of overbooking. Conversely, in the two unstable failure scenarios, the failure was pictured as uncommon due to the hotel's policy of not overbooking. In the two unstable recovery scenarios, the hotel was portrayed as generally being overbooked with no extra rooms available, and upgrading the guest to a suite was depicted as an atypical circumstance due to a cancellation. With stable recovery, the hotel was described as usually having many extra guestrooms available. To reiterate, in all four conditions, the recovery was the same upgrade to a suite, i.e., a positive recovery outcome.

Prior to their exposure to stimulus information, participants were asked to provide the name and location of a hotel where they had stayed during the past year. Next, they were asked to evaluate the service quality of the hotel based on their actual experiences there (based on three survey questions), and were asked how likely they would be to return to the hotel in the future (based on one question) on a scale of 1 to 5. Then, participants were asked to read a scenario, imagining that the encounter had occurred at the hotel where they had named in the previous question. This procedure is similar to that employed by Smith and Bolton (1998) and is a methodology that assures accurate pre-scenario attitudes and eliminates any necessity to manipulate or impose pre-scenario attitudes. Finally, participants were asked to evaluate post-scenario service quality (based on three questions), outcome satisfaction (based on three questions), general satisfaction (based on three questions), and intent to return (based on one question). A sample of the unstable failure/stable recovery survey is included in the appendix.

SAMPLE AND MEASURES

The sample consisted of 613 hotel guests originating from 30 different countries. Most respondents (539) were from the U.S., while the most common nationalities of those respondents who were not from the U.S. were Canada (14 respondents), Jamaica (10 respondents), Aruba (5 respondents), and England (5 respondents). The mean age of respondents was 32.9 years old, with a range of 19 to 75 and a standard deviation of 12. A total of 46.4 percent of the respondents were male and 53.5 percent were female.

Trained graduate students, who randomly assigned potential respondents into the four experimental conditions, and who administered surveys in person, randomly selected participants. Due to some missing responses for some items, the sample size varies slightly by analysis. A total of 151 respondents participated in the stable failure/stable recovery scenario, 158 participants were in the unstable failure/unstable recovery scenario, 149 respondents were in the unstable failure/stable recovery scenario, and 155 respondents were in the stable failure/unstable recovery scenario.

Existing scales were used wherever possible (see appendix for the actual scales). Confirmatory factor analysis (CFA) using structural equation modeling (SEM) was performed to examine the reliability and validity of the outcome satisfaction, overall satisfaction, and service quality scales. CFA was chosen over an exploratory factor analysis because the goal was to provide a confirmatory test of well-established measures. SEM was chosen because it is an appropriate methodology for the subject research design. The results from the CFA show that the item reliabilities for all scales were above 0.50, hence suggesting adequate construct validity. Moreover, the model achieved a good fit, with a goodness-of-fit index (GFI) of 0.97, and on adjusted goodness-of-fit index (AGFI) of 0.95. The root mean square error of approximation (RMSEA) was 0.06, demonstrating an acceptable fit (Schumacker and Lomax, 1996). The $\chi 2$ value was significant at 76.8 (df = 24, p<0.05). However, as the sample size increases (generally above 200), the $\chi 2$ test has a tendency to indicate a significant probability level (Schumacker and Lomax, 1996, pp. 124-125). In this present study, the large sample of 613 respondents might have contributed to the significant $\chi 2$ value. However, interpreted alongside the other goodness-of-fit statistics, the model fit appears to be very acceptable.

The internal reliability of all scales exceeds the conventional minimum of .70 (Rosenthal and Rosnow, 1991). Specifically, the three questions making up the pre-scenario service quality factor resulted in a Coefficient Alpha of .91, the three questions making up post-scenario service quality had an Alpha of .91, the three questions comprising the overall satisfaction factor had an Alpha of .92, and the three questions comprising the general satisfaction factor had an Alpha of .89.

FINDINGS

The use of a MANCOVA procedure incorporating outcome satisfaction, overall satisfaction, service quality and return intent as multiple response variables was justified because these measures correlated positively with each other (for correlation coefficients between the response measures, please see Table 1). Since prior experiences with the hotel might bias the consumer's future evaluations, the subject's pre-exposure service quality assessment was run as a covariate in the data analysis.

Table 1. Correlation Coefficients between Outcome Satisfaction, General Satisfaction, Post-Scenario Service Quality, and Return Intent

	Outcome Satisfaction	General Satisfaction	Post Scenario Service Quality	Return Intent
Outcome Satisfaction	1.000			
General Satisfaction	0.569*	1.000		
Post Scenario Serv. Qual.	0.506*	0.835*	1.000	
Return Intent	0.441*	0.768*	0.799*	1.000

* correlation is significant at the .01 level

The mean ratings by failure and recovery attribution for all four response measures are presented in Table 2. The Wilks lambda F approximations for failure and recovery attributions were significant (Wilks lambda = .901 for failure and Wilks lambda = .861 for recovery effect, p<.001 for both). The interaction effect was insignificant. The means and standard deviations for our response variables are presented in Table 2.

Table 2. Response Variable Means by Failure and Recovery Attribution

	Post-Scenario Service Quality		General Satisfaction		Return Intent		Outcome Satisfaction	
	Stable recovery	Unstable recovery	Stable recovery	Unstable recovery	Stable recovery	Unstable recovery	Stable recovery	Unstable recovery
Stable Failure	3.85 (0.88*)	3.13 (1.06*)	3.98 (0.89*)	3.31 (1.10*)	3.76 (1.19*)	2.96 (1.35*)	4.56 (0.69*)	4.47 (0.73*)
Unstable Failure	4.34 (0.74*)	3.77 (0.94*)	4.38 (0.78*)	3.87 (0.86*)	4.26 (0.94*)	3.74 (1.16*)	4.71 (0.54*)	4.54 (0.74*)

* standard deviation

Univariate F-tests for recovery attribution were significant at $p < .05$ for all four response measures. For service quality, $F = 85.29$, $p < .001$; for overall satisfaction, $F=67.51$, $p < .01$; for return intent $F=55.79$, $p < .01$, and finally, for outcome satisfaction, $F = 3.07$, $p < .05$. When failure was stable (i.e., likely to happen again), the mean rating for post-scenario service quality was 3.49 (3.85 with stable recovery and 3.13 with unstable recovery), whereas when failure was unstable (i.e., unlikely to happen again), the mean rating for post-scenario service quality increased to 4.05 (4.34 with stable recovery and 3.77 with unstable recovery). The same pattern was observed for our general satisfaction scale. When failure was stable, the mean rating for general satisfaction was 3.64 (3.98 with stable recovery and 3.31 with unstable recovery), whereas when failure was unstable, the mean rating for general satisfaction increased to 4.12 (4.38 for stable recovery and 3.87 for unstable recovery). Taken together, these results support Hypothesis 1.

When recovery was stable, the mean rating for outcome satisfaction was 4.63, whereas in an unstable recovery condition the mean was 4.52. The guests who believed that failure was unstable and recovery was stable (mean = 4.71) were significantly more satisfied with the compensation method than their counterparts in the stable failure and unstable recovery condition (mean = 4.47). This finding provides support for Hypothesis 5. With return intent, the mean rating for return intent was 3.36 when failure was stable. Conversely, when the guest perceived the failure as unstable, the mean return intent increased to 3.99. This finding supports Hypothesis 3.

For failure attributions, the univariate F-tests were significant for service quality, overall satisfaction and return intent, $F=55.89$, $F=39.85$ and $F=42.91$ respectively, $p<.001$. When recovery was stable, the mean rating for post-scenario service quality was 4.09 (3.85 with stable failure and 4.34 with unstable failure), whereas when recovery was unstable, the mean rating for post-scenario service quality decreased to 3.45 (3.13 with stable failure and 3.77 with unstable failure). The same pattern was repeated with general satisfaction. When recovery was stable, the mean rating for general satisfaction was 4.18 (3.98 with stable failure and 4.38 with unstable failure), whereas when failure was unstable, the mean rating for general satisfaction dropped to 3.60 (3.31 with stable failure and 3.87 with unstable failure). Therefore, Hypothesis 2 was supported.

With stable recovery, the mean rating for return intent was 4.01, whereas when failure was unstable, the mean rating dropped to 3.35. The guests who were most likely to return believed that failure was unstable and recovery was stable (mean = 4.26), while the guests who were least likely to return believed that failure was stable and recovery was unstable (mean = 2.96). These results provide support for Hypothesis 4.

The attribution framework postulates that consumers are concerned with explanations for product or service failures (Weiner, 2000; Folkes, 1984). In this study, we found that hotels guests' overall satisfaction and service quality assessments are higher when the guests believe that the service failure is unstable (i.e., unlikely to happen again in the future) and the service recovery is stable (i.e., likely to be similarly resolved should a service failure occur). Moreover, guests are more likely to return to the same hotel when they believe that service failure is unstable and recovery is stable.

DISCUSSION, RESEARCH IMPLICATIONS AND MANAGERIAL IMPLICATIONS

When services or products fail, people tend to engage in causal attributions (e.g., Weiner, 2000). Yet research investigating consumer attributions in a service recovery context is relatively scarce (e.g., Bradley and Sparks, 2002; Maxham and Netemeyer, 2002). To bridge that gap, this study examined how guests' stability attributions influenced their satisfaction with the hotel stay and return intent.

Overall, many of our findings with actual hotel guests are consistent with previous work that employed student samples (McCollough, 2000). However, unlike previous research, we found that hotel guests are more satisfied with the upgraded guestroom when they perceive recovery as being stable rather than unstable. Further, unlike previous research in this area, our results indicate that stability attributions influence the guests' intent to return.

Due to the intangibility and inseparability of services like hotel accommodations, consumers' perceptions of satisfaction may include contextual cues that they use to evaluate quality and to decide whether to return (Choi and Chu, 2001). Thus, the manner in which the upgraded guest room is presented to the guest may be a contextual cue used by guests to evaluate their satisfaction with the room accommodation itself. Seasoned travelers, who are likely to encounter overbooking in real life, seem to be sensitive to the hotel's ability to recover from service failures in a consistent manner. Our findings provide additional support for Barsky and Labagh's (1992) contention that the manner of guest reception is directly linked to return intent.

Service recovery strategies and tactics should be matched to the specific incident (Davidow, 2000; Levesque and McDougall, 2000; Smith et al., 1999). The subject study found that the optimal tactical match in the incidence of overbooking is that the guest ultimately needs to be convinced that service failure is unlikely, and in the rare instances when service failure occurs, that recovery is stable, e.g., in this case, that an upgraded room is almost always available. Ultimately, however, most hotel guests seem to be indicating that had they truly desired to have an upgraded guest room (a suite), they probably would have been willing to pay for it. It goes without saying that lodging managers should be attentive to their yield (i.e., overbooking should occur to the extent of no-shows and cancellations).

For practicing managers, this research provides some strategic direction regarding the handling of service failure and recovery, in general, and specifically regarding the common practice of overbooking. Strategic management is often discussed in terms of strategies and tactics (e.g., David, 2001). The strategy of concern in the subject study is hotel guest room yield management, i.e., revenue management. Essentially, a hotel manager may take either a conservative or an aggressive approach with respect to the strategy of revenue management. Based on the results of the subject study, hotel managers should be aware that if they take an aggressive approach regarding overbooking, there exists a strong likelihood that when the hotel fails to deliver on its promise to guests, the guests' entire experience (including their satisfaction with facilities) may be tainted, and the guests may even be less likely to return. As Levesque and McDougall (2000, p. 20) ultimately concluded, "Getting it right the first time is the best strategy".

As with any research study, the findings of this work should be interpreted with caution for several reasons. First, to maximize internal validity, hypothetical scenarios, rather than an actual consumption experience, were used as stimuli. Second, data came from a single sample in the US. It can be argued that consumers' attributional processes are heavily influenced by their cultural backgrounds (e.g., Mattila and Patterson, 2004), and therefore, replications across other cultural groups will be needed to fully understand the implications for international travelers. Third, our manipulations were limited to a single type of recovery method (room upgrade) and to a single form of service failure (unavailable room). Other compensation methods (e.g., vouchers for future stays) or other types of service failures (e.g., a rude employee) might produce different results.

Our research builds on previous research because we found that hotel guests are more satisfied with an upgraded guestroom when they perceive recovery as being stable rather than unstable. Further, unlike previous research in this area, our results indicate that stability attributions influence the guests' intent to return. Future research should continue to develop this area of research by using actual guest samples, as we did, but also should continue to expand on the diversity of the sample studied. In particular, undertaking cross national stability research could provide invaluable information for managers operating in a multinational context.

REFERENCES

Barsky, J. D., and Labagh, R. (1992). A strategy for customer satisfaction. *The Cornell Hotel and Restaurant Administration Quarterly*, 33(5), 32-40.

Boshoff, C. (1997). An Experimental Study of Service Recovery Options. *International Journal of Service Industry Management*, 8(2), 110-30.

Bradley, G., and Sparks, B. (2002). Service Locus of Control: Its Conceptualization and Measurement. *Journal of Service Research*, 4(4), 312-324.

Brown, S. (1997). Service recovery through IT: complaint handling will differentiate firms in the future. *Marketing Management*, 25-27.

Choi, T.Y., and Chu, R. (2001). Determinants of hotel guests' satisfaction and repeat patronage in the Hong Kong hotel industry. *International Journal of Hospitality Management,* 20, 277-297.

Collie, T., Sparks, B., and Bradley, G. (2000). Investing in interactional justice: A study of the fair process effect within a hospitality failure context. *Journal of Hospitality and Tourism Research,* 24, 448-472.

David, F.R. (2001). *Strategic Management Concepts.* (8th Ed.), Upper Saddle River, NJ, USA: Prentice Hall.

Davidow, M. (2000). The bottom line impact of organizational responses to customer complaints. *Journal of Hospitality and Tourism Research,* 24, 473-490.

Folkes, V., Koletsky, S., and Graham, J. (1987). A field study of causal inferences and consumer reaction: the view from the airport. *Journal of Consumer Research,* 13(March), 534-39.

Folies., and Valarie. (1988). Recent Attribution Research in Consumer Behavior: A Review and New Directions. *Journal of Consumer Research,* 14(March), 548-65.

Folkes, V.S., (1984). Consumer reactions to product failure: An attributional approach. *Journal of Consumer Research,* 10(4), 398-409.

Fornell, C., and Wernerfelt, B. (1987). Defensive marketing strategy by consumer complaint management: a theoretical analysis. *Journal of Marketing Research,* 24(November), 337-346.

Goodwin, C., and Ross, I. (1992). Consumer Responses to Service Failures: Influence of Procedural and Interactional Fairness Perceptions. *Journal of Business Research,* 25, 149-163.

Levesque, T., and McDougall, G. (2000). Service problems and recovery strategies: an experiment. *Canadian Journal of Administrative Sciences,* 17(1), 20-37.

Liu, C., Warden, C., Lee, C., and Huang, C. (2001). Fatal service failures across cultures. *Journal of Hospitality and Leisure Marketing,* 8(1/2), 93-113.

Mattila, A. (1999). Consumers' value judgments. *The Cornell Hotel and Restaurant Administration Quarterly,* 40(1), 40-46.

Mattila, A., and Patterson, P. (2004). The impact of culture on consumers' perceptions of service recovery efforts. *Journal of Retailing,* 80, 196-206.

Maxham, J. III., and Netemeyer, R. (2002). A Longitudinal Study of Complaining Customers' Evaluations of Multiple Service Failures and Recovery Efforts. *Journal of Marketing,* 66(4), 57-71.

McCollough, M.A. (2000). The effect of perceived justice and attributions regarding service failure and recovery on post-recovery customer satisfaction and service quality attitudes. *Journal of Hospitality and Tourism Research,* 24(4), 423-447.

McCollough, M.A., Berry, L., Yadav, M. (2000). An empirical investigation of customer satisfaction after service failure and recovery. *Journal of Service Research,* 3(2), 121-137.

Miller, J., Craighead, C., Karwan, K. (2000). Service recovery: a framework and empirical investigation. *Journal of Operations Management,* 18, 387-400.

Mount, D.J., Mattila, A. (2000). The final opportunity: the effectiveness of a customer relations call center in recovering hotel guests. *Journal of Hospitality and Tourism Research,* 24(4), 514-525.

Richins, M.L. (1983). Negative word-of-mouth by dissatisfied consumers: a pilot study. *Journal of Marketing,* 47, 68-78.

Rosenthal, R., Rosnow, R.L. (1991). *Essentials of behavioral research: methods and data análisis.* New York, USA: McGraw Hill.

Schumacker, R.E., Lomax, R. (1996). *A Beginner's Guide to Structural Equation Modeling.* NJ, USA: Lawrence Erlbaum Associates.

Smith, A.K., Bolton R.N. (1998). An experimental investigation of customer reactions to service failure and recovery encounter: paradox or peril?. *Journal of Service Research,* 1(1), 65-81.

Smith, A., Bolton, R., Wagner, J. (1999). A model of customer satisfaction with service encounters involving failure and recovery. *Journal of Marketing Research,* 34(August), 356-372.

Sparks, B.A., and McConnell-Kennedy, J. (2001). Justice Strategy Options for Increased Customer Satisfaction in a Services Recovery Setting. *Journal of Business Research,* 54, 209-218.

Susskind, A. (2005). A content analysis of consumer complaints, remedies and repatronage intentions regarding dissatisfying service experiences. *Journal of Hospitality and Tourism Research,* 29, 150-169.

Susskind, A. (2004). Consumer frustration in the customer-service exchange: The role of attitudes toward complaining and information adequacy related to service failures. *Journal of Hospitality and Tourism Research,* 28, 21-43.

Tam, J. (2000). The effects of service quality, perceived value and customer satisfaction on behavioral intentions. *Journal of Hospitality and Leisure Marketing,* 6(4), 31-44.

Tax, S., Brown, S. (1998). Recovering form learning from service failure. *Sloan Management Review,* Fall, 75-88.

Tax, S., Brown, S., and Chandrashekaran, Murali. (1998). Customer Evaluations of Service Complaint Experiences: Implications for Relationship Marketing, *Journal of Marketing,* 62(April), 60-76.

Tax, S. and Brown, S. (2000). *Service Recovery: Research Insights and Practices,* in Handbook of Services Marketing and Management, (T. Swartz and D. Iacobucci, Eds.), Thousand Oaks, CA, USA: Sage, 271-286.

Taylor, S. (1994). Waiting for service: the relationship between delays and evaluations of service. *Journal of Marketing* 58(April), 56-69.

Weiner, B. (2000). Attributional thoughts about consumer behavior. *Journal of Consumer Research* 27(3), 382-387.

Weiner, B. (1980). Cognitive (attribution)-emotion-action model of motivated help giving. *Journal of Personality and Social Psychology* 39(2), 186-200.

Zemke, R. (1999). *Service recovery: turning oops into opportunity.* In Best Practices in Customer Service (R. Zemke and J. Woods, Eds.), AMACOM, AMA Publications, New York, USA, 279-288.

APPENDIX

1. Date _____ , 200_
2. Name of interviewer_____
3. Name of interviewee_____
4. Address _____
   _____
   _____
5. Phone number _____
6. E-mail address _____

7. Interviewee sex (circle one number):
1   Male
2   Female
8. Interviewee Age (round to nearest year) _____
9. List the name and city of a hotel where the interviewee has stayed during the past year:
   Hotel/motel name _____
   Hotel/motel city/location _____

10. For each of the following questions, circle the one number that most applies.

Low   High

1 2 3 4 5   How would you rate the overall quality of service provided by the hotel/motel where you stayed?
                     This variable was coded as "Overall 1"

1 2 3 4 5   Based on your past experiences with this specific hotel/motel, your attitude toward its overall service quality is …
                     This variable was coded as "Past 1"

1 2 3 4 5   To what extent do you believe that this hotel/motel provides high quality service?
                     This variable was coded as "Extent 1"

1 2 3 4 5   How likely would you be to return to this hotel/motel in the future?
                     This variable was coded as "Return 1"

11. *The interviewee should read the following information and complete the following questions*:

Imagine that you are traveling and are staying overnight at the hotel/motel that you indicated above where you stayed in the past year. You made your reservation several weeks ago and have a confirmed, guaranteed reservation for a standard "economy" room with a double bed. You give your name to the clerk on duty at the front desk. The following dialogue then takes place:

Clerk: 'I'm sorry, but we're overbooked and don't have your reserved room. This almost never happens as we have a policy not to overbook I can't remember the last time this happened'.

The clerk looks very concerned and begins pushing buttons on his or her computer terminal.

Your response: 'Is there anything you can do for me?'

Clerk: 'We rarely run out of rooms and are almost never full. So, if you'd like, I can upgrade you to our best room at no extra charge. It's a very nice suite with two rooms, a king-size bed, and a great view. Will that be acceptable?'

Your response: 'Yes, that will be fine'.

The clerk pushes some more buttons, prints out a registration card, and hands you a key. You notice that the registration is for a suite at no extra charge.

Clerk: 'Again, I'm very sorry about the confusion. This rarely happens, so we don't usually have this problem. Please enjoy your stay, and let us know if there is anything we can do to make your visit more pleasant'.

You thank the clerk and leave the desk area. Your room proves to be a beautiful, spacious suite with plenty of amenities, and you have no complaints.

Low				High	
1	2	3	4	5	Given the situation you read, how would you rate the overall quality of service provided by the hotel/motel where you stayed? **This variable was coded as "Overall 2"**
1	2	3	4	5	Based on your past experiences with this specific hotel/motel, including the events described, your attitude toward its overall service quality is … **This variable was coded as "Past 2"**
1	2	3	4	5	Considering the event you read about, to what extent do you believe that this hotel/motel provides high quality service? **This variable was coded as "Extent 2"**
1	2	3	4	5	How satisfied would you be with the room provided? **This variable was coded as "Satisfied"**
1	2	3	4	5	How well did this room meet your needs? **This variable was coded as "Needs"**
1	2	3	4	5	Overall, how satisfied would you be with the room? **This variable was coded as "Room"**
1	2	3	4	5	How satisfied did this experience leave you feeling? **This variable was coded as "Feeling"**
1	2	3	4	5	How well did this overall service experience meet your needs? **This variable was coded as "Experience"**
1	2	3	4	5	Overall, would you be very satisfied with this service encounter? **This variable was coded as "Encounter"**
1	2	3	4	5	How likely would you be to return to this hotel/motel in the future? **This variable was coded as "Return 2"**

In: Tourist Satisfaction and Complaining Behavior
Editor: Atila Yüksel

ISBN 978-1-60456-002-2
© 2008 Nova Science Publishers, Inc.

Chapter 13

A COGNITIVE APPRAISAL PROCESS MODEL OF EMOTIONS AND COMPLAINING BEHAVIOR

Heejung Ro and Anna S. Mattila
Pennsylvania State University

INTRODUCTION

Highly competitive markets are increasingly common in many industries (e. g. hotel, restaurant, and airline industries), and hence, defensive marketing strategies are gaining popularity (Fornell and Wernerfelt, 1987). Service recovery aims at regaining customer satisfaction through responsiveness. In other words, service recovery rests on the manager's understanding of when consumers complain, given that recovery cannot occur without a "complaint" (Singh and Wilkes, 1996). Therefore, it has been paradoxically argued that dissatisfied customers should be encouraged to complain (Rust, Zahorik, and Kenningham, 1996). Unfortunately, research on consumer dissatisfaction suggests that up to two thirds of typical consumers do not report their dissatisfaction (Andreason, 1985; Richns, 1983). The majority of dissatisfied customers simply fail to communicate with the service provider about receiving poor service. However, they may quietly switch companies, engage in negative word-of-mouth (Richins, 1983 a), or do both.

An unhappy customer who fails to voice his/her dissatisfaction is of great concern to service organizations for several reasons: (1) the firm loses the opportunity to remedy the service failure and to retain the customer (Hirschman, 1970; Blodgett and Anderson, 2000), (2) the firm's reputation can be damaged from negative word-of-mouth (Richins, 1983 a) resulting in the loss of current and potential customers, and (3) the firm is deprived of valuable feedback about the quality of its services (Fornell and Wernerfelt, 1987). Therefore, insightful managers want to understand not only customers who voice their complaints but also those who fail to do so (Stephens and Gwinner, 1998).

It should be noted that prior research has mainly centered on complainers and only a few studies have considered the silent majority of noncomplainers (e.g. Stephens and Gwinner,

1998). Though a substantial body of research has addressed various topics of consumer complaining behavior and proposed diverse models to explain the process, several important gaps remain. First, most previous research has focused on behavioral dissatisfaction responses. Although some researchers acknowledge that consumers may take non-behavioral responses such as no-action (Day and Landon, 1977), this category has been largely ignored. To bridge that gap, we suggest that the "no action" response warrants immediate attention even if it is less visible than other types of behavioral responses.

Second, while it is acknowledged that emotions are triggered and customers engage in cognitive appraisal during service failure, relatively little is known about the interplay between emotions and cognition in the context of service failures (Bennett, Hartel, McColl-Kennedy, and James, 2003). At what point do consumers react affectively to service failure situation? We attempt to explore the relationship among affective responses, emotions, and dissatisfaction in the context of the consumer's cognitive appraisal process.

Finally, although previous research has addressed various forces motivating complaining behaviors, there are additional factors that warrant attention. For example, perceived effort might influence the likelihood of choosing various complaining options. Simply stated, it takes effort to complain. Not only does complaining require physical effort and time, the consumer must also invest cognitive effort to decide whether or not to complain and how to go about it (Huppertz, Mower and Associates, 2003).

The main objective of this study is to propose an integrated conceptual framework of consumer complaining behavior by using a cognitive appraisal theory as a framework. Specific focus is placed on no-action response, interplay of emotion and cognition, and consumer effort. In the following section, we review relevant literature in consumer complaining behavior and cognitive appraisal-emotion-coping process. Next, based on the literature review, we propose a conceptual framework and discuss each stage of the process and related components. Finally, a brief summary and conclusions are presented.

LITERATURE REVIEW

Consumer Complaint Behavior

Most consumer complaining behavior studies acknowledge Hirschman's exit, voice, and loyalty conceptualization as a theoretical starting point. Basically, his theory suggests three alternative responses to deteriorating relationships: exit, voice, and loyalty (Hirschman, 1970). Exit is a voluntarily termination of an exchange relationship and it results in switching patronage to another product/service. Exit decisions involve some effort, such as switching cost and searching for alternatives. The voice option is viewed from a proactive perspective as "any attempt at all to change rather than escape from an objectionable state of affairs" (p. 30). Similar to the exit option, the voice response entails effort and motivation on the part of the consumer. By contrast, Hirschman views the loyalty option as a passive response. That is "loyal" consumers neither exit nor voice. Rather, they continue to remain in the relationship with the dissatisfying product/seller and "suffer in silence confident that things will soon get better" (p. 38). His framework has inspired voluminous research in areas such as psychology, organizational behavior, and consumer complaining behavior.

In consumer complaining research, Day and Landon (1977) introduced the generally well received public-private distinction in complaint response. According to their conceptualization, dissatisfied consumers would either "take action" or "take no action". If action was taken, it was labeled as either public (e.g. redress seeking complaint, legal action, third-party complaint) or private action (e.g. personal boycott of the brand, negative word-of-mouth). Conversely, the "take no action" response is described as 'forget about the incident and do nothing at all'.

In an effort to develop consumer complaining behavior (CCB) taxonomy, Singh (1988) specified three dimensions: (1) voice, reflecting actions directed toward the seller; (2) private, involving negative word-of-mouth (WOM) and exit; (3) third party, relating to actions directed toward external agencies such as the Better Business Bureau and legal options. In consumer behavior, negative word of mouth is often considered as a distinct construct (Singh, 1990; Richins, 1983 a), and consequently, four responses commonly used in consumer complaining studies are (1) voice, (2) third-party action, (3) exit/switch, and (4) negative word-of-mouth (e.g. Blodgett and Granbois, 1992; Boote, 1998). The diagram (Figure 1) shows the taxonomy of consumer complaining behavior.

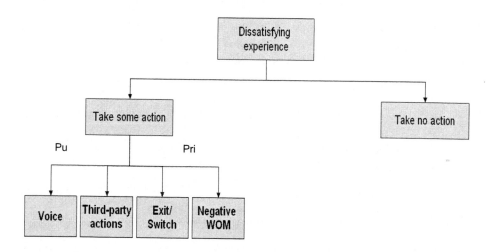

Figure 1. Consumer Complaining Behavior Taxonomy
(Based on Day and Landon, 1977; Singh, 1988; Singh, 1990; Blodgett and Granbois, 1992)

Unfortunately, "no action" response is often ignored by researchers or alternatively it is mixed in with other categories. Singh (1988), for example, included the "no action" response in the voice response by arguing that failing to take action appears to reflect feelings toward the seller. Based on Day and Landon's (1977) classification, the "no action" response is described as 'forget about the incident and do nothing,' yet it is not clear whether this response translates into doing nothing or whether it leads to other responses such as switching or return. Recently, Zeelenberg and Pieters (2004) introduced a similar concept called "inertia". Inertia reflects a passive response and accordingly customers fail to take action in response to a service failure. We suggest that the "no action" response warrants more attention because it is a dissatisfaction response that many consumers might engage in.

Therefore, we included "no action" response in our model along with other behavioral responses (e.g. voice, negative WOM).

COGNITIVE APPRAISAL – EMOTIONS – COPING BEHAVIOR

In psychology and consumer research, a number of theories have been offered to specify the particular appraisals of events that elicit different emotions (Lazarus, 1991; Roseman, Antoniu, and Jose, 1996). Cognitive appraisal has been described as "a process through which the person evaluates whether a particular encounter with the environment is relevant to his or her well-being, and if so, in what ways" (Folkman et al., 1986). Lazarus (1974) suggested that emotions are the outcomes of the cognitive appraisal and an emotion-evoking situation calls for a coping mechanism. During the service encounter, the customer makes an evaluation known as cognitive appraisal to determine whether a dissatisfying experience is actually stressful. These stressful appraisal outcomes, in turn, elicit emotive reactions that, in conjunction with cognitive appraisal, influence the consumer's coping strategies (Stephens and Gwinner, 1998).

Lazarus and his colleagues postulate that emotions are a result of primary and secondary cognitive appraisals (Lazarus, 1991). While primary appraisal focuses on goal conflicts, secondary appraisal assesses an individual's coping strategies. Folkman and Lazarus (1988) suggest various distinct coping strategies with two basic coping styles: problem-based coping and emotions-based coping. The former involves direct actions to resolve the situation, while the latter reflects indirect actions to minimize emotions (e.g., removing oneself from a stressful situation or blaming someone else for a personal failure).

In the marketing literature, these two styles of coping behavior have been categorized as complaining (problem-based coping) and non-complaining (emotions-based coping) behaviors (Chebat, Davidow, and Codjovi, 2005). Problem-based coping requires the consumer to directly act on the service failure while emotions-based coping calls for more passive strategies such as controlling one's emotions or seeking support from others (Menon and Dubé, 2004).

PROPOSED MODEL OF CONSUMER COMPLAINING BEHAVIOR

Model Overview

The proposed conceptual model (Figure 2) starts with service failure as an input into the process. A service failure will trigger an immediate affective response (initial dissatisfaction) that enables consumers to engage in a cognitive appraisal process. A cognitive appraisal process consists of four components: importance of the event, seriousness of the problem, attribution, and coping potential. Negative emotions are generated as a result of the cognitive appraisal and the elicited emotions influence the type of coping strategies used by the consumer. Problem focused coping and emotion focused coping are manifested as consumer complaining behaviors. Voice and third-party actions are considered as problem focused coping strategies, while negative word-of-mouth, switch, and no-action are considered as emotion-focused coping strategies.   Individual differences (personal factors such as demographic characteristics, prior complaining experience etc.) and industry characteristics (market factors such as switching convenience and typicality of the service failure) also influence cognitive appraisals thus having an impact on complaint behaviors.

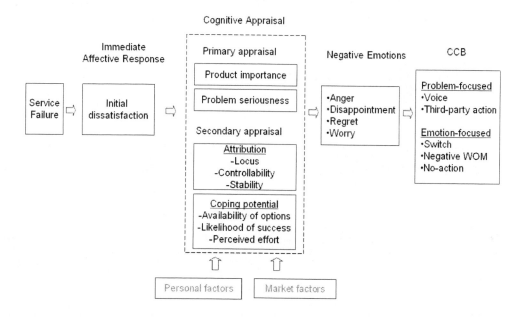

Figure 2. A Cognitive Appraisal Process Model of Emotions and Complaining Behavior (Based on Stephens andGwinner, 1998; Bennett et al., 2003; Yi and Baumgartner, 2004)

SERVICE FAILURE

A service failure can be described as dissatisfying service event in which consumers' performance perceptions fall short of their pre-consumption standards, thus leading to dissatisfaction [e.g., poor-quality restaurant meals, rude service representative, long waiting, losing luggage during the airline travel (Stephens and Gwinner, 1998)]. A large amount of theoretical debate and empirical research has revolved around the question on what standard(s) people use in the comparison process (Wirtz and Mattila, 2001). This line of research has resulted in six broad classes of pre-experience standards. They are (1) predictive expectations (Oliver, 1980), (2) ideal performance (Sirgy, 1984), (3) needs and wants coined as value-percept (Westbrook and Reilly, 1983) or desires (Spreng and Olshavsky, 1993), (4) experience-based standards (Cadotte et al., 1987), (5) comparisons with social norms (Swan, 1983), and (6) multiple standards (Sirgy, 1984; Spreng, MacKenzie and Olshavsky, 1996).

Expectancy-disconfirmation theory is the dominant framework for explaining consumer (dis)satisfaction (Oliver, 1997). This framework suggests that consumers form expectations about the likely performance of the product, evaluate the actual performance of the product, and compare performance to expectations. If performance is greater than their expectations, consumers experience positive disconfirmation, and if performance is less than their expectations, consumers experience negative disconfirmation (Oliver, 1997).

In summary, a service failure is often defined as service performance that falls below the customer's expectations (Hoffman and Bateson, 1997) and it serves as a potentially stressful event that will be evaluated via the cognitive appraisal process (Stephens and Gwinner, 1998). Therefore, service failure becomes a starting point of our model.

INITIAL DISSATISFACTION (IMMEDIATE AFFECTIVE RESPONSE)

Day (1984) suggests that it is not the judgment of dissatisfaction per se that motivates the consumer to complain but rather the negative emotional state that arises from the appraisal of unfavorable product/consumption outcome. There is ample evidence to suggest that emotions play an important role in determining satisfaction with a product/service (Westbrook and Oliver 1991; Oliver, 1997; Phillps and Baumgartner, 2002; Liljander and Stranvik, 1997; Price, Arnould, and Tierney, 1995). However, the interplay between emotions and dissatisfaction is quite complex.

For example, Oliver (1989) suggests that specific types or categories of emotional responses might be causal antecedents to satisfaction. Thus, negative emotions are aggregated together and lead to a general dissatisfaction judgment. In contrast, Bougie, Pieters and Zeelenberg (2003) suggest that dissatisfaction is an antecedent of a specific emotion (anger) and that dissatisfaction does not have a direct impact on complaint behaviors, negative WOM, or third-party actions. While most of the previous research (e.g. Oliver, 1997; Phillps and Baumgartner, 2002) conceptualize dissatisfaction as an accumulated overall feeling, Bougie, Pieters, and Zeelenberg (2003) consider dissatisfaction as an affective response relating to a specific service encounter. Bougie et al.'s (2003) conceptualization of dissatisfaction might thus be understood as initial dissatisfaction because it is not a cognitive summary judgment but rather it is negative affect arising from the service failure.

Although most appraisal theories propose that stressful events, including service failures, lead people to engage in a cognitive appraisal process, some researchers suggest that a service failure will trigger an 'immediate affective reaction' that involves autonomic emotional appraisal that can be manifested in facial/posture expressions (Bennett et al., 2003; Weiss and Cropanzano, 1996).

Following Bennett at al.'s (2003) framework, we propose that consumers feel immediate negative affect from the service failure and this affective reaction in turn triggers a cognitive appraisal process to assess the situation. This immediate affective response is termed as initial dissatisfaction. Our conceptualization of initial dissatisfaction is congruent with Bougie et al.'s (2003) framework where they consider dissatisfaction as an antecedent of other specific negative emotions.

COGNITIVE APPRAISAL

Lazarus and his colleagues postulate that cognitive appraisal composes of two parts: primary and secondary cognitive appraisal (Lazarus, 1991). While primary appraisal focuses on goal conflicts, secondary appraisal assesses an individual's coping strategies. Although cognitive models of emotion in psychology cover a wide variety of factors, importance of the event, problem seriousness, attribution, and coping potential seem most relevant in the context of CCB.

Primary appraisal evaluates whether there is anything at stake in the service encounter. It is a process through which the person evaluates whether the dissatisfying experience is relevant to his or her well-being, and if so, in what way (Lazarus and Folkman, 1984). Two specific components of primary appraisal are: goal relevance and goal incongruence (Lazarus, 1991; Stephens and Gwiner, 1998) and they can be viewed as importance of the event and problem seriousness in the consumer context.

Importance of the event refers to the extent to which an event or an outcome is personally relevant to the individual. Hirshman (1970) suggest that consumers are more likely to voice their complaints when dissatisfied with an important product. Indeed, empirical evidence indicates that product importance is a significant determinant of complaining behavior (Richins, 1987). Problem seriousness, on the other hand, indicates the extent to which an event or outcome is congruent or incongruent with an individual's wants and desires. Personally relevant products/services and serious problems are likely to result in strong emotional responses (Nyer, 1997).

Secondary appraisal consists of consumers' assessments of their ability to cope with the dissatisfying experience (Stephens and Gwinner, 1998). The two key components of this process are attribution and coping potential (Nyer, 1997).

Attribution

Consumers typically assign blame for the incident, which requires knowing who is responsible. Without this, consumers have no target for coping action (Stephens and Gwinner, 1998). Previous research has shown that consumer attributions about the failures that they experience influence their attitudes and behavioral intentions toward the firm (Bitner, 1990; Folkes, 1984; Folkes, Kolesky, and Graham, 1987). Attribution can be examined by three properties: (1) locus of causality - whether the service failure is due to the service provider (an external attribution) or due to the consumer (an internal attribution), (2) controllability - whether the consumer perceives that the service provider could have prevented the problem, or whether it was accidental, and (3) stability - the dissatisfied consumer's perception of whether the service failure is likely to happen again (Folkes, 1984; Weiner, 1985). Folkes (1984) examined relationships between attributional processes and consumer complaining reactions. Her findings suggest that consumers who make external attributions of blame are more likely to ask for a refund, an exchange, and/or an apology, while consumers who make internal attributions, are less likely to seek redress.

Coping potential

Consumers also evaluate their own coping potential, the extent to which they feel they can manage the demands of the service failure encounter and their perception of the availability and likely success of various coping alternatives (Stephens and Gwinner, 1998).

The availability of coping options is influenced by the extent of to which the service provider makes the complaint handling process available. Regarding the likelihood of success of coping alternatives, Singh (1990) measured expectancy-value that represents the consumer's probability assessment of obtaining a certain complaint response outcome.

While coping potential reflects consumers' assessment of how they can go about the service failure situation, two slightly different but related concepts are perceived responsiveness and service recovery expectations. Perceived responsiveness is the service provider's willingness to provide a remedy for the situation (Richins, 1987) and service recovery expectations refer to customers' predictions regarding the extent to which a firm will handle their complaint (Boulding, Karla, Staelin, and Zeithaml, 1993). In multiple service failure/recovery situations, the past service failure/recovery experience offers a cue for future recovery expectations (Maxham and Netemeyer, 2002). These two factors, perceived responsiveness and service recovery expectations, might jointly influence consumer' responses to the failure situation. For example, it is likely that employee responsiveness influences the perceived ability to voice dissatisfaction while service recovery expectations based on past experiences have an impact on the likelihood of success of a voice option.

We add one more component to coping potential – that is perceived effort. Consumers' perceived effort is often neglected in complaining behavior research. However, according to Voorhees et al.'s (2006) qualitative investigation of non complainers, the shortage of time and effort are the most common reason cited for not complaining. It is known that time constraints prompt individuals to limit the amount of effort they invest in a variety of problem-solving tasks (Garbarino and Edell, 1997). Owens and Hausknecht (1999) suggest that the level of difficulty associated with the complaint process will influence consumers' time and effort perceptions. A long and complicated complaining procedure will obviously make consumers feel that more time and effort is required. By simplifying the complaint process, customers are significantly more likely to return voice their dissatisfaction to the firm. Also, the decision of whether or not to complain about a dissatisfying product or service has been thought to be dependent on the expectation of effort required to lodge the complaint (Owens and Hausknecht, 1999). Similarly, Huppertz et al. (2003) suggest that anticipated effort mediates the relationship between complaining behavior and its antecedents such as product importance and attitude toward complaining. In addition, Richins (1983 a) suggested three alternative responses to dissatisfaction by the level of effort involved. "Doing nothing, for instance, requires no effort or resources, while making a complaint often involves a great deal of effort and inconvenience. Telling others about the dissatisfying experience requires low to intermediate level of effort expenditure (p.70)." In sum, prior literature suggests that effort should be considered as a significant and powerful predictor of the consumer's decision whether or not to lodge a complaint.

Another important aspect of the cognitive appraisal theory is the interplay between primary and secondary appraisals. For example, an event that might be first evaluated as harmful or threatening to well-being might not subsequently be perceived as stressful if an individual has the ability to successfully cope with the event (Stephens and Gwinner, 1998).

NEGATIVE EMOTIONS

Negative emotions are regarded as an outcome of stressful cognitive appraisals and researchers suggest that different people can have differential emotional reactions to the same event (Folkman and Lazarus, 1988; Bagozzi, Gopinath, and Nyer, 1999). It is the combination of a subjective appraisal of the situation and coping potential that determines the specific emotions to be evoked (Lazarus, 1991). Nyer (1997) has empirically demonstrated that positive and negative emotions mediate the link between some cognitive appraisal elements and word-of-mouth behaviors. While emotions have been shown to have significant influence on various consumer behaviors, cognitive appraisals linked to consumption emotions have not been fully explored (Ruth, Brunel, and Otness, 2002).

Emotions are often conceptualized as general valenced dimensions, such as positive and negative affect. Yet according to the specific emotions approach (Zeelenberg, van Dijk, and Manstead, 1998; Zeelenberg and Pieters, 2004; Laros and Steenkamp, 2005), it is not the mere valence of emotions that influences consumer responses, but different emotions are believed to lead to varying behavioral responses. This argument is consistent with research in psychology showing that specific emotions can have a differential impact on people's evaluations (DeSteno, Petty, Rucker, Wegener, and Braverman, 2004) and behavioral consequences (Frijda and Zeelenberg, 2001; Frijda, Kuipers, and ter Shure, 1989; Shaver, Schwartz, Donald, and O'Connor, 1987). For example, anger and sadness might result in different types of responses although they both are negative emotions (DeSteno, Petty, Wegener, and Rucker, 2000). Specifically, sadness tends to result in withdrawal while anger typically energizes people to act (Shaver, Schwartz, Donald, and O'Connor, 1987). In addition, recent studies demonstrate that specific negative emotions have a direct impact on behavior, over and above dissatisfaction (Laros and Steenkamp, 2005; Pieters and Zeelenberg, 2005). Service encounters, especially failed ones, often result in specific negative emotions and these discrete emotions partly determine subsequent behaviors (Zeelenberg and Pieters, 2004).

Several taxonomies have been proposed to classify the variety of subjective feelings into a small set of fundamental or primary affects such as Izard's (1977) 'Differential Emotions Scale (DES)' and Roseman's (1991;1996) 'Appraisal Theory of Emotions (ATE)'. Since these emotion taxonomies are developed by psychology researchers, some of their emotions are not applicable in the consumer consumption context.

In order to overcome this limitation, Richins (1997) developed Consumption Emotion set (CES). Richins's CES covers most emotional reactions one encounters in typical consumption situations, and it has been applied by other research (Ruth, Brunel and Otness, 2002). Table 1 provides comparisons of negative emotion taxonomies from Izard (1977), Roseman et al (1996) and Richins (1997).

Table 1. A comparison of negative emotion taxonomies

DES (Izard, 1977)	ATE (Rosman et al.,1996)	CES (Richins, 1997)
Anger	Anger	Anger
Contempt	Contempt	
Disgust	Disgust/ Frustration	
	Dislike	
		Discontent
Sadness	Sadness/ Distress	Sadness
Fear	Fear	Fear
		Worry
Shame	Shame	Shame
Guilt	Guilt	
	Regret	

COPING STRATEGIES

Lazarus and Folkman (1984) defined coping as "constantly changing cognitive and behavioral efforts to manage specific external and/or internal demands that are appraised as taxing or exceeding the resources of the person" (p. 141). They believe that people either engage in 1) problem-focused coping when they feel they have personal control over the outcome or recurrence of the problem in the future, or 2) emotion-focused coping when they feel they have little control. Because different negative emotions involve distinct appraisals of the events that led to them (Lazarus, 1999), they are likely to be associated with different ways of coping with the situation. Yet even in psychology, there is little systematic research on the linkage between specific emotions and particular coping strategies.

Recently, Yi and Baumgartner (2004) examined the relations between four negative emotions (anger, disappointment, regret, and worry) and coping strategies in a consumer context. Their findings suggest that distinct strategies are employed by consumers to cope with different emotions, however, the relations between specific coping methods and complaint responses were not examined. Although the links between coping methods and complaint responses have not been investigated, we expect that problem-focused strategies are associated with public responses (e.g. voice, third-party) while emotion-focused strategies are linked to private responses (e.g. exit, WOM) or no action response.

LINK BETWEEN SPECIFIC EMOTIONS AND COMPLAINING BEHAVIORS

In a cognitive-emotive process model (Stephens and Gwinner, 1998), the authors posit that attributing responsibility for what is happening to someone else (external attribution) produces feelings of anger, disgust, or contempt, whereas blaming oneself or the situation (internal attribution) generates emotions of shame and guilt. Also, believing that an event cannot be helped and that blame for it is situational (situational attribution) leads to the emotions of sadness or fear (Stephens and Gwinner, 1998).

Relying on the specific-emotion approach and attribution theory, we include the following three negative emotions in our model: anger resulting from controllable causes attributes to others, disappointment resulting from uncontrollable attributed the situation, and regret from self-blame. In psychology, anger, sadness, guilt, and anxiety are considered as distinct negative emotions (Lazarus, 1990) and prior research in consumer behavior suggests that these surface as anger, disappointment, regret, and worry in the consumer context (Yi and Baumgartner, 2004). Thus, four negative emotions from different attribution cause are chosen for our model and some of previous findings are discussed as following.

Anger occurs when another person is blamed for the problem (Lazarus, 1999; Smith, 1991; Smith and Ellsworth, 1985). Yi and Baumgartner (2004) found that consumers cope with anger by aggressive efforts (e.g. confrontive coping). Bougie, Pieters and Zeelenberg (2003) also suggest that angry customers behave aggressively and complain about the problem.

Disappointment is felt when an outcome is worse than expected and it is typically associated with blaming others or circumstances (Zeelenberg and Pieters, 2004). Zeelenberg et al. (1998) found that disappointment was associated with feelings of powerlessness and a tendency to get away from the situation. Yi and Baumgartner (2004) state that consumers cope with disappointment by mentally escaping the situation (e.g. mental disengagement) and by giving up the pursuit of a goal that cannot be attained (e.g. behavioral disengagement).

Regret occurs when a foregone alternative turns out to be (or is imagined to be) a better choice than the selected alternative (Zeelenberg et al., 2000). Regret usually involves self-blame and an acknowledgement that one has made a mistake (Zeelenberg et al., 1998). Yi and Baumgartner (2004) found that consumers cope with regret by accepting the responsibility (e.g. acceptance). Bearing responsibility for the mistake also encourages consumers to see something positive in what has happened (e.g. positive reinterpretation).

Worry is related to prospects of undesirable events and uncertainty about what to do (Yi and Baumgartner, 2004). For example, consumers may feel worried when a flight is delayed and might become a cancellation yet they don't know what do about the situation. Yi and Baumgartner's (2004) findings suggest that worry led to diverse assortments of coping strategies. When the threat is relatively tangible and consumers want to adopt a more proactive stance toward the problem, they may engage in planful problem solving and seeking social support. While the perceived threat is relatively intangible and one's option for coping are not clear, consumers may try to adapt to the situation and manage the emotion, using self-control and mental disengagement.

PERSONAL FACTORS

As shown in the model, personal factors are characteristics possessed by individuals that influence the manner in which they conduct cognitive appraisal of service failure situations. From previous studies, several personal factors are identified. Socio-Demographics have been examined and consumers with higher levels of education and more disposable income have been found to be more likely than others to voice complaints (Warland, Hermann, and Willits, 1975). Prior experience of complaining refers to the extent (frequent/infrequent) of past complaining experiences and it is found to influence voice and third-party actions (Singh and Wilkes, 1996). Marketplace experience refers to participation or experience as buyers of goods and services (Huppertz, Mower and Associate, 2003). Similarly, Singh and Wilkes suggest that a consumer who feels relatively alienated from the marketplace is less likely to voice his or her complaint but is more likely to engage in private responses. Attitude toward complaining refers to an individuals' predisposition toward complaining to sellers (Richins, 1983 b, 1987; Bearden and Mason 1984). This personal tendency partially explains why some people are assertive and will seek redress whenever they are dissatisfied with a product, while others are reluctant to seek redress even when highly dissatisfied (Blodgett et al., 1993).

MARKET FACTORS

Market factors may also influence consumer complaining behaviors but only a few studies have investigated market factors or industry characteristics in CCB research. For example, Singh (1990) examined complaining behaviors in three different service categories based on the degree of loose monopolies. In this paper, we propose two factors that are most likely to be relevant in CCB research.

Switching convenience refers to the degree of difficulty in changing to another company in case of dissatisfaction. When consumers have numerous choices and switching is relatively easy, voicing complaints is harder than simply switching brands, stores, or service providers (Fornell and Didow, 1980; Keaveney, 1995). By contrast, when alternatives are limited, dissatisfaction does not usually prompt switching (Andreasen, 1985). The second is typicality of the failure that is described as the customers' belief that specific failures are a common occurrence within a particular industry (Hess et al., 2003). Cadotte, Woodruff, and Jenkins (1987) showed that typicality matters because normative expectations based on a representative group of similar brands affect customer satisfaction with the focal brand. Thus, the typicality or atypicality of a failure may mitigate or enhance the detrimental effects of a failure.

SUMMARY AND CONCLUSIONS

In summary, during the service failure, consumers have an immediate affective response labeled as initial dissatisfaction with service failure. Then customers make an evaluation known as a cognitive appraisal process to assess the significance of the dissatisfaction for the consumer's well-being (primary appraisal) and the availability and likely success of various coping options (secondary appraisal) that might be used to manage the dissatisfying consumption experience. This cognitive appraisal process involves factors such as importance of the event, problem seriousness, attribution, and coping potential. The cognitive appraisal outcomes, in turn, elicit emotive reactions (e.g. anger, disappointment, regret, and worry) that, in conjunction with cognitive appraisal, influence the consumer's complaining behaviors.

Our framework offers a starting point for broadening our thinking on consumers' complaining processes. Specifically, our model incorporates non-behavioral responses (no-action), immediate affective responses (initial dissatisfaction), and additional components of coping (e.g., perceived effort). There is a dire need for a focused effort to develop conceptually sound models that can guide consumer complaining behavior research on these important topics. We hope that this chapter serves as an impetus for such an effort.

REFERENCES

Andreasen, A. L. (1985). Consumer Responses to Dissatisfaction in Loose Monopolies. *Journal of Consumer Research*, 12 (2), 135-141.

Bagozzi, R. P., Gopinath, M., and Nyer P.U. (1999). The Role of Emotions in Marketing. *Journal of the Academy of Marketing Science*, 27 (2), 184-206.

Bearden, W. O., and Mason, J. B. (1984). An Investigation of Influences on Consumer Complaint Reports, *Advances in Consumer Research*, 11, 490-495.

Bennett, R., Hartel, C., McColl-Kennedy, J. R., and James C. E. (2003). *Emotions and complaining behavior following a service failure*, in Academy of Management Best Paper Proceedings: Democracy in a Knowledge Economy, eds D.H. Nagao, Academy of Management, New York, USA. (http://www.aomonline.org/)

Bitner, M. J. (1990). Evaluating Service Encounters: The Effects of Physical Surroundings and Employee Responses. *Journal of Marketing*, 54 (April), 69-82.

Blodgett, J. G., and Anderson, Ronald D. (2000). A Bayesian Network Model of the Consumer Complaint Process. *Journal of Service Research*, 2 (4), 321-329.

Blodgett, J. G., and Granbois, D. H. (1992). Toward an Integrated Conceptual Model of Consumer Complaining Behavior. *Journal of Consumer Satisfaction, Dissatisfaction and Complaining Behavior*, 5, 93-103.

Blodgett, G., Granbois, D. H., and Walters, R.G. (1993). The Effects of Perceived Justice on Complainants' Negative Word-of-Mouth Behavior and Repatronage Intentions. *Journal of Retailing*, 69 (Winter), 399-428.

Boote, J. (1998). Towards a Comprehensive Taxonomy and Model of Consumer Complaining Behavior. *Journal of Consumer Satisfaction, Dissatisfaction and Complaining Behavior*, 11, 140-151.

Bougie, R., Pieters, R., and Zeelenberg, M. (2003). Angry Customers Don't Come Back, They Get Back: The Experience and Behavioral Implications of Anger and Dissatisfaction in Services. *Journal of the Academy of Marketing Science*, 31 (4), 377-393.

Boulding, W., Karla, A., Staelin, R., and Zeithaml, V. (1993). A Dynamic Process Model of Service Quality: From Expectations to Behavioral Intentions. *Journal of Marketing Research*, 30 (February), 7-27.

Cadotte, E. R., Woodruff, R. B., and Jenkins, R. L. (1987). Expectations and Norms in Models of Customer Satisfaction. *Journal of Marketing Research*, 24 (August), 305-314.

Chebat, J.C., Davidow, M., and Codjovi, I. (2005). Silent Voices-Why Some Dissatisfied Consumers Fail to Complain. *Journal of Service Research*, 7 (4), 328-342.

Day, R. L. and Landon, E. L. (1977). *Toward a Theory of Consumer Complaining Behavior*, In Consumer and Industrial Buying Behavior. Eds. Arch G.. Woodside, Jadish N. Sheth, and Peter D. Bennet. New York, USA: North Holland, 425-437.

DeSteno, D., Petty, R. E., Wegener, D. T., and Rucker, D. D. (2000). Beyond Valence in the Perception of Likelihood: The Role of Emotion Specificity. *Journal of Personality and Social Psychology.* 78, 397-416.

Folkes, V. S. (1984). Consumer Reactions to Product Failure: An Attributional Approach. *Journal of Consumer Research*, 10, 398-409.

Folkes, V. S., Koletsky, S., and Graham, J. L. (1987). A Field Study of Causal Inferences and Consumer Reaction: The View from the Airport. *Journal of Consumer Research*, 13 (4), 534-539.

Folkman, S., and Lazarus, R. S. (1988). *Manual for Ways of Coping Questionnaire.* Palo Alto, CA, USA: Consulting Psychologists Press.

Fornell, C., and Wernerfelt, B. (1987). Defensive Marketing Strategy by Customer Complaint Management: A Theoretical Analysis. *Journal of Marketing Research*, 24 (November), 337-346.

Fornell, C., and Didow, N. M. (1980). Economic Constraints on Consumer Complaining Behavior. *Advances in Consumer Research*, 7, 318-323.

Fornell, C., and Westbrook, R. A. (1979). An Exploratory Study of Assertiveness, Aggressiveness, and Consumer Complaining Behavior. *Advances in Consumer Research*, 6, 105-110.

Frijda, N.. H., Kuipers, P., and ter Shure, E. (1989). Relations Among Emotion, Appraisal and Emotional Action Readiness. *Journal of Personality and Social Psychology*, 57 (2), 212-228.

Frijda, N. H., and Zeelenberg, M. (2001). *Appraisal: What is the Dependent?.* In Scherer, K. R., Schorr, A., and Johnstone, T. (Ed.). *Appraisal Processes in Emotion Theory, Methods, Research.* New York, USA, Oxford University Press, 141-155.

Garbarino, E., and Edell, J. (1997). Cognitive Effort, Affect, and Choice. *Journal of Consumer Research*, 24 (September), 147-158.

Hess, R. L., Ganesan, S., and Klein, N. M., (2003). Service Failure and Recovery: The Impact of Relationship Factors on Customer Satisfaction. *Journal of the Academy of Marketing Science*, 31 (2), 127-145.

Hirschman, A. O. (1970). *Exit, Voice and Loyalty: Responses to Decline in Firms, Organizations and States.* Cambridge, MA, USA: Harvard University Press.

Hoffman, K. D., and Bateson, J. E. G. (1997). *Essentials of Service Marketing.* Fort Worth, TX, USA: Dryden.

Huppertz, J., Mower, E., and Associates. (2003). An Effort Model of First-Stage Complaining Behavior. *Journal of Consumer Satisfaction, Dissatisfaction and Complaining Behavior*, 16, 132-144.

Izard, C. E. (1977). *Human Emotions.* New York, USA: Plenum.

Laros, F. J. M., and Steenkemp, J. E. M. (2005). Emotions in Consumer Behavior: A Hierarchical Approach. Journal of Business Research, 58 (10), 1437-1445.

Lazarus, R. S. (1991). Cognition and Motivations in Emotion. *American Psychologist*, 46, 352-267.

Lazarus, R. S., and Folkman, S. (1984). *Stress, appraisal, and coping.* New York, USA: Springer.

Lazarus, R. S. (1999). *Stress and Emotion: A new synthesis.* New York, USA: Springer.

Liljander, V., and Strandvik, T. (1997). Emotions in Service Satisfaction. *International Journal of Service Industry*, 8 (2), 148-161.

Maxham III, J. G., and Netemeyer, R. G. (2002). A Longitudinal Study of Complaining Customers' Evaluations of Multiple Service Failures and Recovery Efforts. *Journal of Marketing,* 66 (4), 57-71.

Menon, K., and Dubé, L. (2004). Service Provider Responses to Anxious and Angry Customers: Different Challenges, Different Payoffs. *Journal of Retailing,* 80 (3), 229-237.

Nyer, P. (1997). A Study of the Relationships between Cognitive Appraisals and Consumption Emotions. *Journal of the Academy of Marketing Science,* 15 (4), 296-304.

Oliver, R. L. (1980). A Cognitive Model of the Antecedents and Consequences of Satisfaction Decisions. *Journal of Marketing Research,* 16 (June), 39-54.

Oliver, R. L. (1997). *Satisfaction: A Behavioral Perspective on the Consumer.* New York, USA: McGraw Hill.

Owens, D.L., and Hausknecht, D. R. (1999). The Effect of Simplifying the Complaint Process: A Field Experiment with the Better Business Bureau. *Journal of Consumer Satisfaction, Dissatisfaction, and Complaining Behavior,* 12, 35-43.

Phillips, D. M., and Baumgartner, H. (2002). The Role of Consumption Emotions in the Satisfaction Response. *Journal of Consumer Psychology,* 12 (3), 243-252.

Price, L. L., Arnould, E. J., and Tierney, P. (1995). Going to Extremes: Managing Service Encounters and Assessing Provider Performance. *Journal of Marketing,* 59 (2): 83-97.

Richins, M. L. (1983 a). Negative Word-of-Mouth by Dissatisfied Consumers: A Pilot Study. *Journal of Marketing,* 47, 68-78.

Richins, M. L. (1983 b). An Analysis of Consumer Interaction Styles in the Marketplace. *Journal of Consumer Research,* 10 (1): 73-83.

Richins, M. L. (1987). A Multivariate Analysis of Responses to Dissatisfaction. *Journal of the Academy of Marketing Science,* 15 (3), 24-31.

Richins, M. L. (1997). Measuring Emotions in the Consumption Experience. *Journal of Consumer Research,* 24 (2), 127-146.

Roseman, I. J. (1991). *Appraisal Determinants of Discrete Emotions, Cognition and Emotion.* 5, 161-200.

Roseman, I. J., Antoniou, A. A., and Jose, P. E. (1996). *Appraisal Determinants of Emotions: Constructing a More Accurate and Comprehensive Theory, Cognition and Emotion,* 10 (3), 241-277.

Rust, R. T., Zahorik, A. J., and Kenningham, T. L. (1996). *Service Marketing.* New York, USA: HarperCollins.

Ruth, J. A., Brunel, F. F., and Otnes, C. C. (2002). Linking Thoughts to Feelings: Investigating Cognitive Appraisals and Consumption Emotions in a Mixed-Emotions Context. *Journal of Academy of Marketing Science,* 30 (1), 44-58.

Singh, J. (1988). Consumer Complaint Intentions and Behavior: Definitional and Taxonomical Issues. *Journal of Marketing,* 52 (1): 93-107

Singh, J., and Wilkes, R. (1996). When Consumers Complain: A Path Analysis of the Key Antecedents of Consumer Complaint Response estimates. *Journal of the Academy of Marketing science,* 24 (4), 350-365.

Sirgy, Joseph (1984). A Social Cognition Model of Consumer Satisfaction/Dissatisfaction. *Psychology and Marketing,* 1 (2), 27-45.

Smith, C. A. (1991). *The Self, Appraisal, and Coping*. In C.R. Snyder and D. R. Forsyth (Eds.). Handbook of Social and Clinical Psychology: The Health Perspective (116-137). New York, USA: Wiley.

Smith, C. A., and Ellsworth, P.C. (1985). Patterns of Cognitive Appraisal in Emotion. *Journal of Personality and Social Psychology*, 48, 813-838.

Spreng, R. A., and Olshavsky, R. W. (1993). A Desires Congruency Model of Consumer Satisfaction. *Journal of the Academy of Marketing Science*, 21 (Summer), 169-177.

Spreng, R. A., Mackenzie, S. B., and Olshavsky, R. W. (1996). A Reexamination of the Determinants of Consumer Satisfaction. *Journal of Marketing*, 60 (3),15-32.

Stephens, N., and Gwinner, K. (1998). Why Don't Some People Complain? A Cognitive-Emotive Process Model of Consumer Complaint Behavior. *Journal of the Academy of Marketing Science*, 26 (3), 172-189.

Voorhees, C. M., Brady, M. K., and Horowitz, D. M. (2006). A Voice from the Silent Masses: An Exploratory and Comparative Analysis of Noncomplainers. *Journal of the Academy of Marketing Science*, 34 (4), 514-527.

Warland, R. H., Herrmann, R. O. and Willits, J. (1975). Dissatisfied Consumers: Who gets Upsets and Who Takes Action. *The Journal of Consumer Affairs*, 9 (2), 148-164.

Weiss, H. M., and Cropanzano, R. (1996). *Affective Events Theory: A Theoretical Discussion of The Structure, Causes and Consequences of Affective Experiences at Work, Research in Organizational Behavior*. 18, 1-74.

Weiner, B. (1985). An Attributional Theory of Achievement Motivation and Emotion. *Psychological Review*, 92 (October), 548-573.

Westbrook, R. T., and Reilly, M. (1983). *Value-Percept Disparity: An Alternative to the Disconfirmation of Expectations Theory of Consumer Satisfaction*. Advances in Consumer Research, 10. Eds. Richard Bagozzi and Alice M. Tybout. Ann Arbor, MI, USA: Association for Consumer Research, 256-261.

Westbrook, R. T., and Oliver, R. L. (1991). The Dimensionality of Consumption Emotion Pattern and Consumer Satisfaction. *Journal of Consumer Research*, 18 (1), 84-91.

Wirtz, J., and Mattila, A. S. (2001). Exploring the role of alternative performance measures and needs-congruency in the consumer satisfaction process. *Journal of Consumer Psychology*, 11 (3), 181-192.

Yi, S., and Baumgartner, H. (2004). Coping with Negative Emotions in Purchase-Related Situations. *Journal of Consumer Psychology*, 14 (3), 303-317.

Zeelenberg, M., van Dijk, W. W., and Manstead, A. S. R. (1998). Reconsidering the Relation Between Regret and Responsibility. *Organization Behavior and Human Decision Process*, 74 (3), 254-272.

Zeelenberg, M., van Dijk, W. W., Manstead, A. S. R., and Van der Plight, J. (2000). On Bad Decisions and Disconfirmed Expectancies: The Psychology of Regret and Disappointment. *Cognition and Emotion*, 14, 521-541.

Zeelenberg, M., and Pieters, R. (2004). Beyond Valence in Customer Satisfaction: A Review and New Findings on Behavioral Responses to Regret and Disappointment in Failed Services. *Journal of Business Research*, 57, 445-455.

In: Tourist Satisfaction and Complaining Behavior
Editor: Atila Yüksel

ISBN 978-1-60456-002-2
© 2008 Nova Science Publishers, Inc.

Chapter 14

CUSTOMER RECOVERY JUDGMENTS: EFFECTS OF VERBAL AND NON-VERBAL RESPONSES

Atila Yüksel and Serhat Cengiz
Adnan Menderes University, Turkey

INTRODUCTION

The concepts of consumer dissatisfaction (CD) and consumer complaining behavior (CCB) continue to receive growing attention from researchers and practitioners (Yuksel, Hancer and Kilinc, 2006). Considering that most dissatisfied customers never bother to complain, customers seeking redress for their complaints provide destinations/companies with opportunities to improve their management and marketing programs so as to enhance customer satisfaction and profitability (Huang, Huang and Wu, 1996). Ineffective handling of customer's complaint was reported to increase frustration and dissatisfaction, reinforce negative consumer reactions and harm a marketer's reputation (Hart, James and Earl, 1990; Hoffman and Chung, 1999; Mattila, 2001). In other words, failure to promptly handle consumers' complaints provokes consumers' unfavorable behaviors (e.g., negative word-of-mouth or exit intentions) and this can have catastrophic effects on an organization's business.

Previous studies have identified different causes and consequences of service failures (Boshoff and Staude, 2003; Jonhston and Fern, 1999). These studies note that the majority of responses to customer complaints are far from restoring customer satisfaction (Boshoff and Leong, 1998; Hart et al., 1990). Bitner, Booms and Tetrault's (1990) study indicates that the greater part of dissatisfying service encounters is the result of frontline employees' inability to respond to service failure situations. Customers often switch to an alternative service provider, not because of core service failures, but because of the unacceptable response of employees to customer attempts to redress failure (Keaveney, 1995, p. 77). This can be attributed to existence or absence of many factors (see Yuksel et al., 2006 for a review of these issues). Broadly speaking, in any service recovery encounter there are at least three elements: i) environmental elements (physical setting), ii) technical elements (essential performance skills), and iii) personal presentation (verbal behavior and nonverbal behavior

(Sommers, Greeno and Boag, 1988). Since the provision of a service recovery requires interaction, the various forms of verbal and nonverbal communication rest at the heart of service delivery and evaluation processes (Hashimoto and Borders, 2005; Sommers et al., 1988). "Non-verbal communication takes place every time one person interacts with another, it may be intentional or unintentional and is part of the rapid stream of communication that passes between two interacting individuals" (Gabbott and Hogg, 2000, p. 385). The nonverbal components are reported to be at least as important as the verbal components of interpersonal communication in shaping the outcome of employee-customer interactions (Barnum and Wolniansky, 1989; Burgoon et al., 1990, cf. Sundaram and Webster, 2000). According to Mehrabian, nearly half of the variations in response to interpersonal communication can be attributed to nonverbal factors (Mehrabian, 1981, Barnum and Wolniansky, 1989, cf. Sundaram and Webster, 2000; Sommers et al., 1988). Furthermore, studies show that verbal interactions need the support of non-verbal communications (Sommers et al., 1988).

In a service recovery situation, nonverbal communication may determine how the service recovery strategy, conducted by the employee, is perceived by the customer. Customers' responses to service delivery, perceived service quality or satisfaction, could be dependent largely on their interpretation of various non-verbal signals during the encounter and their decoding of the meaning associated with them (Enz, 2002). Previous studies revealed unpleasant or displeasing nonverbal behavior as one of the major reasons for customer dissatisfaction (Bitner et al., 1990; Miller, 1992; Morris, 1983). Nonverbal aspects of employee-customer interactions in the context of service failures have however remained almost unexplored in the hospitality and tourism literature (Sommers et al., 1988; Sundaram and Webster, 2000). Interpersonal encounter holds significance in customers' evaluations of service quality. It is thus crucial for service managers and researchers to take a closer look at the service encounter to analyze better how each element of employee nonverbal behavior is likely to influence customers' perceptions (Sundaram and Webster, 2000). Departing from inadequate research on this subject, this Chapter explores whether nonverbal communication in the form of body posture and eye contact would affect customers' perceptions of service personnel's affective qualities, customer emotions and their behavioral intentions in a service recovery situation. It further sets out to explore whether ratings differ as a result of the questioning style (i.e., whether scores would differ when the effect of the same recovery response questioned in nonverbal or verbal format). The following is divided into three sections. The first section undertakes a review on customer complaint behavior and nonverbal communication. The second section presents details of the methodology followed in the study. The final section discusses research findings in the light of previous results.

NONVERBAL RESPONSES AND SERVICE RECOVERY

Previous research suggests that customers evaluate service encounters on three dimensions: outcome, the benefits customers receive as a result of the encounter; procedure, the organization's policies and methods that guide the encounter, and interaction, the quality of the interpersonal treatment and communication during the encounter (Mattila, 2001). Similarly, social exchange theory assumes that people will have expectations with regard to outcome, procedure and interpersonal treatment in a complaint situation and that perceived justice on these dimensions will influence how people evaluate exchanges (McCollough, 2000). More specifically, distributive justice, which involves resource allocation and perceived outcome of an exchange; procedural justice, which involves by means by which decisions are made and conflicts are resolved, and interactional justice which involves the manner information is exchanged and the outcome is communicated will impact on the quality of exchange relationships (Smith, Bolton and Wagner, 1999).

Sundaram and Webster rightly argue that following a service failure, customers would be desirous of getting their problems or elements of their dissatisfaction resolved as quickly as possible. Service failures would evoke anxiety in customers and thus they would be particularly vigilant to notice nonverbal cues in an attempt to discern the service provider's intentions and attitudes regarding helping them (Sundaram and Webster, 2000). "In such situations, the display of inappropriate nonverbal cues (e.g. frowning, lack of eye contact, closed body posture, etc.) is likely to create even more negative feelings on the part of the customer, probably resulting in negative word-of-mouth communication and intentions to discontinue their patronage with that particular service provider" (Sundaram and Webster, 2000, p. 378). Affective characteristics of service personnel, such as their friendliness, responsiveness, and enthusiasm, have been argued to positively influence customers' overall evaluation of service consumption experiences and perceptions of service quality (Sundaram and Webster, 2000; Elizur, 1987). Empirical evidence suggest that nonverbal cues play a significant role in shaping receivers' perceptions of communicators' credibility (Burgoon et al., 1990), persuasive power (Mehrabian and Williams, 1969), courtesy (Ford, 1995), and interpersonal warmth (Bayes, 1972 cf. Sundaram and Webster, 2000). How service personnel dress, their body language, vocal characteristics when speaking to a customer determines whether they and their organization are perceived credible (Chaney and Green, 2006). Conditioned by the culture, people are likely to expect certain nonverbal signals (e.g. smiles and head nods) as indications of approval or attention during conversations (Sundaram and Webster, 2000). Failure on the part of service personnel to provide such signals is likely to affect the customer in a negative manner. Thus, in service encounters it becomes particularly important for service employees to understand and implement the nonverbal signals that will assure the customers that they are receiving complete attention and concern (Sundaram and Webster, 2000).

Sundaram and Webster have developed a conceptual model with an attempt to highlight the role of nonverbal communication in service interactions (Figure 1). The model suggests that both verbal and nonverbal elements of communication between the service provider and the customer influence customers' affect or subjective feelings, which in turn influence their evaluation of the service encounter. Sundaram and Webster's model groups multitude of nonverbal communication cues into four major categories: paralanguage, kinesics, proxemics, and physical appearance. Bodily appearance is the first noticeable nonverbal communication behavior and conveys specific information about a person's character and social behavior (Breytenbach, 2001). Kinesics entail all facial expressions, movements and eye contact and can be defined as the study of body movements (Breytenbach, 2001). Paralanguage entails all forms of verbal communication, which are produced by the voice. Proxemics refers to spatial relations of individuals (closeness/distance). Of particular interest here are the two non-verbal communication variables of eye contact and body posture[1]. Eye contact and body posture have been studied in numerous laboratory and natural settings but very few empirical studies were conducted in a service recovery context. Studies on these kinesics variables show that taken in combination, "high" levels lead to both greater liking of the sender of the message and greater agreement with the message itself (Mehrabian, 1972, cf. Sommers et al. 1988). Eye contact with the individual in a service recovery context can be claimed as perhaps the most important characteristic a frontline staff should have. Experts advise connecting with individuals rather than letting the eyes sweep over the place without making an eye contact with the individual (Chaney and Green, 2006). Eye contact, accompanied by a smile gives the impression that the staff is happy to be there. Posture is another important aspect of nonverbal communication projecting a positive image when listening to/talking with a customer. It is suggested that the extremes of being too stiff, which is perceived as being uptight, or too loose, which comes across as sloppy or careless, should be avoided.

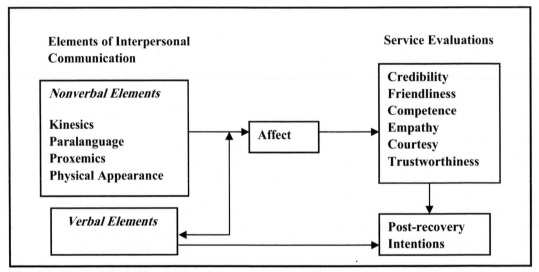

Figure 1. Conceptual Model
Source: Sundaram and Webster (2000)

The model postulates that NVB influences customer emotions, which in turn influence their evaluations. Emotions evoked due to service failure and subsequent recovery attempts are likely to be decisive in customers' evaluations (Yuksel, 2006). Chebat and Sluarsczyk (2003) identified a strong relationship between negative/positive emotions and customers' exit and loyalty behaviours. They suggest that contact employees should be aware of the emotional climate of customer's complaints and should be trained to monitor it. They state that even if the problem, which triggered the complaint can be fixed, the customers do not necessarily remain loyal if the emotions are not properly attended to. Most service failure/complaint handling studies however have not taken into account that failures and

---

[1] Due to space limitation this article only tests effects of kinetics on service recovery evaluations. It is important to note that nonverbal responses of staff may be shaped by customers' verbal and/or nonverbal communication (Sundaram and Webster, 2000).

subsequent recovery attempts, through perceived nonverbal cues, could trigger emotional responses in addition to cognitive appraisal (Dolen et al., 2001; Yu and Dean, 2001).

Proposition 1.Positive nonverbal response would induce favorable customer emotions, perceptions about staff and behavioral intent toward the hotel.

Proposition2 Negative nonverbal response would induce unfavorable customer emotions, perceptions about staff and behavioral intent toward the hotel.

Proposition 3.Verbal response only would produce different evaluation scores than non-verbal response would.

THE STUDY

A quasi experiment was conducted to examine effects of nonverbal behavior, in this case eye contact and open/closed body posture on customers' evaluation of service personnel's affective qualities in a service recovery situation, and on customers' recovery emotions and their behavioral intentions. A questionnaire, based on a scenario, was developed for this purpose. Respondents were instructed to put themselves in the presented situation and asses how they would feel and act. More specifically, the scenario presents a situation in which the customer checks-in a hotel room where the shower malfunctions. Instead of phoning the reception, the customer decides to talk with the receptionist and describes what is wrong. Two pictures (Figure 2), displaying staff-customer interaction, have been used. We have manipulated staff' body posture and eye contact in the experiment. In the first picture, the receptionist displays an open body posture with an appropriate eye contact. In the second picture, the receptionist displays a closed body posture with no eye contact. In each case the receptionist "apologizes and tells the customer she would be taking care of the problem immediately".

After reading the scenario and seen the picture of the receptionist, the respondent is required to indicate what emotions they would feel most, how s/he thinks that the receptionist behaves, and how they would react to the recovery offered. A similar set of questions, excluding interaction pictures, has been used to see whether nonverbal communication has lesser/higher influence on customers' evaluation of staff and service recovery effort than verbal communication does. The scale offered by Sundaram and Webster was used to measure staff affective qualities. This scale consisted of six items (e.g., credible, friendly, competent, emphatic, courteous, and trustworthy). The items were followed by a seven point strongly agree-strongly disagree Likert type scale. An 11 item emotion scale, developed from a review of literature, was used (Yuksel, 2006). Four items were borrowed from Zeithalm et al.'s (1996) study to measure respondents' behavioral intentions. An additional question was asked the probability of getting in touch with the same staff in case of other problems experienced during stay. Seven point very likely/very unlikely scale accompanied these items. Demographic details, such as nationality, gender, age, education and marital status were also collected. The survey was administered to conveniently sampled 200 foreign tourists staying in the selected hotels of Didim, Aydin province in Turkey in the summer months of 2006.

Positive NVB   **Negative NVB**

Figure 2. Positive and Negative NVB

DATA ANALYSIS

Reliability checks of the scales were conducted. A series of pairwise t-tests were run to understand whether two different style of kinesics (positive and negative NVB) have any different effect on respondents' evaluations of affective qualities, emotions and behavioral intentions. A MANOVA test was then utilized to explore differences among the ratings to the set of questions assessing customer reactions to verbal and nonverbal responses.

RESULTS

Eighty-six percent of the respondents were from the UK, followed by tourists from Ireland, Holland, Germany, Poland and others. Fifty four percent of the sample were male. The majority of respondents were in the over 40 age-band (44%). These figures conform to general tourist profile that the Didim region attracts. Reliability tests show that each of the three scales used in the research has acceptable coefficients (0.98 for staff affective qualities, 0.99 for emotion scale, and 0.97 for behavioral intentions). The results of the t-test indicate a significant difference between respondents' assessment of the affective qualities of the service personnel in cases of negative and positive NVB. Table 1 shows that an open body posture, accompanied with an appropriate eye contact would lead to favorable perceptions of the service personnel. The findings clearly indicate that staff displaying such a positive NVB is likely to be seen more credible, competent, courteous and trustworthy by the customer. In contrast, a negative NVB would result in negative perceptions of staff affective qualities. This is important for proper management of service recovery encounters, as the outcome in such situations relies heavily on the development of positive perceptions of service providers. That is, appropriate NVB would imply the competency in providing services, which would influence likelihood of positive perception of a recovery effort (Reisinger and Warzyak 1996). Our findings provide support for the contention that non-verbal response of the employees will have a great impact on the success of a service recovery encounter (George and Tan, 1993). How staff is perceived during the recovery encounters will largely determine how customers would perceive the quality level of the transaction. Thus, the quality of service recovery rendered cannot be separated from the favorability of the NVB displayed by the service provider (George and Berry, 1981). The service provider's nonverbal behavior and verbal skills may lead to more satisfaction than the pure mechanistic system of delivery to a customer. In some cases, the right NVB would be capable of redeeming the poor recovery strategy. Conviviality conveyed in the form of open body posture of service personnel during a recovery encounter may compensate for the low quality procedural or distributional (i.e., outcome) dimension of a service recovery.

Table 1. Perceptions about Staff's Affective Qualities

	NVB (+)	NVB (-)	t	Sig
Credible	6.1087	1.8641	51.199	.000
Friendly	6..1902	1.9239	48.807	.000
Competent	6.1141	1.9239	45.187	.000
Empathic	6.1304	1.9293	46.833	.000
Courteous	6.0707	1.9620	44.674	.000
Trustworthy	6.1902	1.8207	48.314	.000

The findings of the study indicated that staff' display of NVB could influence customers' positive or negative emotions in a recovery situation (Table 2). Respondents in this study reported that they would feel unwelcome when the staff body posture was closed and there was no eye contact.

Table 2. Ratings on emotions by NVB

Emotions measured	NVB (+)	NVB (-)	t	Sig
Comfortable	6.0815	1.9076	47.572	.000
Relaxed	6.0815	2.0054	43.863	.000
Happy	6.0543	1.9022	45.558	.000
Satisfied	6.0598	1.8152	47.221	.000
Important	5.9457	1.9239	44.552	.000
Privileged	5.8913	1.7989	48.135	.000
Contended	6.1087	1.9565	45.094	.000
Glad	6.1576	1.8859	46.429	.000
Cheerful	6.0761	1.8913	48.884	.000
Calm	6.1196	1.8152	49.846	.000
Welcome	6.2772	1.6467	55.204	.000

However, when the body posture is open and there is an appropriate eye-contact, the respondents appear to feel welcome in otherwise a very anxious situation. Management of customer emotions during a complaint handling is ultimately important. Customers will be more emotionally involved in and observant of recovery than in routine or first-time services (Bitner et al., 1990). This implies that customers' behaviors during/after a complaint-handling situation may be emotionally driven (Smith and Bolton, 2002). Experience of distinct emotions may influence their expectations for and perceptions of the recovery performance, and/or their expressions and behaviors (Dube and Menon, 2000). Although affective reactions are influenced by both verbal and nonverbal cues, inferences about relationships and feelings (affect) may be more heavily influenced by nonverbal cues (Zajonc, 1980). Thus, whether customers' affective state will be influenced in a positive or a negative direction would depend on the nature of the verbal responses and on whether they received the anticipated nonverbal cues. While it is not tested in this study, it is possible that negative emotions caused by unfavourable NVB will bias customers' perceptions, evaluations and their complaint behaviours.

Once a customer lodges a complaint, the original transaction may become less relevant to the consumer's ultimate satisfaction than events that follow the complaint (Goodwin and Ross, 1992). Simply acting quickly and autonomously to fix the problem may not generate positive affect unless it is accompanied by empathy and courtesy (Hocutt and Stone, 1998). In other words, dissatisfied customers would expect not only to receive fair settlement, but, more importantly, to be treated with courtesy and respect (Blodgett et al., 1997). Our results show that complainants who receive a fair settlement, but who are treated rudely, most likely will not visit the organization again, and are likely to tell their friends and relatives about their negative experience. As Sparks et al. (1996) noted, recovery will be beneficial only when the frontline staff use an appropriate style of communication during a service failure handling. In parallel with these arguments, our results demonstrate that NVB holds a significant role in determining customers' behavioral intentions following a service recovery effort. While the front-office clerk's verbal response was the same in both cases, positive body posture and eye contact appeared to have increased customers' likelihood of engaging in favorable behaviors. Table 3 clearly demonstrates that likelihood of positive word-of-mouth recommendation and repeat business with the company in the future received significantly higher ratings from respondents in the case of open body posture, accompanied by an appropriate eye-contact. Expressing preference for the company over others, increase the volume of their purchase, saying positive things about the company to others and remaining loyal to the company are signals that customers would be bonding with a company (Zeithalm et al., 1996, p.34).

Table 3. Behavioral Intentions by NVB

Behavioral Intentions Measured	NVB(+)	NVB (-)	t	sig
Say positive things about this hotel to other people	6.03	1.93	5.17	.000
Recommend this hotel to someone who seeks your advice	6.07	1.89	45.50	.000
Encourage friend and relatives to stay at this hotel	6.13	1.78	48.35	.000
Consider this hotel your first choice in the next few years	6.07	176	47.62	.000
If any problems occur during your stay which hotel you stay at, how likely is it that you would get in touch with the same staff again?	6.08	1.75	6.15	.000

In order to test the third proposition of the study, we have conducted a MANOVA test. Table 4 demonstrates that there is a significant difference among the scores of the respondents. They tended to give significantly different perception scores when they are exposed to verbal response only from scores that they rate in NVB case. An analysis of verbal response sample shows that the average rating for the credibility of staff was 5.5; however this rating decreased to 1.8 in the case of negative NVB, and increased to 6.1 in the positive NVB (see Table 4).

Table 4. Verbal vs. NVB ratings: Perceptions about Staff

	NVB (+)	NVB (-)	Just Verbal	F	Sig.
Credible	6.1087	1.8641	5.5385	1227.659	.000
Friendly	6.1902	1.9239	5.5077	1190.072	000
Competent	6.1141	1.9239	5.4308	977.576	.000
Empathic	6.1304	1.9293	5.3538	1051.465	.000
Courteous	6.0707	1.9620	5.3077	924.371	.000
Trustworthy	6.1902	1.8207	5.1538	898.239	.000

It also appears that verbal responses accompanied by NVB influences respondents' ratings on emotions (Table 5). When the respondent is presented with verbal response only, the average rating for "feeling comfortable" was 5.3. This rating was however significantly higher in positive NVB (6.08) and lower in negative NVB (1.9). Another critical emotion "satisfaction" appears to have been influenced when the NVB is included in the question format. The average satisfaction rating obtained from evaluation of just verbal response had risen (fallen) significantly when the same respondent evaluated the recovery response accompanied with the NVB (Table 5).

Table 5. Verbal vs. NVB ratings: Emotions

	Positive	Negative	Just Verbal	F	Sig.
Comfortable	6.0815	1.9076	5.3231	832.972	.000
Relaxed	6.0815	2.0054	5.0923	838.248	.000
Happy	6.0543	1.9022	5.0615	860.715	.000
Satisfied	6.0598	1.8152	4.8615	723.766	.000
Important	5.9457	1.9239	4.7077	845.566	.000
Privileged	5.8913	1.7989	4.8462		.000
Contended	6.1087	1.9565	4.9538	872.640	.000
Glad	6.1576	1.8859	5.0462	915.445	.000
Regretful	6.0761	1.8913	5.0462	968.194	.000
Calm	6.1196	1.8152	5.4462	1253.221	.000
Welcome	6.2772	1.6467	5.3692	1340.026	.000

Inclusion of nonverbal cues thus matters. If the just-verbal format was chosen as the research approach then this would have produced a satisfaction level at 4.83 level. It is possible to deliver the same verbal message with a negative manner and this decreases the rating to 1.81 level.

A consistent finding was observed in the analysis of contrast between verbal response only ratings and NVB-exposed ratings (Table 6). Respondents showed significantly favorable (unfavorable) intention toward the hotel in the case of positive (negative) NVB than in the case of just verbal response.

Table 6. Verbal vs. NVB ratings: Behavioral Intentions

	Positive	Negative	Just Verbal	F	Sig.
Say positive things about this hotel to other people	6.0326	1.9348	4.8462	775.875	.000
Recommend this hotel to someone who seeks your advice	6.0761	1.8913	4.6769	794.858	.000
Encourage friend and relatives to stay at this hotel	6.1359	1.7826	4.6308	830.057	.000
Consider this hotel your first choice in the next few years	6.0761	1.7609	4.4615	725.424	.000
If any problem occur during your stay which hotel you stay at, how likely is it that you would get in touch with the same staff again?	6.0815	1.7554	5.3538	1036.834	.000

CONCLUSION AND RECOMMENDATIONS

Like any spoken language, body language has words, sentences and punctuation. Each gesture is like a single word and one word may have several different meanings. Nonverbal behavior can have several functions in a service recovery. It can clarify verbal message (i.e., communication depends largely on what you are doing vocally and bodily while saying it). NVB can also help establish a relationship between staff and customer and help establish staff credibility (i.e., customer's perception of staff competence, trustworthiness and character). Service recovery is a very delicate, interaction-intensive and emotionally-driven moment-of-truth in which customer may become extremely vigilant to any kind of cue. Empirical negligence of the likely effects of nonverbal behavior on customers' recovery emotions and how customers evaluate service provider is therefore curious. This study explored whether staff's NVB during a service recovery could shape customers' emotional reactions, their evaluation of the staff and their behavioral intentions. Empirical evidence in the study suggests that NVB during a recovery could determine customers' cognitive and affective states. An open body posture, accompanied with an appropriate eye contact leads to positive emotion and favorable perceptions of the service personnel. Staff displaying such positive NVB is likely to be seen more credible, competent, courteous and trustworthy. Favorable NVB appears to have significantly increased the respondents' ratings on behavioral intentions and contacting with the same staff (i.e., trust and empathy building). This has significant implications on the perceived effectiveness of the recovery effort and maintaining long-term relationship with customers. Another important finding relates to the effect of including NVB cues in a study. It seems that respondents are likely to give significantly different ratings for the same recovery response when they are let to evaluate NVB cues and when only verbal response is given. This finding is not surprising, as nearly two-thirds of meaning in the interaction is conveyed in nonverbal ways such as kinesics and that verbal interactions do need the support of nonverbal communication (Hashimoto and Borders, 2005). A person may say "yes" verbally but the body language may be saying "no" (Hashimoto and Borders, 2005), and that customers are likely to make their recovery judgments by taking in both the verbal and nonverbal aspects of the message. Negligence of nonverbal aspects in studies attempting to understand customer decision-making may produce misleading results. Thus, future recovery studies should strive to work out separate and combined effects of verbal and nonverbal aspects on customers' service recovery judgments.

The limitations of the study should be noted. The same respondents were required to rate their evaluation in all situations examined. Recruiting the same respondents may result in respondent fatigue. Respondents were required to put themselves in the depicted situation. Their perception of the NVB and verbal response may be shaped by their cultural background, familiarity with the situation, perceived severity of the problem and so on. Thus, more controlled studies are needed. Their reactions to NVB may differ in different failure situations. These respondents were having holiday in Turkey, thus their recovery judgments may have been determined by overall (dis)satisfaction with their present holiday. Observational methods in real life situations may have been a more suitable research method, as individuals would naturally react in a negative manner to negative verbal signs. This study partially dealt with effects of kinesics on perceptions, emotions and did not examine likely effects of proxemics, tone, haptics etc. Further research is needed to understand their effects. Nevertheless, this study has potential to initiate more research interest on this much neglected issue. One of the interesting areas would be contrasting the effects of verbal responses and NVB (separate and combined effects) on customers' affective and cognitive states. The majority of previous research have followed a methodology in which only verbal recovery responses were provided and assessed (i.e., without visual aids for respondents to feel the NVB accompanying the verbal response). This is curious. Service experience is communication, and that NVB occupies a central role in communication. Exclusion of NVB obscures our understanding of how customers evaluate the complaint handling. Research based on recollection of recovery situation seems to be unable to account for the effects of NVB on customers' recovery evaluations. Limited understanding of NVB's functions during a service recovery may explain why the majority of verbal-based recovery efforts could not move customers' from a state of satisfaction to a state of dissatisfaction.

REFERENCES

Barnum, C., and Wolniansky, N. (1989). Taking Cues From Body Language. *Management Review,* June, 59-60.

Bayes, M.A. (1972). Behavioral Cues Of Interpersonal Warmth. *Journal of Consulting and Clinical Psychology*, 39 (2), 333-339.

Bitner, M. J., Bernard, H. B., and Tetreault, M.S. (1990). The Service Encounter: Diagnosing Favorable and Unfavorable Incidents. *Journal of Marketing*, January, 71-84.

Blodgett, J.G., Hill, D.J., and Tax, S. (1997). The Effects of Distributive, Procedural and Interactional Justice on Postcomplaint Behavior. *Journal of retailing*, 73 (2), 185-210.

Boshoff, C. ve Leong, J. (1998). Empowerment, Attribution and Apologizing as Dimensions of Service Recovery an Experimental Study. *International Journal of Service Industry Management*, 9 (1), 24-47.

Boshoff, C., and Staude, G. (2003). Satisfaction With Service Recovery: Its Measurement and Its Outcomes. *South African Journal of Business Management*, 34 (3), 9-16.

Breytenbach, D. (2001). The Use Of Nonverbal Communication In Assisting The Law Profession: A Focus On Selected Criminal Cases In The High Court Wıtwatersrand Local Division, Johannesburg. *Institute For Human Rightsand Criminal Justice Studies,* December.

Burgoon, J. K., Birk, T., and Pfau, M. (1990). Nonverbal Behaviors, Persuasion And Credibility. *Human Communication Research*, 17(Fall), 140-169.

Chaney, H.L., and Green, G. C. (2006). Presenter Behaviors: Actions Often Speak Louder Than Words. *The American Salesman*, April, 51 (4), 22.

Chebat, J., and Slusarczyk, W. (2003). How emotions mediate the effects of perceived justice on loyalty in service recovery situations: an empirical study. *Journal of Business Research*.

Dolen, W., Lemmink, J., Mattsson, J., and Rhoen, I. (2001). Affective consumer responses in service encounters: The emotional content in narratives of critical incidents. *Journal of Economic Psychology*, 22, 359-376.

Dube, L., and Menon, K. (2000). Multiple roles of consumption emotions in post-purchase satisfaction with extended service transactions. *International Journal of Service Industry Management*, 11 (3), 287-304.

Elizur, D. (1987). Effect of Feedback on Verbal and Non-Verbal Courtesy in a Bank Setting. *Applied Psychology: An International Review*, 36 (2), 147-56.

Enz, C.A.(2002). The Role Of Emotions In Service Encounters. *Journal of Service Research*, JSR. May. 4, 4.

Ford, W.S.Z. (1995). Evaluation of The Indirect Influence of Courteous Service On Customer Discretionary Behavior. *Human Communication Research*, September (22), 65-89.

Gabbott, M., and Hogg, G. (2000). An Emprical Investigation Of The Impact Of Non-Verbal Communication On Service Evaluation. *Europen Journal Of Marketing*, Bradford, USA: 34 (3/4), 384.

Goodwin, C., and Ross, I. (1992). Consumer Response To Service Failures: Influende of Procedural and Interactional Fairness Perceptions. *Journal of Business Research*, 25, 149-163.

Hart, C.W.L., Heskett, J.L., and Sasser, W.E. (1990). The Profitable Art of Service Recovery. *Harvard Business review*, 68 (4), 148-156.

Hocutt, M.A., and Stone, T.H. (1998). The Impact of Employee Empowerment on the Quality of a Service Recovery Effort. *Journal of Quality Management*, 3 (1), 117-132.

Hoffman, D.K., and Chung, B.G. (1999). Hospitality Recovery Strategies: Customer Preference Versus Firm Use. *Journal of hospitality and Tourism Research*, February, 23 (1), 71-84.

Huang, J.H., Huang, C.T., and Wu, S. (1996). National character and response to unsatisfactory hotel service. *International Journal of Hospitality Management*, 15 (3), 229-243.

Johnston, V.S. (1999). *Why We Feel: The Science Of Emotion*. Cambridge, Massachussets, USA: Perseus Books.

Keaveney, S.M. (1995). Customer Switching Behavior in Service Industries: An Exploratory Study. *Journal of Marketing*, 59 (2), 71-82.

Mattila, S. A. (2001). The Effectiveness of Service Recovery in a Multi – industry Setting. *Journal of Services Marketing*, 15 (7), 583-596.

Mehrabian, A., and Williams, M. (1969). Nonverbal Concomitants Of Perceived and Intended Persuasiveness. *Journal of Personality and Social Psychology*, 13 (1), 37-58.

Mehrabian, A. (1981). *Silent Messages*. Belmont, CA, USA: Wardsworth.

Mehrabian, A. (1972). *Nonverbal Communication*. Aldine-Atherton. New York, NY, USA.

Miller, E. J. (1992). *Menu Pricing and Strategy*. 3rd Edition, Van Nostrand.

Reisinger, Y., and Waryszak, R. (1996) Catering to Japanese Tourists: What Service do They Expect from Food and Drinking Establishments in Australia?. *Journal of Restaurant and Foodservice Marketing*, 1 (3/4), 53-71.

Smith, A.K., and Bolton, R.N. (2002). The Effect of Customers' Emotional Responses to Service Failures on Their Recovery Effort Evaluation and Satisfaction Judgements. *Journal of the Academy of Marketing Science*, 30 (1), 5-23.

Smith, A., Bolton, R., and Wagner, J. (1999). A Model of Customer Satisfaction With Service Encounters Involving Failure And Recovery. *Journal of marketing research*, (34), 356-72.

Sommers, M. S., Greeno, D. W., and Boag, D. (1989). The Non-Verbal Communication In Service Provision And Representation. *The Service Industries Journal*, 9 (4), 162.

Sparks, B., Bradley, G.L., and Callan, V. J. (1996). The impact of staff empowerment and communication style on customer evaluations: the special case of service failure. *Journal of Service Management*, 11, 12-26.

Sundaram, D.S., and Webster, C. (2000). *The Nonverbal Communication In Service Encounters*. Santa Barbara, USA, 14 (5), 378.

Yu, Y., and Dean, A. (2001). The Contribution of Emotional Satisfaction to Consumer Loyalty. *International Journal of Service Industry*, 12 (3/4), 234-50.

Yuksel, A. (2006). Customers' Emotional and Behavioural Responses to Complaint Handling. In Parul Parihar (Ed.). *Promises and Perils in Hospitality and Tourism Management*.

Yuksel, A., Hancer, M., and Kilinç, U.K. (2006). Empowerment Levels and Complaining Behaviors: A Case of Hote Customers' Intentions. (in Ed.). Dixit, S.K. *Promises and Perils in Hospitality and Tourism Management*. New Delphi: Aman Publications, 438.

Zeithaml, V. A., Berry, L. L., and Parasuraman, A. (1996). The behavioural consequences of service quality. *Journal of Marketing*, 60, 31-46.

In: Tourist Satisfaction and Complaining Behavior
Editor: Atila Yüksel

ISBN 978-1-60456-002-2
© 2008 Nova Science Publishers, Inc.

Chapter 15

CUSTOMER INDIRECT VOICES TO SERVICE FAILURES: CONTENT ANALYSIS OF E-COMPLAINTS

Abdullah Tanrısevdi
Adnan Menderes University, Turkey

INTRODUCTION

The issue of satisfying customers has become one of the most important strategic aims (Naumann, Jackson and Rosenbaum, 2001). Management of customer satisfaction and customer retention, prerequisites of organizational success, has thus gained further importance (Maxham III, 2001) due to increasing number of alternatives in a competitive business environment (Eccles and Durand, 1998). Complaint management philosophy of an organization could affect both customer retention and profitability (McAlister and Erffmeyer, 2003). This is particularly important in today's business in which customers have become more sophisticated (Sujithamrak and Lam, 2005); and they search more in the process of purchasing (Hoffman, Kelley and Rotalsky, 1995); demand to have more options (Peterson, 1995); and respond boldly when encounter service failures. They may easily complain in case of dissatisfaction and/or they may negatively react against the service failures (Smith, Bolton and Wagner, 1999; Mattila, 2001). Unresolved complaints not only cause loss of existing customers, but also if the recovery expectations are not fulfilled, customers will not hesitate to tell their problem to family members, colleagues, and friends (Lewis, 1983; Huang and Smith, 1996). An upset customer, experienced a dissatisfactory service, can convey the service failure at least nine to twenty people (Hart, Heskett and Sasser, 1990; Carson and Carson, 1998; Eccles and Durand, 1998; Mattila, 2001; Chu, 2002). Failure also destroys loyalty (Miller, Craighead and Karwan, 2000). Organizations cannot afford losing customers due to the cost of gaining new customers, which could cost five times compared to the cost of sustaining existing customers (Lewis, 1983; Hart, Heskett and Sasser, 1990; Carson and Carson, 1998; Hui and Au, 2001; Chu, 2002; Mueller et al., 2003; Tyrell and Woods, 2004).

The rapid development of information technology (IT), particularly Internet makes it possible for customers to search more alternatives in connection with their pre/post purchase behaviors than traditional settings (Harris et al., 2006). Technology enthusiasts are more demanding of a quick response than others are (Matilla and Mount, 2003). Judging from the growing number of discussion forums, it can be speculated that customers tend to share their experiences with forum members for several reasons. The forum sites can be taken as a cooling-off vehicle for complainants and deliver a varied functions to the members, including informing, motivating, supporting like what travel agencies generally do. Although complaint management continues to receive growing attention, little is known about why these sites are opted as a medium, their impact on purchase decisions, and the contents of customers' complaints delivered via Internet (Lee and Hu, 2004; Tyrell and Woods, 2004).

The chapter aims to contribute to the literature by undertaking an extensive analysis of complaints submitted to the Internet sites and gain insight into service failure experiences of Turkish customers staying at hotels in Turkey. To this end, this chapter first undertakes a review of literature on service failure and recovery. Customer complaints submitted to the selected Internet sites have been categorized in accordance with failure types identified by previous studies. Implications of the study are discussed and suggestions for future work are provided.

LITERATURE REVIEW

Service Failures and Recovery Efforts

Service failures may be defined as "...consumer-perceived breakdown in a firm's system or any service-related mishaps that occur during a customer's experience with a firm" (Maxham III, 2001, p.11). Most authors agree that even if strict checking procedures are applied (Carson and Carson, 1998) failures, mishaps, and mistakes are almost inevitable (Hart, Heskett and Sasser, 1990; Boshoff and Leong, 1998; Webster and Sundaram, 1998; Mueller et al., 2003; Wong, 2004; Lee and Hu, 2004, Yuksel, 2006). While service mistakes/delays are inevitable, dissatisfied customers are not (Wong, 2004). Appropriate recovery efforts can remove negative feelings and turn dissatisfied customers into a loyal customer (Hart, Heskett and Sasser, 1990; Huang and Smith, 1996). From an operation perspective, service providers should make every effort to provide the customer with a positive experience the first time (Miller, Craighead and Karwan, 2000).

There are many studies indicating service failures and each of them is very important for understanding unique characteristics of services (Bitner, Booms and Tetreault, 1990; Hoffman, Kelley and Rotalsky, 1995; Manickas and Shea, 1997; Licata, Mills and Suran, 2001; Naumann, Jackson and Rosenbaum, 2001; Chu, 2002; Mueller et al., 2003; Gursoy, Chen and Kim, 2005). These studies show that customer problems should be solved promptly, even though they may not be stemming from that particular firm (Hart, Heskett and Sasser, 1990).

Understanding failure mode enables to find the sources of existing problems (Bae, Ha and Park, 2005) and allows determining the way of recovery efforts. For instance, economic losses require economic recoveries (e.g. compensation) whereas social related failures can be managed by using social recovery strategies (Smith, Bolton and Wagner, 1999). Offering refund and discounts following product/service failures is likely to increase satisfaction with recoveries and indirectly affect WOM intent (Maxham III and Netemeyer, 2002). Zemke (1991 cf. Mueller et al., 2003) asserts that if a failure appears, companies have to apologize, offer a fair fix, correct the failure and more importantly show and demonstrate that the firm cares about customers. Promptness of the firm to customer problems and proactive approach to guest relations in failure situations are significant to deliver what Carson and Carson (1998) termed, psychological service recovery and concrete service recovery.

CUSTOMER COMPLAINT BEHAVIORS

Customer complaint behavior refers to how customers, exposed to mishaps or failures, do behave during a service delivery process and post – purchase intentions and it is directly related to dissatisfaction (Sujithamrak and Lam, 2005). Singh (1988) categorized customer complaint behaviors into three groups: voice (when people investigate redress seeking directly from service provider), private complaints (people do not hesitate engage in word – of – mouth concerning dissatisfying experiences with others), and complaint to third party organizations (complaints directed to some independent organizations, that is people seek an outside party to redress). Singh and Pandya (1991) grouped complaint behaviors into four: Exit (people leave the organization and not desire to be patron), negative word of mouth, voice and complaint to third parties. Exit is usually performed when voice is useless (Lyons, 1996). Hunt (1991) classified complaint behaviors into three groups: voice (high, middle and low), exit (high, middle and low), and retaliation (high, middle and low). Hansen, Swan and Powers (1997) added two different complaint behaviors as 'no action or private action'. No action intentions refer to 'do not do anything'. They think that the case is hopeless or they do not want to make it a big case (Hart, Heskett and Sasser, 1990). Blodgett, Hill and Tax (1997) explain consumers who are reluctant to get their rights prefer negative WOM instead of leaving business silently. Oh (2003) breaks voice into two sub-groups: direct and indirect. Direct voice explains complaints registered directly with the firm at the time of dissatisfaction whereas indirect voice covers complaining cards, e-mail and so on.

Scholars have studied how dissatisfied customers cope with their dissatisfaction and in what conditions they complain. According to Day (1984) the importance of consumption (the amount of money which is paid), customer's knowledge and experiences (knowledge of brand and product, and their numbers of type before), difficulty of complaint (requires time etc.), and the idea which is about that complaint is successful end are critical determinants of how customers react to service failures. Oh (2003) asserts that complaining takes a lot of time, require efforts, and disrupt routines. According to Lyons (1996) complaining is inevitable in case the problem is external, reappearance probability is high, and it can be prevented but the organization did not take sufficient precautions. Therefore, the type, frequency, and magnitude of failures are critical in complaining decisions (Bolton and Wagner, 1999; Hoffman, Kelley and Rotalsky, 1995).

ELECTRONIC-BASED CUSTOMER COMPLAINTS

Internet and electronic texts are becoming widely available. An important advantage of Internet is that it has a great potential to encourage users to express thoughts and feelings openly as it does not require face-to-face communication (Esterberg, 2002 cf. Binik, Mah and Kiesler, 1999, p.125-126). However, there is still no consensus among scholars concerning purposes and objectives of technology - driven complaint intentions. Tyreel and Woods (2004) argue that all types of complaint behaviors can be observed in a single e-complaint. Oh (2003) claims electronic based complaints are covered in indirect voice behavior. Furthermore, McDougall and Levesque (1999) classified e-complaints in terms of negative word of mouth behavior, whereas Matilla and Wirtz (2004) evaluate it as remote channel (Sujithamrak and Lam, 2005).

Web-based complaint forums can be utilized by customers for indirect voice, negative WOM, third party and middle level retaliation. Indeed, this type of communication can be considered a unique source for e-consumers (Shea, Enghagen and Khullar, 2004). As Internet is an anonymous tool, it encourages customers who avoid voicing to the service provider, to use regardless of whether the organization wants to listen or not (Tyrell and Woods, 2004). Another aspect is the characteristics of the complainants. As Mattilla and Wirtz (2004) indicate, shame-prone customers would use internet to avoid confrontation (cf. Sujithamrak and Lam, 2005).

An increasing number of consumers share their problems about their hotel experiences on popular Internet sites (Lee and Hu, 2004). Customers may hope that the company that causes a complaint will pay attention to the problem and give feedback (Lee and Hu, 2004). Additionally web-based complaining provides confidentiality while sharing negative experiences with the public. Besides, sites inform the prospective customers that the company supports the problems in question or not (Lee and Hu, 2004 cf. Gelb and Sundram, 2002).

The main objective of electronic-based complaint forums is not likely to back bite firms that complained about. In contrast, they try to contribute to development of quality approach. These sites allow internet users to identify a firm by name and industry (Tyrell and Woods, 2004), and thus, they represent a highly significant customer feedback. In doing so, they play a role in letting firms follow sites where their products and services are likely to be discussed (Lee and Hu, 2004 cf. Gelb and Sundram, 2002), force them to remedy the problem areas (Tyrell and Woods, 2004 cf. Harrison-Walker, 2001) further, allow publishing suggestions expressed by customers. These types of sites also provide a means of two-way communication. The system watches customer interaction history. Complainants easily login to their account to read and analyze the data. Besides, firms are registered in these forum sites as an institutional member to learn whether they have received any complaint or not. In this way, successful companies in terms of complaint handling are scored and rated on their own site, according to their performance, such as speed of solution, and full solution. Webmaster shows various graphics in accordance to these companies' performance.

In electronic-based complaint forums, the web editor automatically notifies complaints. Received complaints are first pre-evaluated and filtered by eliminating swearwords and slang. An advising board (lawyer, judge, technician, and academician) generally codes. Then webmaster recodes them to the related sub files by their categories. Finally, all cases submitting to webmaster are categorized into different industries. Tour companies, rent a car firms, time-sharing organizations and hotels are placed into the tourism file.

THE STUDY

Previous studies about complaint handling process are mostly related to laboratory or scenario-based experiments (Karatepe, 2006) (Table 1 shows a brief distribution of the methods used in the previous research). Although these studies have contributed to our understanding of service failure, it seems that customer-originated data (i.e., complaint records of actual customers) may be more useful for several reasons (Lee and Hu, 2004). First, this type of data involves nominative cases. Indeed, customers could unlimitedly express their feelings, thoughts, projections, or suggestions. Second, the researcher does not initiate the cognitive/emotive process so the data would not be artificially manufactured. Data through customer-registered episodes are collected in an unobtrusive way and thus it is not contaminated by the research methodology (Esterberg, 2003; Lee, Cai and O'Leary, 2006; Wagenaar and Babbie, 1989). Thus, contrary to forcing participants to fill in questionnaires or read scenarios, gathering data through customers' e-complaints have several advantages (Cresweel, 1994).

A content analysis was utilized to gather and analyze the words, concepts, and relationships within the recorded texts (McAlister and Erffmeyer, 2003). Content analysis has been used in analyzing a variety of marketing concepts and it has been especially useful in examining customer complaints (Mueller et al., 2003). To explain contents of cases, a frequency analysis was employed, and the frequency of cases was counted and compared with other cases (Bos and Tarnai, 1999).

The data collection involved Turkish holidaymakers who had stayed at hotels in a certain period and expressed their complaints via the Internet. Three specialized electronic based consumer complaint forums were selected for the analysis[1]. E-forums are chosen because they are conducive to study the actual records of actual customers. Forums make it easy to collect various types of complaints from few databases during a limited study period. Forums are free of charge for customers, hence access is easier than other sources such as official applications to centers of consumer rights, trade courts etc. Forum enables users to openly express thoughts and feelings without fear of confrontation. Finally, forums are generally traced by prospective customers before buying.

The study was carried out between the 24 – 28 of February 2007. The process started with searching 'sikayet' (complaint) as keyword on the 'Google in Turkey'. Totally 686 hotel complaints were identified during the research period. A random sampling was utilized, and after a random start, every third complaint case was selected and 227 were used for the final analysis. The procedure for analyzing the content began with establishment of categories (Bos and Tarnai, 1999). To minimize potential subjectivity, an independent researcher was invited to participate into the study. Each text was read independently and codes were generated.

---

[1] One of these sites (http://www.sikayetvar.com) was awarded with "Golden Spider Reward of 2005 and 2006", by Turkish NGOs.

Table 1. Distribution methods used in previous researches

Year	Author (s)	Data Collection Method	Sample
1980	Hannigan	Content analysis	40 tourist complaints gathered from Canada and USA newspapers
1983	Lewis	Questionnaire	120 hotel guests
1991	Singh and Pandya	Critical incident technique	172 bank customers
1994	Kelley and Davis	Quasi-experimental	156 customers
1995	Hoffmann, Kelley and Rotalsky	Critical incident technique	Five students in a service marketing class at a university, 373 critical incidents
1995	Glenn	Critical incident technique	467 tourism administration students
1995	Ostrom and Iacobucci	Scenario	98 MBA students
1996	Lyons	In-depth interview and focus group	10 restaurant customers
1996	Sparks and Callan	Role playing	292 businessman and businesswoman
1996	Brown, Cowles and Tuten	Scenario	424 undergraduate students
1996	Bejou, Edvardsson and Rakowski	Critical incident technique	Airline passengers in Switzerland and USA
1998	Boshoff andLeong	Scenario	239 undergraduate students
1998	Chung and Hoffmann	Critical incident technique	Restaurant customers
1999	Bolton and Wagner	Mixed design experiment	375 undergraduate students and 602 hotel customers
2000	Becker	Critical incident technique	382 critical incidents
2001	Licata, Mills and Suran	Questionnaire	227 bank customers
2001	Matilla	Scenario	441 undergraduate students
2001	Colgate and Norris	Face- to- face in-depth interview	20 bank customers
2002	Chu	Questionnaire	402 international traveler
2003	ABTA	In-house information and survey	ABTA members
2004	Lee and Hu	Content analysis	222 self-selected hotel customers' online complaints over five-year period
2004	Shea, Enghagen and Khullar	Content analysis	1000 email responses submitting for a web-based complaint
2004	Tyrell and Woods	Literature review	-
2005	Sujithamrah and Woods	Questionnaire	250 hotel restaurant customers
2005	Susskind	Critical incident technique and questionnaire	358 mall patrons
2006	Yuksel, Kilinc and Yuksel	Scenario and questionnaire	700 Turkish, Dutch, British and Israeli tourists

The results of the independent reviewing process indicated 91% consistency between the coders. Finally, a single coding scheme was generated that captures twenty-four sub-groups under eight main categories. In addition to defining main categories of complaints, we attempted to understand the reasons for using forums. In other words, this part of the analysis helped us to figure out whether forums are used as a means for a redress expectation from the company or as a means for retaliation.

RESULTS AND DISCUSSION

Totally 227 complaint cases were examined. In general, two categories of complaints appear to occupy a larger portion of the analyzed complaints. Depending on their contents, we have named these two major categories as service delivery and corporate policy failures. 71.3% of the cases were in the category of service delivery failures (f: 917), and 12.4% were in the category of corporate policy (f: 160). Frequencies of other complaint categories were relatively less, and hence they are not discussed here. A summary of the e-complaint categories are presented in Table 2.

Category of service delivery failures includes seven complaint themes. Three hundred ninety-seven cases resulted from inappropriate employee behaviors (43.29%). Within this category, five sub-complaint groups were identified. Inhospitable employee behaviors ranked the first. Some examples derived from the texts indicate that customers are largely shocked by unacceptable behaviors. A holidaymaker expresses that: "...but in this time with a sharp reaction, receptionist first warned me to be polite and gentle, then uttered a threat against me as saying: do not bust up! Otherwise, I get someone to kick you out" (Case number: 47). Another case sounds a terrible experience: "...the receptionist asked me: Here is a hospital? How can you hold us responsible for everything? You pay for something, I see, but not hotel. Then he sets out to beat me..." (Case number: 114). Last but not least, one upset customer says: "...the receptionist tried to beat us at the lobby. So our holiday was ruined by rude staff to end at police station. Oh! I cannot believe that! My request was just to get an invoice on my account..." (Case number: 95).

Table 2. Content analysis of e-complaints

Categories	Rank	Frequency	Percent
A) Service Delivery	1	917	71.30
1) Inappropriate Employee Behaviors *		397	43.29
• Inhospitable behaviors		324	
• Lack of professional knowledge		54	
• Inexperience actions		9	
• Physical appearance		6	
• Sexual harassment		4	
2) Core Products*		320	34.89
• Food and Beverages		219	

Table 2. (Continued)

Categoties	Rank	Frequency	Percent
• Tasteless dishes		105	
• Lack of diversity		80	
• Stale foods		34	
• Room		101	
• Equipment		34	
• Cleanliness		28	
• Not ready to use		24	
• Quietness		8	
• Heath		7	
3) Slow and undelivered services*		131	14.28
• Queue		108	
• Waiting for food and drink service		12	
• Check-in and out procedures		10	
• Other		1	
4) Reservation*		15	0.01
5) Equipment failures*		31	0.03
6) Stocks*		16	0.01
7) Wrong charging*		7	0.008
B) Corporate Policy	2	160	12.44
• All-Inclusive		82	
• Cost reduction		42	
• Unfair practices		28	
• Other		8	
C) Hygiene	3	80	6.22
• Swimming pool		64	
• Ancillary services		16	
D) Lack of Reliable Information	4	56	4.35
• Purposely wrong advertisement		34	
• Inability to communicate to staff		15	
• Missing information		7	
E) Physical Appearance of Hotels	5	48	3.73
F) External Factors	6	11	0.08
G) Service Disasters	6	11	0.08
H) Failure caused by Customer	7	3	0.002
Grand Total		1.286	100

* Percentages in main failure category

Three incidents above show the extreme inhospitality of the employee. We have defined them as "unacceptable behaviors". Furthermore, following cases reflect less rude still, but inhospitable behaviors: "the receptionist says: ....seeing that you do not like, take a holiday for a five star hotel by paying 200 YTL for one night" (Case number: 11) or as in case 11: "...if you cannot enjoy yourself what can I do?". Responses of hotel employees to customers appear to vary by their position in the hotel. A holidaymaker explains: "...even if they were in a state of insolvency in order to express the way of hotel, in spite of the fact that we were customers of them, they behaved us as if we had disturbed them..." (Case number: 87). Further, several cases show that employees cannot perform contemporary marketing practices. According to one of the reported episodes: "…although the hotel we stayed and foods we tasted were fine, negative attitudes towards customers were really irritating" (Case number: 14). Following case indicates a similar incident: "….when I called the hotel, I was shocked hearing such expressions: …but who told you all foods and beverages were free of charge? This is the first time I've heard" (Case number: 88). Lack of professional knowledge was another frequently mentioned factor (f: 54). A customer, stayed in a five star hotel, expressed: "…it was very interesting and surprising experience for me! The waiter did not know whether to add ice into my red wine (!)…" (Case number: 53). As commonly known in the international hotel industry, honeymooners expect special care during their holiday. The report of case 117 shows that: "…housekeeping stuff did not care our special situation. But we were honeymooners!".

The second largest share of the dissatisfying encounters was related to the core products (f: 320). Nearly one third of the complaints (34.89%) in service failure category was rising from inefficiencies of core products including food and beverage (f: 219), and in-room facilities (f: 101). All-inclusive practices at the resort hotels may account for the low quality of food and beverages. Tasteless dishes appear as a common problem (f: 105). For instance, "…the menu that they call as all-inclusive contained just 8-10 different dishes. Chickens were not well cooked, and tasteless. Teas were served in plastic glasses with only two-different cookie. Additionally, the labels of cokes we've not heard up to now…" (Case number: 96). Eighty cases indicated poor hygiene as a problem whereas room-based problems were stated more frequently (f: 101). The majority of complaints relate to insufficient equipment (e.g. TV, and Ac remote control) Holidaymakers also complained about beverage quality at the hotels. As expressed by the cases 59 and 24: "…thanks to beers I had drunk at hotel bar! I did not need to drink any water. Because, nearly half of the bottles of beer were filled with water!" Another customer says, "…this was the first taste I have ever had- raki (a Turkish traditional alcohol) – brand, oh! I have never heard of it. What a pity, you had to take it. Because there was not alternative…". Diversity of foods in hotel restaurants appeared another area receiving frequent complaints (f: 80). This could be again the result of all-inclusive practices. Case 31 explains that: "…I stayed for three-nights. They told before, the menu was open buffet, however during three days, I had to have just the same or similar foods such as – chicken, chicken with rice, chicken with onion and so on. That is, I did not see any red meat dish on the buffet during all holiday…"

Corporate policy related failures are the second major complaint category (12.44 %). This category involved all-inclusive practices, billing mistakes, and unfair practices (e.g. treat differently to foreign and domestic tourists). The most frequently mentioned complaint was about all-inclusive (f: 82). Following case reflects that: "…in an all-inclusive hotel that we stayed for one week, the manager asked us, as if so nice; oh! Please take less food and beverage, otherwise we become bankrupt!" Congestion, crowd, and other irritating factors that would be resulting from all-inclusive had a potential to cause dissatisfying encounters, as indicated by some cases. Waiting time for services in the areas of open buffet, aqua-park, and fitness, etc. received considerable number of complaints. A customer, stayed at a resort hotel with all-inclusive, says: "…We were shocked! Only one tea machine was set during breakfasts, so guests had to wait for a long time in a queue just for a cup of tea! I have a real difficulty in understanding how a five star hotel certificate was given to this dormitory!" (Case number: 134). Another guest implies a similar incident: "… there were lot queues – like a student canteen – even if you would like to take drinks; you had to wait for at least 15 minutes…" (Case number: 11).

We tried to understand why electronic forums are used by analyzing certain phrases within the submitted complaint texts (Table 3). It appears that some of these individuals had not sought redress while staying at the hotel (108 complainants of 227). Convenience to express the experienced problem via a cyber forum could be a significant reason of choice. A holidaymaker explains: "…this was a great lesson for us. After coming back home, I had sent an e-mail directly to their website, but I could not get any response. So I decided to voice here" (Case number: 29). Another guest states: "…I would like to address hotel via this forum. You are losing customers! Furthermore, you will receive more this type of complaints." A few complainants tend to draw conclusions and assume that these problems are peculiar to the Turkish tourism. Cases 153 and 45 both stated: "…the problems we faced with in a short period reflect current situation in Turkey. ….In my opinion; all holiday villages and five star hotels are similar…service quality suffers" Forty-nine cases show that the hotel guests not only voice via cyber forums, but also they claimed to be redressed during their holiday. This behavior fits into complaint behaviors - direct voicing, and indirect voicing – stated in the literature. A hotel guest explains: "I and my wife tried to express the problem about AC to the receptionist one more time, but she did not care! She just said: OK. I would immediately go to contact technical department. But we did not hear a positive sound from that department during the five days" (Case number: 169). Another customer, using cyber forum, had also voiced directly to hotel management about a serious health problem. She explains: "My kid is nearly 3 years old. She had been festered from the swimming pool. We immediately took her to the hotel doctor. The doctor confirmed that infection seriously affected my daughters' eyes. We were shocked! Then, I directly told to assistant director of the hotel. He said: we are sorry, but everyone could be exposed to such a problem. These words had driven me crazy. Hence, I write here so that everybody knows" (Case number: 209). Negative WOM intend (14 %) and exit (13.1%) ranked the third and fourth as the reasons for usage of e-forums. Findings indicate that the majority of complainants use internet forums as a tool to indirect voice after consumption in order to warn prospective customers to avoid: "…Because I do not wish other prospective customers encounter these types of disappointments, I would like to inform them in advance" (Case number: 71). Case 168 indicates that: "…I will not take a holiday at this hotel one more time, so I wanted to share you my feelings and bad experiences. Please be careful!" Thirty of the complainants interrupted holidays and returned homes (13.2%). This type of complaint behavior generally falls into the category of exit. As one case shows, exit behavior is generally performed when voice is useless (Lyon, 1996): "…The delivered services at the hotel was such that we looked forward to leaving the hotel" (Case number: 148). Another guest explains: "We had to leave hotel 2 days ago from the scheduled date. But we were forced to do that" (Case number: 201). Individuals using forums not only expect to be heard but also to be compensated. Case 149 states: "…my request is that please find a solution to my problem, the hotel management should apologize".

Table 3. Complaint behaviors gathered from the contents of the records

	Cases	Percent
Not seeking redress while at hotel	108	47.57
Redress seeking at hotel	49	21.58
Negative WOM	32	14.09
Exit	30	13.21
Third party intentions	6	0.02
Not mention	2	0.008
Total	227	100

CONCLUSIONS AND IMPLICATIONS

Customer complaint management continues to receive growing attention in the marketing discipline. However, little research has been conducted on e-complaints. In this chapter, frequently mentioned service failures within e-complaints of Turkish domestic tourists were examined. Employee behaviors account for the majority of dissatisfying encounters, followed by core product and corporate policy related problems. The findings share similarities with those of previous studies. Bitner, Booms and Tetreault (1990) found staff behaviors as the most complained category. Similarly, Hoffman, Kelley and Rotalsky (1995) and Kılınc (2004) identified service delivery failures as a significant category. Although, Kılınc explained that service delivery failures were about one-fourth of all complaints in hotels, and the core product complaints are the most complaint receiving category, our findings indicate otherwise. Analogously, Chu (2002) reports employee behaviors as the most important complaint category.

This study has important implications. While previous studies assume that no-action type of customers do nothing (presumably at the premise), our study shows that there is no guarantee that they would engage in e-based actions against the company. The analysis clearly shows that the majority of customers have not tried to voice their problems while staying at the hotel, but they use the forum as a platform to disseminate the experience. Literature presents several reasons for not to complain, including the case is hopeless or does not want to make it a big case (Hart, Heskett and Sasser, 1990). In line with suggestions of Mattilla and Wirtz (2004), our findings support the view that shame-prone customers would use internet to avoid confrontation (Sujithamrak and Lam, 2005).

Features of service encounter create an environment where service failure is almost inevitable (Mueller et al., 2003). Service providers should learn to find effective solutions although they may not be able to prevent all complaints (Karatepe, 2006). The results of the study show that non-complaining customers in fact carry their cases elsewhere. Thus, hotel managers are advised to develop schemes to break customer silence by encouraging them to complain. Customer who could not have an opportunity to voice should be seen as he/she deprived of his/her valuable suggestions (Kılınc, 2004). The study findings clearly indicate that cyber channels provide website users with information and retaliation. Learning negative experiences and promptly acting for resolutions would prevent companies from costly results. Thus, hotel managers are advised to install online terminals in-house so that some of the shame-prone customers can utilize those as a voicing medium. Alternatively, it would be beneficial for hoteliers to follow up e-forums and to be an institutional member.

As with most research, this study has some limitations. First, written complaints as drawn from complaint forums should be considered carefully as a data source by taking into account their probability of inaccuracy (Tyrell and Woods, 2004). Second, due to the methodology and sampling, the results of underlying categories about electronic based complaint behaviors cannot be generalized. Extensive research is needed to understand functions of e-complaints on prospective and actual customers' decisions.

REFERENCES

ABTA. (2003). Travel statistics and trends. London, UK.

Bae, S. M., Ha, H. S., and Park, S. C. (2005). A web-based system for analyzing the voices of call center customers in the service industry. *Expert Systems with Applications*, 28, 29-41.

Becker, C. (2000). Service recovery strategies: the impact of cultural differences. *Journal of Hospitality and Tourism Research*, 24 (4), 526-538.

Bejou, D., Edvardsson, B., and Rakowski, J. P. (1996). A critical incident approach to examining the effects of service failures on customer relationship: The case of Swedish and US airlines. *Journal of Travel Research*, Summer, 35-40.

Bitner, M. J., Booms, B. H., and Tetreault, M. (1990). The service encounter: Diagnosing favorable and unfavorable incidents. *Journal of Marketing*, (54), 71-84.

Blodgett, J. G., Hill, D. J., and Tax, S. S. (1997). The effects of distributive, procedural and interactional justice on postcomplaint behavior. *Journal of Retailing*, 73 (2), 185-210.

Bos, W., and Tarnai, C. (1999). Content analysis in empirical social research. *International Journal of Educational Research*, 31 (1999), 659-671.

Boshoff, C., and Leong, J. (1998). Empowerment, attribution and apologizing as dimensions of service recovery: An experimental study. *International Journal of Service Industry Management*, 9 (1), 24-47.

Brown, S. W., Cowles, D. L., and Tuten, T. L. (1996). Service recovery: its value and limitations as retail strategy. *International Journal of Service Industry Management*, 7 (5), 32-46.Carson, P. P., and Carson, K. D. (1998). Does empowerment translate into action? An examination of service recovery initiatives. *Journal of Quality Management*, 3 (1), 45-79.

Chu, R. (2002). Stated-importance versus derived-importance customer satisfaction measurement. *Journal of Service Marketing*, 16 (4) 285-301.

Chung, B., and Hoffmann, K. D. (1998). Critical incidents service failures that matter most. *Cornell Hotel and Restaurant Administration Quarterly*, (June), 66-71.

Colgate, M., and Norris, M. (2001). Developing a comprehensive picture of service failure. *International Journal of Service Industry Management*, 12 (3), 215-233.

Day, R. L. (1984). Modeling choices among alternate responses to dissatisfaction. *Association of Consumer Research Proceedings*, (11), 496-499.

Eccles, T., and Durand, P. (1998). Complaining customers, service recovery and continuous improvement. *Managing Service Quality*, 8 (1), 68-71.

Esterberg, K. G. (2002). *Qualitative Methods in Social Research*. USA: McGraw – HillHigher Education.

Glenn, F. R. (1995). Negative visitor-hospitality industry staff interaction: response styles of potential employees. *The Tourist Review*, 3, 50-64.

Gursoy, D., Chen, M. H., and Kim, H. (2005). The US airlines relative positioning based on attributes of service quality. *Tourism Management*, 26 (2005), 57-67.

Hannigan, J. A. (1980). Reservations cancelled consumer complaints in the tourism industry. *Annals of Tourism Research*, 7 (3), 367-384.

Hansen, S. W., Swan, J. E., and Powers, T. L. (1997). Vendor relationships as predictors of organizational buyer complaint response styles. *Journal of Business Research*, (40), 65-77.

Harris, K. E., Grewal, D., Mohr, L. A., and Bernhardt, K. L. (2006): Consumer responses to service recovery strategies: The moderating role of online versus offline environment. *Journal of Business Research*, 59 (2006), 425-431.

Hart, C. W. L., Heskett, J. L., and Jr. Sasser, W. E. (1990). The profitable art of service recovery. *Harvard Business Review*, (July-August), 149-156.

Hoffman, K. D., Kelley, S. W., and Rotalsky, H. M. (1995). Tracking service failures and employee recovery efforts. *Journal of Service Marketing*, 9 (2), 49-61.

Huang, C. H., and Smith, K. (1996). Complaint management: Customers' attributions regarding service disconfirmation in restaurants. *Journal of Restaurant and Food Service Marketing*, 3 (4), 121-133.

Hunt, H. K. (1991). Consumer satisfaction, dissatisfaction and complaining behavior. *The Society for the Psychological Study of Social Issues*, 107-117.

Hui, M. K., and Au, K. (2001). Justice perceptions of complaint-handling: a cross-cultural comparison between PRC and Canadian customers. *Journal of Business Research*, 52, 161-173.

Karatepe, O. M. (2006). Customer complaints and organizational responses: the effects of complainants' perceptions of justice on satisfaction and loyalty. *Hospitality Management*, 25, 69-90.

Kelley, S. W., and Davis, A. M. (1994). Antecedents to customer expectations for service recovery. *Journal of Academy of Marketing Science*, 22 (1), 52-61.

Kılınc, U. K. (2004). *Sikayet yonetimi ve yetkilendirme: resort otel incelemesi, Aydın, Adnan Menderes* Universitesi Sosyal Bilimler Enstitusu Turizm Isletmeciligi Anabilim Dalı (yayinlanmamis yuksek lisans tezi).

Lee, G., Cai, L. A., and. O'Leary, J. T. (2006). www.Branding.States.Us: An analysis of brand - building elements in the US state tourism websites. *Tourism Management*, 27, 815-828.

Lee, C. L., and Hu, C. (2004). *Analyzing hotel customers' e-complaints from an internet complaint forum*. In J. E. Mills and R. Law (Eds), Handbook of Consumer Behavior, Tourism, and Internet (167-181), NY, USA: The Haworth Hospitality Press, Inc.

Lewis, R. C. (1983). When guests complain. *The Cornell H.R.A. Quarterly*, August, 23-32.

Licata, J. W. Mills, G. N., and Suran, V. (2001). Value and satisfaction evaluations during a service relationship. *Service Marketing Quarterly*, 22 (3), 19-41.

Lyons, J. (1996). Getting customers to complain: A study of restaurant patrons. *Australian Journal of Hospitality Management*, 3 (1), 35-50.

Maniskas, P. A., and Shea, L. J. (1997). Hotel complaining behavior and resolution: A content analysis. *Journal of Travel Research*, 6 (2), 68.

Maxham III, J. G. (2001). Service recovery's influence on consumer satisfaction, positive word-of-mouth, and purchase intentions. *Journal of Business Research*, 54, 11-24.

Maxham III, J. G., and Netemeyer, R. G. (2002). Modeling customer perceptions of complaint handling over time: the effects of perceived justice on satisfaction and intent. *Journal of Retailing*, 78, 239-252.

Mattila, A. S. (2001). The effectiveness of service recovery in multi-industry setting. *Journal of Service Marketing*, 15 (7), 583-596.

Mattila, A. S., and Mount, D. J. (2003). The impact of selected customer characteristics and response time on E-complaint satisfaction and return intent. *International Journal of Hospitality Management*, 22 (2), 135-145.

McAlister, D. T., and Erffmeyer, R. C. (2003). A content analysis of outcomes and responsibilities for consumer complaints to third-party organizations. *Journal of Business Research*, 56, 341-351.

McDougall, H. G. G. and Levesque, J. T. (1999). Waiting for service: effectiveness of recovery strategies. International Journal of Contemporary Hospitality Management, 11 (1), 6-15.

Miller, J. L., Craighead, C. W., and Karwan, K. (2000). Service recovery: a framework and empirical investigation. *Journal of Operations Management*, 18, 387-400.

Mueller, R. D., Palmer, A., Mack, R., and McMullan, R. (2003). Service in the restaurant industry: an American and Irish comparison of service failures and recovery strategies. *Hospitality Management*, 22, 395-418.

Naumann, E., Jackson, D. W., and Rosenbaum, M. S. (2001). How to implement a customer satisfaction program. *Business Horizons*, January-February, 37-46.

Oh, D. G. (2003). Complaining behavior of public library users in South Korea. *Library and Information Science Research*, 25, 43-62.

Ostrom, A. and Iacobucci, D. (1995). Consumer trade-offs and the evaluation of services. *Journal of Marketing*, 59 (January), 17-28.

Peterson, R. A. (1995). Relationship marketing and the consumer. *Journal of the Academy of Marketing Science*, 23 (4), 278-281.

Shea, L., Enghagen, L., and Khullar, A. (2004). *Internet Diffusion of an e-complaint: a content analysis of unsolicited responses*. In J. E. Mills and R. Law (Eds), Handbook of Consumer Behavior, Tourism, and Internet (145-156), NY, USA: The Haworth Hospitality Press, Inc.

Singh, J. (1988). Consumer complaint intentions and behavior: definitional and taxonomical issues. *Journal of Marketing*, 52 (January), 93-107.

Singh, J., and Pandya, S. (1991). Exploring the effects of consumers' dissatisfaction level on complaint behaviours. *European Journal of Marketing*, 25 (9), 721-733.

Smith, A. K., Bolton, N. R., and J. Wagner (1999). A model of customer satisfaction with service encounters involving failure and recovery. *Journal of Marketing Research*, 36, 356-372.

Sparks, B., and Callan, V. (1996). Service breakdowns and service evaluations: the role of customer attributions. *Journal of Hospitality and Leisure Marketing*, 4 (2), 3-24.

Sujithamrak, S., and Lam, T. (2005). Relationship between customer complaint behavior and demographic characteristics: a study of hotel restaurants' patrons. *Asia Pacific Journal of Tourism Research*, 10 (3), 289-307.

Suskind, A. M. (2005). A content analysis of consumer complaints, remedies, and repatronage intentions regarding dissatisfying service experiences. *Journal of Hospitality and Tourism Research*, 29 (2), 150-169.

Tyrrell, B., and Woods, R. (2004). *E-Complaints: Lessons to be learned from the service recovery literature*. In J. E. Mills and R. Law (Eds), Handbook of Consumer Behavior, Tourism, and Internet (183-190), NY, USA: The Haworth Hospitality Press, Inc.

Wagenaar, T. C., and Babbie, E. (1989). *Practicing Social research: Guided activities to accompany the practice of social research*. USA: Wadsworth Publishing Co.

Webster, C., and Sundaram, D. S. (1998). Service consumption criticality in failure recovery. *Journal of Business Research*, (41), 153-159.

Wong, N. Y. (2004). The role of culture in the perception of service recovery. *Journal of Business Research*, 57, 957-963.

Yuksel, A. (2006). Customers' *emotional and behavioural responses to complaint handling*. In Dixit, S. (Ed.). Promises and Perils in Hospitality and Tourism Management (356-392), New Delhi, India: Aman Publications.

http://www.sikayetvar.com

http://www.sikayetim.com

http://www.otelsikayet.com

In: Tourist Satisfaction and Complaining Behavior
Editor: Atila Yüksel

ISBN 978-1-60456-002-2
© 2008 Nova Science Publishers, Inc.

Chapter 16

TOURIST'S ONSITE PERCEPTIONS, EVALUATIONS AND THEIR APPROACH/AVOIDANCE BEHAVIORS: POSITIVE REINFORCEMENT THROUGH MEDIA EXPOSURE

Atila Yüksel and Ergün Efendi
Adnan Menderes University, Turkey

INTRODUCTION

A review of literature suggests that managers, through use of appropriate means, should strive to stimulate customers' approach behaviors (Mehrabian and Russell, 1974). *Approach behaviors* include all positive behaviors that might be directed at the environment; for example a desire to remain in a store, place, attraction etc. and explore its offerings could be stated as approach behavior. *Avoidance behaviors* reflect contrasting responses; that is, a desire to leave a place or not to browse represents avoidance behaviors (Spangenberg, Crowley and Henderson, 1996). *Approach behaviors* are suggested by increased willingness to interact with others (including salespeople) in an environment, increased willingness to spend time and return to an environment, and an increased willingness to spend money. Individuals are expected to have greater approach behaviors in pleasant environments creating positive affects and greater avoidance behaviors in unpleasant environments creating negative affects (Mehrabian and Russell, 1974; Yuksel, 2006).

Research in-so-far has provided empirical evidence about effects of such environmental cues as noise, lighting, color, atmosphere, crowd density etc. on customers' perceptions, evaluations and approach-avoidance behaviors. Recent arguments suggest that there are yet other factors in the direct control of destination authorities which can have effects on tourists' onsite evaluations and approach/avoidance behaviors (Yuksel, 2006). Marketing efforts that decrease the level of uncertainties associated with a service experience, as well as, unawareness level about a place and its attractions may induce positive evaluations and approach behaviors. Provision of additional information (e.g., what is available, at what cost and how to get there) through exposure of onsite promotions/advertisements, for example may help reduce uncertainties and associated risk concerns. Continuous communication with visitors in this form can increase interest and awareness about offerings of the place. It can compensate likely inefficiencies and incompleteness resulting from initial (if any) communication efforts which are likely to be constrained by time, space and other limitations.

According to Siegel and Ziff-Levine (1990), through properly managed advertising/promotion campaigns, National Tourism Authorities (NTAs) can generate advertising awareness among the target audience, generate awareness of the destination as an acceptable place to visit, create a positive image of the destination *vis-à-vis* its competitors, motivate consumers to travel to the destination in the near future, and influence travel behavior by converting those motivated by advertising to actually visit the destination (cf., McWilliams and Crompton, 1997). NTAs practices support the contention that promotional efforts of a destination would be only influential in customer decision-making prior to leaving. In other words, these practices are transactional and sales oriented, not relational (Woodside and Sakai, 2001). "No efforts or budget is planned for development of an ongoing relationship with the inquiring prospective visitors" (Woodside and Sakai, 2001, p. 378). We argue that, in addition to attempts to influence decision making at "prior-to-leaving" stage, it is possible that marketing efforts can affect decisions/evaluations while "en route", and/or "after arriving" at the destination (Perdue and Pitegoff, 1990 cf. Kaplanidou and Vogt, 2003[1]).

While it is generally pursued, transactional marketing - only sales-driven pre-purchase marketing activities - has a number of limitations. These marketing activities tend to be designed for generation of first-time buyers, and thus they may not be effective for another significant segment (e.g., repeat customers). Attempts to create first-time buyers require large resources in order to be effective. Many NTAs may lack such resources. NTAs appear to believe that once their destination has been announced to public at large there is no need to advertise it further. Pre-purchase marketing efforts are likely to be inefficient when they do not reach as many potential and interested visitors as wished. Initial advertising when a destination is launched may not be seen 100% of potential buyers. Even seen, a significant proportion may not pay attention or be interested in. Evidence suggests that while a large number of potential customers may request information from an advertising campaign, they may never read the brochure at all (Woodside, 1996). It is possible that in a situation where numerous messages reach the consumer, s/he may neglect the message due to selective perception and/or superiority of competitors' offers. Timing and duration of promotion/advertisement at tourist-originating countries/regions is crucial. If consumers have only a short time to examine the message, are not repeatedly exposed to the message, and if there are many distractions (e.g., other messages), processing of the message by the individual will be unlikely (Reiser and Simmons, 2005). This may explain why in some cases promotional expenditure compared to other determinants of demand, appeared to have a minimal effect on tourist flows to a country (Uysal, 1983; Uysal and Crompton, 1984, cf. Faulkner, 2003).

---

[1] Since the purpose of this chapter is not to undertake a model comparison, interested readers are referred to Kim et al., (2005) for a review on their strengths and limitations.

Advertising can be used more effectively when further materials are provided to those customers who notice and respond to advertisers' offers of these materials (Woodside et al., 1997). "Too often awareness advertising leaves the prospect dangling, with no idea of what to do next, where to buy, or how to obtain more information. At the very least, the ideal advertising and marketing process should bridge this gap between the advertising and the sale by offering-and providing-additional information. We call this 'linkage'" (Rapp and Collins, 1987, p. 17). Linkage advertising "links the up-front advertising to the sale with additional arguments and benefits which the up-front advertising [i.e., the print or broadcast advertisement that includes the linkage offer] didn't have space or time to include" (Rapp and Collins 1987, p. 17, cf. Woodside 1997). According to Woodside et al. (1997) linkage (two-step) advertising may be particularly effective in increasing brand-affect, and intentions to return to the destination among visitors with prior visits to the destination because it stimulates deeper mental processing of current and former experiences by the visitor. Destination linkage advertising may serve as an album that helps to build, maintain, renew, and strengthen mental connections of places/events and outcomes experienced (Woodside et al., 1997, p. 217). Running an onsite advertising strategy, dependent or independent of initial advertising at tourist-originating countries, may benefit a destination in other ways. NTAs may not be able to include all places/attractions of interest to customers in their pre-purchase advertising due to cost of advertising, characterized by budget, space and time limitations. They can however bring forward those additional areas into the attention of actual visitors through subsequent onsite advertisements.

There is a paucity of research on the third stage of holiday (i.e., after arriving destination) in terms of whether onsite media exposure of a destination (e.g., at airports, hotels, restaurants, tour buses, streets etc.) increases visitors' perceptions and approach behaviors. Practices, at least at Turkish destinations, show that post-purchase promotions/advertisements to visitors on holiday are not widely used. This is surprising, as post purchase promotions/advertisements can increase preference of the product in the future through purchase reinforcement (DelVecchio et al., 2006) and relationship building (Woodside et al., 1997). Display of promotional materials onsite, independent or dependent of initial advertising, would help building continuous communication with customers. In other words, carefully crafted onsite promotion materials, preferably consistent with initial promotions/advertisements used at the pre-purchase stage, can serve an Instructor Manual. Availability of information to reduce potential uncertainties, largely arising from the buyer's inexperience with the product may hold significance in evaluation of the overall product experience. Tentatively speaking, even the most experienced visitors to a place may miss some aspects of that place which would otherwise have boosted the experiential quality of total holiday. Probability of missing experience opportunities is exacerbated in the case of visitors who tend to engage in low information search behavior at the pre-purchase or onsite stage of the holiday. Multiple and proper message exposures give tourist more opportunity to internalize destination attributes and to develop more positive attitudes (Shiffman and Kanuk, 2004).

LITERATURE REVIEW

The role of marketing in communication with customers is comprehensive (Dore and Crouch, 2003) and it is conducted in a variety of ways. Marketing requires a detailed planning, and large amounts of time and money (MacKay and Smith, 2006). Promotions and advertising are among the frequently used communication tools in marketing. Promotion is used "to communicate with individuals, groups, or organizations with the aim of directly or indirectly facilitating exchanges by informing and persuading one or more of the audiences to accept a firm's products" (Dibb et al., 1994, p. 376). Advertising is defined as "a paid form of non-personal communication about an organization and its products that is transmitted to a target audience through a mass medium such as television, radio, newspapers, magazines, direct mail, public transport, outdoor displays or catalogues" (Dibb, et al. 1994, p. 386). Holloway (2004) notes that promotional literature in the form of travel brochures, guides etc. can be defined as a form of advertising. These vehicles make consumers aware of products, inform about the product and demonstrate how these products can satisfy their needs and wants (Holloway, 2004). Despite the studies showing minimal effect of promotion on tourism demand and tourist flows to a country (Uysal, 1983; Uysal and Crompton, 1984), statistically significant impacts and long-term effects of advertising have been reported. Papadopoulos (1987) concluded that promotional expenditure by the Greek National Tourist Organization did have an impact on tourist arrivals, and the strength of this impact varied among the major markets. Crouch, Schultz, and Valerio (1992) found that the international marketing of the Australian Tourist Commission played a statistically significant role in influencing inbound tourism to that country. Industry Canada's (1994) report concluded that advertising has had a small but significant effect on the U. S. and Japanese markets. In a comparison of 15 NTAs actively engaged in promotions in the U. S. market, Hunt (1991) noted that in general those with above average marketing expenditure achieved better growth rates in their share of this market (cf. Faulkner, 2003).

PROMOTION EFFECTIVENESS

Studying the effects of advertising (TV, radio, posters, newspapers, magazines etc.) has received a huge volume of research attention in academic and practitioner literature (Givon and Horsky, 1990; WTO, 2003). Effectiveness is typically assessed by conversion or by tracking studies (Kim, Hwang, and Fesenmaier, 2005). Conversion studies measure the number of inquiries that are "converted" into actual visitation (Kaplanidou and Vogt, 2003). Conversion model assumes that conversion/behavior derives after a sequence of stages over time and that motivation to travel comes after inquiring for information and eventually leads to conversion (Kaplanidou and Vogt, 2003). Advertising tracking model, however argues that inquiry fulfillment may facilitate conversion but it is not a necessary condition and that consumers may be converted solely by advertising based on awareness and image building impacts (Kaplanidou and Vogt, 2003). Tracking studies are designed to monitor changes in the markets' awareness, interest, preference, and intentions as a consequence of exposure to advertising campaigns (Faulkner, 2003). In support of tracking studies, Davidson (1994, p. 358, cf. Faulkner 2003) notes that "In essence, the science of predicting human behavior – of which advertising evaluation research is a branch – is at best imprecise. The relationship between message and a change in the mind set is more direct and easier to study; and if the effect of advertising begins in the potential customer's mind then advertising evaluation research should also begin in the potential customer's mind". According to Siegel and Ziff-Levine (1994) "It is only rarely that definitive conclusions can be drawn about the impact of advertising on travel behavior. Instead, tracking research is more valuable, from a diagnostic perspective, in pin-pointing the strengths and weaknesses of a campaign for the fine-tuning of creative development and media buying" (p. 563).

Promotion/advertising requires large amounts of NTAs' funds (Dore and Crouch, 2003), and thus it is imperative to understand not only how potential customers respond to such activities but how relations with customers can be maintained and sales in existing markets can be increased (MacKay and Smith, 2006). How communication effectiveness can be enhanced is another important managerial issue. The ways in which tourism destinations and NTAs measure the effectiveness of their activities, in attracting tourism, is still developing (WTO, 2003). According to the WTO report, current approaches vary significantly between NTAs. The extent to which measurement takes place is dependent upon the types of activity undertaken, the objectives behind these activities and, of course, the budgets available (WTO, 2003). It is reported that "in some cases the cost of evaluating some promotional activities could be more than the cost of the activity itself". "Many evaluations to date have been ad hoc in the sense that they have relied on one or two techniques that address only part of the problem…" (Faulkner, 2003, p. 26). Nevertheless, NTAs should ensure that public resources are used wisely and seek to measure the benefits that they produce relative to the costs2. Onsite promotion/advertisements may increase return of marketing investments.

PURCHASE REINFORCEMENT

Advertising matters. Ehrenberg (1972) suggests that "the key role of advertising is in reinforcing previous purchase decisions, rather than in persuading people to make a first-time or brand-switching decision". Ehrenberg's model Awareness-Trial-Reinforcement (ATR)

---

[2] However, evaluating the effects of NTAs activities on a destination's tourism performance is especially problematic due to a number of reasons. i) Distinguishing the separate effects, on destination performance, of individual components of the destination e.g. disaggregating the effect of NTAs promotions from the impact of, say, new product developments such as a major new attraction is problematic. ii) Distinguishing the separate effects, on destination performance, of individual components of the marketing mix e.g. disaggregating the effect of media relations, advertising, brochure distribution, websites and trade exhibitions is difficult. iii) Another problematic area is the isolation of impacts of uncontrollable external, environmental variables, negative (war, terrorism, weather, unfavourable exchange rates etc.) or positive (a hit film featuring a destination such as "Lord of the Rings" in New Zealand), from impacts of NTAs activity. iv) Similarly, isolating the effects of NTAs activities from those of organizations within the same destination, over which the NTAs has no control e.g. the direct marketing activities of tour operators, hotels, transport companies etc. is a complicated issue. v) Finally, assessing the residual effects of NTO activities, and those of other organizations, after the activities themselves have ceased i.e. the 'wear-out' factor compounds the accurate measurement (WTO, 2003).

emphasizes that potential visitor's first gain awareness and interest in a destination, then try it. Satisfaction with the experience would reinforce desire to return in the future. This model recognizes that previous visitors would use their experience with a destination in order to make a selection decision, and attitudes developed from previous visits are likely to be resistant to persuasive advertising whose messages may be counter to that experience, but receptive to advertising that reinforces it (McWilliams and Crompton, 1997). Individuals on holiday would continue to be receivers of messages (Krugman, 1969). Thus, repeated exposure to destination promotion materials/messages may result in gradual learning and ultimately further visitations, and extra buying behaviors on holiday (McWilliams and Crompton, 1997). Donnelly and Ivancevich (1970) argue that after a purchase a buyer would be highly receptive to advertising and sales promotion put out on the product s/he bought. Literature on post sales promotion and advertising further shows that buyers would feel reassured that a wise purchase decision has been made when they are presented with such postpurchase promotions. For existing customers, promotion reinforcement takes place by reminding customers to buy the brand thereby supporting their preference for it. For non-users, promotions may induce trial thereby buttressing attitudes and likelihood of purchase (DelVecchio et al., 2006). Post-purchase promotions may however raise questions in customer minds as to why the brand needs to promote (DelVecchio et al., 2006). Effect of post purchase advertising on customers evaluation and preferences have been tentatively supported by two studies in the automobile industry. One study found that automobile buyers exhibited high readership of advertisements for the make of the car they had recently bought. Another study revealed that back-out rates were significantly lower when the buyers were positively reinforced by the salesman (Donnelly and Ivancevich, 1970). Supporting information that reinforces a purchase decision is expected to reduce likely dissonance in individuals.

Onsite destination promotions/advertisements by NTAs can prompt favorable perceptions, and this may enhance image that visitors hold for the destination (Braun-LaTour et al. 2006). Destination image, conveyed through multiple channels including promotional literature, the opinions of others, and the general media, is a key factor in the pleasure travel decision-making process to a destination (Baloglu and McCleary, 1999; MacKay and Fesenmaier, 1997). Image plays a significant role in the success of tourist destinations, since image, seen as a mental picture formed by a set of attributes that define the destination in its various dimensions, exercises a strong influence on tourist behavior (Beerli and Martin 2004; Bigne, Sanchez and Sanchez, 2001). Image fulfils a fundamental function in the choice process, as tourists generally have a limited knowledge of destinations that they have not been previously (Beerli and Martin 2004). Studies have revealed that influence of image is not just limited to the selection process but post-visit image influences tourist satisfaction and intention to repeat visit in the future (Bigne, Sanchez and Sanchez, 2001).

Image that an individual holds for a destination/attraction may change as a result of experience and also exposure to advertising. Repeated exposure of a destination to actual holiday makers through promotional materials/advertising can stimulate further interest and alter perceptions about a destination (Kim and Richardson, 2003). Viewing visitable and previously unknown places other than the main destination through promotional films/advertising may be an experience in itself to some extent. At least, it gives an opportunity to gather information about a place (Kim and Richardson, 2003). Displaying promotional films on highly-patronized places (e.g., outdoor places, billboards, shopping places, banks, restaurants, etc.) may act as a shopping window for a destination. Destination images can be recrafted through such regular displays (Connell, 2005).

Repetitive display of promotional materials3 on-site may facilitate tourist information search behavior. Previous research suggests that a significant amount of planning and information search is conducted en-route (1-3 days prior to an activity). Once in the country, tourists rely heavily on word of mouth, guidebooks and visitor centers as information sources (Reiser and Simmons, 2005). That is, tourists would seek to enhance quality of their holiday by decreasing the level of associated uncertainty through information search not only prior to a trip but also during trip (Fodness and Murray, 1997). Whilst on vacation, visitors will need information on what opportunities are available, where they are to be found, and at what cost (Raitz and Dakhil, 1989, cf. Fodness and Murray, 1997). Repeated and planned exposures of a destination through promotion materials/advertising, a directly controllable information source from a destination's standpoint, tourists' perceptions and behaviors may be favorably influenced. Cost of advertising on-site (destination) would be relatively cheaper and it can be met under a sponsorship scheme of a local government.

Woodside et al., (1997) argue that advertising may be particularly effective in increasing brand-affect and intentions to return to the destination among visitors with prior visits to the destination because it stimulates deeper mental processing of current and former experiences by the visitor (p. 217). Based on learning theory of preferences (Krugman) Woodside et al., argue that repeat visitors who have been exposed to advertising are likely to spend the most money, partly because the advertising increases their knowledge of things to do at the destination area, they have the most positive attitude about the activities available at the destination. Repeated visitors who have not been exposed to such advertising can be expected to engage in fewer activities and spend the least because they focus their visiting time on repeating activities they enjoyed on prior visits, do not repeat marginally enjoyable activities. Similarly, the new visitors who have been exposed to the advertising is expected to spend more money as s/he will learn about and do more activities than new customer who have not been exposed (Woodside et al., 1997, p. 217). Woodside et al. provide some extent of support for different effects of linkage advertising on repeat and first-time buyers. The study shows that advertising has greater effect on repeat customers' expenditure patterns. Based on the reviewed literature we suggest that:

P1: Exposing destination promotion material/advertising whilst on holiday would significantly affect visitors' perceptions and evaluations of a place/product and their approach behaviors.

P2: Exposing destination promotion material/advertising whilst on holiday would significantly influence visitors' present and future behavioral intentions.

P3: Effects of exposure would differ between first time and repeat visitors.

CONCLUSION

As image is not just what tourists know, but also what they think or feel, understanding and managing destination image sources affecting travelers' thinking and feeling is vital

---

3 How promotions can be designed and executed is a topic of another study.

(Yuksel, 2006). Travelers are not only motivated by the appearance of destinations and attractions prior to visit, but also by the location's emotional qualities which help fulfill their psychological needs (Kim and Yoon, 2003; Pearce, 1988). Exposing promotion material whilst on holiday may benefit destination authorities in several ways. It would be appropriate to speculate that such exposures can stimulate favorable consumption emotions. Properly repeated exposures may intensify tourists' interest in exploring other areas at the destination. Onsite promotions could induce more sales, particularly within the existing market, as it can be used to move the customers from a stage of unawareness to awareness. The exposed material should however be effective in seizing attention, awaking interest, arousing a desire to try or buy the product and urging customer to take action (Yadin, 2002). Having seen diversity of things to do/visit whilst on holiday may lead to previously unplanned actions, visits, and/or spending.

REFERENCES

Baloglu, S., and McCleary, K. W. (1999). A model of destination image formation. *Annals of Tourism Research*, 26 (4), 868-897.

Beerli, A., and Martin, J. D. (2004). Tourists' characteristics and the perceived image of tourist destinations: a quantitative analysis- a case study of Lanzarote, Spain. *Tourism Management*, 25, 623-636.

Braun-LaTour, K. A., Grinley, M., J., and Loftus, E. F. (2006). Tourist Memory Distortion. *Journal of Travel Research*, 44 (4), 360, 367.

Connell, J. (2005). Todlers, tourism and tobermory: destination marketing issues and television- induced tourism. *Tourism Management*, 26, 763-776.

DelVecchio, D., Henard, D. H., and Freling, T. H. (2006). The effect of sales promotion on post-promotion brand preference: A meta-analysis. *Journal of Retailing*.

Donnely, H. J., and Ivancevich, J. M. (1986). Post-purchase reinforcement and back-out behavior. *Journal of Marketing Research*, 399.

Dore, L., and Crouch, G. I. (2002). Promoting destinations: An exploratory study of publicity programmes used by national tourism organisations. *Journal of Vacation Marketing*, 9 (2), 137-151.

Ehrenberg, A. S. C. (1972). *Repeat-buying*. Amsterdam North-Holland.

Faulkner, B. (2003). Why marketing practices to reinforce the purchase and to convince actual visitors to visit more attractions/places during their stay are very limited is curious.*Aspects of Tourism*, 9, 19.

Fodness, D., and Murray, B. (1998). A typology of turist information search strategies. *Journal of Travel Research*, 37 (2), 108-119.

Fodness, D., and Murray, B. (1997). Tourist information search. *Annals of Tourism Research*, 24 (3), 503-523.

Givon, M., and Horsky, D. (1990). Untangling the effects of purchase reinforcement and advertising carryover. *Marketing Science*, 9 (2), 171-187.

Holloway, J. C. (1994). *The Business of Tourism* (4th edt). Great Britain, UK: Pitman.

Kaplanidou, K., and Vogt, C. (2003). *A new series of marketing and research papers to better inform Michigan's tourism industry.* http://www.prr.msu.edu/economicimpacts/pdf/otherpdf/conversionsurvey.pdf, accessed 18 July 2006.

Kim, D. Y., Hwang, Y. H., and Fesenmaier, D. R.(2005). Modeling tourism advertising effectiveness. *Journal of Travel Research*, 44 (1), 42-49.

Krugman, H. E. (1962). The learning of consumer preferences. *Journal of Marketing*, 24(fall), 621-631.

MacKay, K. J., and Fesenmaier, D. R. (1997). Pictorial element of destination in image formation. *Annals of Tourism Research*, 24(3), 537-565.

MacKay, K. J., and Smith, M. C. (2006). Destination advertising age and format effects on memory. *Annals of Tourism Research*, 33 (1), 7-24.

McWilliams, E. G., and Crompton, J. L. (1997). An expanded framework for measuring the effectiveness of destination advertising. *Tourism Management*, 18 (3), 127-137.

Mehrabian, A., and Russell, J.A. (1974). The basic emotional impact of environments. *Perceptual and Motor Skills*, 38, 283-301.

Pearce, P. L. (1988). *The Ulysess factor: evaluating visitor in tourist settings.* New York, USA: Springer-Verlag. Fundamentals of tourist motivation.

Rapp, S., and Collins, T. (1987). *Maximarketing.* New York, McGraw-Hill.

Reiser, A., and Simmons, D. G. (2005). A quasi-experimental method for testing the effectiveness of ecolabel promotion. *Journal of Sustainable Tourism*, 13 (6), 590-615.

Siegel, W., and Levine, W. Z. (1990). Evaluating tourism advertising campaigns: Conversion vs. advertising tracking studies. *Journal of Travel Research*, 28 (3), 51-55.

Spangenberg, E.R., Crowley, A. E., and Henderson, P. W. (1996). Improving the store environment: do olfactory cues affect evaluations and behaviours. *Journal of Marketing*, 60, 67-89

Woodside, A. G., Trappey, R. J., and MacDonald, R. (1997). Measuring linkage-advertising effects on customer behaviour and net revenue: Using quasi-experiment of advertising treatments with novice and experienced product-service users. *Canadian Journal of Administrative Sciences*, 14 (2), 214-228.

Woodside, A. G., and Sakai, M. (2001). Meta-Evaluations of Performance Audits of Government Tourism-Marketing Programs. *Journal of Travel Research*, 39, 369-379.

Yuksel, A., and Yuksel, F. (in press). Shopping risk perceptions: Effects on tourists' emotions, satisfaction expressed loyalty intentions. *Tourism Management*, in press.

In: Tourist Satisfaction and Complaining Behavior
Editor: Atila Yüksel

ISBN 978-1-60456-002-2
© 2008 Nova Science Publishers, Inc.

Chapter 17

DESTINATION PERSONALITY AND FAVORABLE IMAGE CREATION THROUGH MEDIATED EXPERIENCES - HOLIDAY POSTCARDS

Yasin Bilima[a] and Atila Yüksel[b]

[a]Mustafa Kemal University, Turkey
[b]Adnan Menderes University, Aydýn, Turkey

INTRODUCTION

Understanding tourist decision-making process in the choice of a holiday destination is critical for developing effective tourism marketing plans. Several scholars have proposed various frameworks to explain how a selection decision is made (Hong, Kim, Jang and Lee 2006; Sirakaya and Woodside 2005; Chen and Gürsoy 2001; Morrison 1996). Tourist decision-making is generally described as a consecutive process (Hong et al. 2006; Decrop and Snelder 2005), and this process involves assessment of several aspects in the form of symbols, images, words, pictures, etc. (Cai, Feng and Breiter 2004). These elements may have relative weights on the process and its outcome. Purchase of a holiday is complex due to a number of features that are peculiar to the tourist product. Unlike tangible products, the tourist doesn't have a chance to test the holiday product and see the destination before the purchase (Kim and Richardson 2003; Eclipse 2003; Cai 2002). The tourist, however, may envisage the destination through the images that the destination releases via direct or indirect channels, (including word-of-mouth communication).

Choice of a particular destination among others largely depends on favorable images that the individual holds for the destination, as well as, the degree of the fit between the push (i.e., motivation) and pull factors (i.e., attractions or what a destination can offer) (Yoon and Uysal 2005; Hankinson 2004; Bansal and Eiselt 2004; Cai 2002; Leisen 2001). Destination choice may also rest upon the extent of congruency between the individual's self-image(s) and the image that the destination conveys. Recent studies provide empirical evidence suggesting affective image (Hong et al. 2006; Ajzen 2001; Sorolla 1996), brand personality (Hosany,

Ekinci and Uysal 2006; Ha 1998; Aaker 1997; Cohen, Martin and Athola 1972), and self-image congruency (Chon and Olsen 1991; Sirgy 1982) greatly impact on tourist decision-making and subsequent behaviors. If this is the case, then understanding causes of affective image, brand personality and image congruency is indispensable.

The power of a brand resides in the consumer' mind from both lived (purchase and usage) and mediated (advertising and promotion) experiences (Shiffman and Kanuk, 2001, p. 141). Despite the recognition that choice of a tourism destination is led by motivation-based attitudes (Lam and Hsu 2006, p. 589), the role of images rendered through destination advertisements in formation of tourist attitudes, feelings, and behaviors has been under researched (Jenkins, 2003). For example, contrary to its wide usage and potential power, holiday postcards have captured very limited academic attention (Markwick 2001; Jenkins 2003; Day et al. 2002). Researchers have rarely focused on tourist postcards to explore how the nature of photographic images symbolizes desired experiences; how they sustain particular motivations and how they would evoke emotions about the destination (Markwick, 2001). Equally interesting, likely effects of image congruency and destination personality conveyed by postcards on the decision process have been inadequately dealt with (Hong et al. 2006; Chen and Gürsoy 2001). The power of photograph in depicting images on picture postcards is considerable, since postcards are a direct representation of reality, a "true" reflection of actual places, people and events (Markwick 2001, p. 420). Taking a photograph or buying a postcard on holiday effectively serves to represent and signal the genuineness of the tourist experience. Postcards are not only a representative of experience (i.e. destination), but also a marketing agent for attributes, characteristics, concepts, values and ideas (Yüksel and Akgül 2007; Mackay and Fesenmaier 1997). It is thus appropriate to argue that visual images portrayed by postcards can become a powerful destination marketing tool that produce awareness, further information-search action, favorable attitudes and behavioral intentions. This however depends on the degree to which images depicted by the postcard are congruent with the person's self-image, holiday motivations and desired destination characteristics. This chapter discusses potential relationships between depicted images on holiday postcards and such elements as self-image congruency, affective image and destination personality that are deemed to be significant in tourist's decision-making process. Understanding these relationships would help destination authorities in designing effective postcards, which in turn helps develop communications that appeal to various personality types.

TOURIST DECISION MAKING

Previous studies highlight the key function of attitudes (i.e., predispositions or feelings toward a tourism destination or service) in predicting tourist behavior (Sirakaya and Woodside 2005; Chen and Gürsoy 2001; Lam and Hsu 2006). Attitudes are positive, negative or neutral views of an "attitude object": i.e. a person, behavior or event (wikipedia). Individuals may be "ambivalent" towards an attitude object, meaning that they simultaneously possess a positive and a negative bias towards the attitude in question. Attitudes come from judgments and they develop on the ABC model (affect, behavioral change and cognition) (wikipedia). The affective response is a physiological response that expresses an individual's preference for an entity. The behavioral intention is a verbal indication of the intention of an individual. The cognitive response is a cognitive evaluation of the entity to form an attitude. In other words, attitudes can be explained by a tri-component model, containing cognitive component (i.e., the knowledge and perceptions that are acquired by a combination of direct experience with the attitude object and related information from various sources), affective component (i.e., a consumer's emotions or feelings about a particular product or brand), and conative component (i.e., the likelihood or tendency that an individual will undertake a specific action or behave in a particular way with regard to the attitude object).

Ajzen (2001) suggests that an individual hold one, and only one attitude toward any given object or issue. Similarly, Kraus (1995, p. 64) states that specific attitudes are significantly better predictors of specific behavior than general attitudes. Different theories have been postulated to explain attitude-led human behavior in different situations. Theory of Planned Behavior (TPB) and Theory of Reasoned Action (TRA) by Ajzen and Fishbein (1975) are the two most widely used theories in the literature. According to these theories, attitudes capture the intentions and these intentions determine the behavior. Individuals are usually quite rational and make systematic use of information available to them. People consider implications of their actions before they decide to engage or not engage in a given behavior" (Ajzen and Fishbein, 1980, p. 5). According to the TRA, the most important determinant of a person's behavior is behavior intent. The individual's intention to perform a behavior is a combination of attitude toward performing the behavior and subjective norm. The individual's attitude toward the behavior includes; behavioral belief, evaluations of behavioral outcome, subjective norm, normative beliefs, and the motivation to comply.

Most attitudes are a result of observational learning from their environment and unlike personality, attitudes are expected to change as a function of direct and/or indirect experience. The formation of attitudes is also strongly influenced by the influence of family and friends, direct marketing, mass media and the Internet (Shiffman and Kanuk, 2001). Mass media communications in the form of special-interest magazines, and television channels provide an important source of information that influence attitude formation. Research has shown that consumers are exposed to an emotionally appealing advertising message is more likely to create an attitude toward the product than for consumers who have beforehand secured direct experience with the product category (cf. Shiffman and Kanuk, 2001).

POSTCARD: ATTITUDE BUILDER?

Attitude that travelers hold about a destination can be significantly influenced by several information sources (Baloglu and Mangaloglu, 2001). Postcards are one of the potential sources. The old cliché of a picture being worth a thousand words is particularly true for the promotion of places as holiday destinations (Jenkins, 2003). Pictures can be perceived and processed more quickly than words (Henderson et al. 2003; Day et al. 2002). Pictorial elements are better recalled and affect both positive and negative brand/product beliefs, images and attribute perceptions (Mackay and Fessenmaier, 1997). Postcards contain visual tangible cues which are likely to influence recipients' perception of the place and enhance buying intentions toward the destination. If executed properly, information relayed through postcards can have promotional value that communicates the benefits of a particular destination to potential travelers. Postcards are inexpensive (i.e., its delivery cost is met by the buyer), it is a commercial commodity (i.e., it generates income for the locals), easy to produce and they can transmit a great deal of visual information. Some postcards have dual lives (Winiwarter, 2001). They can be either a piece of mail or an enjoyed treasure in the personal album (Winiwarter, 2001). Postcards would reach more than a single individual. Postcards, generally accompanied by favorable impressions about the place and the holiday, would hold a significant role in raising awareness about the destination not only of the recipient but also others within the social circle of the recipient. It is customary to display a received postcard from a close friend abroad on office boards or show the postcard to visiting friends or relatives at home. Thus postcards can help raise awareness of the destination and probably place it within the consideration set of the prospective traveler. Additionally, since there is a social bond between the sender and the recipient, credibility of information transmitted through postcards can be greater compared to specific commercial efforts of the destination (Yuksel and Akgul, 2007). In contrast to their small size, properly executed postcards can generate positive attitudes and purchase intentions (Stafford, 1996 cf. Back 2001, p. 295). The main aim of postcard industry should therefore be to enhance awareness of the destination and convert a potential tourist into an actual tourist through capturing his/her interest and desire to purchase the holiday product. One should however note that the advertising of a destination through postcards are only successful if they establish a link between the individual's motivations, goals of preferences and the target destination (Uzzell, 1984, cf. Jenkins, 2003, p. 11). As Markwick (2001) states, postcard images must relate to particular motivations and desires associated with holiday.

POSTCARD: MOTIVATION FIT

Travel is basically need-related (Cooper, Fletcher, Gilbert and Wanhill, 1993) and the inner urges, which initiate travel demand, are called travel motivations. Motivation refers to a state of need that exerts a push on the individual toward certain types of action that are likely to bring satisfaction (Moutinho, 1986). Tourists have different travel reasons and motives based on psychological and/or biological needs and desires, and these are integral forces that evoke, direct and integrate a person's attitude and behavior to activate the decision (Chang, Wall and Chu 2006; Yoon and Uysal 2005; Sirakaya and Woodside 2005; Beerli and Martin 2004a; Kotler et all. 1999; Mill and Morrison 1985). Travel is often stated to be a complex form of behavior through which the traveller seeks to satisfy not one single motivation but several distinct needs simultaneously (Baloglu and Uysal, 1996). Some theories stress the need for balance and harmony, considering the traveller to be satisfied with the expected, and to be uncomfortable with the unexpected. Others suggest that the unexpected is satisfying and the individual will seek for complexity, not the sameness (Moutinho, 1986). In general, holidays are seen to arise from the need to escape from everyday surroundings for purposes of relaxation and discovering new things, places and people, and may be periods of self-discovery (Ryan, 1997). According to Mannel and Iso-Ahola (1987), the desire to change from one's daily routine (i.e., escaping) and the desire to gain intrinsic personal and interpersonal rewards (i.e., seeking) operate simultaneously to bring about travel behaviour.

According to Urry (1990), tourists seek escape from work and their ordinary everyday lives. Seeking different experiences is the prime motivator for travel. Difference equates with excitement, curiosity and interest. According to Jenkins, each traveler considers the images of destinations in order to assess the balance between similarities (i.e., likeliness to home with safety, comfort, confidence and ease of travel) and differences. Escape from the everyday life and work is one of the most significant motives for a holiday and postcards depicting spectacular environments, idyllic settings, secluded places and luxurious surrounds all link with the desire to escape in the minds of the recipient. People travel because they are "pushed" into making travel decisions by internal or psychological reactions, and "pulled" by the external forces of the destination attributes (Yoon and Uysal 2005). Although destination attributes (pull factors) are the initial factors filtering the choice process, personal motivations have the greater power on deciding where to go (Hong et al. 2006; Bansal and Eiselt 2004; Klenosky 2002; Goossens 2000; Gnoth 1997). The push factors that include emotional-dominant or inner-directed elements (affective outcomes and self-congruency) and personality elements related to a destination (brand, personal motivations) are associated with outside objects (visual elements; postcards, brochures, photos, etc.) (Gnoth 1997; Lam and Hsu 2006). Postcards can be a useful tool in tourists' strive for matching their inner-directed elements and destination personality factors, which are assumed to correlate positively with decision and purchase behavior intentions and brand preferences (figure 1) (Decrop and Snelder 2005; Kastenholz 2004; Morrison 1996). The images portrayed by postcards hence must symbolize particular desires and fantasies that are central to the motivating structures of the tourist process (Markwick, 2001). We argue that:

P1: Postcards with images that are congruent with individual's holiday motivations would induce more favorable affective images and this would result in positive attitudes toward that particular destination than motivation-incongruent postcards.

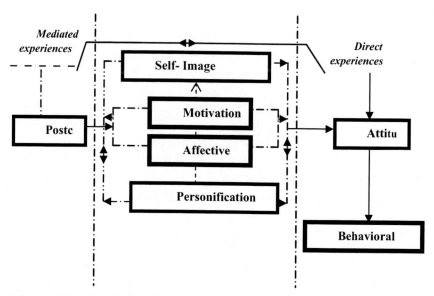

Figure 1: Proposed Model: Likely effects of postcard-images on attitude building

POSTCARDS: AFFECTIVE IMAGE MAKER

Majority of researchers in tourism marketing appear to have treated image as a construct similar to attitude. The term image generally refers to a compilation of beliefs, and impressions based on information processing from various sources over time, resulting in an internally accepted mental construct (Crompton, 1979). Destination image can also be defined as the sum of beliefs, ideas, expectation, feelings and impressions that an individual has of a place or destination (White 2004; Kar and Litvin, 2003; Jenkins 1999; Baloğlu and Brinberg 1997). Leisen (2001, p. 50) argues that, "the image represents the destination in the traveler's mind and gives him/her a pre-taste of that destination; it determines the traveler's consideration of a given area as a vacation destination. Then, once the destination is in the evoked set, its image is modified by further information and evaluated against the images of alternative destinations". Destination image is made up of three distinctly different but hierarchically interrelated components: cognitive, affective, and conative (Gartner, 1996). Cognitive image is defined as an evaluation of the known attributes of the product (Gartner, 1996). From a cognitive viewpoint, tourist destination image is assessed on a set of attributes that correspond to the resources or attractions that a tourist destination has at its disposal (Stabler, 1995, cf. Beerli and Martin 2004). Affective image relates to motives in the sense that it is how a person values the object under consideration (Gartner, 1996). "It is the feelings that we hold about any object" (Gartner 1996, p. 457). The conative image is analogous to behavior because it is the action component (Gartner 1996). After processing external and internal stimuli about a destination, a decision is made whether or not to travel to the area (Gartner 1996).

Like attitudes, the formation of image is the development of a mental construct based upon impressions chosen from a flow of information (Reynolds 1965, cf. Echtner and Ritchie, 1991). According to Gunn (1972) tourists form an image of a destination after undergoing a multiple stage process. These include accumulating mental images of the destination (i.e., forming an organic image); modifying the initial image after more information (i.e., forming an induced image); deciding to visit the destination, visiting the destination, sharing the destination, returning home and modifying the image based on the experience in destination. Two types of image, organic and induced are argued to be influenced by different information sources. Organic image (person-dependent) is based on the non-commercial sources of information, such as new about the destination in the mass media, information received and opinion of friends and relatives. The induced image (destination-dependent) is based on commercial sources of information, such as different forms of advertising and information from travel agents and tour operators. The third type of image (complex image) will be affected and modified by actually visiting the destination (Echtner and Ritchie, 1991). Gunn (1972) states that individuals can have an image of a destination even if they have never visited or even been exposed to commercial forms of information. Using Gunn typology, Gartner (1996) has developed an image formation process as a continuum consisting of eight distinctly different components. One of these components - un/solicited organic - suggests that information received from individuals who have visited an area or believe they know what exists there carries a higher level of credibility in the image formation since it comes from an acquaintance (Gartner, 1996).

Empirical evidence suggests that affective image has more impact on developing destination image than do cognitive image components. This is because the physical components and attractions can not encourage the tourists to visit destination without destination's emotional qualities, which help fulfill the tourists' psychological needs (Mackay and Fesenmaier 1997). Postcards can be an important source of affective image building. Postcards suggest a level of intimacy of experience which appeals directly to the tourist's desires and attitudes emotionally, and have an ability to accomplish desires that are fed through affective imaginary (Edwards, 1996). Postcard–induced feelings about the place appears to determine, at least to some extend, the degree to which the destination would be valued highly as a travel destination. Yüksel and Akgül (2007) report that postcards generate affective images and which in turn result in positive attitudes toward holiday destinations. Attitudes have been defined as an evaluative formation and in this formation affective component derived from emotions is regarded as attitude. Affective attitude is the quick, automatic evaluative response as immediate evaluation, distinct from more temporarily delayed and cognitively mediated responses, because affective attitudes are derived from consciously accessible emotions and feelings rather than external factors (environment, physical attributes) (Sorolla, 1996). This immediate evaluation is also related to the behavioral intention that is assumed to be the immediate antecedent of behavior (Bamberg et al., 2003). Therefore, we propose:

P2: Postcards can generate (un)favorable affective destination image which then in turn impacts on attitude and behavioral intent.

POSTCARDS: SELF IMAGE CONGRUENCY

Current consumer behavior literature holds the view that the consumer's purchase decision making process involves the evaluation of not only the utilitarian or functional attributes of a product but also the value-expressive or personality-related attributes of the product (Chon and Olsen, 1991). Each person has an image of herself/himself as a certain kind of person, with certain traits, skills, habits, possessions, relationships and ways of behaving. Products and brands have symbolic value for individuals who evaluate them on the basis of their consistency with their personal pictures or images of themselves. In a similar line, Kastenholz (2004, p. 719) notes that "product-self-congruity – the perceived match between a product's or its user's personality and consumer's self-image – is assumed to correlate positively with brand preference and/or purchase and this phenomenon is often ignored in destination image research". It has been theorized that purchase decision-making (i.e., product preference, purchase intention) is generally affected by person's self-image through the activation and operation of the self-consistency motives (Litvin and Kar 2003; Sirgy 1982). Self-image (self-congruity, self-concept) can be defined as the totality of the individual's thoughts and feelings having reference to himself/herself as an object or how individuals perceive themselves to be (Litvin and Kar 2003; Chon and Olsen 1991) and as a mental picture of themselves (Morrison 1996; Chon and Olsen 1991).

Consumers attempt to preserve or enhance their self images by selecting brands and products with images or personalities that they believe are congruent with their own images and avoid products that are not (Shifmann and Kanuk, 2001, p. 139; Decrop and Snelder

2005; Morrison 1996). Empirical evidence suggests that the self-image-product image congruity (commonly known as self-image congruence) can affect consumers' product preferences and their purchase intentions. Self-image congruence can also facilitate positive behavior and attitudes toward destinations. A recent research reported that respondents with higher levels of self-image congruity were more likely to prefer the brand and enjoy higher levels of satisfaction with the brand as compared to those with lower levels of self-image congruity (Jamal and Goode, 2001). A recent research by Sirgy and Su (2000) shows that travel behavior is influenced significantly by both self-congruity and functional congruity. Self-congruity is the match between the destination visitor image and tourists' self-concept (actual, ideal, social, and ideal social self-image). Functional congruity is the match between the utilitarian attributes of the destination and the tourist's ideal expectations related to those attributes. Self-congruity is found to influence functional congruity. Their research concludes that the destination environment influences the formation and change of the destination visitor image and the tourist-perceived utilitarian destination attributes. Kastenholz (2004) suggests a relationship between self-image and affective destination image. That is destination image congruency is considered to be a result of a direct comparison between self-image and affective destination image. According to her study, only the affective dimension is significant on destination self-image measurement, while the cognitive dimension is not. Several other studies have shown that congruency between a person's self-image and destination image is an important factor in evaluating the attractiveness of destinations and tourist satisfaction (Foley and Fahy 2004; Litvin and Kar 2003; Eclipse, 2003; Jenkins 1999). As Jenkins (2003) notes, a postcard may affirm individual's (sender) identity with that scene, attraction, landmark, resorts, destination, etc. We propose:

P3: Images depicted by postcards may correspond to the individual's self-image. Postcards can facilitate development of favorable attitude/ behavioral intentions toward that particular destination, provided that images rendered by postcards are in congruence with the recipient's self-image.

P4: Destination image congruency is strongly determined by affective image-self image match than by the match between cognitive image and self image.

POSTCARDS: DESTINATION PERSONALITY

A brand is a collection of images and ideas representing an economic producer; more specifically, it refers to the concrete symbols such as a name, logo, slogan, and design scheme (wilkipedia). Brand recognition and other reactions are created by the accumulation of experiences with the specific product or service, both directly relating to its use, and through the influence of advertising, design, and media commentary (wilkipedia). A brand is a symbolic embodiment of all the information connected to a company, product or service. A brand serves to create associations and expectations among products made by a producer. A brand often includes an explicit logo, fonts, color schemes, symbols, sound which may be developed to represent implicit values, ideas, and even personality (wilkipedia). Personality can be defined as a dynamic and organized set of characteristics possessed by a person that uniquely influences his or her cognitions, motivations, and behaviors in various situations (Ryckman, 2004 wilkipedia). Based on the premise that brands can have personalities in much the same way as humans, Brand Personality describes brands in terms of human characteristics. Brand personality is seen as a valuable factor in increasing brand engagement and brand attachment, in much the same way as people relate and bind to other people. Lively brand personality reaches out to the consumer, helps them to express themselves, and thus bestows meaning to the relationship. It is not unusual to see the consumer choose brands that better fit his or her personal style, or that aptly compliment his or her status.

The power of a brand resides in the consumer' mind from both lived (purchase and usage) and mediated (advertising and promotion) experiences (Shiffman and Kanuk, 2001, p. 141). From a semiotic perspective, an advertisement may be defined as: "a sign, representing the actual product image (or object), the meaning of which is dependent on the interpretation of the ad recipient (interpretant), which in turn is based on the context in which the ad (sign) occurs" (Dingena, 1994, p.36). Brand Personality Creation through Advertising Hans Ouwersloot and Anamaria Tudorica, 2001. Brand personalities are created in different ways and with different tools. However the creation always involves active communication on the side of destination. The set of human characteristics associated with a brand is a crucial bridge that makes the brand relevant to the consumer, and advertising tools are the carriers to bring forth the brand personality. The psychographic variables like emotions associated with the brand image constitute the personality of a brand. Although the experiences of the consumers with the brand cultivate such personality, advertising plays a dominant role in personality creation. Brand personality traits are formed and influenced by any direct or indirect contact that the consumer has with a brand. A brand, unlike a person, cannot think, feel or act. A brand has no objective existence at all; it is simply a collection of perceptions in the mind of the consumer. Consumers accept the marketing actions to humanize brands. One explanation for this can be found in the theories of animism. This theory suggests that there exists need by people to anthropomorphize objects in order to facilitate interactions with the nonmaterial world (Fournier, 1998). Anthropomorphization occurs when human qualities are attributed to nonhuman objects, e.g. brands. Consumers easily assign personality qualities to inanimate objects like brands in thinking about brands as if they are human characters (Blackston, 1993; Fournier, 1998; J. Aaker, 1997). Indirectly, the brand personality is created by all the elements of the marketing mix. Betra, Lehmann and Singh (1993) suggest that the personality of a brand is created over time, by the entire marketing mix of the brand – "its price (high or low, odd or even), retail store location (imagery associations), product formulation (ingredients, benefits), product form (solid/liquid, etc.), packaging details (color, size, material, shape), symbol used in all phases of the brand communication, sales promotion, and media advertising" (p. 93). Travellers will attempt to preserve, enhance, alter, or extend their self-images by preferring holiday products or services believed to be consistent with their relevant self-image and by avoiding products and destinations that are not. Examples for existing personalities include unspoiled –pristine natural and/or socio-cultural aspects "100% Pure New Zealand", diversity - beach +, different segments," Amazing Thailand, Incredible India", Old and New, Traditional and Modern –variety Culture –"Malaysia: Truly Asia". In branding Australia, authorities use a logo of yellow kangaroo against red sun over background of green and blue sea. This is done to brand Australia as youthful, stylish, vibrant, diverse, and adventurous. Colors are carefully used to signify, coolness and endless (blue), cleanliness (green), warmness, life, energy, youth ness, friendliness (yellow) (Fabricious, 2006). We propose:

P₅: Emotions that destinations evoke in consumers through mediated experiences (e.g., viewing postcards) are likely to result in personification of that destination and this will in turn affect their behavioral intentions toward that particular destination.

P₆: Congruence between destination personality and individual's self image would lead to preference (consideration) of that particular destination depicted in a postcard.

CONCLUSION

Destinations may possess a personality that consumers either use as an avenue for self-expression or to experience the anticipated emotional benefits that differentiate one destination from another. These perceived destination personalities emerge through the different ways destinations present themselves, including postcards. However, research on brand personality and the symbolic use of brands largely has been restricted to how consumers express themselves by choosing brands and has ignored how destinations themselves perceive their brand personalities. Moreover, brand personality often has been discussed with clear reference to products and corporate brands, but not to destinations and how this is communicated via holiday postcards. The contention of this study is that congruence between travelers' motivation and image that the destination releases through postcards can shape how the destination is personified, and that personality and self image congruence can be related to travelers' choices (Hankinson 2004; Wee 2004; Wysong et all. 2002; Kim, Han and Park 2001). For example choice of colors in postcards can help authorities in their attempt for building favorable personalities.

Aaker (1997) proposed a 5-dimensional instrument to assess "the set of human characteristics associated with a brand" (p. 347): Sincerity (e.g., honest, down-to-earth, wholesome, cheerful), Excitement (e.g., daring, spirited, imaginative, up-to-date); Competence (e.g., reliable, intelligent, successful); Sophistication (e.g., charming, upper class, feminine); Ruggedness (e.g., outdoorsy, tough, Western). According to Aaker (1997, p. 348), brand personality attributions are based on (i) Person-related associations: Perceived personality traits of people associated with a brand come to describe the brand's personality (e.g., typical user/ user imagery, testimonials, employees of company, CEO, etc.), and (ii) Product-related associations and inferences: Personal or others' experiences while using the brand, product category associations and associations induced by the brand name, symbol or logo, the advertising style, the price, and the distribution channel. While adapted for the use of destination personality measurement, this instrument has inherent flaws. Conceptually problematic items (among others): ´competence´ (reflects abilities, not personality), ´feminine´ (descriptive?, value judgment?), ´Western´ (values?), as well as recent findings pinpointing fundamentally different processes at the neural level suggest different knowledge structures being used while making "personality" judgments about people or brands, respectively raises questions about the validity of the instrument. Brand personality should thus be redefined as "the set of human personality traits that are both applicable and relevant for brands." (Bosnjak, Rammstedt and Tuten, 2004).

REFERENCES

Aaker, J. L. (1997). Dimensions of brand personality. *Journal of Marketing Research*, 34, 347-356.

Ajzen, I. (2001). Nature and operation of attitudes. *Annual Review of Psychology*, 52, 27 – 58.

Back, K. (2001). *Effects of price, brand name, and advertising information on travelers' hotel evaluations*. In Second Graduate Conference, Las Vegas (pp. 289-303).

Baloğlu, S., and Brinberg, D. (1997). Affective images of tourism destinations. *Journal of Travel Research*, 35 (4), 11-15.

Baloğlu, S., and Mangaloğlu, M. (2001). Tourism destination images of Turkey, Egypt, Greece, and Italy as perceived by US-based tour operators and travel agents. *Tourism Management*, 22; 1-9.

Bamberg, S., Ajzen, I., and Schmidt, P. (2003). Choice of travel mode in theory of planned behaviour: the roles of past behaviour, habit, and reasoned action. *Basic and Applied Social Psychology*, 25 (3), 175 – 187.

Bansal, H., and Eiselt, H. A. (2004). Exploratory research of tourist motivations and planning. *Tourism Management*, 25, 387-396.

Beerli, A., and Martin, J. D. (2004a). Tourists' characteristics and the perceived image of tourist destinations: a quantitative analysis – a case study of Lanzarote, Spain. *Tourism Management*, 25, 623 – 636.

Beerli, A., and Martin, J. D. (2004b). Factors influencing destination image. *Annals of Tourism Research*, 31 (3), 657-681.

Betra, R., Lehmann, D., and Singh, D. (1993). *The brand personality component of brand goodwill: some antecedents and consequences*. In Aaker and Biel, Brand Equity and Advertising: Advertising's Role in Building Strong Brands (pp. 83-95). Hillsdale, USA: Lawrence Earlbaum Associates Publisher.

Blackston, M. (1993). *Beyond brand personality: building brand relationships*. In Aaker, D. A., and Biel, A., Brand Equity and Advertising: Advertising's Role in Building Strong Brands (pp. 83-95). Hillsdale, USA: Lawrence Earlbaum Associates Publisher.

Bosnjak, M., Rammstedt, B., and Tuten, L. T. (2004). *What does Aaker's brand personality scale actually measure?*. University of Mannheim, Dept. of Psychology II, ZUMA Mannheim, Germany, Virginia Commonwealth University, Richmond, VA, USA. (http://www.psyconsult.de/bosnjak/media/presentations/CPR2005_Bosnjak_Ramstedt_Tuten_BPS.pdf ?wb_session_id=d55fef214ab34d134f5f8bb2e37271f8)

Cai, L. A. (2002). Cooperative branding for rural destinations. *Annals of Tourism Research*, 29 (3), 720-742.

Cai, L. A., Feng, R., and Breiter, D. (2004). Tourist purchase decision involvement and information preferences. *Journal of Vacaiton Marketing*, 10 (2), 138-148.

Chang, J., Wall, G., and Chu, S. T. (2006). Novelty seeking at aborginal attractions. *Annals of Tourism Research*, 33 (3), 729-747.

Chen, J. S., and Gürsoy, D. (2001). An investigation of tourists' destination loyalty and preferences. *International Journal of Contemporary Hospitality Management*, 13 (2), 79-83.

Chon, K. S., and Olsen, M. D. (1991). Functional and symbolic congruity approaches to consumer satisfaction / dissatisfaction in tourism. *Journal of International Academy of Hospitality Research*, 28 (3), 1-11.

Cohen, J. B., Fishbein, M., and Athola, O. T. (1972). The nature and uses of expectancy – value models in consumer attitude research. *Journal of Marketing Research*, 9, 456 – 460.

Cooper, C., Fletcher, J., Gilbert, D., and Wanhill, S. (1993). *Tourism: Principles and Practice*. Pitman Publishing, UK.

Crompton, J. L. (1979). An assessment of the image of Mexico as a vacation destination and influence of geographical location upon that image. *Journal of Travel Research*, 17 (4), 18-24.

Day, J., Skidmore, S. ve Koller, T. (2002). Image selection in destination positioning: a new approach. *Journal of Vacation Marketing*, 8 (2), 177 – 186.

Decrop, A., and Snelder, D. (2005). A grounded typology of vacation decision making. *Tourism Management*, 26, 121-132.

Dingena, M. (1994). *The creation of meaning in advertising: Interaction of figurative advertising and individual differences in processing styles*. Amsterdam, Netherlands: Thesis Publishers.

Eclipse (2003). *Destination image. Eclipse* (the periodic publication from Moonshine Travel Marketing for destination marketer. edition 1: 4-5. www.moonshine.org

Edwards, E. (1996). *Postcards – greetings from another world*. (197 – 221), Selwyn, T. (Editor), The Tourist Image Myths and Myth Making in Tourism, John Wiley and Sons Publication, USA.

Etchner, C. M., and Ritchie, J. R. B. (1991). The meaning and measurement of destination image. *Journal of Tourism Studies*, 2 (2), 2-12.

Fishbein, M., and Ajzen, I. (1975). *Belief, attitude, intention, and behaviour: an introduction to theory and research*. Boston, Addison – Wesley.

Foley, A., and Fahy, J. (2004). Incongruity between expression and experience: The role of imagery in supporting the positioning of a tourism destination brand. *Journal of Brand Management*, 11 (3), 209-217.

Fournier, S. M. (1998). Consumers and their brand: developing relationship theory in marketing. *Journal of Consumer Research*, 24(3). 343-373.

Gartner, W. J. (1996). *Tourism Development: principles, process and policies*. New York, USA: Van Nostrand Reinhold.

Gnoth, J. (1997). Tourism motivation and expectation formation. *Annals of Tourism Research*, 24 (2), 283-304.

Goossens, C. (2000). Tourism informations and pleasure motivation. *Annals of Tourism Research*, 27 (2), 301-321.

Gunn, C. (1972). *Vacationscape: Designing Tourist Regions*. Austin: Bureu of Business Research, University of Texas.

Ha, C. L. (1998). The theory of reasoned action applied to brand loyalty. *Journal of Product and Brand Management*, 7 (1), 51 – 57.

Hankinson, G. (2004). The brand images of tourism destinations: a study of the silency of organic images. *Journal of Product and Brand Management*, 13 (1), 6-14.

Henderson, P. W., Cote, J. A., Leong, S. M., and Schmitt, B. (2003). Building strong brands in Asia: selecting the visual components of image to maximize brand strenght. *International Journal of Research in Marketing*, 20, 297-313.

Hong, S., Kim, J., Jang, H., and Lee, S. (2006). The role of catagorization, affective image and constraints on destination choice: an application of the NMNL model. *Tourism Management*, 27, 750 - 761.

Hosany, S., Ekinci, Y., and Uysal M. (2006). Destination image and destination personality: An application of branding theories to tourism places. *Journal of Business Research*, 59, 638-642.

Jamal A., and Goode, M.M.H. (2001). *Marketing Intelligence and Planning*. 19 (7), 482-492.

Jenkins, O. H. (2003). Photography and travel brochures: the circle of representation. *Tourism Geographies*, 5 (3), 305-328.

Jenkins, O. H. (1999). Understanding and measuring tourist destination images. International Journal of Tourism Research, 1 (1), 1-15.

Kar, G.H., and Litvin S. W. (2003). Destination image. Eclipse (the periodic publication from Moonshine Travel Marketing for destination marketer). *Research Report*, 1, 1-4.

Kastenholz, E. (2004). Assessment and role of destination-self-congruity. *Annals of Tourism Research*, 31 (3), 719-723.

Kim, H., and Richardson, S. L. (2003). Motion picture impacts on destination images. *Annals of Tourism Research*, 30 (1), 216 – 237.

Kim, C. K., Han, D., and Park, S. B. (2001). The effect of brand personality and brand identification on brand loyalty: Applying the theory of social identification. *Japanese Pyschological Research*, 43 (4), 195-206.

Klenosky, D. (2002). The "pull" of destinations: a means-end investigation. *Journal of Travel Research*, 40, 385-395.

Kotler, P., Bowen, J., and Makens, J. (1996). *Marketing for Hospitality and Tourism*. Second Edition, Prentice-Hall International Inc. U.S.A.

Kraus, S. J. (1995). Attitudes and the prediction of behavior: a metaanalysis of the empirical literature. *Personality and Social Psychology Bulletin*, 21, 58–75.

Lam, T., and Hsu, C. H. C. (2006). Predicting behavioral intention of choosing a travel destination. *Tourism Management*, 27, 589 – 599.

Leisen, B. (2001). Image segmentation: the case of tourism destination. *Journal of Services Marketing*, 15 (1), 49-66.

Litvin, S. W., and Kar, G. H. (2003). Individualism / collectivism as a moderating facyor to the self-image congruity. *Journal of Vacation Marketing*, 10 (1), 23-32.

Mackay, K. J., and Fesenmaier, D. R. (1997). Pictorial element of destination in image formation. *Annals of Tourism Research*, 24 (3), 537 – 565.

Mannell, R., and Iso-Ahola, S. (1987). Psychological nature of leisure and tourist experiences. *Annals of Tourism Research*, 14, pp. 314–331.

Markwick, M. (2001). Postcard from Malta: image, consumption, context. *Annals of Tourism Research*, 28 (2), 417 – 438.

Martin, J. L. E. (2003). Modelling determinants of tourism demand as a five-stage process: a discrete choice methodological approach. *Tourism and Hospitality Research*, 4 (4), 341-354.

Mill, R. C., and Morrison, A. M. (1985). *The Tourism System: An Introductory Text*. First Edition, Prentice-Hall International Inc., USA.

Morrison, A. M. (1996). *Hospitaliy and Travel Marketing*. Second Edition, Thomson Publishing Inc., U.S.A.

Moutinho, L. (1987). Consumer behaviour in tourism. *European Journal of Marketing*, 21, 10; 5 – 7.

Ryan, C. (1997). *The tourist experience*: The new introduction, Cassell, London.

Ryckman, R. M. (2004). *Theories of personality* (8th ed.). Belmont, CA, USA: Thomson.

Sirakaya, E., and Woodside, A. G. (2005). Building and testing theories of decision making by travellers. *Tourism Management*, 26, 815-832.

Sirgy, J. M. (1982). Self-concept in consumer behaviour: A critical review. *Journal of Consumer Research*, 9 (3), 287-300.

Sirgy, J. M., and Su. (2000). Destination Image, Self-Congruity, and Travel Behavior: Toward an Integrative Model. *Journal of Travel Research*, 38 (4), 340-352.

Shiffman, L. G., and Kanuk, L. L. (2001). *Consumer Behavior*. Prentice Hall.

Sorolla, R. G., Garcia, M. T., and Bargh, J. A. (1999). The automatic evaluation of pictures. *Social Cognition*, 17 (1), 76 – 96.

Sorolla, R. G. (1996). *Affective and Cognitive Influences on the Immediate Expression of Attitudes: Are Feelings Really First?*. Submitted Doctoral Dissertation, New York University.

Stabler, M. J. (1995). *The image of regions: theoretical and empirical aspects*. In B. Goodall and g. Ashworth (Eds). Marketing in Tourism Industry: The Promotion of Destination Regions (pp. 133-159). London.

Stafford, B.M., 1996. *Good Looking: Essays on the Virtue of Images*. MIT Press, Cambridge, MA.

Urry, J. (1990). *The consumption of tourism*. Sociology, 24 (1), 23-35.

Uzzell, D. (1984). An Alternative Structuralist Approach to the Psychology of Marketing. *Annals of Tourism Research*, 4, 12–24.

Wee, T. T. T. (2004). Extending human personality to brands: the stability factor. *Journal of Brand Management*, 11 (4), 317-330.

White, C. F. (2004). Destination image: to see or not to see. *Internaional Journal of Contemporary Hospitality Management*, 16 (4/5), 309-314.

Winiwarter, V. (2001). *Buying a dream come true*. Rethinking History, 5(3), 451-454.

Wysong, S., Munch, J., and Kleiser, S. (2002). An investigation into the brand personality construct, its antecedents and its consequences. *American Marketing Association Conference Proceedings*, 13, 512-518.

Yoon, Y., and Uysal, M. (2005). *An examination of effects of motivation and satisfaction on destination loyalty: a structural model. Tourism Management*, 26, 45-56.

Yüksel, A., and Akgül, O. (2007). Postcards as affective image makers: an idle agent in destination marketing. *Tourism Management*, 28.

In: Tourist Satisfaction and Complaining Behavior
Editor: Atila Yüksel

ISBN 978-1-60456-002-2
© 2008 Nova Science Publishers, Inc.

Chapter 18

DO WE NEED TO CHANGE THE RESEARCH PERSPECTIVE TO BETTER UNDERSTAND CUSTOMER DISSATISFACTION? HOW COULD IT BE?[1]

Burak Mil and Atila Yüksel
Adnan Menderes University, Turkey

INTRODUCTION

It is complained about that the number of the sufficiently scientific high quality studies at miscellaneous platforms are not increasing and it is emphasized that the specific contribution made to the related literature cannot be at the required level. Nevertheless that the determination is appropriate, for our colleagues who will create an effect, there shall not be ruled out the deficiencies of the environment which will create such effect. Furthermore, the courses and/or administrative loads taken with different reasons are affected by habituations, no exhortation, stagnancy, etc. many other reasons which are among the preliminaries of the specific contribution mentioned above. In the balance of encouragement of the candidates to researching and/or giving a lecture according to the requirements and their talents it is seen that the equilibrium of the balance is tending in favor of this latest. While restructuring the desired equilibrium, question of "How is the researcher" shall storm the brains. At this question which has beside the quorum of the opinions regarding to its significance and on the other side a polemical definition/application will not be correct to dogmatize. However due that the question has not a satisfactorily answer, it will lead to the growing the researchers who will affect the shaping of the future by means of "wrong tradition" maybe, and also to be emaciated.[2] The humans tend to make only those things that they could see.

---

[1] A Turkish version of the paper was published in Seyahat ve Otel İşletmeciliği Dergisi, 2007.
[2] All the opinions expressed herein are reflecting the observation of the academician whose education is continuing and shall not be deemed as a sequence of strict rules. Is licit the more expanding or constricting in the future of this approach.

Is the answer of this question laying in the question of "who is not researcher?" Is the answer of "Why is the research made" question describing the researcher? Should the researcher identity be defined by means of features of a good researcher? Is correct to ascribe to the researcher titles as "innovator/traditionalist, good/bad, dogmatic/pragmatic, international/national etc.? Although that the research and researcher are an integral overall, is normal that the "research" to affect the researcher? The kind, content, complexity, frequency of the research is effective in the maturation of the researcher and the difference creates worth. [3]

Is being a researcher, trying to find out new things in an obsessive way, not looking from a different perspective to the currently existing things for just to be the first, to make himself spiritual unapproachable beyond the enigmatic sentences, to really break off and to be neurotic, to be monopolistic at knowledge/share, to be neuter/unresponsive, to not tolerate to alternative, to not issue more knowledge/consideration than that taken, to be protuberant/ hollow and to not give pleasure? Is the "researcher" this one taking refuge in the knowledge maybe not existing but created in the shade of the scales easily accepted based on the dexterous eulogies related to who is improved by others? Is the "researcher" awakening to the elimination by the averages of the deepness from the extremes? Is the researcher this one running to catch the truth or this creating the truth? Or is researcher this one believing to the end or this creating a cradle at the end? Is the researcher the edifier or the nurturer? Is the researcher this one continuing the candidates with whom he is interfering in the research/development focused working branches? Is the researcher the describer or the analyzer? Is the researcher this one developing the scale? Is the researcher finding out that while measuring a concept, a fact the items used in the scale maybe will never reflect the emotions of the researched persons? Is the researcher the reason of the concept and application decoys? Is the researcher being assertive? Is the researcher at the durability or at the transience? Is the researcher at the authenticity or at the painstaking? Is the researcher the occupation or the life style/philosophy? Is the researcher seeing or looking? Is the researcher this one believing to what he is seeing or seeing this that is he believing? Is the researcher taking refuge beyond the power of the mass of number or awakening to the qualitative of the numbers? Is the researcher the one scanning or assessing? Is the researcher this that takes the points or take the points gotten? Is the researcher at the "I think therefore I exist (cogito ergo sum)" or "I discuss (get discussed) so I exist"? Is the researcher the adventure or the refuge? Is the researcher leaving trace or scenting? Is the researcher the sovereignty or the facilitation?

The considerations about how the researcher is (or who should be) firstly shall be the subject of the academic discussions. Being aware that we are under the decisiveness of the numbers from the columns of the daily newspaper the scientific articles published in the most distinguished academic magazines, the purpose of herein study written with the ideal of querying the certainly seen matter is to get asked to the precise the question of "wonder I".

---

[3] Here, until the achieving by different means the accumulated and traditional knowledge the process of the research keeps a significant place regarding to being open to the ability of teaching, of being distinctive, convertible and to renew itself. However, one of the miscue of the researcher of accepting the knowledge and approaches located by means of essays, without being persuaded could be the creator of the further miscues. Generally the studies are ascribing to the derivatives of the original instead of the original study. These kinds of applications are rising as the products of the by "theories" instead of "main" theory.

WHAT IS POSITIVISM?

Positivism, is a deductive approach using the quantitative data due to generalizing about the nature of the facts and human behaviors by means of empirical analyzes and to set to the rules. With other works, it is an philosophical current which is based on the empiric knowledge idea (Günay, 2004) and argues that it is the single valid method of the science and scientific management to reach to the knowledge and tries to explain in general the nature of the world by means of a systematic thought(Neyhouse, 2002). Many scientists and philosopher tried to explain the positivism in different ways; however, the term of positivism has firstly been used by Auguste Comte (Sunata, 2005).

The fact of positivism shaped and developed with such knowledge base by time has to change its form due to the separation of every derivation from the original and has ignored the metaphysic speculation and accepted the apparent as reality (Marshall, 1999). Positivism is an epistemological approach explanative regarding the outside world and aiming to gather foreseeable knowledge related to the future. It provides that the relations between knowledge obtained by mean of observation and experiment, acts and facts to be understood (Keat and Urry, 1994). Positivism is a continual – usual – current until the antic eras.

The application of the positivist methodology which is the most popular method of creating of the scientific knowledge has gone further even that its own rules of the positivism. Especially in the explanation of the studies the belief of the need of numerically explanation of every concept, is not gone further again that the qualitative comments. The numbers have distinctiveness in today's world in every field. The amount of the income, the expression of the way gone as distance and the number of the lived years and read books are, confront us such the most critical measure. Well, is it really true? Shall it be so delusive to speak about the characters of the numbers other than their numerical properties inside of them?

In the positivism the dialectic of the science is one. The dialectic and method of the explanation and affirmation used in the science is one, is single (unification of science). The methods used in the Physical Sciences and Social Sciences and the perspective to these sciences is the same. We cannot talk about a different method of the Social Sciences. In the positivism an expression is meaningful only if may be verified or falsified. There is not the third option. It is called verifiability principle. So the human may know the meaning of such expression under the situations in which an expression is true or false. This may be completely defined in the conditions where under the principle of verifiability the answer of a question is "yes" or "not". In the way the question is made independent, the conditions are defined by making the question independent and this is called specification principle (www.akademikkariyer.net, 05.10.2006).

It is said that in the positivism a third possibility does not exist. The answer to be given to this question is yes or not. However, in the research methods, the role of the researcher is not reflected within a research made. Because, the fact that the observation may change the observed thing can be clearly seen by examples from the daily life. In an example it is said that just the existence of the anthropologist there who has made research in a little local county which has been isolated from the modern life has changed the life of the county. The matter which was the aim of the knowledge that he wanted to obtain has been changed as a result of his analyze.

The principle of verifiability is coming at the top of the most queried principles which the "verity" is queried within the positivist methodology. The famous physician who developed the waive theory of the quantum physic, is drawing the attention to a special connection related to the verity fact. The physician who prepared a fictive experiment is imagining that in the box is a cat and near the cat is a mechanism related to the beaming to be made by a radioactive elements which made the beta disintegration. If the beta particle spread in the mechanism crashed into the detector, the poison gas to be effused will kill the cat; if the gas will not be effused that cat will remain alive. When it is looked at the box the possibility of see the cat alive it is seen half at half as certain "verity". However, it is not possible to understand the situation of the cat without opening the box. When the box will be opened it will be seen if the cat is alive or death. But, in this stage there shall be mentioned an interesting situation. The (researcher) who made the experiment may defer as long as he wants the last step, the attempt to open the box. Here, due that the clear situation of the cat is not known is appearing a deferred aliveness-deadness situation and so it express the mixing up in an affair possibility for the research. Namely, the result of the research has the possibility of a third option. If it is presupposed that the cat is seen alive together with the opening of the box, in this stage the all other main and middle possibilities are declining to the possibility which is true and which may be supported. So as the meaning earned from this fictive experiment it could mean that at every research at least one possibility may exist. So minimally the researcher shall keep this in his mind.

POSITIVIST RESEARCH

The scientific research is the overall of the processes which have got a certain system, are consistent, related to each other and complementing each other. The research made with the positivist methodology have a hypothetic and deductive structure. The researcher is verifying the hypothesis resulted from the theory. These hypotheses are made by establishing causative binds between the elements which are effective in its occurring (Kuş, 2003). With other words, the research question or the hypothesis is shaped. The design which will provide the credible and valid answer for the hypothesis is designed and is applied. The results of the research are evaluated by propound the relations with the previously knowledge (Erdoğan 2003).

The philosophy has interested with the nature of the existence and knows ability due to bring a rationalistic explanation about the existence against to the mythology which means the dignifying of the truth make it imaginary. The scientific knowledge increasing by time has created its own sub branches (such mathematics, medicine). By its effect the philosophic currents and ecoles have been appeared. Even that production of the knowledge has begun in pre-modern period, "the science as a discipline" has been established in the modern period. The two main branches of the philosophy which at first were seen as the base of the science the occurred natural sciences and social sciences has became the two different "total of the disciplines" of the philosophy. At the being of the 17th and 18th centuries the term of "science" has been used only as the natural sciences called as basic sciences and their technological applications. The natural sciences are including the overall systematic knowledge of the basic laws related to the object (Sunata, 2005). The main appearing point of the philosophy is the relation of knowing with existence and spirit with the object. In fact the answers given to these questions have made the camps. Yet, these who are taking as base the spirit and subjective are creating the idealist camp and these taking as base the nature and the objective are creating the materialist camp.

The scientists many times are trying to reveal this relation by means of observations made by them. These relations entering in our life as "facts" are available as far as may be comprehended as a physical reality. Due that the main aim of the scientific explanations shall be based on the observation of the "real" facts the brittle relation between the comprehending and misapprehension is come to light. As every banal human the scientists are presupposing in majority as real the ideas and facts which are supported by the comprehensions and realities. Many things are constructed on this "reality" scenario. Whereas, some times the perceptions may confuse the human. A person who is looking for a while directly to a light source even that he closes his eye the imagination of the light continues to be still before of him. Even that the retina is not exposed to the light, our brain with the stimulus taken from the retina keeps continuing the light play. Due to these explanations we may reach the result that the events and facts which easily are seen as reality do not need to be real.

Additionally to all of these explained it should be not ignored that the beliefs and expectations are playing a key role in the perception of the reality and it is affected by these. The comprehension knows what find out our senses, and the thing made by our intellect is the commenting or making sense of these perceptions. As Charles Wynn and Arthur Wiggins said in their book called "Quantum bouncing in wrong way" instead of the phrase of "I wouldn't believe if I wouldn't see" becomes more meaningful. The positivist approach, is accepting the data source as the transferring wire of the natural knowledge and neuter. Is not the researcher the persons which shaping the research and continues to researching with the energy and sense taken from that? The peccable circle from this approach shall be certainly criticized. The researcher is a part of the research and the research is a part of the researcher. Not its reason, result or excuses.

CRITICAL APPROACH[4]

The Frankfurt philosophers, have been interested to critic the limits which have been tried to be adopted by force to the ethical mind at the positivist philosophies. The criticism of the positivism in this respect has become one of the most central interests of the thought which will be called post facto as critical theory. The most important element within the critical theory is the defense of the "intellect" which is comprehended as a critical talent joining

---

[4] The critical theory is the product of the new Marxists a group of German who are disturbed from the economical determinism tendency especially of this theory from the situation of the Marxist theory. The Frankfurt School is taken its name from the Frankfurt Social Researches Institute which has been found in Germany in 1923. The school has been officially founded on February 23 in 1923 in Frankfurt. Its members have been active before this officially foundation. In 1930s together with the acceding of the Nazis, mostly of the leader members have immigrated to States and continued their scientific studies there. They have continued these activities at an institute which was in collaboration with Colombia University. After the Second World War some of the criticism theoreticians have go back to Germany. The others remained in the States. The criticism theory has today been carried out of the borders of Frankfurt School. (www.felsefe.gen.tr, 05.10.2006).

together with the knowledge the integration of the human in a way to forward the freedom with the transforming of the world (www.felsefe.gen.tr, 05.10.2006).

Basically the positivism is trying to expose the relations between social fact and language which determines these and words by means of staying far from the approaches based to the opinionated presumptions especially within the frame of the limitations created by language and filtrations (www.merih.net, 01.10.2006). Due that the perception is based on the presumption it is asserted that the resource of the knowledge is the outer world or represents the out world as it is (Günay, 2005). Due that is both not opened to the comments and also deals with the subject within the frame of the world, the positivism may carry the meaning that has not the criticism aspect (Günay, 2004). However, according to Lundberg (1939) the results achieved from so detailed research could not be always successful and some times the positivist social thoughts may lead to absurd results. This situation may be due to both the empirical and methodologist problems. In this case the deficiencies of the positivist approach could be removed only by means of other methods (Clark, Riley, Wilkie and Wood, 1998). Beside to this as mentioned before the positivism is insufficient regarding the subjects such human behaviors and attitudes. In this case according to the positivist approach making use of critical bases to reach to the objective knowledge may be healthier. Nevertheless, the point that shall be taken into consideration here is that the critical approaches have never conclusiveness (Clark et al. 1998).

One of the other part criticized of the positivism it that it is accepting that all the studies are applicable with a single scientific method. For all the disciplines it is dealing with the physical relation as a reliability criterion. The positivists admit that the knowledge is naturally neuter. Beginning from this point, they are arguing that the positivism is materializing the social life and is accepting it as a natural process. According to the critical ecole, positivism ignores in a process these that are in effecting situation and see the same as passive elements determined by natural powers. Therefore, the critical ecole does not admit that the science may be applied to the human acts without querying the general rules. Another point is that it is contended with assessing the sufficiency of the materials related to the aims of the positivism. However, it not tends to the similar assessment of the similar aims. Naturally, the current order is materialized and the facts are dealt within the certain lines. The positivism is pushing the actor and social scientist to the passivity (www.felsefe.gen.tr, 05.10.2006). While the positivist approaches are subjecting the outlying realities with the models or statistical method, non positive knowledge related to the social subject with critical approaches among the subjective signs. There it is important to select the data which are objective and these which aren't objective in an equilibrate way and reach to the essential (Abbott, 1990).

The quantitative research among the eligibilities as collecting the data in big amounts, having a focus point, giving to the researcher the possibility of having the control in hand, comparability of data easily, has also weak aspects as not providing flexibility in the stage of collecting the data, remaining insufficient in understanding the social processes and is not revealing the meanings ascribed by the persons to the social facts.

The essential base of the critics forwarded to the positivist deductive approach and quantitative research on this subject are on the non suitability of performing the researches made on the humans and their behaviors with the researching techniques based on the positivism (prescriptive and severe) due that the social facts are a result of the human behaviors. On the other hand, when the human aspect of the researcher is taken into consideration, there are persons arguing that the even when taking the decision of the subject of the research it is not possible that the researcher to behave neuter and objective (Akgül, 2004).

WHAT IS THAT REAL?

Realism is the current admitting that the existence is available as free and objective from the human intellect. The reality is created from the objective and material structure of the relations. This structure cannot be directly observed. The things observed by us shall actually be explained with the structure of the material relations lying under. (Ozan, 2006).

In terms of philosophy it may be discussed about two kinds of realities. One of these is related to the structure of "tings" and the other to the "things". In the first is admitted the existence of an entity independent from the mind and in the second is admitted the existence of the experiment objects independent from the mind and perceptible which are holding their basic properties even when are not seen. According to the realistic approach there exists a world independent from the intellect. The trees, soils, and rocks are not made by the intellect of the conscious. Because they existed long before the humans existed (www.dogakoleji.com, 09.10.2006).

The critical realism is an approach appearing at beginning of 1980s and which especially has been spread in the field of the geographic and social sciences. The most important envoy of this current is Roy Bhaskar. He admits that the critical realism is a realism out of our perception and observation. The realism is made of the objective material structure. This structure cannot be directly observed. The things which we cannot observe shall be actually explained by means of the structure of the material relations lying under (Ashworth et al., 1990). Among the basic properties of the approach, presumptions of admitting the existence of an independent world from the knowledge, the knowledge related to this to have the property of being falsified, the existence of the exigency in the world and the availability of the natural or social objects compulsively to causative power and act methods and the ability of the existence of these structures even when they don't cause to the chain of the regularly facts, are taking place (Ozan, 2006).

The social and the natural realism are created by the real entities and their relations. The social realism is a world product of the cognitive sources created by the social actors of every social event within it and where the social regulations are the product of the material relations but which cannot be observed. In the positivist approach the realism is created from the event which can be observed apart. While is admitted that the positivism with its entities which could be not observed and attitude ignoring the structures and the causal power, it is clear that the critical realism is explaining the events and structures which can be observed and which not and makes these understandable. What is the power of the reality? Is it the number of the persons believing to something? Is it the power of persuading?

When it is looked at the studies made is can be easily seen that a style far from this querying and abstaining from discussing has been developed. Especially the tendency of call on numbers as the proof of every reason at the studies (admitting the complexity of the quantitative) mostly is going beyond the real research problem in the research. Another important point which it is ignored is the not being aware or ignoring the fact the numbers in every quantity have always qualitative meaning other that the numeric meanings. Yet, every numerical multiplication is not only related to the numbers. After a certain point the quantitative increasing is bring together the change from the quality. The most suitable example to that is the cancer from a tissue. Due that the cancer is the uncontrolled sharing of the cells it represents the most critical model effecting the change from the quality of the numerical increase. After a certain point the increasing occurring in the tissue and which cannot be controlled brings together the results of non ability of such tissue to perform its duty. It is completely clear in this example that may deceptive to percept always the numbers only as number. However, this who wants to be deceived is deceived. As it is mentioned in the letter written by Tevfik Frikret to its son: "Deception is an endless cure" (cf. Meriç, 1998: 238).

The researcher is the person searching the "reality". So how is caught or may be caught the "reality"? The researcher shall accept in advances that the "reality" is not stable. The reality is dynamic because it is alive. The desire of find out the reality shall be at all the searching peoples regardless their fields, educations, judges. Maybe at first it may be seen as an empty endeavor or a meaningless endeavor. Whereas this search is the course of curiosity, which is the essence of all science fields. Maybe Kemal Tahir is one of the writers summarizing this endeavor in the most beautiful way: "The reality confides itself hard, because it is alive, it is changeable. Due that it is alive and changeable once it is confided it does not remain in our hands forever. Therefore, the war to be made with the reality is endless. The victory of this war is from its continuity" (cf. Meriç, 2006: 250). The researcher shall be the discussing one more than the thinking one. The discussing and maybe the "loser". As Cemal Meriç said in its diary at the discussion the both parts are searching the reality together and due that it could not show to the other it is a victory (Meriç, 2006).

At first it became to search the god shaped with the belief that the universe is created from numbers, in the number and with the support of the pagan beliefs to make the numerical formulas from the orders of the commands of god and foresee the future. According to the kabala belief the god has created the world using the 10 numbers. The Arabians have prophesied using the ancient numeric system. Other than the Arabian and Hebrew applications the availability of a numerical meaning and provision of every letter in the Roman letter order, it gives clues about the effects of the numbers at that period on the daily life. Even that in our days this belief hasn't been lost it seems that it has only changed the target. In some of the fields the numbers have became worth more that themselves are expressing. In the world of the science the effects of this are clearly coincided.

When we are looking to the tourism research in an ample frame especially in the last years we are coinciding with studies interested so much with the number, tending so much on the numbers, which are emphasizing the numbers more than their aim, process, method and results. As one of its results beginning of use of the numerical based and computer aided statistical programs may be shown. However, it shall be not forgotten that the essential matter is not the numbers themselves is what they are showing. To see the reality shall have a look to what the hand shows not to the hand. The fact showed here is the qualitative notion beyond the numbers.

In a far east story is referring to two brothers keeping the budged book of the king. The two brothers who for month get stifled in the works of calculation and books firstly begin to not think anything other than the numbers. After a while everything for them became numbers. Without need to count they knew the number of the rice from the palm and the numbers of the sands from the sand of the shore. However they could not see either the rice or the sands. The only thing that they could see was the numbers.

CONCLUSION: ON THE EXISTENCE

What is the method or what shall be the method of querying the existence of something? Doesn't searching the existence of black in the black leading to the perspective error? Before searching an answer to these questions maybe the discussion that shall be made is again on the perception of the existence. In the process of a research, when the adaptation from the writing related to the problem of the research is joining with the preconception of the method used and advanced ascendancies of the researcher, we were witness for many times to the difference of the result to the firstly dealt with. As a reason of this the scientific contribution may be showed. However, is it also an ignoring? Maybe the thing that shall be thought is whether the found thing is that searched or not. The coincidence of Archimedes with the solution of the problem which has going into his mind at a time when he wasn't looking for cannot be submitted as its reason. Because, it isn't the same thing that the acquired thing to be approved to that searcher and coincide with the searched thing in a different place.

If we had to go into deeper details on thinking about the dilemma of where the existence shall be searched, it may be possible to reach to the hypothesis that the existences admitted as contrary to each other may be the approver of each one. The method of the applications which we make in the course of our daily life within being aware about sometimes may be more substantive that our research designs. As example the researcher who wants to measure the satisfaction of the customers, if asks always its questions on the satisfaction is there really the thing measure the level of the satisfaction? Where is beginning, is ending or how is shaped the concept of the satisfaction? Without querying the dissatisfaction may the satisfaction be learned? Let presume that we are searching a black fleck on a surface formed by black and white colors. In which part are we looking for? In the black part or in the white part? If we searching in the black part, we cannot see any difference because trying to differ the black on the black is just loss of time. However, on the white part even the smallest fleck is conspicuous. As in other sample it is the black stones from the rice which is white may be easily hand picked.

The presumption that the existence shall be searched at a contrary existence is creating a very critical point in the research developed with a qualitative point of view. Because it is based on completely contrary facts against the positivist methodology. However, taking place in the counter camp of the positivist ecole in a field where the subject is the human such in the social sciences it doesn't always give the negative result. Over than that, by doing so the positivism is completely rejected or it is wrong to give the statement that every positivist research example is previously denied. If we have to go back to the black fleck, it is inevitable that the colors of the black on the black surface to be most distinguished. So the colors of the black are observed more clearly on the black surface. In such case the argumentation is returning to the beginning. The essential ideal is to determined what to be looked for, where to be looked for and how to be looked for. Related to this subject the perspective shall be determined and in this way the making of the error of dealing with, within the research is avoided.

The researcher shall be this searching. Searching but maybe this that never reaching to what he is searching. May be he shouldn't reach. The researcher in the social sciences is this running on the continuously changing "truth" and using the philosophy for this. The philosophy shall not be the method of find out of the researcher, shall be the method of continuously searching.

If it shall be tough on the searching process of the knowledge and experience qualification of the researcher – and thanks to that on the effect of the research- to itself, we may be easily be witness to the fact that this is before of all resulting from its own internal dynamics of the researcher. Even that the density of the mentioned qualification is not following a linear course, it may leave the researcher in the contradiction of courage-scare. The belief in respect of the assuredness of the "certain" knowledge is closely related to the principle of verifiability of advanced preconception of the positivist methodology and falsifiability principle of Popper. In this way the verifiable and not falsifiable is "admitted". However, if the admitted is just an illusion?

It may be discussed about an argumentation related to the subject and method of the research and ambivalence of the researcher. The reason of the ambivalence of researcher is many times the conscious. The researcher has got an intense accumulation of the comparative abstract knowledge related to the subject of the research will approach to the subject for imperturbable. The main reason of the care showed to this approach is knowledge. The consciousness researcher cannot create causal theory and designs its philosophy according to its knowledge. May be the most meaningful word was said by Shakespeare in his Hamlet called tragedy on the existence of this internal agent which rises at the formation of a research: "Consciousness makes coward of us all".

The researcher is not only this "finding out" what he is looking for. The thing that made the human researcher is the desire of tasting the ambition created by finding out answer to what he is looking for, more than the answer taken to his question at the end of the study promoted by him. This shall be like that.

REFERENCES

Abbott, A. (1990). Positivism and interpretatiton in sociology: lessons for sociologist from the history of stress research. *Sociological Forum,* 5 (3), 435 – 458.

Akgül, O. (2004). Tümdengelim ve Tümevarım Yaklaşımları ve Uygulamaları. *Seyahat ve Turizm Araştırmaları Dergisi,* 137-142

Ashworth, C. (1990). *The Strucuture of Social Theory*, Londra, USA: Macmillan.

Blaikie, N. (1993). *Approaches to Social Inquiry*, New York, USA: Harvester.

Clark, M. A., Riley, M. J., Wilkie, E., and Wood, R. C. (1998). *Researching and Writing Dissertations in Hospitality and Tourism.* International Thomson Business Press, 1. Ed. USA.

Erdoğan, İ. (2003). Pozitivist Metodoloji Bilimsel Araştırma Tasarımı İstatistiksel Yöntemler Analiz ve Yorum. Ankara, Turkey: ERK.

Günay, M. (2004). *Metinlerle Felsefeye Giriş.* Karahan Publishing, Birinci Basım.

Lundberg, G. A. (1939). "Contemporary positivism in sociology". *American Sociology Review,* 4 (1), 42 – 55.

Keat, R., and Urry, J. (1994). *Bilim Olarak Sosyal Teori,* İmge Publishing.

Kuş, E. (2003). *Nicel-Nitel araştırma Teknikleri.* Anı Publishing: Ankara.

Meriç, C. (2006). Bu Ülke. Iletişim Publishing, 27. Ed., İstanbul.

Meriç, C. (1998). Jurnal, Cilt 1. Iletişim Publishing. 5. Ed. İstanbul.

Marshall G. (1999). *Sosyoloji Sözlüğü.* Bilim ve Sanat Publishing. Ertem Matbaası.

Neyhouse, T. J. (2002). *Positivism in Criminological Tought: A Study in History and Use of Ideas,* LFB Scholarly Publishing, A.B.D..

Ozan, D.,E. Sosyal Bilimlerde Gerçekçi-İlişkisel Yaklaşımın Ana Hatları (httppraksis.orgfiles003Ozan.pdf#search=%22ele%C5%9Ftirel%20ger%C3%A7ek%C3%A7i%20yakla%C5%9F%C4%B1m%22, accessed 09.10.2006).

Sunata,U. (http://www.delidumrul.com/sb/modules.php?op=modloadandname=Newsandfile=article andsid=23, accessed 05.10.2006)

Wynn, C., and Wiggins, A. (2005). Yanlış Yönde Kuantum Sıçramalar. Tübitak Populer Bilim Kitapları, 4. Ed.: Ankara.

http://www.akademikkariyer.net/archive.asp?caid=214andaid=156 (09.10.2006)

http://www.dogakoleji.com/Dogaloji/menu.asp?bolum=icerikandicerik_id=186 (09.10.206)http://www.felsefe.gen.tr/elestirelsosyoloji.asp (05.10.2006)

http://www.merih.net/rhp/positivism.htm (01.10.2006)

LIST OF AUTHORS

Abdullah Tanrisevdi (BA in Tourism and Hotel Management, Dokuz Eylul University; MSc in Business Administration , Hacettepe University; PhD at Adnan Menderes University. E-mail: atanrisevdi@adu.edu.tr) is currently lecturer in the Aydin Vocational School – Marketing Program - Adnan Menderes University. His research interests are mainly in the area of electronic commerce, CRM, complaint management, and special interest tourism.

Ahmed Salih holds a Bachelors of Business Degree in Tourism Management from University of Queensland, Australia, and a Masters Degree in Tourism from University of Otago. Currently, he is reading for a Ph.D. in School of Hotel and Tourism Management at The Hong Kong Polytechnic University. He worked as Director (Trade Standards) at Ministry of Tourism and Civil Aviation, Government of Maldives prior to commencing studies for a Ph.D. His research interests include marine tourism, human resources in tourism industries in, sustainable tourism development, and tourism impacts.

Alison McIntosh (Ph. D) is Associate Professor, Department of Tourism & Hospitality Management, University of Waikato, New Zealand. Her main research interests are in tourists' experiences of heritage and culture, spiritual dimensions of tourism, and qualitative and critical approaches to tourism research. Alison has published in leading journals such as *Annals of Tourism Research, Journal of Travel Research, Tourism Management* and *Journal of Sustainable Tourism.*

Anna S. Mattila, is an Associate Professor at Pennsylvania State University. She holds a Ph.D. from Cornell University, an MBA from University of Hartford and a B.S. from Cornell University. Her research interests focuses on consumer responses to service encounters and cross-cultural issues in services marketing. Her work has appeared in the *Journal of the Academy of Marketing Science, Journal of Retailing, Journal of Service Research, Journal of Consumer Psychology, Psychology & Marketing, Journal of Services Marketing, International Journal of Service Industry Management, Cornell Hotel & Restaurant Administration Quarterly, Journal of Travel Research, International Journal of Hospitality Management, Tourism Management* and in *the Journal of Hospitality & Tourism Research.* She is a recipient of John Wiley & Sons Lifetime Research Award and The University of Delaware Michael D. Olsen Research Achievement Award. Web-link: www.personal.psu.edu/faculty/a/s/asm6

Atila Yüksel (BA in Tourism and Hotel Management, Dokuz Eylul University; MSc in Tourism Management, the University of Wales; Ph. D. at Sheffield Hallam University, ayuksel@adu.edu.tr) is an associate professor at the School of Tourism and Hospitality

Management, Adnan Menderes University. He has published articles, book chapters, conference papers on tourist satisfaction and complaint management, destination planning and marketing, and tourism research in prestigious scientific journals, including *Annals of Tourism Research, Tourism Management, Journal of Hospitality and Tourism Research, Journal of Travel and Tourism Marketing, Journal of Vacation Marketing, the Cornell Hotel and Restaurant Administration Quarterly, and the Journal of Travel and Tourism Research.*

Bettina Grün (MSc and PhD in Applied Mathematics, Vienna University of Technolgoy; E-mail: Bettina.Gruen@ci.tuwien.ac.at) is a Research Assistant at the Department of Statistics and Probability Theory of the Vienna University of Technology. Her main research interests are finite mixture modeling, statistical computing and quantitative methods in marketing research and tourism.

Burak Mil (BA in Tourism and Hotel Management, Mersin University; MSc in Tourism and Hotel Management, Mersin University, burakmil@gmail.com) is a lecturer at Didim Vocational School, Adnan Menderes University. He is currently a Ph. D. candidate at School of Tourism and Hospitality Management, Adnan Menderes University. He has a professional experience on tourism and hospitality industry and published articles and conference papers on HRM and tourism, and research methods. His research areas are gastronomy, research methods in tourism and tourist satisfaction.

Ergün Efendi holds a B.S. degree in Tourism and currently a research assistant and a postgraduate student at the Graduate School of Social Sciences, Adnan Menderes University (E-mail: eefendi@adu.edu.tr).

Fisun Yüksel (BA in Tourism and Hotel Management, Dokuz Eylul University; MSc in Tourism Management, Sheffield Hallam University, Ph. D. at Sheffield Hallam University: fisunyuksel@yahoo.com) is a faculty of School of Tourism and Hospitality Management, Adnan Menderes University. She has published articles on destination management, planning and marketing, tourist satisfaction and complaint management, and tourism research in prestigious scientific journals, including *Annals of Tourism Research, Tourism Management, Journal of Hospitality and Tourism Research, Journal of Travel and Tourism Marketing, Journal of Vacation Marketing, and the Journal of Travel and Tourism Research.* Her recent research is in the field of actor-network relationships.

Héctor San Martín (BA in Business Administration and Ph.D. at Cantabria University; smartinh@unican.es) is a Lecturer in the Faculty of Economics, Cantabria University. He has published articles, book chapters and conference papers on service marketing, tourist satisfaction, destination marketing, and marketing and tourism research in prestigious scientific journals, including *Industrial Marketing Management, Tourism Management,* and other Spanish journals.

Heejung Ro (Bachelor in Geography, Kyung Hee University; Master in Hotel Administration, University of Nevada Las Vegas; Master in Applied Statistics and Ph.D. in Hospitality Management, Penn State University) is an assistant professor of the Rosen College of Hospitality Management, University of Central Florida (Email: heejungro@hotmail.com). Her research focuses on consumer behavior, including consumer dissatisfaction and complaining behaviors, negative emotions and coping strategies, and service failure and service recovery.

Huong Le is a researcher in School of Management and Marketing, Faculty of Commerce, University of Wollongong (Northfields Ave, Wollongong, 2522 NSW, Australia. E-mail: huong@uow.edu.au). Huong has completed her PhD at the University of Sydney in Australia, she has published a number of journal articles, books chapters and conference papers relating to aspects of marketing, and management. Her research interests are arts management, arts marketing, and tourism marketing.

Ignacio A. Rodríguez del Bosque (BA in Business Administration and Ph.D. at Oviedo University; rbosquei@unican.es) is a Marketing Professor in the Faculty of Economics, Cantabria University. He has written and co-authored numerous journal articles and book chapters relating to destination marketing, business communication and service marketing. His works have previously published in the *Tourism Management, the International Journal of Research in Marketing, the Journal of Retailing and Consumer Services, the Journal of Targeting, Measurement and Analysis for Marketing, the Industrial Marketing Management, the Journal of Business Ethics,* and other Spanish journals.

Jesús Collado is a Bachelor in Business Administration and Ph.D. at Cantabria University, where he is a Lecturer in the Faculty of Economics, Cantabria University (Email: colladoj@unican.es). His research experience focuses on distribution channels and relationship marketing, tourist satisfaction and service marketing. He is the author and co-author of several publications in *Industrial Marketing Management, Tourism Management,* and other Spanish journals.

John W. O'Neill holds a B.S. degree in Hotel Administration from Cornell University, an M.S. degree in Real Estate from New York University, and a Ph.D. degree in Business Administration from the University of Rhode Island. Dr. O'Neill, an Associate Professor, teaches and researches in the area of lodging strategy and real estate at Penn State, and has received the Favorite Professor Award. Prior to his professorship at Penn State, he was Professor in the International Hotel School at Johnson & Wales University in Rhode Island for seven years, where he was named Teacher of the Year. Dr. O'Neill has served as a consultant to Marriott International, Hilton Hotels, Holiday Inn, Choice Hotels International, numerous banks, and others. Dr. O'Neill is frequently quoted on a variety of topics related to the hospitality industry in *USA Today, Business Week, Business Travel News, Hotel & Motel Management, Hotels, Lodging, New York Times, Crain's New York Business, Philadelphia Inquirer, Philadelphia Business Journal, Providence Journal, Kansas City Star,* and *U.S. Japan Business News.* In addition, he has written articles for *Lodging, Lodging Hospitality, Commercial Investment Real Estate, Cornell Hotel and Restaurant Administration Quarterly,* and the *Journal of Hospitality and Tourism Research,* having received the *Article of the Year Award* from the latter two.

Philipp E. Boksberger is a senior lecturer of tourism management at the University of Applied Sciences HTW Chur (philipp.boksberger@fh-htwchur.ch). Since completing his Ph.D. at the University St.Gallen and a research fellowship at the School of Tourism at the University of Queensland, he acts as deputy director of the Institute for Tourism and Leisure Research. His research interests cover consumer behavior, marketing as well as strategic management issues in tourism in which he published various journal articles, conference papers and book chapters.

Sara Dolnicar is a Professor of Marketing at the School of Management and Marketing at the University of Wollongong (Northfields Ave, Wollongong, 2522 NSW, Australia. E-mail:

sarad@uow.edu.au) and the Director of the Marketing Research Innovation Centre (MRIC). Sara has completed her PhD at the Institute for Tourism and Leisure Studies at the Vienna University of Economics and Business Administration. Her research interests include market segmentation, measurement in marketing, tourism marketing and social marketing.

Serhat Cengiz holds a B. S. Degree in Tourism and currently a postgraduate student at the Graduate School of Social Sciences, Adnan Menderes University (E-mail: serhatcengiz@gmail.com). His research interests include hospitality management and organization, organizational commitment, employee performance, non-verbal communication and tourist satisfaction.

Yasin Bilim (BA in Tourism and Hotel Management, Erciyes University; MSc in Tourism and Hotel Management, Mustafa Kemal University. E-mail: ybilim@yahoo.com) is a research assistant in Tourism and Hotel Management School, Mustafa Kemal University. He is currently a Ph. D. candidate at School of Tourism and Hospitality Management, Adnan Menderes University. He has published articles and conference papers on destination marketing and tourists' security. His research areas are tourism marketing, research methodologies in tourism, and destination marketing tools.

INDEX

B

C

D

F

G

H

I

M

N

O

P

S

T

U